THE FIELD OF SOCIAL WORK

THE FIELD OF
Seventh Edition

CO-AUTHORS

Andrew W. Dobelstein

George Hoshino

H. Carl Henley

Janice H. Schopler

Maeda J. Galinsky

Lois R. Taber

Richard H. Taber

Jane H. Pfouts

Morris H. Cohen

CONTRIBUTORS OF CASE MATERIAL

George Hoshino

Arthur L. Leader

Barbara L. Glaser

Edith C. Woodard

Gertrude I. Cohen

Shirley Morris

Rendell A. Davis

Donald D. Hughes

Ann Bilas Johnson

SOCIAL WORK
ARTHUR E. FINK

HOLT, RINEHART AND WINSTON
New York Chicago San Francisco Dallas
Montreal Toronto London Sydney

To Kathleen Boles Fink

Copyright 1942, 1949, © 1955, 1963, 1968, 1974 by Holt, Rinehart and
Winston, Inc.; © 1978 by Holt, Rinehart and Winston

Library of Congress Cataloging in Publication Data

Fink, Arthur Emil, 1903–
   The field of social work.

   Includes index.
I. Title.   1.   Social service—Addresses, essays, lectures.
 HV40.F5   1978   361   77-89733
 ISBN 0-03-022196-X

Designed by Scott Chelius

Printed in the United States of America

   90 038 9 8 7 6 5 4 3

Preface

As was true of six previous editions, this volume aims to serve the undergraduate student in the liberal arts college. This student is most likely to be a junior or a senior who has enrolled, knowingly or unknowingly, in an elective course—called the Field of Social Work, or Introduction to Social Work, or Contemporary Social Work, or some variation on these.

However, through the years these editions have served a useful purpose in acquainting other audiences with the usefulness of the social services as social work has become recognized increasingly as furthering the welfare of individuals, groups, and communities.

It may not be too presumptuous to suggest that an understanding of the social services and the skills of social workers could be of value to teachers, physicians, hospital chaplains, ministers, policemen, lawyers, judges, correctional administrators, public health workers, nursing home personnel, board members of voluntary and public agencies, city officials, and county commissioners—indeed, all those who touch the lives of others in a helpful, or potentially helpful, relationship.

A glance at the Table of Contents reveals the active participation of many persons as co-authors of chapters and as contributors of material illustrative of the range of contemporary services. All of these associates are identified appropriately by their agency affiliation. They have all shared in the rigors of composition and should feel genuine satisfaction in their productivity.

Gratitude must be expressed to Mrs. Lucille Hollifield of the Spruce Pine, North Carolina, Public Library for her unfailing diligence and courtesy in checking many bibliographical inquiries.

This volume is dedicated to Kathleen Boles Fink. Although not a social worker, she has shared in the labors of seven editions as typist, proofreader, indexer, and critic.

Arthur E. Fink

Little Switzerland, N.C.

Contents

THE FIELD OF SOCIAL WORK

PART ONE

BASES FOR SOCIAL WORK PRACTICE

1

INTRODUCTION: SOCIAL RESOURCES, HUMAN NEED, AND THE FIELD OF SOCIAL WORK

ANDREW W. DOBELSTEIN
School of Social Work, University of North Carolina

The panorama of activities addressed by the field of social work has become, truly, a window on modern society. This book, *The Field of Social Work*, discusses the methods and techniques which persons employ in a variety of occupational endeavors in order to assist individuals, families, social groups, and community associations to meet the challenges of modern society. The field of social work is a field of action. The field of social work engages problems in society and seeks solutions to them. The problems addressed are not only those individuals may have at some time during their lives—problems of getting a job or obtaining an adequate income, or personal difficulties with family members and friends—but also problems within the social system itself—problems of slum housing, criminal justice, racial and social justice, and adequate distribution of the social and economic wealth of America.

The field of social work has become one of the most complex social endeavors of twentieth-century American life. This complexity derives from the increasing demands for a greater number and variety of services which all citizens are placing upon both voluntary associations and government. One hundred years ago, when the Charity Organization Societies were the primary agencies providing social services, Mary Richmond was able to define the field of social work by the seventeen social services which were then available. Today, however, there are over twenty different social services offered by municipal governments, over one hundred ninety different social services offered by the federal government, and over ninety-five different social services offered by voluntary organizations which are members of the United Way.[1] When social services provided by state governments, regional governmental units, special districts, and less formal voluntary agencies are added, Americans possess an extraordinary array of resources to help them live satisfying lives.

The student who faces social services of such magnitude for the first time might well ask which of these social services comprise the field of social work today. Alfred Kahn, the well-known authority on social services in America, describes social services as "communal provisions to promote individual and group well being and to aid those in difficulty."[2] Such a description suggests that the whole array of social service programs and activities comprises the field of social work. Health services, educational services, family counseling services, housing services, as well as many other activities would be included in Kahn's definition. Thus the field of social work stirs up images of activities so comprehensive as to leave the student wondering whether any service offered to people might be included.

BOUNDING THE FIELD OF SOCIAL WORK

Although all social activity might be considered to comprise the field of social work, social work, as it is known today, is a special field of social service. The field of social work might be better understood by discussing the types of agencies which provide social services, the types of persons who provide these social services, the types of help given, and the special methods used to provide social services.

---

[1]*Municipal Yearbook* (Washington, D. C.: International City Management Association, 1975), esp. pp. 121–48; *Catalogue of Federal Domestic Assistance* (Washington, D. C.: U. S. Government Printing Office, 1975); *United Way of America Identification System* (Fairfax, Va.: United Way of America, 1972).

[2]Alfred J. Kahn, *Social Policy and Social Services* (New York: Random House, 1973), p. 4.

The Types of Agencies

Although the agencies included in the field of social work may be categorized in a number of ways, voluntary and public social service agencies provide a convenient distinction for this discussion. Generally, voluntary social service agencies are private, nonprofit corporations which exist to provide social services which the members of those corporations wish to have provided. The best example of a voluntary social service agency is suggested by a retirement home operated by a large denominational church. Voluntary agencies are further characterized by a board of directors which is composed consistent with the agency's charter, and which has final responsibility for determining what kinds of social services should be provided to which persons, and how these services should be financed. Usually the funds to support voluntary agencies come from private sources.

Voluntary agencies have played a crucial role in shaping the field of social work since the beginning of this nation. Most social services were provided voluntarily, by churches and philanthrophic organizations, before the twentieth century.[3] Particularly during the nineteenth century social services from voluntary agencies were preferred over those provided by public agencies, largely because there was fear that public agencies were politically corrupt, and the belief that only voluntary agencies could supply truly helpful social services.[4]

The Great Depression (1929–1935) produced a dramatic expansion of the field of social work. The personal economic problems precipitated by the depression were so great as to make the task of providing social services voluntarily virtually impossible. The federal government initiated several important social service programs, while public agencies of state and local government redoubled their foundering social service efforts. Private funds were not sufficient to meet the massive need during the depression, and many voluntary agencies were too particularistic to be able to administer large-scale social programs. Many voluntary social agencies were forced to close under the weight of such economic pressures.[5] When the Social Security Act was legislated in 1935, a foundation was created for the development and strengthening of public social service agencies at all levels of government.

The public agency differs from the voluntary agency in several respects. By nature of its incorporation as a nonprofit public agency, the public agency

---

[3]June Axinn and Herman Levin, *Social Welfare, A History of the American Response to Need* (New York: Harper & Row, 1975).

[4]Mary E. Richmond, *The Long View* (New York: Russell Sage Foundation, 1930), esp. p. 142.

[5]Josephine C. Brown, *Public Relief, 1929–1939* (New York: Henry Holt & Company, 1940).

must serve everyone. The public agency may be an extension of an existing unit of government, or it may exist as a public corporation separate from a formal governmental structure. The best example of a public social service agency in contemporary America is suggested by a local Department of Social Service which provides a wide range of social services to anyone who is eligible to use them. A public agency may also be governed by a public board, as prescribed by its charter of incorporation, but perhaps the most distinguishing feature of the public agency is that it is financed with public funds—tax money collected from the general public.

Although some distinctions between voluntary and public social service agencies still exist in the field of social work, the distinctions have become less important since the 1960s. It was during the period of the "Great Society" programs, initiated by former President Lyndon B. Johnson, that voluntary agencies were called upon to direct many social service activities toward the goals set for the Great Society programs, and public funds were easily made available to voluntary agencies to achieve these purposes.[6] Thus there developed less autonomy and independence within the voluntary agency as to what kinds of social services would be provided to which persons once public funds were used to support those services. Today, the precise relationship between the public and voluntary agency is still under debate,[7] but regardless of the outcome of the realignment, the boundaries of the field of social work will still depend upon the nature and purpose of both the public and voluntary agency.

The People Who Perform the Social Services

Another distinguishing characteristic of the field of social work is provided by those who deliver social services. In general, the field has been staffed by social workers. Social work originated from the method of "scientific charity," first described in 1813 by Thomas Chalmers, a minister from Glasgow, Scotland,[8] and later incorporated as the method and philosophy of the Charity Organization Societies, the primary social service agencies of the nineteenth century.[9] A leading American charity organization worker, Mary

---

[6]David L. Sundquist, *Politics and Policy* (Washington, D. C.: The Brookings Institution, 1968).

[7]Herman Levin, "The Essential Voluntary Agency," *Social Work* 4, no. 1 (January 1966): 98–106.

[8]Thomas Chalmers, *On Political Economy in Connection with the Moral State and Moral Prospects of Society* (New York: Daniel Appleton, 1832).

[9]Frank D. Watson, *The Charity Organization Movement in the United States* (New York: Macmillan, 1922).

Richmond, refined the methods of scientific charity and formed them into a unique helping method, which she called Case Work.[10]

Mary Richmond worked tirelessly to improve the abilities of those who provided these early social services—persons who were frequently called "friendly visitors." She organized meetings, spoke at public gatherings, and wrote prolifically. Eventually, as Charity Organization Societies began to offer training sessions to their workers, regular study programs were organized in colleges and universities. The first formal program of study specializing in charity work was offered in a newly organized New York School of Social Work, in 1904, and within fifteen years, fifteen similar educational programs were developed in universities across the country to prepare persons for charity work.[11] The social work profession was born, and those who worked in the field of social work were called social workers.

The young social work profession was immediately involved in what has become a continuing debate as to what constituted a "profession," and whether the experience and education of social workers was sufficient to award them that mark of esteem. Several questions have dominated this debate. Should education be in a university or a social agency? Should social work education be at the graduate or undergraduate level? Should the education be directed toward the development of special skills, and if so, what should they be? What theories should be taught as a foundation for social work education? Most of these crucial issues still remain as points for debate.

In 1939, the Association of Schools of Social Work somewhat arbitrarily determined that social work education would be graduate-level education at a university. Yet the fact has remained that those who work in the field of social work with undergraduate educations in social work have always outnumbered those with master's degrees. Furthermore, undergraduate schools also outnumber graduate schools by about twenty to one. Undergraduate schools are known for the ability to develop flexible educational programs in keeping with the needs of the field of social work. In 1972 the National Association of Social Workers opened membership to graduates of undergraduate social work schools, thus formally acknowledging the professional status of undergraduates, and the Council on Social Work Education gives full recognition to undergraduate schools in its membership. Today, undergraduate social work education is acknowledged fully as professional education for the field of social work.

---

[10]Ralph Pumphrey and Muriel Pumphrey, *The Heritage of American Social Work* (New York: Columbia University Press, 1961), pp. 223 ff; and Mary E. Richmond, *Social Diagnosis* (New York: Russell Sage Foundation, 1917).

[11]Elizabeth G. Meier, *A History of the New York School of Social Work* (New York: Columbia University Press, 1954).

Although the field of social work is characterized by people educated in this profession, there are other groups of people who provide manpower to the field. Many people working in the field of social work have no formal social work education but have other professional credentials—psychologists, psychiatrists, nurses, physicians, lawyers, for example. These persons work with social workers in both public and voluntary agencies. For example, public health centers and mental health centers are characterized by their rich variety of persons from different professional backgrounds, while, somewhat by contrast, local Departments of Social Services are characterized by a prominence of social workers. In the latter situation, where social workers are the dominant professional group, the agency is frequently referred to as a "primary agency," while in the former situation, where social workers are not the primary professionals, the agency is referred to as a "host agency." Both primary and host agencies are well within the field of social work.

Another group of persons working in the field but not specifically educated in social work are those with job responsibilities directly related to the successful achievement of the social service mission of a particular agency. In the departments of social service, these persons might be eligibility workers. In the Community Action agency, these persons might be the outreach workers. In the mental health agency, these persons might be case aides. Such persons are an integral part of the social service team and often have considerable special experiences and perhaps some limited exposure to principles of social work practice.

The Type of Help Offered

No two individuals face the same situations in the same way; thus the social services offered by the field of social work are endlessly varied. Yet the field of social work is directed toward efforts to provide assistance which will enhance "social functioning wherever the need for such enhancement is either socially or individually perceived."[12] This means that the type of help offered through the field of social work is concerned with efforts which will assist individuals to realize their full potential in order to attain a satisfying, productive, meaningful way of life in this society. A contemporary report on social services describes their purpose as follows:

> At the core of the social services concept is the idea of expertise and responsibility for helping the primary units of social care, social support and social growth, namely the individual and the family. The objectives of help are: (1) to avoid where

[12]Werner W. Boehm, *Objectives of the Social Work Curriculum of the Future* (New York: Council on Social Work Education, 1959), p. 46.

possible and to better manage problems that impair the ability of both families and individuals to cope with life; and (2) to assist individuals and families to more fully develop their social capacities essential to productive and useful lives in our society.[13]

Heated discussions regarding the proper focus of this helping activity have occupied considerable attention of those who serve in the field of social work. The first discussion has dwelt on whether the individual or the surrounding environment should be the primary recipient of helping activities. In other words, should the help offered by the field of social work be directed toward changing or improving the capacity of the individual so as to make better use of the resources of this society, or should the help be directed toward changing or improving the social resources of the society to better meet the needs of individuals?

This problem of the focus of help in the field of social work emerged clearly during the early years of development of the profession. Mary Richmond believed that the individual should be the focus of social work help. She recognized that the society was far from perfect but that social reform took place on a case-by-case basis as change took place through individuals.[14] In sharp contrast to this philosophy stood a growing number of social and municipal reformers who believed that the level of social functioning could only be improved as society provided greater social benefits for persons with pressing problems.[15] Led by Grace and Edith Abbott, Lillian Wald, Jane Addams, and others, these social reformers argued for a place for social reform in the field of social work.[16] When Jane Addams was elected president of the National Conference of Charities and Corrections in 1909, the field acknowledged both emphases.

The focus of help has continued to be a problem. Theories of scientific charity, the case-by-case approach, and the techniques of social diagnosis and treatment designed by Mary Richmond were crude professional tools compared to those tools possessed by medicine, law, and even education. Following World War II, the widespread application of Freudian psychology offered social work the potential for deepening its theoretical foundations and refining its helping skills. As the field of social work adapted Freudian theory to its purposes, social work once again became heavily committed to achieving social adjustment through individual change. Several years later, how-

---

[13]John B. Turner, ed., *The Future for Social Services in the United States* (Preliminary Report) (Washington, D. C.: National Conference on Social Welfare, 1977), p. 15.

[14]Richmond, *Long View,* p. 352 ff.

[15]Thomas H. Greer, *American Reform Movements: Their Patterns since 1865* (New York: Random House, 1949).

[16]Allen Davis, *Spearheads for Reform* (New York: Oxford University Press, 1967), p. 2.

ever, adoption of national programs to promote social change balanced the emphasis in the field of social work. The juvenile delinquency prevention programs and the War on Poverty programs were predicated upon the assumptions that unless the society could expand its social resources, individual satisfaction was impossible to achieve.[17] The social unrest characterized by the severe racial disorders several years later echoed this emphasis,[18] while thoughtful scholars hypothesized that the social order exploited those with serious social problems, and only major social realignments could achieve a desirable society.[19] The field of social work quickly responded to these new programs. Social workers were employed by new social agencies while social work educators designed new theories and advanced new helping approaches. Thus today the field is characterized by a rich mixture of theories and treatment techniques directed at both the individual and society.

Another controversy over the helping focus of the field of social work has been directed toward the relationship between the provision of financial aid and the provision of other helping services, sometimes called "personal care" services. One of the most pronounced disputes between Mary Richmond and the social reformers concerned the use of financial aid in the helping process. Mary Richmond held that social services should be restorative and rehabilitative, and that through social services individuals and families should achieve social and economic independence. The very need for financial aid, in Mary Richmond's view, was an indication that help beyond the granting of money for food, clothing, and shelter was necessary. Indeed, Mary Richmond argued that good social services kept people off relief.[20]

The social reformers argued that government had the responsibility to provide cash grants for the needy, and lobbied for state relief plans to serve dependent mothers, children, and the elderly. By the time the Great Depression of the 1930s required intervention by the federal government, all states had some form of public aid program. The Social Security Act, legislated at a time when social services were considered superfluous, contained no social service provisions at all, and those social reformers who testified in Congress in support of the act never suggested that services had any part in dealing with the economic dependency which the Social Security Act addressed.

---

[17]Lillian B. Rubin, "Maximum Feasible Participation: The Origins, Implications and Present Status," *Annals of the American Academy of Political and Social Science*, no. 385 (September 1969):14–29; and Richard A. Cloward and Lloyd E. Ohlin, *Delinquency and Opportunity* (Glencoe, Ill.: The Free Press, 1960).

[18]Office of the President, *Report of the National Advisory Commission on Civil Disorders* (Washington, D. C.: U.S. Government Printing Office, 1968).

[19]Frances Fox Piven and Richard A. Cloward, *Regulating the Poor* (New York: Pantheon Books, 1971).

[20]Mary E. Richmond, *Friendly Visiting among the Poor* (New York: Macmillan, 1899).

Curiously enough, however, as local welfare departments began to implement the public assistance programs, they encountered considerable difficulty handing out money without also giving recipients some advice and counsel. It soon became clear that the people who needed public assistance needed help with other problems as well, and those early social workers who set up the budgets for public assistance clients counseled about other pressing problems as well. In 1943 the Federal Security Agency authorized federal matching monies to states to help defray the costs of these rudimentary social services, and the following year the Federal Security Agency looked to Charlotte Towle to define the nature of social services in public assistance work.

Charlotte Towle was intimately familiar with public assistance work, and she concluded that social services should both cushion the personal trauma of asking for financial assistance and facilitate the client to use all the help the public assistance agency had to offer. Towle argued that the Social Security Act expressed the American conviction "that the needy individual has a claim on society of the right to financial assistance," and that social services were needed to preserve this right that had been established by law.[21]

Towle encountered stormy resistance from the Federal Security Agency over her views. Her ideas stirred resentment and controversy in professional social work circles, and the Federal Security Agency was forced to seek advice about social services from another well-known social worker, Grace Marcus. Marcus concluded that "no single point of view exists in the general social work field or among the staff of the bureau [of public assistance] with regard to the character of service in public assistance."[22] Thus the contest abated, for the time being, with the general view that informal, "differentially viewed," services as part of public assistance were permissible, and that more comprehensive social services were to be provided by agencies separate from public assistance.

Continued pressure from two sources, however, forced a reassessment of the purpose for social services, so carefully adopted in 1946. Both the U. S. Congress and a large number of social workers wanted social services which would get people off the relief roles. In 1950 the American Public Welfare Association (APWA) conducted a well-planned nationwide study of families with dependent children who received Aid to Families With Dependent Children (AFDC). The study concluded that AFDC kept families together and gave children a good start in a secure home environment. Further, the study found evidence to suggest that experienced, well-trained social case workers

---

[21]Charlotte Towle, *Common Human Needs* (New York: American Association of Social Workers, 1952), p. vi.

[22]Grace Marcus, *The Nature of Service in Public Assistance*, Public Assistance Report No. 10 (Washington, D. C.: U.S. Government Printing Office, 1946).

were an asset in helping families become stable, and eventually these stable families became economically self-sufficient.[23]

At about the same time, the U. S. Congress was also seeking ways to help persons get off relief. Between 1947 and 1949 over twenty pieces of legislation were proposed to Congress to reduce welfare roles by making deserting fathers provide financial support for their children. In 1949, Republican Representative Gerald Ford of Michigan proposed legislation which would make it possible for the federal government to trace deserting fathers and make them pay for the upkeep of their children, and this legislation was appended to the Social Security Act in 1950.[24] The legislation was unenforceable and presumed, by social workers, to be going about the problem in the wrong way. Thus social workers proposed expanding social services as instruments of social rehabilitation. Congress legislated amendments to the Social Security Act of 1956 which authorized the provision of social services to maintain and strengthen family life.

In 1962 Congress reaffirmed its commitment to social services as an important part of giving welfare, owing in part to the growing national mood that social services were helpful to people and in part to President John F. Kennedy's stirring welfare message—a landmark statement which proposed that public assistance "must be more than a salvage operation, picking up the debris from the wreckage of human lives. Its emphasis must be directed toward prevention and rehabilitation."[25] The subsequent 1962 amendments to the Social Security Act contained broad authority and generous funds to provide social services.

Congress grew impatient, however, with the lack of progress from social service programs. Welfare roles were increasing, not decreasing. Welfare costs were soaring by the late 1960s. Thus Congress legislated the Work Incentive Program in 1967, later *requiring* that able-bodied mothers seek employment. Finally, President Richard M. Nixon proposed a welfare reform to Congress which would have, according to Daniel Moynihan, then a domestic affairs advisor to President Nixon, substituted an "income strategy" to replace the "social service strategy" of the Kennedy-Johnson years.[26] After considerable uncertainty Congress passed a form of welfare reform in 1972

---

[23]Gordon W. Blackwell and Raymond F. Gould, *Future Citizens All* (Chicago: American Public Welfare Association, 1952).

[24]Maurine McKeany, *The Absent Father and Public Policy in the Program of Aid to Dependent Children* (Berkeley and Los Angeles: The University of California Press, 1967).

[25]John F. Kennedy, Message to Congress, *Congressional Record*, February 1, 1962, 108, pt. 1: 1405.

[26]Daniel P. Moynihan, *The Politics of a Guaranteed Income* (New York: Vintage Books, 1973).

(P. L. 92–603), but Congress did not deal specifically with social services until 1974 when it passed Title XX to the Social Security Act. This latest amendment to the Social Security Act clearly states the purposes for social services and removes the obligation that social services are primarily responsible for keeping persons off relief.

The field of social work encompasses those helping activities designed to improve the standard of living for individuals who experience disruptive and disabling social and economic problems. The help offered is designed to assist individuals improve themselves in order to make better use of existing social resources and at the same time seek social changes which will improve the quality of life for everyone. The field of social work recognizes that income maintenance is an indispensable element of social service help, but income maintenance without accompanying social services does not easily fit within the boundaries of the field.

THE SKILLS AND TECHNIQUES USED IN GIVING HELP

Social work methods are the skills and techniques by which workers in the field provide social services. As might be expected in a dynamic field of work, these methods are in a constant state of refinement, redevelopment, reassessment, and reformulation. Although social work methods are used in many fields, the field of social work can be defined by its unique application of these methods with respect to the type of help given, the persons who give it, and the agencies in which it is given.

The first of these methods was introduced and refined by Mary Richmond and is presently called social casework. The early efforts of the social reformers quickly led to the development of a second method, social group work. This method developed because the social reformers worked more with groups of people than with individuals. Settlement houses, in particular, were focal points for considerable social reform activity at the turn of the twentieth century, and the social group work method originated from this work.[27] Partly from a need to better coordinate and organize sources of funding for the early voluntary agencies, and partly from a need to carry forward the work of social reform, a third method of social work was added. This method has been called community organization.[28] These three methods of providing help have had high visibility over the years, and although the special techniques of implementing these methods have been subjects of discussion and refine-

---

[27]Grace Coyle, *Group Work with American Youth* (New York: Harper & Row, 1948).

[28]Murray Ross, *Community Organization Practice* (New York: Harper & Row, 1967).

ment, the methods remain the major ways of giving help in the field of social work.

In addition to these major methods, the field of social work also uses research, social planning, administration, social program management, and social policy development to provide social services. These latter methods of providing help are not unique to the field of social work and occupy a place of lesser importance in the activities undertaken within it. Often these methods are supportive of the major methods of casework, group work, and community organization. The development of these methods, the special skills required to implement them, and the various subtleties in their application in the field of social work comprise the subject of a considerable portion of this book.

In Summary

The field of social work seems at first to encompass the whole range of service undertakings by voluntary and public organizations in America, but upon closer examination, it is seen to be a unique combination of activities which can be defined in respect to the types of agencies which provide social services, the people who provide those services, the purpose of those services, and the methods employed. Yet, even with this greater specification, the field of social work still covers an impressive array of undertakings, and frequently the boundaries of the field appear unclear, shifting, and a source of consternation for many who prefer precise order in their lives. The advantages of a more flexible definition of the field of social work often outweigh the confusions which develop; however, the field is a dynamic milieu of activity reflecting current human needs and social conditions. Through the field of social work, relevant activities to meet some of the most serious social problems are available to most of the members of our nation.

PREPARATION FOR SOCIAL WORK PRACTICE

The extent of the field of social work suggests the need for wide-ranging preparation for those who wish to work in it. Preparation takes place over many years and includes formal academic work, structured, supervised, learning experiences in actual work situations, and a considerable amount of independent vocational experience. To a very great extent preparation for the field of social work never ends. There is always something new to learn—new service programs, new educational opportunities, new vocational responsibilities.

Preparation takes place in respect to elements of the work to be done within the field. Preparation requires a knowledge and understanding of the persons seeking help, sometimes called clients, the problems they present, the programs designed to deal with these problems, the public policies which direct the formation of those programs, and the procedures by which client needs are satisfied. The remainder of this book deals with all these elements in some detail, and only an introductory statement about each element is necessary at this point.

The Persons

While no two persons are alike in personality characteristics and specific needs, every person goes through a chronological process of development —from the newest born child to the oldest senior citizen. It has been possible to identify several stages, or periods, in any person's life, which suggest specific life-shaping events that are likely to dominate the concerns for that individual at that period of life.[29] For example, the period of early childhood is characterized by a struggle for survival and development of self, while the period of adolescence is frequently one of turbulence, characterized by a struggle for independence.

Identification of those struggles which each person is likely to encounter at a particular stage of chronological development is important for understanding what each person seeks from the social services offered by the field of social work. For example, a young mother is often responsible for the care of babies and very young children at a stage of young adulthood, precisely when she is seeking self-identity in the adult world. Thus child care becomes a burden rather than an opportunity for self-fulfillment. Such a mother might seek social services which would provide her with the opportunity to realize her own potential as a person and at the same time enable her to provide adequate care for her children. Educational and vocational services for the mother and day care services for the child would satisfy the social service expectation for this hypothetical mother.

Practice in the field of social work requires further knowledge about the person who seeks its services. Each person has a unique personality which determines what that person believes he needs to help him with a problem. Although it is impossible to develop categories for all personalities, some writers have attempted to describe dominant personality types, such as aggressive, passive, and dependent. When the type of personality is identified, it is often possible to anticipate how the person is likely to behave in respect to the particular situation that person is facing, at that particular stage in the life cycle.

---

[29]Erik H. Erikson, *Identity, Youth and Crisis* (New York: W. W. Norton, 1968).

The Problems

Persons seek social service from the field of social work to assist them in resolving problems. As suggested earlier, the problem might have its origin in the personality of the individual, or in the structure of society, or both. Regardless of the origin of the problem, however, the field of social work is concerned about the social manifestation of the problem. This regard for all problems in a social context is unique to the field of social work.

Almost any personal problem or any economic or political problem might be identified as a social problem. Yet certain elements are often present which suggest that a problem is appropriately addressed by the field of social work. Personal problems become social problems when they handicap persons from carrying out necessary social roles, such as being a parent or earning a living. When the person is not able to command social resources sufficient for survival and development, personal problems also become social problems. In addition, personal problems become social problems when personal behavior is disruptive to others or conflicts with social norms.

From the perspective of the political and economic order, problems become social problems, relevant to solution by the field of social work, when they become recognized by a significant element of the society as public concerns, and when there develops a significant public commitment to address these concerns.[30] For example, unemployment is clearly a social problem when an individual is unable to carry out an appropriate social role of earning a living. It is also an economic problem which affects the supply of labor and the productive capacity of the nation. Unemployment might also be re-identified as a social problem when a significant element of the population becomes concerned about unemployment and a public commitment develops to address unemployment as a public issue. Although many social conditions exist which are not conducive to the development of a healthy social life for all, these conditions do not necessarily become social problems until sufficient public concern is generated about them.

The Programs

Preparation to work in the field of social work requires considerable knowledge about the wide range of programs designed to address social problems. A program might be thought of as a series of activities, or a combination of services directed toward a specific set of objectives. In other words, programs are a specific set of services which are organized in such a way as to produce

---

[30]John B. Turner, "In Response to Social Change: Social Work at the Crossroad," *Social Work* 13, no. 3 (1968):16–22.

specific results and which are provided by specific agencies. For example, the Work Incentive Program consists of social service activities which attempt to assist certain welfare mothers to identify their potential skills for gainful employment, to develop these skills through education and training, and to utilize these skills through placement in appropriate employment settings; the program also helps these mothers utilize other social resources for care and protection of themselves and other members of their families. The objective of this particular combination of services is to provide these mothers with opportunity for economic self-sufficiency. The program is offered by the Department of Social Service with the help of state employment agencies.

The programs offered by the field of social work are quite varied, and the combination of services is virtually unlimited. Until recently, the objectives of social programs were likewise restricted only by a general social purpose. However, the latest amendment to the Social Security Act (Title XX) specifies five goals or objectives for those social programs supported by funds under this act.[31] While there still is no agreement that only programs that seek to achieve those objectives are relevant programs in the field of social work, the program goals specified by Title XX are an important source of knowledge for the beginning social worker in developing knowledge about the social programs which are currently available.

The Policies

The programs, the problems, and, to some extent, the persons who seek social services from the field of social work are largely determined by existing public policies. Public policies take many different forms. Laws are a clear form of public policy. Judicial decisions are public policies. Sometimes statements from outstanding public figures are a form of public policy, as when President Lyndon B. Johnson declared a "war" on poverty. Agencies which administer social programs constantly make public policy by deciding who should receive what services under specific conditions.

Regardless of its form, public policy provides the direction which should be taken in order to achieve the objective of many social programs. An analogy might be drawn between the purposes of public policy and a road map. As one begins a trip, the destination may be clear but difficult to reach if the right roads are not followed. In the case of social programs, public

---

[31]Paul E. Mott, *Meeting Human Needs: The Social and Political History of Title XX* (Columbus, Ohio: National Conference on Social Welfare, 1976). Many of these programs are described in later sections of this book. In addition, see Sheila B. Kamerman and Alfred J. Kahn, *Social Services in the United States* (Philadelphia: Temple University Press, 1976).

policies guide the manner in which programs are provided to those who seek them.

Often when programs fail to reach specific objectives it is evident that new policies are needed. The Work Incentive Program (WIN), for example, was designed to help persons get off welfare. The policy underlying WIN in 1967 was that it should be up to each eligible welfare recipient whether to participate in this program. But when the program failed to achieve this objective, Congress changed the policy and made WIN a mandatory program. Later, President Nixon proposed a different policy for WIN as part of his proposals for "workfare" instead of welfare.

Thus an important element in the field of social work is the knowledge about major public policies, since these policies are likely to affect how social services are provided. The beliefs which people hold are the primary forces in the development and redevelopment of public policies. For example, if people believe that "anyone can make it if they work hard enough," then public policies are likely to reflect this view. In America, many social programs are administered with a strong orientation toward the idea that hard work should come before welfare, since this is a dominant belief in American society. Since public policies determine the direction of public programs, public policies based upon humanistic beliefs are the most helpful for programs in the field of social work. Yet the beliefs of any society might not be adequate to generate policies which would produce better social programs.[32]

The Provision of Social Services

The final element which must be understood in order to work in the field of social work has to do with how services are made available to those who need them. It is characteristic of the field that these services are made available through other people. In other words, the services are not provided by mechanical or electronic means but by other human beings. The services are provided by activities of persons. Obviously, provision of social services takes interpersonal skills in any or all of the methods of social work practice.

Yet something in addition to skill is necessary in provision of social services. This extra something is a philosophy, an attitude, or a point of view, regarding persons with social problems who seek social services. The field of social work soon introduces the social worker to some of the extreme limits of personal deprivation and deplorable social conditions. Many persons who seek social services are hostile and belligerent, and criticize rather than thank social workers for help. Some who seek help do not want to help themselves.

---

[32]Jeffrey Galper, The Politics of Social Services (Englewood Cliffs, N. J.: Prentice-Hall, 1975).

Some try to "beat the system" by dishonesty. A social worker needs a certain kind of attitude—a nonjudgmental attitude—in order to perform his work successfully.

A nonjudgmental attitude means that a social worker does not come to a conclusion regarding the worth of the person seeking help. The social worker accepts the person simply as someone who needs help. There are always reasons why people act as they do. Often they are frightened or depressed over their situation. Many times they are frustrated over the lack of opportunities available to them. Regardless of the reason, however, the social worker must be able to provide the service to the person with objectivity, warmth, and sincerity if the services are to be used effectively.[33]

THE FUTURE

An introduction to the field of social work would not be complete without a brief look to the future. The future for the field of social work is as promising as it is challenging. More and more workers are needed, and to a great extent the increased demands for manpower are being met through undergraduate social work programs of study. These new undergraduate programs represent one of the most exciting developments in the field of social work, since, for the first time in the history of social work education, undergraduate social work education holds a clearly defined position within the social work educational hierarchy.[34]

The future of the field of social work is also challenged by the need for more useful social services and better methods of social work practice to bring these services to those who need them. New public issues require new programs, and the field of social work is constantly challenged to relate itself to new concerns. President Carter's interest in "welfare reform" is a good example. Many welfare critics, including the President, argue that our present welfare programs discourage enthusiasm for work and tend to challenge the integrity of the family. The proposed welfare changes emphasize work and family stability. The field of social work will have to respond to these changes in welfare emphasis. Social workers will have to be able to help clients find and hold jobs. Social workers will also have to take more aggressive steps to hold families together.

The field of social work is also challenged by rapid geographical growth and has taken on an international aspect through the work of the United

---

[33]National Association of Social Workers, *Code of Ethics* (New York: NASW, 1967).

[34]See *Report on the Task Force on Structure and Quality* (New York: Council on Social Work Education, 1975) and *An Analysis of the Responses to the Reports of the Task Force on Structure and Quality in Social Work Education and the Task Force on Practice and Education* (New York: Council on Social Work Education, 1976).

Nations, the United States Agency for International Development, the United States Department of Health, Education, and Welfare, the International Conference on Social Welfare, and many other organizations within nations around the world. One of the most pressing issues in international social work is the protection of human rights. In the words of the United States Committee to the XVII International Conference on Social Welfare, "Human rights, respected and protected, are the necessary conditions of social development —certainly as important as economic growth and citizen involvement."[35]

Most of all, the field of social work will be challenged to meet the expanding demands for social services with high-quality and useful social programs. This will require better educated, more highly skilled social workers at all levels within the field. Estimates suggest that well over 100,000 social workers are needed. What kind of social workers these persons will be is an important question. Only highly qualified, dedicated social workers will meet the challenge of providing high-quality services. Thus those who study this book represent the answer to whether the field of social work can meet this challenge.

Finally, the future of the field of social work is promising. Increased social technology has the potential to end human misery. Increased economic productivity and social wealth provide the resources to implement new technologies around the world. Improved educational programs promise highly skilled, dedicated workers. Perhaps never in the history of mankind have the promises been so capable of realization, and never have the challenges been so great. The future of the field of social work begins with what social work students learn today.

BIBLIOGRAPHY

Axinn, June, and Herman Levin. *Social Welfare: A History of the American Response to Need.* New York: Harper & Row, 1975.

Blackwell, Gordon W., and Raymond F. Gould. *Future Citizens All.* Chicago: American Public Welfare Association, 1952.

Davis, Allen F. *Spearheads for Reform.* New York: Oxford University Press, 1967.

Galper, Jeffrey. *The Politics of Social Services.* Englewood Cliffs, N.J.: Prentice-Hall, 1975.

Mott, Paul E. *Meeting Human Needs: The Social and Political History of Title XX.* Columbus, Ohio: National Conference on Social Welfare, 1976.

---

[35]John B. Turner, ed., *Development and Participation: Operational Implications for Social Welfare* (Washington, D.C.: U.S. Department of Health, Education, and Welfare, 1975), p. 3.

Moynihan, Daniel P. *The Politics of a Guaranteed Income.* New York: Vintage Books, 1973.

Piven, Francis Fox, and Richard A. Cloward. *Regulating the Poor: The Functions of Public Welfare.* New York: Pantheon Books, 1971.

Richmond, Mary E. *The Long View.* New York: Russell Sage Foundation, 1930.

Sundquist, David L. *Politics and Policy.* Washington, D.C.: The Brookings Institution, 1968.

Towle, Charlotte. *Common Human Needs.* New York: American Association of Social Workers, 1952.

Turner, John B. ed. *Development and Participation: Operational Implications for Social Welfare.* Washington, D.C.: U.S. Department of Health, Education, and Welfare, 1975.

2
THE ASSUMPTION OF RESPONSIBILITY

ARTHUR E. FINK
**Professor Emeritus, School of Social Work,
University of North Carolina**

A. EUROPEAN BACKGROUND

The records of earlier civilized peoples reveal, despite the rigors of the times, a compassion for others—for the sick, the old, the handicapped, the poor. This was true of Egyptians, Jews, Greeks, Romans, and those who adopted Christian teachings. Throughout the centuries that mark the Christian era, benevolence and mutual aid were enjoined. It was so during feudalism, and it was only as the modern state began to evolve that the relation of serf and master, man and his church, underwent change.

It is in one of these emerging states, Great Britain, that these and other changes will be traced briefly as a prelude to our experience as American colonies and later as a nation. Not only was the feudal system in the process of dissolution, but also England had been struck, in 1348, with the Black

Death, which within a period of sixteen months had reduced (according to the historian Trevelyan) the English subjects "from perhaps four million to perhaps two and a half million souls." A decreased supply of workers, coupled with considerable aimless wandering of the landless, moved the landed gentry to prevail upon Edward III to initiate repressive measures. Whereupon the king issued in 1349 a proclamation, the famous Statute of Laborers, which required able-bodied workers who were without means of support to accept employment tendered to them, forbade them to leave their own parish, and prohibited alms to able-bodied beggars.

Not only were there recurrences of pestilences, although none so scourging as the Black Death, but also there were crop failures and famines, and wars on the Continent. Added to all these were the Acts of Enclosure (the conversion of tilled land into pasture for more profitable sheep raising), which dislocated rural laborers. The accumulation of a century and a half of such ills finally obliged Henry VIII to seek the enactment of a statute in 1531, which in effect was the first expression of a positive responsibility for the relief of economic distress. Mayors and justices of the peace were required to seek out the aged poor and those compelled to live by alms and to authorize such persons to restrict their begging to designated areas. In order to control unauthorized begging by the able-bodied unemployed, fines were imposed on persons who gave money or lodging to such beggars. Furthermore, an able-bodied beggar was to be whipped and returned to his place of birth and there to "put himself to labour as a true man oweth to do."

This legislation was but a beginning and within five years was supplemented by the Statute of 1536, as a further acceptance of governmental responsibility. Local officials, including church officers, were to secure funds through church collections, to be used to help the poor, impotent, lame, sick, and diseased so that they would not be reduced to begging. Justices and other local officers were given authority to take children between the ages of five and fourteen who had been begging and to appoint them to masters to be trained to earn a suitable living. Sturdy vagabonds and "valiant beggars" were to be whipped and even mutilated if found guilty of continual loitering and idleness. Severe and primitive though this may have been, in the sixteenth century it signaled the transition of poor relief from an unregulated dispensing of aid by the church to the beginnings of regulation by the state.

During this same year, 1536, and again in 1539, Henry VIII expropriated the monasteries. Not a few of those whose lives had been within these monasteries—monks and nuns and the many families that had been sheltered or employed in the monasteries and convents—were turned out. Some of these joined the ranks of the other poor and wanderers.

It was not long before it was generally recognized that a system of voluntary collection under voluntary agents furnished neither the necessary funds nor the essential stability of personnel to ensure even a modicum of relief.

By 1572, overseers of the poor were appointed as civil officers to direct the expenditure of tax funds levied upon the local community for the purpose of relieving the poor. Within four years the justices of each county were empowered to secure by purchase or lease the buildings to be used as houses of correction. Here, materials for work were to be provided for the unemployed to the end that work habits might be instilled and, it was hoped, the necessity for relief be lessened.

Commenting on these early years, Karl de Schweinitz in the volume so aptly titled *England's Road to Social Security* wrote in 1943:

> The statutes from Henry VIII to Elizabeth established a principle and a tradition of relief locally financed and locally administered for local residents, with the overseer of the poor as the responsible official, and a system of public assistance that included direct grants of aid to the unemployable and a policy of work for the able-bodied. After two centuries of attempts to control poverty by repressive measures, government slowly and reluctantly came to accept positive obligation for the help of people who could not provide for themselves. The experience of the years between 1349 and 1601 had convinced the rulers of England of the presence of a destitution among the poor that punishment could not abolish and that could be relieved only by the application of public resources to individual need.[1]

The Elizabethan Poor Law

Queen Elizabeth I, daughter of Henry VIII and Anne Boleyn, acceded to the throne in 1558 and reigned for forty-five years, until her death in 1603. On a number of occasions, notably the years 1563, 1572, and 1576, laws were enacted relating to the poor—taxes and enforced contributions, putting rogues and vagabonds to work, providing work for the needy willing to work as well as overseers, almshouses, and houses of correction. Toward the end of her reign, these assorted enactments were codified in the Acts of 39 Elizabeth, 1597, and 43 Elizabeth, 1601, since referred to as the Elizabethan poor law. Provision was established for three categories of relief recipients: the able-bodied poor, the impotent poor, and dependent children. For the able-bodied poor, employment was to be provided under pain of a session in jail or in the stocks for refusal to work. The almshouse was to be the sanctuary of the second group, the unemployables. Children who could not be supported by their parents or grandparents were to be apprenticed, the

---

[1]Karl de Schweinitz, *England's Road to Social Security* (Philadelphia: University of Pennsylvania Press, 1943), p. 29. This volume is invaluable as a record of England's efforts over six centuries to deal with the welfare of people as a governmental responsibility. Every student who would understand developments in America as well as England should familiarize himself with it.

boys until they were twenty-four years old and the girls until they were twenty-one or married. For the execution of these legal provisions a tax was to be levied in the parish upon lands, houses, and tithes, which was supplemented by private charitable bequests of land or money and by the use of fines for the violation of certain laws. Commenting upon these statutes, the British historian S. Reed Brett wrote in 1962:

> Their terms were based upon three clear principles. First, they tacitly recognized that it was the State's duty to care for those unable to care for themselves. Second, they continued the distinction between the impotent poor and the "sturdy beggars"; the former were to be cared for, and the latter punished. Third, the unit of Poor Law relief was the parish (whose authorities were likely to know, or to be able to discover, the truth about the needs of the parishioners).[2]

Although there were some who regarded these laws as the model for all time, the model soon yielded to an addition here, a repair there, an alteration in some other place. Inevitably the poor moved from one place to another, from parishes where relief was lean to parishes where, if relief was not ample, at least it was comfortable. Several hundred years before, by the Statute of Laborers of 1349, Parliament had ordered laborers to stay in their own parishes; but so acute had the condition of laborers become that no man would root himself to a spot where he was doomed to slow starvation. By the Settlement Act of 1662 each parish became responsible only for those who had legal residence within its bounds, which usually meant residence by birth. Furthermore, those without legal settlement were returnable to their proper parish, while newcomers could be accepted only upon posting surety against becoming public charges.

Another extension of the poor law was the development of the workhouse test. Despite the supposedly deterrent or therapeutic effects of a parish list of relief recipients and their grants, there seemed no letup in the size of the list. If anything, the public list grew longer and longer until, in desperation it may be, the workhouse test was devised. Bristol's experience after the enabling act of 1697, whereby expenses were reduced, gave impetus to this method of work relief. Parishes were permitted to join forces for the purpose of establishing workhouses in which the poor might be lodged and worked. To refuse to work, however, was to court dismissal and to be denied any relief. To make matters even worse, at least so far as the able-bodied poor were concerned, parishes were permitted to "farm out" the poor on contract.

---

[2]S. Reed Brett, *The Tudor Century, 1485–1603* (London: George C. Harrap & Co., Ltd., 1962), p. 122.

This amounted, in essence, to an invitation to the lowest private bidder to exploit human labor to the utmost. So criminal and so degrading had such practices become through the years that finally, in 1782, Parliament was obliged to abolish "farming out."

A system of allowances was later devised, which added to the miseries of the unemployed as well as those who were barely managing to eke out a living. It is not intimated here that there was any deliberate effort on any individual's part to demean the condition of English labor, but the fact remains nevertheless that the effect of legislation presumably designed to improve the lot of the worker actually achieved the opposite result. The able-bodied poor were to be provided with work by the overseers of the poor and could retain their own domiciles. However, when the overseer had collected the wage and found it insufficient to support the worker and his family, a supplementary grant from relief funds was to be made. Such a wage subsidy, as might have been foreseen, depressed wages throughout England and tended to pauperize the entire working population. What employer would not pay a low wage if he knew the government would supplement it? What incentive was there to pay a "living" wage when the "dying" wage was sure to be added to? Was it any consolation to the poor that the same Parliament that enacted the allowance system also rescinded the workhouse test? Surely, here was firsthand material for the pen of the English cleric, Thomas Malthus, upon which to base his population theory and his dire predictions of the tendency of population to outrun the food supply.

The Poor Law Revision of 1834

For two centuries England had struggled with the problem of a changing social order: the feudal system had disintegrated, the control of the church over the lives of communicants had been slackened, a commercial and industrial economy had gained a dominant position. All the while, however, the lot of the worker and his dependents had fallen to lower and lower estate. In 1834 a parliamentary commission presented a report that aimed to revise the Elizabethan and post-Elizabethan poor laws. Upon the basis of the committee's report, legislation was enacted enunciating the following principles: doctrine of least eligibility, reestablishment of the workhouse test, and centralization of control.

An analysis of these principles substantiates the penetrating description of them, by the Webbs, as the "framework of repression." The doctrine of least eligibility meant "that the condition of paupers shall in no case be so eligible as the condition of persons of the lowest class subsisting on the fruits of their own industry." It mattered not how low the standard might be of the lowest paid common workman in Great Britain; no person receiving aid was to be as well off. Then, as if this were not enough, the authorities could always hold out as a threat the ever-impending workhouse. Able-bodied poor could apply for assistance to the public workhouse, but refusal to accept the lodging and fare of the workhouse disbarred them from qualifying for any aid. Outdoor relief, that is, outside of an institution, was reduced to an absolute minimum. The third principle, centralized control, was the only one that could be said to look forward rather than backward. A central authority consisting of three Poor Law commissioners had power to consolidate and coordinate poor-law services throughout the land. Parishes were no longer to be the administrative units; in their stead were to be poor-law districts or unions administered by an unpaid board of guardians. This was really the beginning of the recognition that the problem of relief was larger than any single local unit.[3]

Between 1834 and 1909 there were numerous changes in poor-law legislation, the cumulative effect of which was to veer the entire system away from the principles of 1834. The most important changes were those that began to develop specialized care for certain disadvantaged groups. District schools and foster homes were provided for dependent children; hospitals, dispensaries, and infirmaries for the sick; specialized institutions for the insane and feebleminded; special schools for the blind and the deaf.

Yet even these developments did not alter the fundamental changes taking place in this three-quarters of a century. The effects of the industrial revolution penetrated to the depths of British life. Pauperization, bad housing, poor health, and faulty sanitation—these and many more effects became progressively accumulative, like a snowball rolling downhill. By 1909 Great Britain needed another revision, and judging by the signs of the times, one far more fundamental than that of 1834.

The Poor Law Report of 1909

Great Britain was fortunate to have the dissenting voices of the Webbs (Beatrice and Sidney) on the Royal Commission on Poor Laws and the Unemployed. Through the Webbs (Mrs. Webb was an official member of the commission) was expressed much of the enlightened thought on the fundamental problems of the British social and industrial order. It was no accident that the report of 1909 and its subsequent adaptations gave strength to principles that stressed curative treatment and rehabilitation, universal provision, and what, for lack of a better term, may be called compulsion. Cure was

---

[3]In surveying the problem of relief from the medieval period through this revision, one commentator observed, referring to the reformers of 1834: "Their implication that the able-bodied, brought to destitution by individual fault, made up the vast majority of dependents was no less influential for its being erroneous. In great measure such conclusions reflected a set of mind which, by ignoring the facts of the industrial revolution, justified the insecurities created by it." Blanche D. Coll, "Perspectives in Public Welfare: the English Heritage," *Welfare in Review,* March 1966, p. 11.

to be substituted for repression, and provision for all in the place of the punishingly selective workhouse test. Furthermore, it was recognized that the state on occasion would have to exercise compulsion in the best interests of both the community and the individual, specifically in instances involving restraint of vagrants, isolation of mental cases, removal of children from unfit parents, compulsory vaccination, regulation of child labor, and compulsory schooling.

If the principles of 1834 provided a framework of repression, those of 1909 may be characterized in the Webbs' terms as the "framework of prevention." A positive approach was to be substituted for a negative, an approach that made possible the utilization of human potentialities. The philosophy of laissez faire, which had built and sanctioned eighteenth- and nineteenth-century industrial Britain, was giving way before a philosophy that recognized the interdependence of the individual and the state as well as their mutual obligations. As a measure of this shift, we need only look at the translation into action of the majority and minority reports. The majority report advocated the widening, strengthening, and humanizing of the poor law; the minority favored the breaking up of the poor law and the abolition of the poorhouse, and in its place the establishment of a national minimum of services. In the generation that has followed, the dissenting opinion (as so often happens) has become the majority opinion. Great Britain's present-day organization for social security, although by no means perfect, transcends the Elizabethan poor law as much as the modern airplane transcends the cart of 1601.

Developments after 1909

The legislative enactments after 1909 substantiate the statement that a policy of national minimum service became dominant. In 1911 the National Insurance Act, which provided compulsory insurance against sickness and unemployment, was passed. In 1925, the Widows', Orphans' and Old-Age Contributory Pensions Act extended the insurance principle to cover old age and death. Cash payments provided for: (1) pensions for widows of insured men, with temporary allowances for dependent children; (2) allowances during childhood for the orphans of insured persons; and (3) old-age pensions for insured persons and for insured men betweeen sixty-five and seventy years of age.[4]

---

[4]de Schweinitz remarked that this legislation "applied an innovation only to be compared in importance with the legislation that between 1536 and 1601 established the responsibility of the state for guaranteeing the individual a protection against starvation. A new principle had been introduced in Anglo-Saxon government . . . social insurance as a means of obtaining security." de Schweinitz, *England's Road to Social Security,* p. 208.

The Local Government Act of 1929 moved closer to the breakup of the old poor law, which the minority report advocated. The Boards of Guardians were abolished and their functions turned over to the county (rural) and county borough (urban) councils, which had been established in the latter part of the nineteenth century as the largest unit of local administration. Administration of relief through public assistance committees was to follow the general pattern of administration in health, education, and other activities carried on by the councils.

The Unemployment Act of June 28, 1934, created an Unemployment Assistance Board, operating on a national scale throughout Great Britain. Under its provisions, unemployment assistance was to be available to the unemployed who were not covered by insurance or whose term of benefits had expired. Supplementary pensions were also to be granted to any person "entitled to receive weekly payments on account of an old-age pension, or a person who has attained the age of sixty and is entitled to receive weekly payments on account of a widow's pension." Once more de Schweinitz's observation must be relayed:

> The development of National Assistance affected the unemployed, the aged and widows, and the war sufferers. Outside these categories local relief as administered by the counties continued, but with a diminishing part in the program of social security. That program at the end of the fourth decade of the twentieth century consisted of three defenses against want: social insurance, the largest; then national assistance; and for those not protected by the first two provisions, public assistance.[5]

The Beveridge Report

On November 20, 1942, Sir William Beveridge (later Lord Beveridge), chairman of the Inter-Departmental Committee on Social Insurance and Allied Services, presented the Committee's report to His Majesty's government. During the preceding eighteen months, Sir William and his associates had been executing the charge to survey "existing national schemes of social insurance and allied services, including workmen's compensation, and to make recommendations." The report emphasized four major principles: (1) every citizen to be covered; (2) the major risks of loss of earning power—sickness, unemployment, accident, old age, widowhood, maternity—to be included in a single insurance; (3) a flat rate of contribution to be paid regardless of the contributor's income; (4) a flat rate of benefit to be paid, also without regard to income, as a right to all who qualify.

---

[5]de Schweinitz, *England's Road to Social Security,* p. 226.

At the time the Beveridge report was being prepared, Great Britain was engaged in a war for its very existence as a free nation. A coalition government was in power, but before World War II was over, the report already was receiving consideration in Parliament. In June 1945, legislation was enacted providing for the initiation, a year later, of a system of family allowances, one of the recommendations of the Beveridge report. In July 1945, the Labor party came into power and took favorable action upon most of the other recommendations, including a National Health Service. July 5, 1948, was the date set for the implementation of several programs.

Contemporary Public Services in Britain[6]

Income Maintenance   The foregoing legislation replaced earlier programs and, with subsequent enactments, furnished a substantial social insurance base for Great Britain's contemporary income-maintenance measures. The Department of Health and Social Security has consolidated many earlier agencies and now administers these programs in the form of National Insurance, Industrial Injuries Insurance, Supplementary Benefits, and specialized allowance schemes. The main National Insurance scheme provides cash payments, usually on a weekly basis, to insured residents as follows: unemployment benefit, sickness benefit, maternity allowance, maternity grant, widow's allowance, widowed mother's allowance, widow's pension, guardian's allowance, special child's allowance, death grant, and retirement pension. Grants are typically one-time payments; allowances are ongoing benefits, sometimes for specified periods; and pensions generally refer to payments made when one is no longer working due to the attainment of a specific age. The Industrial Injuries part of the National Insurance scheme is based on workers' weekly contributions and provides cash benefits for personal injuries and certain diseases which arise out of and in the course of employment. Survivors and dependents are also covered by certain Industrial Injuries benefits.

Generally speaking, all persons above school-leaving age (sixteen years) and up to the time they qualify for retirement pension (sixty years for women, sixty-five for men) are insurable and make a weekly contribution. The contribution rates vary according to whether the person is in Class 1 (employed;

---

[6]The sections on Income Maintenance, Family Allowances, National Health Service, and the Personal Social Services were prepared by W. David Harrison, a graduate of the University of Minnesota School of Social Work, presently on the staff of the school and engaged in its doctoral program. During 1975–1976 Mr. Harrison was employed as a social worker in Great Britain by the Northumberland County Council.

that is, those who work for an employer) or Class 2 (self-employed; that is, those who work on their own account), or Class 3 (nonemployed; that is, not in Class 1 or Class 2). The employer also makes a contribution in Class 1, but obviously not in Class 2 and Class 3. The national government also contributes out of its general taxation revenues. The benefits also vary between classes; members of Class 1 have available to them all benefits itemized in the preceding paragraph; those in Class 2, all except the unemployment benefit; and those in Class 3, the benefits listed except for the unemployment benefit, sickness benefit, and maternity allowance. Benefits under the Industrial Injuries schemes are available only to persons in Class 1.

The Beveridge report recommended, and Parliament endorsed, the principle of a flat-rate contribution and a flat-rate benefit, and the original law was shaped accordingly. The original benefit levels were below the subsistence levels Beveridge intended, however, and there has been a trend to allow larger contributions as a worker's earnings increased, with resulting higher benefit levels. This approach was implemented for retirement pensions in 1961, and for unemployment and sickness benefits in 1966. Some legislative intiatives in this decade have completely abandoned the flat-rate principle.

Beveridge had intended that contributory pensions would represent adequate income for a minimum standard of living, but in many cases additional money was needed to reach this standard, largely due to the inflationary forces which have frequently outdated the minimum subsistence level. While there have been increases in both the cash and absolute values of benefits over the years, it has been necessary to provide an additional source of income to some recipients. These Social Insurance and Industrial Injuries claimants, as well as uninsured people who were without adequate income, were helped by the National Assistance Board, which paid cash benefits on the basis of need rather than contributory status. In 1966 a new scheme of supplementary pensions and allowances for needy people who were not in full-time work went into effect and is now administered by the Supplementary Benefits Commission of the Department of Health and Social Security. Supplementary Benefits now provides the income floor below which no British individual or family need fall. A number of other benefits are available through the Department of Health and Social Security, including Family Income Supplements which add an allowance to low-paid full-time workers with dependent children; Attendance Allowances, which provide cash assistance to people so severely physically or mentally disabled as to require constant attention or supervision; and Mobility Allowances, which benefit disabled people who cannot walk, but who can benefit from increased facilities for mobility. There has been a trend toward establishing new noncontributory allowance categories as their benefit to those in certain types of hardship becomes apparent.

Family Allowances   Additional reference must be made to family allowances and the National Health Service. These programs have been integral parts of life in the United Kingdom since 1945 and 1948, respectively. They are noteworthy because of their benefit and use as a matter of right by virtually the entire population, available equally and without a hint of charity or stigma. Family allowances provide a cash payment to families for each child who is below the school-leaving age of sixteen; or for young people up to nineteen years of age who remain in school or are apprentices. The value of a family's allowance depends solely on the number of children, and its only relation to income is the fact that it is taxable as such. Payments are made weekly to parents at neighborhood post offices out of the general revenue of the Exchequer, rather than from National Insurance funds. They were intended originally to reduce poverty in large families with low wages, and to a lesser extent to restore the birth rate which had declined during the Great Depression and World War II. While there is no evidence that British family allowances have stimulated population growth, their benefit to families and children has warranted their maintenance and increasing cash value over the years. Recent developments have expanded the scheme to include payments for first-born children for the first time.

National Health Service   As the United States works toward the goal of making high-quality health care available to all segments of the public, it is useful to examine briefly the basic principles of the National Health Service. As a comprehensive service based upon the citizen's right to medical care, it provides general practice, specialist, hospital, and community physical and mental health services without charge to the patient. Dental services, prescriptions and optometry are similarly covered, although in certain situations some treatments may require nominal payments. This does not mean that any of the services are free, but rather that the patient does not pay for them on an individual transactional basis. The services are available equally to the total population, and they are paid for by the total population through taxation and a small National Health Service contribution which is collected with workers' National Insurance contributions. Regional, area, and community authorities and departments plan, organize, and deliver these centrally funded services.

Since 1948 there have been a number of additions and modifications to the service. The ever-increasing technical, financial, and social complexities of modern health care have contributed to a recent acceleration of the evolutionary process. Various proposals for improving the administrative structure had been discussed for some eighteen years before the reorganization which took place in 1974, corresponding with local government reorganization. Among the objectives of the plan were uniting the hospital and community branches of the service, enabling greater public and professional participation in planning and operations, and improving management and accountability through central government's financial authority. Much of the current discussion of health care provisions in the United States and Great Britain comes from the fact that these are not readily integrated objectives, and that they require time to become practical realities. A forthcoming royal commission report will consider further adaptations of the National Health Service to meet these challenges while maintaining high standards and widespread public confidence.

The simplest and clearest statement of the programs that went into effect July 5, 1948, is to be found in a pamphlet prepared by the British Information Services, entitled *Britain's Charter of Social Security*. Its concluding statement is:

> July 5th, then, marks one more stage on the long road of British social development. No one claims that the new charter is perfect; it will certainly be added to, modified and improved upon as time goes on, and as experience shows where its shortcomings lie. But in spite of whatever shortcomings there may be, it puts Britain well in the forefront of progress toward complete social security. . . .
>
> The charter as a whole is, in effect, an expression of the duty of the community to the individual. By his work and his social conduct the individual helps the community, and in return the community helps him when he is in need of help —and in the long run it is the individual who counts for most. The retention of the principle of contributions means that these social benefits are not simply a form of charity which pauperizes the individual, but the fact that the individual does not have to pay the whole cost himself means that society is not blind to its duties.
>
> In conception the scheme is a compromise between fully government-financed services and services completely paid for by contributions, just as in administration it is a compromise between centralism and devolution of responsibility. In each, the compromise can be adjusted in the light of changing needs, and the scheme retains the advantages of flexibility without losing the other advantages of uniformity.
>
> This division of responsibility between the central government, the local authorities, and the individual himself is perhaps the keynote of the whole but it is the individual for whom the whole exists. In a democratic country such as Britain that is as it should be.[7]

The Personal Social Services   While income maintenance and the administration of other cash benefits are clearly the responsibility of the central government Department of Health and Social Security, local government social service departments are largely responsible for providing the individualized help which people may need when confronted with nonfinancial problems and difficulties. These services cover a wider range than is available

---

[7]British Information Services, *Britain's Charter of Social Security,* July 1948, pp. 22–24.

33

in most communities in the United States and are frequently mandated or suggested by Acts of Parliament. A sample of them might include the provision of telephones, bath aids, and physical adaptations for the homes of disabled people; residential care for certain young or elderly people; help with domestic work in order to allow infirm or greatly distressed people to remain in their homes and communities; interpersonal counseling for overwhelmed parents or children; the provision of free bus passes to the elderly; and child protection services. These and the variety of other services provided by local social service departments are used by a very considerable cross section of social and income groups, and receive broadly based public support.

Like the income maintenance and health services, the "personally tailored" social services developed in uneven, often piecemeal fashion over the years. A serious problem had developed so that by the 1960s many independent public agencies were inefficiently overlapping and duplicating one another, while frequently being inaccessible to potential consumers either geographically or because of narrowly defined functions. In response to these and other difficulties, the personal social services equivalent of the Beveridge report was submitted in 1968 by Lord Seebohm, chairman of the Committee on Local Authority and Allied Social Services. The Seebohm report recommended consolidating many of the existing agencies and expanding the role and responsibility of the new social service departments. The committee recognized the fact that social and personal problems were complex and were not often resolved adequately within departments such as child care or mental welfare. It emphasized the need for preventive, developmental, and coordinated services rather than simply putting the existing departments together under a common roof. Stress was also placed on the need to make the proposed new departments readily available to the communities which they were to serve. In 1970 the Local Authority Social Service Act opened the way for implementation of the basic recommendations of the Seebohm report, including the departments of social services which are now in existence throughout Great Britain. They are characterized by county or metropolitan authority administration and a number of area service teams throughout the community. Some services, such as legal aid, probation and parole, school social work, and housing remain independent.

Since 1970 the transition to unified community-based agencies has been complicated by a nationwide revamping of city and county government boundaries and responsibilities, increasing stringency in public spending, and greatly increased consumer demand for social service department resources due in part to new legislation and increased access to services. The generalist-specialist issue has also come into clearer focus. But the concept of service delivery which is accessible and useful to the entire community, not tied to financial assistance programs, and offering competence in both general and specialized areas of practice has proven itself. It is in all probability a prelude to the model of service which the United States will evolve in the future and carry into the next century.

The British do not view the provision of these services as a condescending charity of the state. They are the services that an enlightened and democratic state, through its elected and accountable representatives, deems to be the right of a responsible people. Furthermore, they are regarded as an investment in the lives of the people as their energies and wills are directed to the survival of their country in this highly competitive contemporary world. This emphasis upon constructiveness and prevention, upon a healthier, more productive, and happier people is in marked contrast to the repressive legislation of the Statute of Laborers of 1349. It is also some measure of the creative humanity of a democratically oriented people.

Voluntary Services: European Background

Even before the rise of modern European states there were social services of a primitive sort provided through the agency of the church. Individual and institutional benevolences, in obedience to religious teachings, were manifested through alms to the poor, shelter to the homeless, and care and comfort to the sick. Monasteries and hospitals, the latter being charitable foundations for the sick, the destitute, and the aged, were most prominently identified in the almsgiving and sheltering role. Throughout the Middle Ages the religious guilds and craft associations also undertook to provide shelter and alms.

Yet, for all the good intentions of individuals or organizations, charity persisted without order or coordination. Rather than reducing begging and vagrancy, the indiscriminate giving of alms only encouraged greater reliance thereon. The Elizabethan poor laws had attempted to bring order out of the chaos of public relief, but it remained for the German cities of Hamburg and Elberfeld in the eighteenth and nineteenth centuries to develop the beginnings of an organized system. In Hamburg the first steps consisted of the establishment of a central bureau followed by the apportionment of the city into districts. To each district an overseer or supervisor was assigned, and associated with him were others who served voluntarily. These visitors called upon the poor in their districts and sought to render assistance as well as to keep themselves informed of conditions producing distress and poverty. Each visitor was to maintain close and friendly relations with the poor within his district. This friendly visiting, together with the districting principle and the overall direction and coordination of a central board for the entire city, was the unique feature of the plan. The only paid and officially constituted person was the chairman of the central bureau. As the work expanded from its beginnings in Hamburg in 1788 to its elaboration in Elberfeld in 1852, greater stress was placed upon the relation of the visitor to the person in need, the enlargement of the power of the visitor actually to grant relief, and the emphasis upon removing the causes of pauperism. While the Hamburg-Elberfeld system began essentially as a voluntary venture and while much of the leadership and support, including the use of volunteers, continued from these sources, it eventually received public funds and operated under municipal ordinances. Its significance lies in its early enunciation of principles that underlay the later charity organization movement in Great Britain and America.

The Charity Organization Society

The various principles and practices as worked out in the Hamburg system, then by Thomas Chalmers in Glasgow, 1843, and later in Elberfeld, found expression in the first Charity Organization Society (COS) in London, 1869. As the name implies, the Charity Organization Society aimed to effect a coordination among existing welfare services and agencies. The granting of relief was the function of the existing agencies, as it had been heretofore. The purpose of the COS was to develop a machinery and a technique whereby relief could be expeditiously and economically administered without duplication and competition. A central committee was established to which district committees were answerable. The district committees served as clearing-house and central registration bureau. They were also to relieve such as fell outside the poor law, but only after making a thorough investigation. Arrangements were worked out between the district committees and the poor-law officials so that there would be no overlapping or duplication of services. This society, while important for what it did for organizing initiative and philanthropy in a coordinated service for the poor of London, is equally famous as a pioneering model, which other cities, principally those in the United States, were to follow.

Within a short time of the formation of the COS, another development was under way—the social settlement. The baleful effects of the industrial revolution were to be found in the large cities, commercial and industrial, and it was in response to these conditions that some clergymen and some Oxford and Cambridge university students and graduates addressed themselves. Beginning in his Whitechapel parish in London's notorious East End, Vicar (later Canon) Barnett worked directly with the poor. With his fellow workers, he sought to improve the lot of distressed individuals as well as to change the environment that enveloped them. One of these workers, Arnold Toynbee (1852–1883), who was a lecturer and tutor at Oxford University, had lived in half-furnished lodgings as far as he could after the manner of workingmen, joining their clubs, discussing with them ". . . things material and spiritual—the laws of nature and of God." In his honor and memory the social settlement was named Toynbee Hall when it opened in 1884. The social settlement idea spread throughout Britain, and within two years the first settlement house (Neighborhood Guild) was opened in New York City by persons who had become familiar with the work of Toynbee Hall.

Contemporary Voluntary Services in Great Britain

Social services under voluntary auspices have continued to expand since the COS days. Many charitable societies were in existence before 1869, many have developed since then, and very few have gone out of existence. There are many organizations, some of them with titled or royal patronage, that continue to provide social services to meet the needs of the British people. In some instances these organizations provide services for which the need persists even beyond the existing tax-supported services. In other instances, organizations will have modified their service offerings or will have developed new programs to meet emerging needs not yet within the scope of the public social services, such as the "meals on wheels" services to older persons, many of whom are housebound but who insist stoutly on maintaining their accustomed habitation. There is hardly a public social service for which there is not one or more like services offered under voluntary auspice —not as competitive but as complementary and occasionally supplementary. Such activity and such organizations attest to the vitality of the voluntary effort throughout Great Britain in family and child welfare, old people's welfare, corrections, welfare of the blind, youth services, legal aid, and so on. It may not be inappropriate to recall the observation of the Nathan Report that "historically, state action is voluntary action crystallized and made universal."[8]

The British have faced directly the respective roles of the voluntary and the statutory (in America, public welfare) services, and have a place for both; indeed, in the British democratic system the two are essential. Dr. W. G. S. Adams, formerly warden of All Souls College, Oxford, expressed it in these words:

---

[8]Report of the Committee on the Law and Practice Relating to Charitable Trusts, 1952, Her Majesty's Stationery Office, cmd. paper, 8710, pa. 39. Likewise, it should be noted that the Introduction to *Social Services in Britain* reinforces the same point: "Nearly all the services now in being were pioneered by voluntary organizations, especially the churches, and many voluntary services still surround and supplement those publicly and statutorily provided. The two types are not competitive but complementary; public authorities often work through voluntary authorities specially adapted to serve specific needs, and their officials co-operate with the workers of the many social service societies." *Social Services in Britain,* prepared by the Reference Division, Central Office of Information, London, rev. February 1969, p. 1.

Great as was the nineteenth century both in the field of state development and of voluntary service, it was only a prelude to the greater developments of the twentieth century. The first quarter of this century, especially the years 1906 to 1912, saw an unparalleled advance of state functions in the field of social security and well-being. The first world war greatly extended the organisation and controls of the state. The movement continued in the second quarter of the century and was carried much further by the extension of state control in the second world war and the period following. But with this great expansion of the state there came also in this country a remarkable development of voluntary organisations. Here, as in the Dominions and in the United States of America—countries with much in common in their idea of constitutional and personal liberty—state action itself encouraged and used the resources of voluntary organisations. It was found in one field after another that, in order to realise the policy of national security and social well-being, the state had in increasing measure to call upon the resourceful co-operation of voluntary organisations. This is characteristic of our way of life. At one time it seemed to some as if the statutory bodies would do away with the need for voluntary organisations. But more and more it came to be realised that we were reaching out to a vision of community life in which the co-operation of voluntary and statutory bodies was essential. Their services were complementary, not competitive, still less antagonistic, in a true view of community development. At least this was the British way of life.[9]

THE VOLUNTARY SERVICES IN AMERICA

From the earliest immigration to America through the succeeding years, concern has been expressed by members of various religious groups for the welfare of people. This was true of Protestants, of Catholics, of Jews, and of members of the Society of Friends from the first day they set foot on American soil. Indeed, this was true once these groups settled in the New World because they had had a similar concern in the countries from which they came. In all religious teachings there is a like commitment, which seeks expression in whatever place and in whatever circumstances the members find themselves. This commitment often finds expression in promoting social welfare through voluntary associations.[10]

---

[9]W. G. S. Adams, "Voluntary Social Service in the 20th Century," in *Voluntary Social Services, Handbook of Information and Directory of Organisations* (London: National Council of Social Service, 1948), pp. 11–12.

[10]Within recent years the term "voluntary" has come to be accepted as more accurately descriptive of certain services and social service agencies then the earlier term "private." The term signifies the voluntary association of citizens to provide services, to secure contributions in support thereof, and to effect legal incorporation to fulfill societally approved purposes. In a similar way, even though the term "public" continues to be used in relation to tax-supported social services, there is a marked trend toward using the terms "governmental," or "statutory."

Later, nationality groups, regardless of religious affiliation, bound them-selves to come to the aid of their compatriots: the St. Andrews Society of New York (1756) for the British, the German Society of New York (1784) for the Germans, the French Benevolent Society of New York (1807) for the French.

Still another early group, but one without religious or nationality affiliation, was the New York Society for the Prevention of Pauperism, formed in 1817. Its purpose was to study the causes of pauperism and to promote measures for its prevention and elimination. The members of the society were con-vinced that the forces making for pauperism were within the individual as well as outside him, and that prevention called for certain actions with respect to the internal as well as to the external. A number of the proposed measures anticipated programs eventually elaborated by the charity organization movement later in the century, as well as by such commercial promotions as savings banks, mutual benefit societies, and life insurance. What seemed to characterize this early society was the disparity between the excellence of many of the proposals and the execution of them through effective action.

The Association for Improving the Condition of the Poor

The most impressive, and the most far-reaching in influence, of the early societies concerned with the immediate problems of the city poor, was the Association for Improving the Condition of the Poor (AICP), organized in 1843 in New York City. According to its first constitution the Association's aim was ". . . the elevation of the moral and physical condition of the indi-gent; and so far as compatible with these objects, the relief of their necessi-ties." Besides the relief-giving function, the AICP aimed to do something about the conditions that beset the poor. Among its earliest efforts were those directed toward the improvement of housing and sanitation. It is said that the report made by a committee to the board of the AICP in 1853 was the first tenement-house report made in America. In 1855 a model tenement, "The Workingmen's Home," was constructed largely through the efforts of the AICP. Other efforts during its early period resulted in legislation to prevent adulteration of milk, the establishment of medical dispensaries for the indigent sick, the construction of a public bath and washhouse, the creation of a special institution for the ruptured and crippled, and, in 1849, the incorpora-tion of the New York Juvenile Asylum, "a reformatory and disciplinary institu-tion, for the education and elevation of vicious children and their subsequent indenture."

From the turn of the twentieth century until its merger with the New York Charity Organization Society in 1939, the AICP furthered its program of improving the conditions affecting people. Many of the enterprises it encouraged, sponsored or initiated have since become a part of the community's social services: tuberculosis hospitals, health services for school children, convalescent homes for mothers and babies, school lunches, dental clinics, work relief projects, legislation for widows' pensions, venereal disease clinics, health centers, vocational guidance bureaus, mental hygiene clinics, apartment housing for the aged, and homes for the aged.

The Charity Organization Society Movement in America

Within four years of the organization of the London COS, the United States encountered the serious depression of 1873 as an aftermath of the Civil War. Despite the hundreds of local relief societies, or perhaps because of them, it was generally recognized that the existing methods of charity were inefficient and inadequate. Organizations in such cities as Philadelphia and Boston had made some use of the Hamburg-Elberfeld system of poor relief, but it was not until 1877 that the first COS was established in America. The Reverend Stephen Humphreys Gurteen, assistant rector of St. Paul's Church in Buffalo, New York, actively promoted, together with a number of prominent business and professional men of the city, a nonsectarian organization to deal with the problems of poverty. Gurteen, who was born in England, had earned a bachelor's degree at Jesus College, Cambridge University, and came to New York in 1863. In the summer of 1877 he had visited London and seen the work of the COS, accompanying district agents in their rounds of investigation. The Charity Organization Society came into being in December, 1877. Buffalo was divided into eight districts, each with a committee and a number of family visitors. No relief funds were administered. The COS let it be known that its sole purpose was to help organize existing local charities, and that each society was to retain autonomy. The new society decided it would cut across religious, political, and nationality lines. The early purpose to investigate cases and refer them to proper existing agencies demonstrated the compelling necessity of effecting some reform in the prevailing system of municipal relief. At the same time it aroused the interest of a number of public-spirited citizens.

Such a movement that met with widespread acceptance must have had much to recommend it. In practically every sense the time was ripe for it, and it was ripe for the time. The niggardliness of the Elizabethan poor law survivals in the United States had reduced, or rather maintained, public outdoor relief to the beggar's level. Charitable bodies that made many beginnings in many places incorporated the individualism of the industrial entrepreneur who had grown wealthy in an expanding economy. Not infrequently a prosperous donor sought to impress his particular philanthropy upon any relief society willing to accept his largess. As a result there was such an overlapping and waste of charity funds that more needs were unmet than were met. Coincident with the creation of large cities and scores of factory towns, much of the neighborliness that characterized a simpler society was gone. Coupled with this was the strong conviction that pauperism indicated a character deficiency and required the maximum of personal influence of the donor or the donor's agent upon the recipient.

Expansion of the COS Movement

As one surveys the whole field of social work today, three main groups of interest and activities centered around them are readily apparent. First, the preoccupation with the individual per se; second, concentration upon the group of individuals as the working unit; and third, concern with developing resources to meet human needs. To these three we have given the terms "social casework," "social group work," and "community organization." The division within the charity organization movement exemplifies the first and third of these, while the social settlement expresses the second. Consideration of group work will be left for later chapters, but the developments within the COS with respect to trends toward individualization and community organization must necessarily be dealt with here.

An attitude that regarded the needy as victims of their own vices and failings tended to absolve the social order of any responsibility for the conditions that reduced individuals to destitution. As long as such an attitude prevailed, it was consistent to make relief as unattractive as possible. A maximum premium was placed upon gratuitous advice, the arts of persuasion, and the rigors of exhortation. But an awakened social conscience, coupled with some comprehension of the interrelationship of the economic and social order, gave pause to so easy and comfortable a proposition and compelled attention to some of the factors that lay outside the individual. This realization was based, understandably enough, upon a rather fragmentary knowledge of "causes," but it tended to shift some emphasis from an internal to an external causation. It may be more accurate to say that the approach became twofold: first, to continue to give an individualized service in the light of a growing insight into human character (the more technical term "behavior" was to appear later); and second, to seek for those changes within the existing framework of society that would produce less devastating effects upon the individual.

Among the earliest of these concerns was housing. Long before the charity organization movement had taken form, proposals had been made for improving housing conditions for the poor in order to reduce the incidence of pauperism. Under the Hamburg-Elberfeld system, efforts had been made toward better housing for the poor. In London, Octavia Hill and Edward Denison, leaders in reform movements, had agitated for years in the same cause. Brooklyn, however, was one of the early American cities to secure the enactment of a tenement-house law in 1879, and later, under the inspired leadership of Alfred T. White, to erect model tenements. Edward T. Devine, in his reminiscent volume *When Social Work Was Young,* recounted the work of the New York Society in making available to the city of New York the services of housing authorities through the organizational channels of COS. Other cities also gave attention to housing reform, among which must be mentioned Chicago, Washington, D.C., and Youngstown and Columbus, Ohio.

The prevention of tuberculosis was another crusade in which COS workers were enlisted. As in the case of housing reform, the initial body was a committee within the New York Society (in 1902), which was still under the leadership of Edward T. Devine. This Committee on Prevention of Tuberculosis wisely utilized the services of capable physicians and lay persons in working out a program of research into the social and medical aspects of tuberculosis, education of the public, encouragement of sanitoriums for the care of patients, and relief of indigent consumptives. Several years later, in 1904, at a meeting of the American Medical Association, the National Association for the Study and Prevention of Tuberculosis was organized. In other cities—Washington, D. C., Minneapolis, Boston, Buffalo, Pittsburgh, and Chicago—the Charity Organization Society or its equivalent was active in tuberculosis work, laying the groundwork for an effective nationalization of a preventive program.

Shortly after the establishment of the first and second juvenile courts in Chicago and Denver, workers within the charity organization movement had become active in the field of juvenile probation. In 1900 the Buffalo Society organized a committee on probation, which was instrumental in the passage of a state law to amend Buffalo's city charter permitting the appointment of two probation officers. Later, the New York Society placed a woman probation officer at the disposal of a magistrate's court to effect a closer relation between the legal aspect of the court and the social rehabilitation of the offender. Societies in other cities followed with close interest the developments within the court structure, particularly within the juvenile court.

One aspect of this concern with the operation of the courts was the effort stimulated by charity organization societies to secure a fairer distribution of legal services to persons with limited means. Too often, clients who came to the attention of social workers were in need of legal services but lacked resources to take advantage of, or even to secure, the protection of their legal rights. Both Baltimore and Buffalo established legal aid bureaus within their own societies to make legal services available to clients, either without cost or at minimum cost.

Other areas in which the societies came to operate were those of desertion and nonsupport cases. Especially was this true in Boston, Philadelphia, and Chicago. Problems within the family also called for action, such as the inadequacies and lack of facilities for dealing with dependent and neglected children. The Children's Aid Society of Pennsylvania was launched in 1882 largely through the efforts of those associated with the work of the Philadelphia Society for Organizing Charity. Beggars and vagrants, whether within or outside a family group, were touched by COS efforts. For a time in New York all beggars and vagrants were turned over by the Police Department to the COS, where aid was administered by means of wayfarers' lodges; these lodges were also provided in Chicago, Philadelphia, and Boston.

Professional Journals, Schools, and Organizations

Three developments in the latter years of the nineteenth century and early twentieth must be mentioned here because of their continuing contribution to the field of social work. One of these was the establishment of a professional journal, another the founding of a professional school for the training of social workers, and a third the beginnings of a professional organization.

The *Survey* and *Survey Graphic* date back to the Charity Organization Society of New York. As long ago as 1891, the society had published the *Charities Review*, and for the next ten years it continued to speak for the social work of that day. In 1897, *Lend-A-Hand*, published in Boston, was merged with the *Charities Review*. At this time the COS had begun a kind of house organ called *Charities*, which aimed to promote directly the work of the organization. Before the merger of the *Charities Review* and *Charities* (to be known as *Charities*) in 1901, each journal had published material of outstanding merit. Mergers were not yet over, for in 1905 *Charities* was joined by Graham Taylor's *Chicago Commons*, and early in 1906 by *Jewish Charity*, to become *Charities and Commons*. After four years, *Charities and Commons* became *The Survey*, taking its name from the monumental study in six volumes of the city of Pittsburgh. During all these years these publications had been under the wing of the New York COS, but in 1912 *The Survey* was incorporated separately. From then until it ceased publication in 1952 it was unequaled in the field of social work publications for pithiness, timeliness, and sprightliness of style.

Just as *The Survey* sprang from the charity organization movement, so also have professional schools of social work. Staff conferences and supervision for employed as well as volunteer workers soon proved inadequate to keep abreast of changing demands of the job. Then followed informal courses and lectures for workers in the various societies, of which perhaps the earliest was Brooklyn, in 1891. The first decisive step was taken when, in 1898, the New

York Society offered its summer school of philanthropy with Philip W. Ayres, assistant secretary of the society, as its director, and with an enrollment of thirty students. For six years this Summer School of Philanthropic Workers continued until it was reorganized upon an eight months' instruction basis. In that year, 1904, the director of the New York Society, Edward T. Devine, along with his other duties, assumed the directorship of the first school of social work in this country. Subsequently, other schools of social work were organized so that by 1977 eighty-five graduate schools of social work were accredited by the Council on Social Work Education. A fast-growing development has been the offer of undergraduate programs in social work. By 1977 the Council had approved such programs in one hundred and eighty-three colleges and universities.

It was not until after World War I that a professional membership organization developed. From its establishment in 1921 it has continued increasingly to bring within its membership workers with appropriate professional training and experience. It has concerned itself with enhancing the quality of performance of those offering the social services; the strengthening of educational preparation for social work practice; the extension of the social services as an essential and positive contribution by governmental as well as voluntary agencies; and the enlargement of the public understanding of social work— to mention but a few of its announced purposes in the exercise of its leadership role as an organization that represents all aspects of the profession. The membership of the National Association of Social Workers numbers approximately seventy-five thousand; its basic journal is *Social Work.*

Although its base is the broad one of social welfare, the core of the National Conference on Social Welfare is professional social work, as judged by its individual as well as agency membership. Growing out of the concerns of the social scientists about social conditions in the last third of the nineteenth century, it took form in 1879 as the National Conference of Charities and Corrections. Always a public forum for the discussion of social welfare issues, it, too, has stood for improvement and extension of social services for all people. Now known as the National Conference on Social Welfare, it meets annually and publishes its official proceedings as *The Social Welfare Forum.*

Everything that has been written here about the charity organization movement is pertinent to family welfare, since it is from that movement that the family societies of today have developed. The immediate relation was the creation of the Field Department within the New York COS in 1905. Four years later this led directly to the Charity Organization Department of the Russell Sage Foundation, with Mary Richmond as director. In 1911 the National Association of Societies for Organizing Charity was formed; Francis H. McLean, formerly secretary of the Field Department of COS, was its first executive secretary. Name changes since then indicate the trend in thinking: American Association for Organizing Charity (to include Canadian societies),

American Assoication for Organizing Family Social Work, the Family Welfare Association of America, and in 1946 the Family Service Association of America. In 1919 the periodical *The Family* was established, and since then has served as an organ of education and opinion on much of the best of casework practice in family welfare and related areas. In October 1946 it was named *The Journal of Social Casework;* in 1950, *Social Casework.*

The Origins of the Social Settlements

At least one other movement must be mentioned in this retrospective survey of the development of social work. It began, understandably enough, in an area that had suffered earliest and most acutely the effects of industrialization —London, England. By the 1880s social work in England consisted largely of the meager grants of a poor relief authority, the unorganized philanthropies (church and private) of benevolent individuals, and the organized efforts of the Charity Organization Society. It will be observed that, in practically every instance, relief was directed toward the individual. It remained for the social settlement to shift this focus from the individual as an individual to the individual within a group. The unit of service had become the group. What was more natural than that such work should emanate from, be supported by, and be engaged in by the class that had benefited most by the industrialization of England—the upper middle class? Toynbee Hall expressed from the moment of its founding in 1884 the conviction that individuals more fortunately endowed with this world's goods could, by taking residence in poorer areas of the city, share their culture and advantages with those to whom opportunity had never come. This sharing process was the substance of the early efforts of the "settlers," a contribution of the more fortunate out of their experience as well as a learning from the poor out of their experience.

The example of Toynbee Hall was carried to America, and in 1886 the first settlement in the United States, Neighborhood Guild, was established in New York City. Industrialization in America had created not only tremendous wealth but also the very conditions that made that wealth unattainable to all but a few. Social work, including the latest addition of the settlements, tried to understand the problems of the disadvantaged and to help them realize opportunities for effective living in a social order that was none too kind to those who had failed to succeed.

Conclusion

It must be obvious from the foregoing account that the beginnings of social work have been inextricably bound up with the fundamental economic conditions and changes within the social order and with the concomitant philosophies expressed therein. From the breakup of the old feudal order, through the successive changes of mercantilism, commercialism, and industrialism, there has persisted the basic and unavoidable fact of human needs. To meet these needs, society established certain services, early based on the premises of individual responsibility. The individual who was in want had brought that condition upon himself through his own shiftlessness, ignorance, or incapacity. The answer was to meet that need as sparingly as possible; relief was not to be attractive enough, for instance, to tempt the lowest paid workman in England away from his job, nor was any individual to be allowed to feel that society approved of his need. This all sounds quite Elizabethan, but it must be remembered that such was the philosophy dominant throughout the two centuries that followed.

Several centuries of attempts at alleviation had clearly shown the limitations of any program that dealt only with the result instead of the cause. Little insight was gained into the nature of social problems until our understanding took in more than merely the fault of the individual. Only after we began to realize that there were factors larger than and beyond any individual did we proceed to the next phase, prevention. Then the role played by the entire nation—its industry and trade, its philosophies and social institutions— became evident. An awakened understanding of these forces showed their relation to the fate of the individual. Only with such understanding could an ameliorative program that saw the connection between cause and effect take hold. Social work became a part of the economy of the nation. As the new profession developed, it became clear that social workers who were called in after the damage to the individual had been done might well be looked on for consultation, direction, and action before the fact. This early concern with social problems gradually expanded (some would say narrowed) to working with those capacities within the individual that enable him to adjust to and use effectively his environment of things and people.

Important and far reaching as public welfare is today, it must be evident how essential a part social work under voluntary auspices has exercised in the overall development of the social services. Even though the bulk of financing is now carried by governmental funds, it was voluntary agencies during the preceding century that developed the basis for the present individualized services in all welfare programs. In many instances it was the voluntary agencies that provided institutional care for disadvantaged persons— children, the aged, the chronically ill, the mentally ill, the feebleminded, the blind, the deaf, the juvenile offender—and then later experimented with noninstitutional services for many of these. They were the agencies that developed the basis of what today is social action; they that developed the basis for current group work services; they whose labors furnished the groundwork for much of present-day community organization.

With all their mistakes, inevitable in any pioneering, the voluntary agencies have consistently and conscientiously pushed for standards that ultimately have been incorporated into sound social work practice. Furthermore, the adoption through public financing of many of the services they developed has enabled them to move into new areas of exploration. What becomes more and more clear, just as in Great Britain, is that there will continue to be a complementary role for the voluntary social service agency and the government agency. As heretofore, their respective positions will undergo redefinition and realignment as needs and conditions change, but their interdependency will be as essential as it will be inevitable, given our democratic system.

BIBLIOGRAPHY

Abbott, Edith. *Some American Pioneers in Social Welfare.* Chicago: University of Chicago Press, 1937.

Beveridge, William H. (Lord Beveridge). *Social Insurance and the Allied Services.* New York: Crowell-Collier and Macmillan, 1942.

Bremner, Robert H. *American Philanthropy.* Chicago: University of Chicago Press, 1960.

Bruno, Frank J. *Trends in Social Work, 1874–1956: A History Based on the Proceedings of the National Conference of Social Work.* 2d ed. New York: Columbia University Press, 1957.

Chambers, Clarke A. *Paul U. Kellogg and the Survey: Voices for Social Welfare and Social Justice.* Minneapolis: University of Minnesota Press, 1971.

Cole, Margaret. *Beatrice Webb.* New York: Harcourt, Brace & World, 1946.

Davis, Allen F. *American Heroine: The Life and Legend of Jane Addams.* New York: Oxford University Press, 1973.

————. *Spearheads for Reform: The Social Settlements and the Progressive Movement, 1890–1914.* New York: Oxford University Press, 1967.

Devine, Edward T. *When Social Work Was Young.* New York: Crowell-Collier and Macmillan, 1939.

de Schweinitz, Karl. *England's Road to Social Security.* Philadelphia: University of Pennsylvania Press, 1943.

Health Services in Britain, Central Office of Information Reference Pamphlet 20. London: Her Majesty's Stationery Office, 1974.

Kahn, Alfred J., and Sheila B. Kamerman. *Not For the Poor Alone: European Social Services.* Philadelphia: Temple University Press, 1975.

Klein, Philip. *From Philanthropy to Social Welfare.* San Francisco: Jossey-Bass, 1968.

Lowell, Josephine S. *Public Relief and Private Charity.* New York: G. P. Putnam's Sons, 1884.

Lubove, Roy. *The Professional Altruist: The Emergence of Social Work as a Career.* Cambridge, Mass.: Harvard University Press, 1965.

Mays, John, ed. *Penelope Hall's Social Services of England and Wales.* 9th ed. London: Routledge & Kegan Paul, 1975.

MacKenzie, Norman, and Jeanne MacKenzie. *The Fabians.* New York: Simon & Schuster, 1977.

Morris, Robert. *Toward a Caring Society.* New York: Columbia University School of Social Work, 1974.

Mowatt, Charles Loch. *The Charity Organization Society, 1869–1913.* London: Methuen, 1961.

Pimlott, J. A. R. *Toynbee Hall: Fifty Years of Social Progress.* London: J. M. Dent & Sons, 1935.

Pumphrey, Ralph E., and Muriel W. Pumphrey, eds. *The Heritage of American Social Work.* New York: Columbia University Press, 1961.

Queen, Stuart Alfred. *Social Work in the Light of History.* Philadelphia: J. B. Lippincott, 1922.

Reynolds, Bertha C. *An Uncharted Journey.* New York: Citadel Press, 1963.

Rich, Margaret E. *A Belief in People.* New York: Family Service Association of America, 1956.

Richmond, Mary E. *The Long View.* New York: Russell Sage Foundation, 1930. *Report of the Committee on Local Authority and Allied Personal Social Services, The Seebohm Report.* London: Her Majesty's Stationery Office, 1968.

Sleeman, J. F. *The Welfare State: Its Aims, Benefits, and Costs.* London: George Allen & Unwin, 1973.

Social Security in Britain. London: Her Majesty's Stationery Office, 1973.

Stein, Bruno. *Work and Welfare in Britain and the U.S.A.* London and Basingstoke: Macmillan Press, Ltd., 1976.

Warner, Amos G. *American Charities.* New York: Thomas Y. Crowell Company, 1894.

Watson, Frank D. *The Charity Organization Movement in the United States.* New York: Crowell-Collier and Macmillan, 1922.

Willmott, Phyllis. *Consumer's Guide to the British Social Services.* Harmondsworth, England, and Baltimore, Md.: Penguin Books, 1975

3
SERVICES AND AGENCIES IN PERSPECTIVE

ARTHUR E. FINK

Professor Emeritus, School of Social Work,
University of North Carolina

A. FROM THE ALMSHOUSE TO SOCIAL SECURITY

The main outlines of the English Poor Law have been presented as the background for the development of American systems of relief. When colonists came to America, they were largely from England, and brought with them English ideas, English common law, English institutions, English customs. The almshouse is a case in point. Pauperism was not to be made respectable. Relief was to be as unpalatable as possible. The catchall institution was the almshouse, into which were herded the old and the young, the sick and the well, the mentally normal and the mentally diseased, the epileptic, the blind, the feebleminded, the alcoholic, and the improvident. As in England, almshouse paupers could be farmed out and children apprenticed. Those who managed to avoid the poorhouse—to call it what it really was—received outdoor relief (that is, in their own homes). We stressed repression, we centered responsibility in the local community, we permitted only a minimum of state supervision and control, and, lastly, a generation later than England we passed our first social security act.

Public welfare is a relatively new term. In the Elizabethan law of 1601 and the revision of 1834, the term was unknown. Destitution was a local problem and even though a governmental unit may have granted relief, the service was termed neither public nor welfare. We of today who speak so glibly of public welfare need some perspective on its development in order to realize the long way we have come and, incidentally, to appreciate the long way we still have to go.

The people and the situations (but not necessarily the problem) with which public welfare has dealt have been essentially local, and the governmental unit that has usually granted assistance has been either the smallest or the one traditionally associated with the relief of distress. In our own country as far back as colonial days it was the parish, the township, the town, the city, or the county rather than the colony which furnished aid. Even with statehood the tradition continued for almost a century in most of the eastern seaboard states.

As long all welfare services were provided by the local community, there was little need for or concern with welfare organization. The overseer of the poor dispensed personally all forms of aid, whether of cash or produce, and operated the poorhouse as well. The only other local service available was that of the jail or house of correction, and that usually came under the direction of the sheriff's office. When, however, the state assumed responsibilities for certain classes of what used to be called the "dependent, the defective, and the delinquent," some definite form of organization was necessary. Massachusetts was the first state to establish a state-wide organization. Created in 1863, the Massachusetts Board of State Charities was charged with the investigation and supervision of the entire system of charitable and correctional institutions and empowered to recommend changes directed toward the economical and efficient operation of such institutions.

From Supervision to Administration

The limitations placed on a state board that could only supervise, investigate, report, and recommend were corrected through the establishment of boards with powers of administration and control. Salaried and full-time members of such boards were charged with the maintenance and direction of the charitable agencies of the state. They hired and fired personnel, controlled financial operations, and established policies for the conduct of the agencies and institutions. Such direct forms of control naturally lent themselves more read-ily to the institutional phase of the welfare program, but services traditionally local were touched as well. Some boards of control sought by suggestions and pressures of various kinds to raise standards of local relief, to encourage additional services for those in need, and to improve already existent ser-vices, particularly in the case of the almshouse and other local institutions such as the jail and the house of correction. State boards of charity or control represented little if any change of belief concerning the unfitness of the poor and handicapped. Their aims were to apply business methods in the realm of "charities and corrections," to increase efficiency of administration, to eliminate waste, and, if not to show a profit, at least to show low operating costs. However, by 1917 a positive approach was beginning to replace the negativism of the past three centuries. Public welfare was coming to be regarded as a service with constructive possibilities. True, there were individ-uals who always would need some kind of help, other individuals who would rather live on the public treasury than by their own efforts; but on the other hand, there were many others, perhaps the bulk of all the disadvantaged, who required efforts directed toward their rehabilitation and self-maintenance. Once this latter conviction began to prevail, it became necessary to imple-ment it with effective organization. Although Kansas City, Missouri, had anticipated this development as early as 1910 with the creation of a Board of Public Welfare, it was not until action by Illinois and North Carolina in 1917 that the movement of state-wide organization really got under way. In that year North Carolina established a State Board of Charities and Public Welfare, consisting of seven unpaid members who appointed a commissioner as the executive officer of the board. The board and the commissioner were charged with certain duties of study, investigation, reporting, licensing, and direct service. The latter pertained particularly to providing for the placement and supervision of dependent and delinquent children. The Illinois commis-sioners had advisory functions only, and the actual power lay with the State Department of Public Welfare and its director, who was appointed by the governor.

From 1917 to 1929 most of the states had joined in the movement toward consolidation and coordination of welfare services into a statewide system. Each state sought to work out its own problems according to the exigencies of the situation and of the time. Thus some states established welfare depart-ments headed by an executive appointed by the governor, with a board solely advisory to the executive. Other states had an appointed board that selected the administrator to operate the welfare department, with certain responsibili-ties allocated to the executive and certain others to the board. A third group of states still retained a salaried board of three or five members performing all the functions of an executive board. In some states, all penal, correctional, relief, health, and mental hygiene services were under the direction of one department or board; while in other states, largely for historical reasons, there were two or more boards, departments, or commissions dividing the field. Some states made an organizational division between the institutional and the noninstitutional services. However, regardless of how administrative responsibility was delegated or whether agencies were single or multiple, there was an unmistakable trend in the direction of coordinating administration and supervision in a state department or board as well as tying in the local communities with the state agency. Yet, throughout all these developments, pauper relief still remained in the local town, township, or county.

The Federal Government and Public Welfare

The very nature of public welfare organization and organizations prior to 1929 reflected the limited role that public welfare played in the life of most communities throughout the United States. Of the three areas of government —national, state, local—the first named offered the least share of services. The national government, narrowly interpreting the welfare clause of the Constitution since President Pierce's precedent-making veto in 1854 of the bill to provide care for the insane, had restricted its public welfare activities to traditionally federal, noncontroversial areas. Four departments carried on services that could be identified as welfare—in a broad sense: Treasury (United States Public Health Service, 1798); Interior (Office of Indian Affairs); Labor (Women's Bureau, Children's Bureau, later placed in Department of Health, Education, and Welfare); Justice (Bureau of Prisons, Board of Parole, Probation, later placed in Administrative Office of United States Courts).

The federal government, however, by subsidies and grants-in-aid (sometimes grants of land, sometimes grants of money) aided many programs operated under state auspices: girls' industrial schools, asylums for the deaf, dumb, and blind; penal and reformatory institutions; welfare and hygiene of maternity and infancy. Before the depression of the 1930s was over, the federal government had been irrevocably committed not only to the principle of contribution but also to the desirability and even the necessity of assuming a partnership role with the states and local communities.

Noninstitutional Services before 1929

Early in the twentieth century certain noninstitutional services such as pension laws for the blind, the aged, and widowed mothers with dependent children began to make their appearance. Although restricted in their original application, these services assumed ever-increasing proportions until they were embodied in the Social Security Act of 1935 and became the predominant and characteristic form of public welfare in the century.

Aid to the Needy Blind   Before 1929 the care of the blind had been assumed in some places by voluntary organizations; in other places, by public
ones. Sometimes it involved institutional care; at other times, educational and
vocational training or retraining. Because the blind are frequently at a disad-
vantage in the labor market and less likely to earn sufficient money for
self-maintenance, the movement for allowances from public funds got under
way long before public aid to dependent children or the aged. As early as
1840 the state of Indiana passed a statute to provide for the support of the
indigent blind. Later, in 1866, the Board of Aldermen and the Board of
Councilmen of New York City passed a resolution outlining a procedure for
handling applications for assistance to the blind. Before the century was out,
one state, Ohio, had enacted a law providing for the relief of the blind. This
law of 1898 was declared unconstitutional, as was that of 1904. However,
in 1908 a further enactment stood the test of constitutionality. In the meantime two other states had acted affirmatively and established a precedent for
pensions for the blind. The Illinois legislature acted in 1903 and Wisconsin
in 1907. Thus, by 1910, before any state had made pension provision for its
widowed mothers or aged, three states had granted public aid to the blind.
In the next decade, beginning with Kansas in 1911 and ending with Nebraska
in 1917, eight other states enacted assistance laws for the blind, and a like
number legislated during the decade ending in 1929.

Aid to Widows and Children   A second departure from the poor-law principles as well as from traditional institutional care was the provision of financial
aid to widows and mothers with dependent children. Several centuries of
poor-law "treatment" of dependent children had revealed the tragic waste
to so many families and children of methods of care that pauperized or
institutionalized the child. The foster-home movement, which originated under voluntary auspices in 1853, was an early innovation in child care, but it
remained for the White House Conference of 1909 to advocate a form of aid
designed to keep mothers and children in their own homes. That conference
went on record as declaring that children should not be deprived of their
homes except for urgent and compelling reasons. Poverty in itself was not
deemed an urgent or compelling reason. When aid was necessary to keep the
home together, the conference declared, it "should be given by such methods and from such sources as may be determined by the general relief policy
of each community, preferably in the form of private charity rather than of
public relief." The recognition of the vital role of the mother in the lives of
her children and of the importance of the early developmental years in the
home had found expression in a new concept of child care.

The first mothers' aid law in the United States was enacted in April 1911
for one county in Missouri, Jackson County. Allowances were made to moth-

ers who were in need, whose husbands were dead or prisoners, and whose children were under fourteen years of age. In June of the same year the first law on the state-wide basis was placed on the statute books of Illinois, known as the "Funds to Parents Act." The juvenile court of each county was empowered to determine the eligibility of parents and children for such assistance and to decide upon the money necessary to provide adequate care for the child. Colorado, in 1912, followed Illinois and adopted a Mothers' Compensation Act.

Once having started, the movement spread rapidly. By the end of 1919, thirty-nine states and two territories had passed laws of various titles—mothers' pensions, mothers' allowances, child welfare, mothers' assistance fund, widows' compensation, aid to dependent children, "an act to promote Home Life for Dependent Children"—all aimed to meet the same need. Within another decade, that is, by the end of 1929, five states and the District of Columbia had followed suit so that at the time of the depression of the 1930s, there were forty-four states, the District of Columbia, and the territories of Alaska and Hawaii that had made provision for aid to children in their own homes.

Old-Age Pensions   Chronologically, assistance to the blind and to mothers of dependent children preceded assistance to the aged. The first state law providing financial aid to the blind was enacted in 1840, the first (state-wide) widows' pension law in 1911. Actually, it was not until 1923 that the first operable old-age pension was on the statute books of an American state. Even though the per capita relief grant was low, the perpetuation of pauperization swelled the grand total of relief to large figures. Almshouse conditions were being exposed to public airing, and the resulting stench often reached the nostrils not only of the social worker or of the sensitive public-spirited citizen, but also the ordinary hardheaded businessman and the equally vociferous taxpayer. Voluntary relief with its best of intentions was in no position to meet so great a need. Institutions reached only a relatively few needy aged. Social insurance schemes had not yet taken hold in the United States. In the face of such convincing reasons for some form of assistance to the needy aged, the wonder is that state aid was delayed so long. Even when the movement for old-age pensions did begin to produce tangible results, the effects were not so pronounced as in the case of the blind or of dependent children. The first state to enact a law that withstood the constitutional test and furnished a statutory base for a program was Montana in 1923. Arizona had passed a law in 1914 that was declared unconstitutional. However, it was the territory of Alaska, now a state, that may rightly claim the first laws that withstood the courts (Pennsylvania's law did not). Wisconsin in 1925, Kentucky in 1926, Maryland in 1927, and four states (California, Minnesota, Utah, Wyoming) in 1929 completed the roll by the close of the predepression era. Nine states and one territory had made their break with the poor-law principle of relief for the aged.

Public Welfare Following 1929

A new way of looking at the problems of people and new ways of dealing with those problems and people began to emerge once we realized that the debacle of 1929 spelled finis to the post–World War I philosophy of the 1920s. Prosperity, despite reassurances from high places, was not around the corner. Depression had come. Translated into human terms, depression meant that millions of workers were unable to earn a living for their families; that people, plain, ordinary people, went hungry and sick; that despair and frustration seized those who became dependent; that rebellion swelled inside people who saw threats of mass starvation in a land of plenty. The social welfare agencies that were supported by voluntary contributions (principally by the annual Community Chest Drive—as it was then called) were carrying an increasing share of the relief load. As the number of unemployed rose from three million in 1929 to an estimated seventeen million in 1933 (out of a gainfully employed population that usually numbered forty-eight million) the task proved beyond the resources of the voluntary agency. The next step was inevitable; namely, the assumption by the state of a share of responsibility. State relief agencies were created to administer the "emergency" programs. This was not enough and the next step had to involve the federal government.

Emergency Relief

On September 23, 1931, the New York Temporary Emergency Relief Administration (TERA) was established by the state legislature to provide state aid for the unemployed. Funds were appropriated to reimburse cities and counties up to 40 percent of their expenditures for unemployment relief. Furthermore, TERA was empowered to make and enforce rules for the proper and efficient administration of relief. In October, Governor Franklin D. Roosevelt appointed Harry Hopkins, an experienced social worker, to be executive secretary of TERA. New Jersey and Pennsylvania also set up emergency relief organizations before the end of 1931, and were followed within the next year by Wisconsin, Rhode Island, Illinois, and Ohio, and subsequently by other states. The problems were no longer "temporary," and despite congressional enactment of the Emergency Relief and Construction Act and its authorization to the newly created Reconstruction Finance Corporation to lend to the states $300 million of federal funds "to be used in furnishing relief and work relief to needy and distressed people and in relieving the hardships from unemployment" the country's situation worsened.

The Federal Emergency Relief Act

An election turned out the administration. Two months later, in May 1933, a new Congress passed the Federal Emergency Relief Act whereby $500 million was appropriated for relief purposes. Grants were made to states, on a matching basis if the state was able to match federal funds or as an outright grant if it was unable to do so. Before a year was over, $1 billion had been appropriated.

The Federal Emergency Relief Act shattered all precedent. It closed the door on three centuries of the "poor law." It signalized the acceptance of federal responsibility for the welfare of more than a hundred million people. It provided for federal leadership and for federal cooperation with the states and local communities in helping them to meet the costs of unemployed relief.

On May 22, 1933, the first day after he assumed office, Administrator Harry Hopkins approved the first grants to seven states. By the end of June, grants had been made to forty-five states. In November of the same year the experiment known as the Civil Works Administration (CWA) was begun for the purpose of putting a large number of workers on civil works projects at current rates of pay. From then until its termination in March, 1934, more than four million workers, half from the unemployed not yet on relief rolls, were placed on work projects. The admitted purpose of the CWA was to give a "shot in the arm" to the economic system by putting men to work and money into circulation. But the expenditure of almost $1 billion in less than half a year proved too costly even for the federal government.

From the end of the CWA to the inauguration of the Works Progress Administration (WPA), several other experiments and expedients were tried. These consisted of programs for the relief of distress in (1) "stranded areas" or with "stranded populations" (such as the cut-over lumber regions, or the worked-out coal areas, and others), (2) rural areas (Resettlement Administration, subsequently Farm Security Administration), and (3) urban areas (Emergency Work Programs with federal funds supplementing local funds).

In January 1935 President Franklin D. Roosevelt declared that "the Federal Government must and shall quit this business of relief." Lest it be feared that this meant a return to the Elizabethan days of 1601, it must be explained immediately that what the president intended was that home relief should be carried on by the local community, but that two other services were to be available. The immediate service was to be a work relief program under federal direction; the contemplated later service was to be the enactment of social security legislation. In theory, then, all needs were to be met; for the employable, a work program; for the unemployed with adequate work records, unemployment insurance and old-age insurance upon retirement; for the unemployable (that is, the young, the aged, the blind), an assistance program; and finally, for those who fall into none of these categories, local relief.

The WPA

The largest governmental work program the world has ever known began to take form under the Works Progress Administration, beginning in May, 1935, with an initial appropriation of almost $5 billion. Despite reshuffling, title changing, and retrenchments, the WPA (subsequently Work Projects Administration) continued to provide a work program, with the federal government paying the wage bill largely and the state or local community serving as sponsor and supplying a share of the materials.

The CCC and the NYA

Two other developments must be mentioned, the Civilian Conservation Corps (CCC) and the National Youth Administration (NYA). The titles obviously indicate the accent on youth. These services were pointed not so much at relief as an end in itself but as a means of maintaining and developing the natural resources of the nation and at the same time of maintaining and developing its human resources. In the CCC camps, young workers, largely from relief families, were to carry on conservation projects such as reforestation, prevention of forest fires, soil erosion control, flood control, and the like. The NYA projects were also for the younger adult group and were directed toward (1) aiding needy high school and college students, (2) assisting other young people on constructive work projects, (3) providing job training, counseling, and placement services, and (4) developing constructive leisure-time activities.

While no one would claim perfection for any of these programs, least of all their leaders, nevertheless one cannot contemplate the imagination, determination, and energy that went into them without realizing the profound changes that had taken place within the span of half a decade. President Pierce's doctrine of a static welfare had given way to a dynamic concept of human welfare. The government—federal, state, local—did exist to ensure the well-being of the people who constituted that government. If the "welfare" of 1854 did not meet the needs of people in 1933, what was more realistic and human than to broaden the area of welfare?

The Social Security Act

The act that President Roosevelt signed August 14, 1935, incomplete though it was, furnished the base for a progressively serviceable social security program. It was a far from perfect document, but time after time (indeed, almost year by year) it has been amended and improved as the Congress responded to the experience of the people and to the testimony of professionals, and as it increased its own understanding. Nor does there seem to be any likelihood, in the foreseeable future, of any cessation of improvement in a program that so basically touches the life of every American and is so fundamental to our country's economy.[1]

B. SERVICES AND AGENCIES, UNDER EITHER STATUTORY OR VOLUNTARY AUSPICES

Care of Children in Institutions

As previously noted, the earliest services in this country were of "poor law" origin—Elizabethan and colonial. Most of these services were minimal in character, providing care in almshouses, sometimes to entire families. Children in so many instances were the most defenseless victims; and it may be quite understandable that efforts were exerted to offer a more humane living experience for some of them. The first instance on record was that of the Sisters of the Ursuline Convent, who had been brought from France to New Orleans in 1727 to found a convent and "to relieve the poor sick and provide at the same time for the education of young girls." The girls taken in charge in 1729 had been orphaned by reason of wars carried on by the Natchez Indians. A second institution, and one still in existence, was the Bethesda Home for Boys near Savannah, Georgia, which owed its origin largely to the zeal of the celebrated English preacher George Whitefield. A third, and the first to be organized and supported by tax funds, was the Charleston Orphan House, organized in 1790 and built in 1794. A fourth was the John de la Howe Industrial School in South Carolina, 1797. The St. Joseph's Female Orphan Asylum under auspices of the Catholic Church in Philadelphia, 1798, was the fifth, and the asylum for the care and education of destitute girls established in 1799 in Baltimore by St. Paul's Episcopal Church was the sixth and the last during the eighteenth century. Throughout the next century more than 400 such institutions were established, and by 1925 there were 1400 in operation throughout the United States. Many of these were under denominational auspice—Catholic, Protestant, Jewish; others were begun and maintained by fraternal order like the Masons, the Moose, the Independent Order of Odd Fellows, the Knights of Pythias, and the Junior Order of United

---

[1] The next chapter deals with the current provisions of the social security program and relates them to the provision of public (statutory) services in the second half of this decade.

American Mechanics; some few were established by private philanthropy and endowment; and occasionally an institution originated as a state, county, or city facility and was supported by tax funds. In addition, provision was made for certain identified groups such as the Association for the Care of Negro Orphans by the Society of Friends in Philadelphia in 1822 and the Association for the Care of Colored Orphans of New York, 1836; other such institutions include ones for destitute Indian children, Buffalo, New York, 1845; one for children of destitute seamen in the city and port of New York, 1846; and an asylum (St. Mary's) in 1852 in Buffalo for widows, foundlings, and infants. Following the Civil War, homes were established for the orphans of fathers killed in the conflict, most of these homes falling under public auspice, that is, tax-supported.

Early in the nineteenth century, children with special disabilities began to receive institutional care, other than in the almshouse. Usually, these institutions were initiated by concerned citizens who constituted themselves an organizing group and undertook a program that, not infrequently, later received subsidies from public funds. Such was the case with the first permanent school for the deaf (1814), the American Asylum in Hartford, Connecticut, later renamed the American School for the Deaf; this was followed by the second, the New York Institute for the Instruction of the Deaf and Dumb, in 1818. The first school for the deaf established directly by a state legislature was in Kentucky in 1823; other states, such as Ohio, Virginia, and Indiana, followed within the next two decades.

Interest was also manifested in the condition of blind children, taking concrete expression in the establishment in 1832 of what subsequently became known as the Perkins Institution and Massachusetts School for the Blind. Eventually as an institution designed to serve the needs of the New England area, it received state appropriation not only from Massachusetts but also from Connecticut, New Hampshire, Vermont, Maine, and Rhode Island. The first institution for the blind to be funded fully by taxes was in Ohio, in 1837, followed by Virginia in 1839, with its institution for both blind and deaf children.

Before the middle of the century, another group—now termed the mentally retarded—began to receive specialized institutional care. The first venture was authorized and funded by the Massachusetts legislature, opening in 1848; within three years the appropriation was doubled and the school became the Massachusetts School for Idiots and Feeble-Minded Youth.

Delinquent youth also were deemed in need of specialized care. New York citizens who had formed (in 1817) the Society for the Prevention of Pauperism became so concerned about the lack of separation of adult and juvenile offenders that, in 1824, the society was renamed the Society for the Reformation of Juvenile Delinquents. In 1825 the society opened, with the aid of a grant of land by the city of New York and an appropriation by the state legislature, the House of Refuge, the first in America. In Philadelphia in 1828, a group of citizens followed the New York plan and opened the Philadelphia House of Refuge, which ultimately received funds from the city as well as from the state of Pennsylvania.

Foster-Home Care

Although institutional care for children increased throughout the remainder of the century, another movement in process provided an alternative way of helping children. The essence of this assistance was to place a child in another home when conditions in his own home were so inimical to his welfare as to make necessary his removal from it. The leadership for this pioneering effort was provided by Charles Loring Brace, who during his training for the ministry had the opportunity to head a children's mission in New York City. The mission in 1853 was renamed the Children's Aid Society, and Brace almost at once began to carry out his idea of withdrawing vagrant and destitute children from the streets of the city and transplanting them into suitable homes in another environment. As originally conceived, the plan was based on the assumption that the child was to carry a share of the work in his foster home, that the foster parents would be relieved of some cares, and the society would bear the expenses of getting the child to the new home or of returning him to his original home if that were necessary, or of finding an alternate foster home. Many of the children were transported as far away as Michigan, Wisconsin, and Minnesota. In all likelihood, these mass migrations of hundreds of children were inspired more by a desire to remove the children from the city streets than by a certain knowledge of the intricacies of child care. For the leaders of the movement, the chief problems were those of gathering children, transporting, housing, and feeding them. Not much thought was given to the problems created when children were separated from family and friends and had to adjust to a different home and strange people. Despite all the shortcomings of the scheme, which were due to ignorance rather than to design, its significance was its departure from indenture, almshouse care, and the available institutions of that day. It was an important step toward adapting services to meet the needs of children, rather than simply warehousing them. Throughout, the basic commitment has been toward the improvement of child-saving services.

Growth of Children's Aid Societies

Developments in other cities spread the work of children's aid societies. In 1860 an agency was founded in Baltimore for the purpose of finding homes for destitute children. Within three years two other organizations were formed: one in Philadelphia, which sought to board Jewish orphans in the homes of relatives or some other worthy family; and the other in Boston, which began to place children in foster homes, in temporary homes, or in its farm school. Other societies were organized in Brooklyn (1866), in Buffalo (1872), in Pennsylvania (Pennsylvania Children's Aid Society, 1882), and in Rochester, New York (1895). Other societies for the most part were privately financed, although in some instances (as in Pennsylvania) the society accepted children from local counties, for whom board was paid from public funds.

Public Sponsorship

While the pioneering work of developing foster-home services for children was privately initiated and directed, only a decade or two passed before a number of states had recognized their responsibilities for the welfare of children and were looking toward means of care other than by indenture and institutions. Massachusetts was the first state to make a beginning (1869) in that direction when it provided a visiting service to all children released from state institutions. This supervision led the way to the state's paying board for many of its children who had been placed in private homes. Ten years later the practice of depositing children in city and town almshouses was outlawed, and in 1882 provision was made for the payment of board for children under ten years of age, in placing them in the State Primary School and requiring that they be committed directly to the State Board of Charities. The most important step in this development of home placement service was the abolition of the State Primary School in 1895 and further extension of the principle of child care in foster homes instead of in institutions. In 1899 New Jersey followed the example of Massachusetts by establishing a state policy of foster-home care for destitute children. The creation of a state board of children's guardians centralized the control and placement of children and made possible the use of private homes as boarding homes until such time as free homes could be found for the children.

Pennsylvania's approach was a recognition of the principle of foster-home care implemented by the services of a voluntary agency. When a state law, passed in 1883, imposed on local communities and counties the care of children, no provision was made for their adequate care. Fortunately, the Pennsylvania Children's Aid Society had been organized the year before as a child-placing agency, and it immediately offered to assist local authorities by working with them on a program of boarding or free homes. Many of the larger counties availed themselves of the society's services, and in such instances payment was made out of county funds for those boarding homes that the agency secured.

61

In the years since these beginnings, foster care had been a service under both private and public auspice. However, as funds have become increasingly available—never enough—from local, state, and federal sources, the foster-care services have tended more and more to be placed within the public sphere. The Social Security Act of 1935 and subsequent amendments, with its Aid to Dependent Children (later, Aid to Families with Dependent Children) and Child Welfare Services, broadened the range of services to children in foster care, but it placed increasing emphasis on keeping children with their own families.

School Social Services

Another area in which services to children have developed is the school. In contrast to the services discussed so far in this chapter, the school program has existed only since the first decade of the twentieth century. Originally referred to as "visiting teacher services," the program is currently called "school social services." These services, with the school as the host agency, developed in response to changes within the educational system. A rising total population, an increasing measure of mandatory school attendance, and a readiness on the part of some educational leaders to question the effectiveness of the school system, all hastened shifts in educational philosophy and practice. Before the days of compulsory school attendance there was no great concern for the child who did not keep up in his class work or who caused too much trouble in the classroom. The easy way to eliminate either problem was to expel him from school: school was for those who could use it as it was. If there was any changing of student attitudes to be done, that was not within the province of the school. In broader conceptual terms, it was the individual's responsibility to adapt to the system, not the system's to the individual. However, the advent of compulsory school attendance (which, significantly enough, placed the compulsory requirement on the state to furnish instruction) created new problems: large classes and the tendency toward regimentation on a mass basis. The lone child stood a good chance of being lost in the school system.

Teachers, and teachers of teachers, were not uninfluenced by thinking in other fields. From psychology (in 1896, Lightner Witmer established the first psychological clinic at the University of Pennsylvania) there emerged concepts of individual differences, of the varying equipment with which individuals come into the world, and of their capacity to adapt to changing demands made upon them. Sociologists were concerning themselves with the nature of the social order as well as with the modifiability of the human personality. Social workers, too, in their day-by-day practice, were learning something about the capacity of the individual to adapt to his environment and how that environment in turn might be altered to meet the individual's needs. As a result of these contributions, more and more attention was focused upon the child in school. Large classes and inevitable regimentation, with stress upon subject matter and pressure on the child to fit himself into the mold of the school, began to yield to a newer philosophy that emphasized the needs of the individual child. Greater attention was directed toward each child's capacity for adapting to the school. This shift signalized a departure from the traditional role of the school in its preoccupation with the intellectual life of the child and introduced a growing concern for the emotional factors that are related to learning and which, indeed, often impede learning. The realignment of objectives also carried with it a revised estimation of the criteria of successful teaching. Rather than the inculcation of a quantity of knowledge, a teacher's success might more rightly be measured by the growth of the child. This newer approach was finding ultimate expression in the increasing efforts of education to adapt the school program to the maturing child.

In a previous paragraph the school was referred to as a "host agency." It is not set up to be a social agency, no more than is a hospital, a court, or a prison. A hospital is a medical agency; a court is a judicial agency; a prison is a correctional agency. However, in order better to accomplish their purposes, a corollary function has been added to each. Thus as host agency the hospital engages in medical social work, the court dispenses probation, and the prison authorizes parole. So it is with the school. The school is primarily an educational agency, but it also does social work so that it can help students who have difficulties that prevent them from making full use of what the school has to offer.

During the period 1906–1907, school social work was introduced in three different cities: New York, Boston, and Hartford. In New York the immediate impetus came from two social settlements that had assigned visitors to school districts in order that the settlement-house staff might keep in closer touch with the teachers of the children who lived in the settlement neighborhood. The initiating group in Boston was the Women's Education Association, which established a home-and-school visitor in one of the city schools for the purpose of ensuring a closer tie between the home and the school. In Hartford the suggestion came from the director of the psychological clinic; at first the worker was known as a "special teacher" who assisted the pyschologist by gathering case histories; later this assignment included the carrying out of the recommendations.

The Commonwealth Fund Support

The subsequent development of school social work gave substance to much of the early promise. Following the pioneering efforts of private agencies, a number of public school authorities introduced visiting teacher projects into the tax-supported school systems. Rochester, New York, may be cited as an early instance. There, in 1913, school social services were supported and controlled by the board of education. The greatest impetus, however, came from the program inaugurated by the Commonwealth Fund, with its fourfold approach to the prevention of delinquency. One part of that program was committed to the National Committee on Visiting Teachers, affiliated with the Public Education Association, whose membership included leaders in the fields of education and social work. Thirty approved centers located in twenty-three states served as bases for the demonstration project. For the first five years, beginning in 1921, the Commonwealth Fund supported these thirty demonstrations; in the ensuing three years its attention was concentrated upon training teachers for such work. It aimed to increase the understanding of behavior problems by teachers in training, to improve the standards of work by field visits and conferences, and to advise school systems that were interested in establishing such programs on a permanent basis. Twenty-one of the original thirty continued as an ongoing service of the school system. The contribution of the fund, however, went far beyond the boundaries of these twenty-one communities. Within the next decade as the conviction mounted that more, not fewer, social services were needed in the schools, an increasing number of both rural and urban school systems inaugurated programs.

From then until now, as more and more communities included school social services as integral parts of their educational programs, the services have broadened. While the original approach had been a direct service to the child and to the parent, this was expanded to include a consultation service to the teacher as well as to the school principal. Later still, the service was extended to consultation with the school administration on curriculum matters and to broadened educational programs that would meet the vocational needs of all students, not simply those who were college bound. The next move, and a quite contemporary one, is toward the community, involving the resources of all social service and civic agencies while at the same time stimulating the kind of community projects and services that will enhance healthful and satisfying living for all its people. For example, in some areas of the country, advisors are brought into the schools from the surrounding minority community to collaborate closely with the school social workers. An additional facet of this is the engagement of parents as volunteers, primarily assisting teachers, with the social workers acting as facilitators in the process. The school program that received its original impact from forces in the community has developed a service within its system that, over a half-century later, has come back full circle to the community.

The Development of Services in the Medical Settings

Although their focus was on different aspects of illness, both psychiatric social work and medical social work began to take shape in the first decade of this century, specifically in the year 1905. As Ida Cannon recorded in her historical volume *Social Work in Hospitals,* the immediate precursors of medical social work were: (1) services provided for the aftercare of the insane in Germany, France, England, and America; (2) services furnished by lady almoners in London hospitals; (3) nursing, especially the visiting nursing service provided by Lillian Wald and Mary Brewster in New York City; and (4) the field-work training of medical students at Johns Hopkins Medical School and Hospital.

On two successive days in October, 1905, social workers were introduced into medical settings in the Boston area—the Berkeley Infirmary (no longer in existence) and the Massachusetts General Hospital (MGH), an increasingly useful and prestigious medical institution throughout the ensuing years. Dr. Richard C. Cabot, a member of the staff of the Massachusetts General Hospital, took the leadership by creating the Social Service Department. Besides being in charge of the Outpatient Department of MGH, Dr. Cabot was a board member of the Children's Aid Society of Boston and consultant to the State Industrial School for Girls. He was firmly convinced "that this work is essentially one of *linking* the patient to all available sources of help . . . to connect the hospital with all the social forces and helpful agencies outside its walls." The social worker was also to be an interpreter, one who not only intepreted the hospital to the patient but also interpreted to the physician and the hospital management the "conditions existing in the patient's home or community, which have a vital bearing upon his disease and upon its treatment." Knowing both the rich and the poor, Dr. Cabot observed "rich people need this service when they are sick almost, if not quite, as much as poor people."

Dr. Cabot deplored the increasing impersonality of the hospital and the elaboration of medical specialties; yet, judged by developments since then, the hospital of his day was a relatively uncomplicated medical institution. Today his criticism is even more applicable, for as the hospital becomes highly compartmentalized, adds clinic to clinic, multiplies specialist by specialist, and ends up with elaborate equipment and an endless line of patients, the point is reached where the sick person is in danger of being lost in the maze. It is quite clear that the original reasons for the introduction of medical social work in 1905 are still as valid and have even greater urgency. For Dr. Cabot, medical social work served to assist the physician in diagnosis and treatment by studying the patient in his social situation and by interpreting the patient and his environment to the physician. In addition, the medical social worker assisted in providing effective medical treatment by organizing resources in the hospital as well as enlisting the aid of the patient's family and the community at large. Dr. Adolph Meyer of Johns Hopkins Hospital (social service was established there in October 1907) believed social work in the hospital was for the purpose of securing facts about the patient while he was in the hospital, ensuring healthy conditions in the home in preparation for the patient's return, and maintaining such conditions after the patient's return home. Throughout all these activities the social worker was to be in constant contact with the physician. For Dr. Henry B. Richardson, medical social service has as its immediate objective the relief of inner and outer pressures, whether these arise from external realities and illness or from personal attitudes and feelings: "The ultimate objective is to enable sick people to draw on their own capacities in seeking and using medical care, in preventing illness or maintaining health."

Within the past two decades, leaders within the medical social work area, while stressing the essential role of the worker in the hospital, also recognize that the patient has a family and that the family lives in a community. Both Elizabeth Rice and Harriet Bartlett insist on the hospital role, but also call for a reaching to the outside. Miss Rice elaborates this in her analysis of the interrelationships of social work and public health, and Miss Bartlett underscores the same points as she identifies the medical social worker as a participant in the multidisciplinary care of the patient—outside as well as inside the hospital.

Other Services within the Hospital While the basic commitment of the medical social worker within the hospital has been direct service to the patient, there has always been a degree of teaching responsibility. As early as 1913, medical social workers at the Massachusetts General Hospital participated in the teaching of medical students at the Harvard Medical School and student nurses in the hospital training school. Within recent years the proliferation of medical knowledge and the compartmentalization of the medical specialties have made the student in the school of medicine, the intern, and the resident better informed about disease but less aware of the patient as a person. On the other hand, the medical social worker has concentrated on personal, familial, and community aspects, and is equipped to help the physician to understand the whole person as he responds to the impact of the inside and the outside influences. The essential areas of knowledge relate to the person, to his family relationships, and to community resources. She or he is the key person qualified to help prepare the patient's family for his discharge—or, in the absence of family, to help make adequate preparation for the patient's care after discharge. This increased awareness of the varying factors influencing the person in well-being and illness will be

66

of value to the physician, whether ultimately he engages in the practice of medicine or becomes associated with a school of medicine or a hospital. The nurse, too, with such knowledge can widen her understanding of the patient. Likewise, the instruction offered by medical social workers in schools of public health has value as the physicians and other public health workers devote themselves to the expanding public health services that communities are demanding.

Other contributions of medical social work within the setting of the hospital are consultation with other professional colleagues, participation in program planning and policy formulation, research, and the training and utilization of baccalaureate case aides. The knowledge gained through practice within the hospital as well as through contacts with the community equip the worker to be of value in sharing that knowledge with colleagues in other areas of the hospital and with administrators. In those instances in which members of the social service department have a research competence, they may be involved directly in a specific project. It is no exaggeration to say that the basic knowledge and skills of the medical social worker reach beyond the confines of any one department and contribute meaningfully to the total purpose of the hospital.

Medical Social Work in the Larger Community

Although medical social work began in this country with a hospital base, it has reached out increasingly to the community. This was the original purpose of relating patient care within the hospital to the family and community outside. As more and more programs have developed—vocational rehabilitation, crippled-children services, maternal and child health aid, services for the chronically ill and the aging, home-care services, as well as public heatlh emphasis on disease prevention, and public welfare participation in Medicaid —the knowledge and competence of the medical social worker have been put to use. This does not so much require that the individualized casework service be concentrated in the hospital, but rather that it be a broad-ranging unit working with other professional persons and groups and with the community as a whole. A number of the services exercised within the hospital, such as program planning, policy formulation, use of aides, and research, have been brought into operation on a wide community scale.

As a worker within the hospital as well as within the community, the medical social worker is vitally related to the accelerating trend toward comprehensive medical care. This has been described as medical care when the patient needs it, where he needs it, and to the extent that he needs it. It may be provided in a hospital bed, a hospital clinic, a physician's office, a group-practice center, the patient's home, or in a long-term care facility. It should be characterized by comprehensiveness, continuity of care, family-centered services, and coordination throughout. The further development of comprehensive medical care, the inevitable stimulation of medical care programs by extensions of the Social Security Act, coupled with the innovative discoveries in medicine and the expectations and needs of citizens will place greater demands on social workers. Professional workers, among them medical social workers, will be required to direct their energies and talents toward the achievement of the highest quality care for all people. This could be one of the many vital social tasks to be accomplished during the remaining quarter of the twentieth century.

The Psychiatric Setting

Throughout much of the nineteenth century in America the emphasis in dealing with deviant behavior was upon institutionalization. In a fascinating review of that period, Daniel Rothman showed that institutions have always been places of first resort, the preferred solution to the problems of poverty, crime, and insanity: "philanthropists and state legislatures also erected imposing insane asylums and doctors and interested laymen urged families to put their mentally ill in institutions as soon as the symptoms appeared." This era of custody was described by Albert Deutsch in 1937 as moral treatment, but always with emphasis upon restraint and isolation. Not infrequently the hospital was far removed from the centers of population and access was difficult. Increasingly, it became the repository for the violent, the old, the hopeless, and those with whom the family could not cope.

It was the brilliant insights of Dr. Sigmund Freud, his associates, and his students that effected a breakthrough. Their analyses of the unconscious and the conscious opened up new avenues of approach in treating deviant behavior. A wholly new orientation of the human mind and personality was made possible. Freud's conception of personality was to modify, if not eventually replace, the older static view. Many American psychiatrists, although not psychoanalysts in any sense of the term and certainly not Freudian, came to express this more dynamic point of view. Thus, by the first decade of the twentieth century, psychiatry had already made its imprint by shifting the emphasis from custody and classification to causes of unsocial behavior and effectiveness of treatment.

The change from custodial care to individualized study and treatment was a new approach to the kind and quality of care accorded mental patients. This first found expression in the newly opened psychopathic hospitals, neurological clinics of hospitals, and hospital social service departments. Psychiatrists were becoming increasingly aware of the effect of emotional experiences on the personality development of the individual. At the same time they realized that environmental pressures upon the individual were factors to be reckoned with in any form of mental disability. The early psychopathic hospitals, of which the first was established in Michigan in 1906, concentrated on the study, diagnosis, and treatment of forms of mental disease that had hopeful prognosis. As part of this study, the psychiatrist gathered material on the life histories of patients. Gradually, however, this assignment was delegated to field workers who functioned under the psychiatrist's direction.

The first instance of the actual employment of a social worker in a hospital occurred in the neurological clinic of the Massachusetts General Hospital under the direction of Dr. James J. Putnam, a colleague of Dr. Richard Cabot. Soon thereafter a social worker was employed in the psychopathic wards of Bellevue Hospital, New York, for the purpose of assisting patients who were recovering from mental illness. The New York State Charities Aid Association, through its committee on mental hygiene, had secured the appointment of an "aftercare worker" to supervise patients discharged from two New York hospitals. It was not until the next year that the first social worker was placed on the payroll of a state hospital for mental diseases, the Manhattan State Hospital. In 1913, two Massachusetts hospitals, Danvers State Hospital and Boston State Hospital, each placed a social worker on the staff.

A substantial impetus to the development of this work came in 1913, when the Boston Psychopathic Hospital began its social service department under the leadership of Dr. Ernest Southard and Miss Mary C. Jarrett. Hardly had this project started than World War I began. By the time the United States became involved in 1917, it had become clear that the development of social service in civilian hospitals would be just as necessary, if not more so, for army hospitals. The practical difficulty to be faced was that there were not enough specially trained social workers to meet emergency needs. Accordingly, plans were made to enlarge the training facilities at the Boston Psychopathic Hospital. Eventually an arrangement was effected whereby an emergency training course was given under the joint auspices of Smith College, the National Committee for Mental Hygiene, and the Boston Psychopathic Hospital, with Miss Jarrett in charge. It is generally believed that the term describing this new specialty, psychiatric social work, was coined by Dr. Southard and Miss Jarrett. In their book, *The Kingdom of Evils,* they expressly stated that this branch of social work was a new emphasis rather than a new function, having grown out of ideas and activities that already existed in scattered forms. In this respect its development is not unlike that of medical social work.

Out of these first training courses of eight weeks' duration (1918) came the establishment, within a year, of a permanent graduate school of social work training at Smith College. Other schools, already established, such as the New

York School of Social Work, the Pennsylvania School of Social and Health Work, and the Chicago School of Civics and Philanthropy, not only continued their interest in the field of psychiatric social work but also added to this rapidly enlarging area, which already was beyond the bounds of the hospital. Within a decade there was not a school of social work that did not pay its respects to the psychiatric point of view, and for some it constituted the cornerstone of the curriculum. The caseworkers who trained in these many schools drew upon a common base and utilized their knowledges and skills in a variety of agencies in which services were offered. In the psychiatric setting, they were essential members of professional teams—psychiatrist, clinical psychologist, and psychiatric social worker—whose services were directed to the treatment of mental illness and the restoration of afflicted persons to sound mental health.

The Child Guidance Clinic: The Commonwealth Fund

A review of developmental years requires more than a word about the contributive role of the Commonwealth Fund in the establishment of child guidance clinics. Within a few years of its organization as a voluntary (non-governmental) foundation in 1918, the Commonwealth Fund called upon representatives in such areas as psychiatry, psychology, education, juvenile court, and social work to formulate a plan for work in child welfare. These representatives had been familiar with the psychological clinic established by Lightner Witmer at the University of Pennsylvania; the Chicago Juvenile Psychopathic Institute founded by Dr. William Healy (from which emanated his monumental study, *The Individual Delinquent,* in 1915); and the Henry Phipps Psychiatric Clinic of Johns Hopkins Hospital, Baltimore, under the direction of Dr. Adolph Meyer. The Fund attempted to explore some of the root problems of juvenile delinquency by adopting, in November, 1921, a five-year experimental program with the following explicit purposes:

1. To develop the psychiatric study of different predelinquent and delinquent children in the schools and juvenile courts; and to develop sound methods of treatment based on such study.
2. To develop the work of the visiting teacher whereby the invaluable early contacts which our school system makes possible with every child may be utilized for the understanding and development of the child.
3. To provide courses of training along sound lines for those qualified and desiring to work in this field.
4. To extend by various educational efforts the knowledge and use of these methods.

A number of organizations already in existence were utilized to help carry into effect the first three of these purposes. The New York School of Social Work was placed in a position to offer additional courses for psychiatric social workers, to provide fellowships for training students in this new field, to establish a psychiatric clinic for the study and treatment of children with special problems, and to offer field training of students. The National Committee for Mental Hygiene, through its newly formed division on the prevention of delinquency, was to carry on the demonstration child guidance clinics, while the Public Education Association of New York, through its National Committee on Visiting Teachers, was to conduct demonstrations of visiting teacher work in different areas of the country. To attain the fourth objective, the fund set up its own agency, the Joint Committee on Methods of Preventing Delinquency, to act as a coordinating agency for the program as a whole and as an interpreter of the work through published articles or special studies.

Early in 1922 the first demonstration child guidance clinic was initiated in St. Louis with a staff consisting of one psychiatrist, one psychologist, and one psychiatric social worker. Children with behavior difficulties were referred by schools, institutions, private homes, and juvenile courts. Three-fourths were sent from the juvenile courts, and it was soon realized that if a preventive service were to be offered, it would have to be done, in a great many instances, long before the child was brought to the juvenile court. If the purpose of the newly established clinic was to give meaning to the title of the committee (Methods of Preventing Delinquency), it was doomed to ineffectiveness because so much of the responsibility for preventing delinquency rested with agencies other than the clinic. Throughout the remainder of the demonstration period in the cities of Norfolk, Dallas, Minneapolis, St. Paul, Los Angeles, Cleveland, and Philadelphia, this fact became more and more self-evident. It was realized that community services such as those of the school and of social agencies—particularly children's agencies—were valuable because they helped the child construct a more realistic objective for himself and because they furnished a more natural medium for approaching the child. At the same time, it became apparent that more stress in the clinic setup would need to be placed upon social work. Accordingly, the ratio of workers was changed to one psychiatrist, one psychologist, and three social workers.

Comprehensive Community Mental Health Services

Despite the increasing awareness of mental illness from the beginning of the mental hygiene movement (sparked by Clifford Beers in his book *A Mind That Found Itself*), until World War II occurred, the country was not prepared for the shock produced by Selective Service examinations of men called for duty in the armed forces. Not only were a large number unfit for military service because of mental and emotional difficulties, but of those inducted an astonishing number proved unequal to the demands of military service. It was reported that by the end of World War II more than 380,000 men had been discharged from the service because of psychiatric disabilities. In the postwar period, the country and the Congress were determined to provide appropriate service for these veterans. Under the aegis of a revitalized Veterans Administration, a nationwide program of services for veterans was established, including a wide distribution of hospitals and community clinics. In addition to providing a high quality of in-patient service, there were extensive outpatient clinic services that demonstrated the value as well as the practicability of psychiatric services at the community level. As part of its total service to all veterans, the Veterans Administration committed its facilities for training purposes in psychiatry, clinical psychology, and psychiatric social work.

The period since then has been characterized by a number of developments that emphasize our awareness of the importance of mental health and the necessity to concentrate services and programs as much as possible within each community. These services have been established and underwritten by federal legislation such as the National Mental Health Act, 1946; the Community Mental Health Centers Act, 1963; and the Comprehensive Health Planning and Public Health Service Amendments of 1966. The overall effect of these federal laws, complemented by state legislation, has been to alert the public with regard to mental problems, to encourage community participation in local mental health facilities and programs together with other community programs, and to further the training of professional personnel. A practical result of these developments has been a reduction of the number of mental hospitals, a decrease in length of the patient's stay, and an increase in the utilization of community halfway houses. However, as the services have moved from mental hospital to community, the necessity for increased facilities, personnel, and funds has been highlighted. All of this is a far cry from the state hospital of a century ago.

Correctional Institutions

Another area that calls for some degree of historical perspective is corrections. In early America the local jail was supplemented by the state prison or penitentiary. One type, the Pennsylvania system of solitary confinement day and night, owed its origins to the Society of Friends in Philadelphia in the late eighteenth century. The other, solitary confinement at night and congregate labor in prison shops, developed in Auburn, New York, in the early nineteenth century. Two other institutions came into being during that century: the house of refuge for young offenders in the 1820s and the reformatory for the group comprising ages sixteen to thirty years, in the 1870s. To this must be added the creation of the juvenile court, and the beginnings of probation and parole.

The Juvenile Court   Illinois enacted the first juvenile court law in July, 1899. The fundamental premise of this pioneering legislation was "that the care, custody and discipline of the children brought before the court shall approximate as nearly as possible that which they should receive from their parents, and that as far as practicable they shall be treated not as criminals but as children in need of aid, encouragement, and guidance." The new law provided for separate and private informal hearings, protection of court records from publicity, detention of children separate from adults, appointment of a probation staff, and one jurisdiction for all cases involving delinquent, neglected, and dependent children up to the age of sixteen years. Within recent years there has been an increasing recognition that the child affects, and is affected by, other family members, and that a court that provides a range of juridical services and social services can serve an enlargingly useful purpose. It is essential that such a court be structured as a court and not as a social service agency, even though certain social services, of necessity, must be provided in order for the court to achieve its maximum usefulness.

Although juvenile courts in each state have stressed individualization of treatment, it has been necessary also to safeguard the legal rights of the child. Two cases involving juveniles reached the U.S. Supreme Court during the 1960s; Kent in 1966 (District of Columbia) and Gault in 1967 (Arizona). The essence of these two decisions by the Court is that the child does not surrender his constitutional rights because he is a juvenile. He is entitled to counsel, he must be given notice in writing of the charges against him, and he has the constitutional privilege against self-incrimination, he has the right to confront witnesses, his counsel has the right of access to records, and the juvenile has the right of appeal. These two cases dealt with procedural matters as noted in the Court's words: "nor do we here rule upon the question whether ordinary due process must be observed with respect to hearings to determine the disposition of the delinquent child." It is not unlikely that at some time in the future the U.S. Supreme Court may have a case before it which will call for a due process interpretation of the juvenile court decision concerning disposition of the juvenile after facts have been ascertained. The importance of due process in relation to treatment was expressed by the Court: "Unless approximate due process of law is followed, even the juvenile who has violated the law may not feel that he is being fairly treated and may therefore resist the rehabilitative efforts of the court personnel."

Probation   Probation is one of a number of possible dispositions following court procedure, whether it be in the juvenile court or the adult criminal court. Although the use of probation has been characteristic of the juvenile court since its founding, actually it antedated the court by many years, beginning first on a volunteer basis. As early as 1841 a Boston shoemaker, John Augustus, at his own request to the court, served as surety for a drunkard and continued to do so and to provide a degree of supervision for many others over a period of years. In 1869 the Commonwealth of Massachusetts made provision by law for an agent of the State Board of Charities to appear in criminal trials involving juveniles, when necessary to provide suitable homes for them, and to make periodic supervisory visits. Probation for adult offenders was undertaken officially in Boston in 1878, and within two years the authorization was state-wide. From that time until the present, each of the 50 states adopted adult probation, and since the establishment of the juvenile court, every state has made provision for juvenile probation.

Social Services within the Correctional Institution   Advanced thinking in the correctional field presses more and more for community-based services, but the present stage of knowledge about human behavior (which includes our persistent fear of the criminal and a desire for retribution) does not permit the abandonment of any of the three most common correctional institutions: the reform (or training) school, the reformatory (or industrial school), and the prison. Social workers (and, it is hoped, others) are convinced that social services have a real beneficial application wherever there is a human and social need, and have urged their utilization within the institutions. Limits are recognized as a part of the reality situations facing both worker and prisoner, and yet those very limits within an institution can be used constructively in the casework process.

The classification clinic affords an opportunity for the worker to be of help to the inmate. In the steps from arrest, to trial, to imprisonment, the offender seldom meets with any individual consideration. Perhaps for the first time, he comes to learn inside the institution that a worker exists who can help him with some of his difficulties. The classification system sets as its object the fitting of the individual into the institutional scheme, and, so far as is practical, the adaptation of the institution to the individual. It is an attempt at individualization in a mass situation by offering proper placement, educational training, housing and recreational facilities, and contacts with home. As such, it must take into account the equipment of the inmate as well as his personality needs, and it is in this area of assisting the inmate in making the institutional adjustment that the worker functions.

Parole   It has been said frequently that preparation for parole begins before an individual ever gets to a correctional institution. The treatment he gets at the hands of police, jailers, prosecutors, and judges leaves its impression with him and may have a good deal to do with his attitude toward such officials and the agencies they represent when he leaves prison. The parole officer's job is not so different from that of the probation officer—both call for skill in helping the offender to deal with his problems and to take advantage of his own resources and those of his environment in moving in a more acceptable direction. The use of community resources may be just as important in work with the parolee as with the probationer. When it comes to the point of discharge from parole, the worker will need to assure himself that the individual is ready to go on his own without further help. If the institutional experience has been a constructive one and parole supervision has managed to help the parolee to accept his share of responsibility for his own feelings and behavior, then the parole officer may feel fairly comfortable about the individual proceeding under his own power.

Work-Release Programs   Within recent years a number of correctional institutions have made legal provision for some form of work release, either for educational purposes or for preemployment. Such a program not only helps to prepare the prisoner for freedom but also enables him to conserve or develop working habits and to earn for himself and his family at the same time. Selected prisoners work during the day at jobs in the community, are paid at prevailing rates, and return to the institution at night. Part of his earnings is charged off against the cost of his maintenance at the institution, another part is committed to the support of his dependents, and the balance is held in trust and given to him when he leaves.

Prerelease Guidance Centers and the Halfway Houses   Many workers in the correctional field believe that the several months following release from an institution are the most critical and that maximum opportunity should be offered to make the transition from confinement to freedom in the community. The work-release program is a step in that direction and the prerelease guidance center or a halfway house is another, the purpose being to provide a living and a working experience as a valid part of the completion of the offender's sentence. The center or halfway house is staffed with qualified personnel in areas of employment as well as in individual and group counseling. It is envisioned as part of the treatment program that began in the institution and is continued outside until full freedom is earned. Most of the centers or halfway houses are under official auspice (that is, state or institutional correctional authority), although some are under the direction of a voluntary agency such as a religious, fraternal, or civic group.

In retrospect, it should be noted here that the community and community services are being increasingly used as alternatives to institutionalization. This can be seen in such areas as mental health, mental retardation, and corrections. Indeed, one state (Massachusetts) has committed itself to closing its juvenile correctional institutions and channeling its resources to development of community services for juveniles.

Services to the Aging and the Aged: The Emergence of the Aged

The interest of the American people in the aged and aging is a comparatively recent development, although most European countries, especially Great Britain, were alert to population changes at least a generation before us. Our awareness goes back to the economic depression of the 1930s, when the poverty among the aged, the helplessness of older people on relief rolls, the dominance of the machine in industry and agriculture, and the displacement of the older worker led to legislative proposals for old-age pensions or insurance, a movement finally culminating in the Social Security Act in 1935. Social workers, with very few exceptions, had their share in this general neglect, as evidenced by the paucity of services for the aged except in a few family service agencies or institutions for the aged. Hardly a paper on any aspect of aging appeared in the social work journals or at the annual meetings of professional organizations during the first third of the present century. It was only when sufficient interest was articulated by workers that organizations devoted some consideration to various aspects of aging, beginning during the fourth decade. The movement was exemplified by such organizations as the American Geriatrics Society (1942), the Gerontological Society (1945), and the National Retired Teachers Association (1947). These were followed by the American Association of Retired Persons (1958), the National Council on Aging (1960), and the National Council of Senior Citizens (1962). Finally, recognition of this nationwide social obligation was highlighted by the significant event of the president of the United States acting as host to the first White House Conference on the Aging in 1961. (Incidentally, this event was preceded more than a half-century before by an earlier president who convened the first White House Conference on Children in 1909.) Ten years later (1971) another president called the Second White House Conference.

As we become increasingly aware of the aging and as we study their conditions and the conditions besetting them, we realize the desirability of offering a wide range of services and programs. Some of these are offered to individuals, some to groups, many relate to community programs, and some require legislation and funding appropriations. Most of these services relate to problems that affect all human beings but which are particularly severe for the aged, such as money, health, housing, and family relations, to mention but a few of the salient ones. The family service agency has been the organization that traditionally has undertaken to meet certain needs of family members, including, of course, the older members. More recently, as public welfare departments have moved more and more toward meeting the needs of family members, it has been possible to offer still more extensive as well as intensive service to aging persons. In some family agencies there has been no differentiation with respect to age, whereas in others there has been sufficient volume to justify a degree of staff specialization. Both kinds of agencies not only have offered individualized services, but also have either made referrals to group agencies or utilized group process within their own agency structure.

Much of the service of these agencies, including that of departments within medical settings, has been to help older persons remain in their own homes, and to counsel them about their various difficulties. For some, friendly visiting by volunteers may prove a genuine source of satisfaction to the older person whose conditions oblige him to remain close to his living base and yet who needs the companionship of other human beings. Not infrequently a home-maker (sometimes called home aide) service will permit the older person to remain in his home while the homemaker performs the essential household tasks.

Other older people may be helped to remain in their own homes through the offer of protective services by either a public welfare department or a family service agency. Somewhere between 5 and 10 percent of persons over sixty-five years of age are unable to manage their own affairs and do not have relatives or friends to help them. They may be living under hazardous conditions, baffled by the difficulties of daily living, confused, ill in body or mind, or both, a possible danger to themselves or to others, and exposed to exploitation. Such persons may need not only medical and nursing care, but also legal services for the conservation of their limited financial resources and the protection of their legal rights, which may relate to guardianship or even commitment to a custodial institution. Primary efforts are directed toward keeping the older person in his familiar setting, and alternative forms of care are resorted to only as they are necessary and appropriate.

For those who require medical care a range of facilities and services has been set up. These vary from community to community; few communities have a full spectrum of services, and no community has enough of them. Hospital care is one of these resources, but no community or hospital is able to provide bed care indefinitely. Most hospitals can provide services for acute illnesses, but because of the increasing demands upon them, other arrangements must be made for the person requiring long-term care. Whenever and wherever possible, it is desirable to have the long-term patient return to his home, assuming that there is room for the patient, that the family members are able to provide the necessary care, and that a physician's services are available. In recent years hospital personnel, public health workers, visiting nurses, and community leaders have been developing what has come to be known as home-care programs. These are designed to make the services of the hospital available to the patient who is not ill enough to require the concentrated technical facilities of a general hospital, but who is unable to attend an outpatient clinic or a physician's office. There is also provision for readmission to the hospital for specific purposes, followed by return to home care. Two other facilities for the long-term patient must be mentioned, namely, the institution for the chronically ill and the nursing home. There is every evidence that both resources in whatever area of the nation need to be updated and improved in order to serve older people effectively and with dignity.

Three significant legislative acts have dealt with aspects of aging: the Social Security Act of 1935 with provision for old-age assistance and old-age insurance; the amendments of 1965, which added Medicaid and Medicare; and the Older Americans Act of 1965. Previous reference has been made to the first two, to which should be added the contribution of the third. The Older Americans Act of 1965 authorized grants to the states to help them establish and strengthen state and local agencies on aging, and to assist them in the development of services and opportunities for the elderly in their home communities. The purpose was to facilitate community planning and coordination, to stimulate demonstration projects of new techniques to serve older people and help them use their skills, to encourage innovative services, and to expand existing programs. Two especially serviceable features of the act are the provisions for training of persons (including the aged themselves) to work in the field of aging, and for research and demonstration projects. States and communities have been responsive to these opportunities and have put into operation a variety of programs such as transportation, shopping and library services, meals on wheels, homemaker services, employment guidance, retirement preparation, and consumer advisory service. Community planning projects involve multipurpose centers, housing, nursing home services, recreational and educational opportunities for older people, community-service work by older people, and programs to facilitate independent living at home.[2]

Older people are speaking up for themselves. They resent being tolerated by those who are younger—and being stereotyped as feeble, sick, on the shelf, ready to die. And their resentment is justified. They have served their country, they have contributed to our productive system, they have raised their families—and now they insist on continuing to be useful, to be a viable part of the economy, to take their stand politically, to cherish their families and friends, and to remain in the mainstream of American life while strength and spirit endure. The strongest affirmation of this just claim was evidenced at the 1971 White House Conference, which was recorded in a two-volume summary entitled *Toward a National Policy on Aging.* Some 3600 delegates (among them over 100 young people between seventeen and twenty-four) identified nine *needs areas* and five *needs-meeting areas.* The needs areas

---

[2]For an elaboration of legislation relating to the aged, see Chapter 18 in Part III, prepared by Ann Bilas Johnson.

were: education, employment and retirement, physical and mental health, housing, income, nutrition, retirement roles and activities, spiritual well-being, and transportation. To deal with these needs there should be: planning, training, research and demonstration, services, programs, and facilities—under either governmental or nongovernmental auspices. These delegates, the persons in the communities and states from which they came, and millions of other fellow Americans are determined that the measures adopted by the conference shall not represent mere talk and pious resolutions but rather shall be the active, ongoing program to make the lives of older Americans (indeed, of all people) more productive and more meaningful. Much progress has been made, and as the present decade ends the continuance of this trend appears promising.

BIBLIOGRAPHY

Abbott, Edith. *Public Assistance: American Principles and Policies.* Chicago: University of Chicago Press, 1940.

Abbott, Grace. *The Child and the State.* Chicago: University of Chicago Press, 1938.

———. *From Relief to Social Security.* Chicago: University of Chicago Press, 1941.

Adams, Henry H. *Harry Hopkins: A Biography.* New York: Putnam, 1977.

Armor, David J. *The American School Counselor.* New York: Russell Sage Foundation, 1969.

Axinn, June, and Herman Levin. *Social Welfare: A History of the American Response to Need.* New York: Harper & Row, 1975.

Bartlett, Harriett M. *Fifty Years of Social Work in the Medical Setting.* New York: National Association of Social Workers, 1957.

Birch, Herbert G., and Joan Dye Gussow. *Disadvantaged Children: Health, Nutrition and School Failure.* New York: Harcourt Brace Jovanovich, 1970.

Breckinridge, Sophonisba. *Public Welfare Administration in the United States.* Chicago: University of Chicago Press, 1938.

Brown, Josephine C. *Public Relief, 1929–1939.* New York: Henry Holt & Company, 1940.

Bruno, Frank J. *Trends in Social Work, 1874–1956.* 2d ed. New York: Columbia University Press, 1957.

Cabot, Richard C. *Social Service and the Art of Healing.* New York: Dodd, Mead & Co., 1928.

Cannon, Ida M. *On the Social Frontier of Medicine.* Cambridge: Harvard University Press, 1952.

Charles, Searle F. *Minister of Relief: Harry Hopkins and the Depression.* Syracuse: Syracuse University Press, 1963.

Deutsch, Albert. *The Mentally Ill in America.* Rev. ed. New York: Columbia University Press, 1949.

Field, Minna. *The Aged, the Family, and the Community.* New York: Columbia University Press, 1972.

Folks, Homer. *The Care of Destitute, Neglected and Dependent Children.* New York: Crowell-Collier and Macmillan, 1902.

Goldstine, Dora, ed. *Expanding Horizons in Medical Social Work.* Chicago: University of Chicago Press, 1955.

Hopkirk, Howard W. *Institutions Serving Children.* New York: Russell Sage Foundation, 1944.

John Augustus—First Probation Officer. New York: National Probation Association, 1939.

Kadushin, Alfred. *Child Welfare Services.* New York: Crowell-Collier and Macmillan, 1967.

————. *Child Welfare Services: A Sourcebook.* New York: Crowell-Collier and Macmillan, 1970.

Kamerman, Sheila, and Alfred J. Kahn. *Social Services in the United States.* Philadelphia: Temple University Press, 1976.

Kempe, C. Henry, and Ray E. Helfer. *Helping the Battered Child and His Family.* Philadelphia: J. B. Lippincott, 1972.

Klein, Philip. *From Philanthropy to Social Welfare.* San Francisco: Jossey-Bass, 1968.

Komisar, Lucy. *Down and Out in the U.S.A.: A History of Social Welfare.* New York: New Viewpoints, 1973.

Kurzman, Paul A. *Harry Hopkins and the New Deal.* Fair Lawn, N.J.: R. E. Burdick, 1974.

Lee, Grace, ed. *Helping the Troubled Child: Selected Readings in School Social Work, 1935–1955.* New York: National Association of Social Workers, 1959.

Lichter, Solomon, et al. *The Drop-Outs.* Glencoe, Ill.: The Free Press, 1962.

Lundberg, Emma O. *Unto the Least of These.* New York: Appleton-Century-Crofts, 1947.

Mencher, Samuel. *Poor Law to Poverty Program.* Pittsburgh: University of Pittsburgh Press, 1968.

Oppenheimer, Julius John. *The Visiting Teacher Movement.* New York: Public Education Association, 1924.

Rich, Margaret E. *A Belief in People.* New York: Family Service Association of America, 1956.

Romanyshyn, John M. *Social Welfare: Charity to Justice.* New York: Random House, 1971.

Rothman, Daniel J. *The Discovery of the Asylum: Social Order and Disorder in the New Republic.* Boston: Little, Brown & Co., 1971.

Rothman, Daniel J., and Sheila M. Rothman, eds. *Sources of the American Social Tradition.* I and II. New York: Basic Books, 1975.

Sarri, Rosemary C., and Frank F. Maple, eds. *The School and the Community.* Washington, D.C.: National Association of Social Workers, 1973.

Schlesinger, Arthur M., Jr. *The Coming of the New Deal.* Boston: Houghton Mifflin, 1959.

Schreiber, Daniel, ed. *Profile of the School Dropout.* New York: Random House, 1968.

Siporin, Max. *Introduction to Social Work Practice.* New York: Macmillan, 1975.

Southard, E. E., and Mary C. Jarrett. *The Kingdon of Evils.* New York: Macmillan, 1922.

Thurston, Henry W. *The Dependent Child.* New York: Columbia University Press, 1930.

Towle, Charlotte. *Common Human Needs.* New York: American Association of Social Workers, 1952.

Trattner, Walter. *From Poor Law to Welfare State: A History of Social Welfare in America.* New York: Free Press, 1974.

————. *Homer Folks: Pioneer in Social Welfare.* New York: Columbia University Press, 1967.

Warner, Amos G. *American Charities.* New York: Thomas Y. Crowell Company, 1894.

Weinberger, Paul. *Perspectives on Social Welfare.* New York: Macmillan, 1969.

White House Conference on Aging. *Toward a National Policy on Aging,* I, II. Washington, D.C.: U.S. Government Printing Office, 1973.

4
PUBLIC WELFARE

GEORGE HOSHINO
School of Social Work, University of Minnesota

CONTEMPORARY PUBLIC WELFARE

Previous chapters have traced the antecedents of contemporary social welfare and social work in broad perspective: the poor laws in England and the colonies, the voluntary organizations such as the Charity Organization Societies and the settlement houses, programs for the care and protection of children, the origins of social insurance in Europe and the United States, and the emergency measures of the Great Depression of the 1930s that culminated in the enactment of the Social Security Act of 1935. What today is called public welfare is a product of that evolutionary process. Indeed, public welfare is still in a state of development and events of the past few years have altered the public welfare system and the role of social workers within it in drastic ways.

What is public welfare? A simple definition might be one that would encompass all of social welfare provided under governmental, or "public," auspices. Such a definition, however, would embrace a vast area of public social policy under which direct benefits and services are provided to individuals and families. Under this rubric could be counted income maintenance of all forms, whether in cash or in kind, health, including mental health, education, housing, the personal social services, and perhaps employment services. In fiscal year 1976, governmental expenditures for social welfare under this broad definition, excluding employment services, totaled $311 billion, or 21 percent of the gross national product.[1] Sixty percent of these expenditures was federal, the balance state and local. The great bulk of the federal expenditures were those of the federal Department of Health, Education, and Welfare. Other federal departments also have social welfare functions, for example: the Interior Department (Bureau of Indian Affairs), the Veterans Administration, the Department of Housing and Urban Development, the Labor Department [the welfare-related Work Incentive Program (WIN) and various youth and manpower programs], and the Department of Agriculture (food stamps).

At the other extreme, a very narrow definition of public welfare is implied in the way the word "welfare" is used in lay terms to mean "relief" or the cash and in-kind assistance programs of state and local welfare departments. "Welfare" in this sense usually refers to the program of Aid to Families with Dependent Children (AFDC) but may include Medical Assistance (Medicaid) and the widely varying general assistance programs provided by state, county, and municipal governments. Such a definition is too narrow, however, and excludes a broad and increasingly important range of direct personal social services that are provided by welfare departments to families and children, the aged, and the physically and mentally handicapped and in which social work plays a pivotal role.

In this chapter, public welfare will refer to the federal-state-local public welfare system and will focus on the public welfare departments and the programs they administer. Because major federal programs impinge on the local welfare agencies, they also will be considered as well as those of the voluntary sector with which the public welfare programs interact.

Although local public welfare agencies and their programs are authorized by a number of separate federal and state statutes, the basic legislation under

---

[1]Alfred M. Skolnick and Sophia Dales, "Social Welfare Expenditures, Fiscal Year 1976," *Social Security Bulletin* 40, no. 1 (January 1977):5, 10.

which they operate is the federal Social Security Act. This act, the country's most fundamental and comprehensive social welfare legislation, has three distinct components: cash transfer payments in two forms, social insurance (Old Age, Survivors, and Disability Insurance and Unemployment Insurance) and public assistance (Supplemental Security Income and Aid to Families with Dependent Children); payments for health care in the form of social insurance (Hospital and Medical Insurance, or Medicare), and Medical Assistance, or Medicaid; and social services as provided by the new Title XX program of grants to the states for social services and the smaller Title IVB, Child Welfare program.

THE FEDERAL DEPARTMENT OF HEALTH, EDUCATION, AND WELFARE

Although the U.S. Department of Health, Education, and Welfare (DHEW) was established in 1953 to consolidate in one cabinet department the federal government's major health, education, and welfare responsibilities, it was preceded by a number of federal agencies. Among them were the Federal Security Agency, established in 1939, the New Deal agencies of the Roosevelt administration, the Social Security Board originally created to administer the public assistance, unemployment compensation, and federal old-age benefit programs of the newly enacted Social Security Act, the Children's Bureau which dates to 1912, and the Public Health Service which dates as far back as 1789.[2] The major impetus for the eventual creation of the DHEW probably was the establishment of a number of major federal agencies during the depression years to administer specific programs, such as the Works Progress Administration and the Federal Emergency Relief Administration. While these emergency programs were abolished in time as more permanent programs took their place or the need for them abated as the depression ended with the beginning of World War II, from that time on the federal government was firmly committed to major responsibilities in the social welfare field. These responsibilities and functions have continued to expand regardless of which political party has controlled the executive branch or Congress. Today, the DHEW is a huge department.[3] Its budget now exceeds that of any other department, including the Defense Department.

---

[2]In 1789, the first Congress enacted legislation providing for a deduction of 20 cents a month, later raised to 40 cents, from the salaries of merchant seamen to pay for medical care. Thus it could be said that health insurance is as old as the Republic.

[3]See the Department of Health, Education, and Welfare, *Annual Report* (Washington, D.C.: U.S. Government Printing Office), for an overview of the department's organization and a summary of its functions and activities.

The DHEW and other federal departments discharge their responsibilities in a number of ways; some programs are directly administered by a federal agency, others are provided through a complex system of grants-in-aid to the states. In the District of Columbia, the District's Department of Human Resources directly operates the welfare program in a manner quite similar to that of a state or county department of welfare. The District's programs and relationship to DHEW are essentially the same as those of any state.

Other federal welfare services are directly provided through specialized administrative units of the federal government such as the Veterans Administration which has an extensive network of hospital and outpatient health and social services programs for veterans and certain of their dependents as well as pensions and educational benefits. The Bureau of Indian Affairs of the Department of Interior directly serves American Indians who are under federal jurisdiction although Indians may also qualify for state and county assistance and social services.

THE SOCIAL SECURITY ADMINISTRATION: OLD AGE, SURVIVORS, AND DISABILITY INSURANCE (OASDHI) AND SUPPLEMENTAL SECURITY INCOME (SSI)

By far the largest and most significant directly administered federal programs are those of the Social Security Administration which has a network of regional and district offices reaching into virtually every locality in the nation. It is at the district offices of the Social Security Administration that residents of the United States have their first contact with "social security." Claimants go to these offices to establish their eligibility for benefits when they reach retirement age, become disabled, or are widowed or orphaned by the death of the breadwinner. Since 1974, the Social Security Administration has also managed the claims of the needy aged, blind, and disabled for SSI.

In fiscal year 1976, a total of $90.4 billion in cash payments was made by the Social Security Administration for OASDHI.[4] Beneficiaries of cash payments as of the end of September, 1976, included 20.7 million retired workers and their dependents, 4.5 million disabled workers and their dependents, and 7.4 million survivors.[5]

The magnitude and significance of these programs is indicated by the fact that over 90 percent of the labor force is covered by social security and about three-fourths of the aged population receive OASDHI payments. For most of

---

[4]Skolnick and Dales, *Social Welfare Expenditures,* p. 5.

[5]"Current Operating Statistics," *Social Security Bulletin* 40, no. 1 (January 1977):44.

the aged, "social security" constitutes their single most important source of income; for others of them it may be their only regular source of income. The activities of the Social Security Administration even reach overseas since many beneficiaries are residents of foreign countries. So pervasive is the system that many parents obtain social security numbers for their newborn offspring and the social security number, for better or for worse, has become the universal identification symbol for countless transactions.

Beginning in 1974, the Social Security Administration was assigned responsibility for the administration of a major new federal program, Supplemental Security Income for the needy aged, blind, and disabled. SSI replaced the former adult public assistance categories of Old Age Assistance, Aid to the Blind, and Aid to the Permanently and Totally Disabled which, although federally aided, were administered by the states. In the month of September, 1976, 4.3 million beneficiaries received federally administered SSI, of whom 2.2 million were aged, 2.0 million disabled, and 0.1 million blind.[6]

As of January, 1977, the basic SSI benefit for persons living in their own homes was $167.80 a month for an individual and $251.80 for a couple. The first $20 a month of unearned income such as social security payments and the first $65 a month of earned income plus half of the rest are excluded in computing the payment. Moreover, $1500 in assets for an individual and $2250 for a couple are ignored as well as a home, and reasonable amounts of certain other assets.

A system of state supplementary payments operates in conjunction with SSI in many states. Although the states may elect to have the Social Security Administration disburse the supplemental payments and thereby be relieved of the costs of administration, eligibility for the state supplement is determined by the state or local welfare department. Thus considerable complexity and a degree of confusion are introduced by SSI in those states that have supplemental programs, even though their combined federal and state payments are higher than in states that do not supplement the federal payment.

SSI represents a significant step in this country's movement toward a comprehensive system of income guarantees that provide adequate and dignified protection against income interruption and poverty. Although a means test program in which the applicant must demonstrate financial need, SSI has little of the stigma that was associated with the state programs that it replaced. It is a national system administered through the same offices of the Social Security Administration that also administer OASDHI. Its eligibility requirements are considerably more liberal than those of most of the former adult assistance programs. In particular, two features of the former Old-Age Assis-

---

[6] *Social Security Bulletin* 40, no. 1 (January 1977):62.

tance programs—property liens and relatives' responsibility—are notably absent. These two provisions were among the most onerous of all assistance policies to administer and the most deterrent and humiliating to the needy aged and their relatives. They were, in fact, part of the poor-law heritage of public assistance laws.

SSI, in effect, is a guaranteed annual income for the aged, blind, and disabled, the first national program of its type for a general population group. It serves as one model of a guaranteed annual income that could be extended to other groups, in particular the working poor who are substantially excluded from AFDC. The enactment of SSI came about in an interesting way. It was part of a bill whose major provisions dealt with a Family Assistance Plan (FAP) introduced and supported by the Nixon administration as a "welfare reform" measure to replace AFDC. FAP failed to pass Congress but SSI was enacted.

OASDHI and SSI are significant for the public welfare agencies because many beneficiaries also need services available only from the local public welfare department. Medicare does not cover most nursing home care or prescription drugs but Medicaid does. Many beneficiaries receive basic maintenance from OASDHI and SSI but need various supportive and protective services which may enable them to remain in the community and avoid institutionalization. By the same token, a client of the welfare agency may be unaware of or reluctant to apply for benefits available from the Social Security Administration. Thus the Social Security Administration's programs constitute a major component of the network of social welfare services within which the local welfare department operates and about which its staff needs to be aware.

HEALTH CARE FINANCING ADMINISTRATION

In a major reorganization of the DHEW in 1977, responsibility for two major health care financing programs, Medicare and Medicaid, was transferred to a new Health Care Financing Administration. Medicare is a program of payments for hospital care (Hospital Insurance). If the eligible individual elects to pay a monthly premium, which the federal government matches with an equal amount, Medicare also covers the physician's services (Medical Insurance). During the fiscal year 1976, payments under Medicare totaled $17.8 billion.[7]

The Health Care Financing Administration also oversees the Medicaid program which is administered by the states with federal financial participation.

---

[7]Skolnick and Dales, *Social Welfare Expenditures*, p. 13.

FEDERAL-STATE PROGRAMS

In addition to administering its direct benefit programs such as OASDHI and SSI, the Department of Health, Education, and Welfare administers an array of grants-in-aid to the states for certain categories of welfare services and assistance as well as such welfare-related services as the crippled-children's program, maternal and infant care, vocational rehabilitation, and the child abuse prevention and treatment program. Among the largest are the two federally aided public assistance programs, Aid to Families with Dependent Children and Medical Assistance (Medicaid), and the program of grants to the states for social services. Although the Department of Agriculture is responsible for the Food Stamp program, a major income maintenance program for lower income individuals and families, eligibility for the stamps is determined by local welfare departments. Under this program, individuals may purchase stamps at a "bonus," which varies according to income, to buy specified food items.

In these federally aided welfare programs, the federal role is to review and approve state plans, exercise surveillance over state operations to ensure compliance with federal law and regulations, and provide guidance and technical assistance to state and local staff. These functions are exercised through a network of regional offices whose field staff acts as liaison between the states and the federal offices in Washington.

STATE PUBLIC WELFARE

By the time of the Great Depression, most states had some kind of state structure of boards, commissions, or bureaus to administer or supervise a diverse collection of eleemosynary and correctional programs such as old-age pensions, Mothers' Aid or Widows' Pensions, correctional facilities, children's institutions, and almshouses. A state Board of Charities and Corrections was common. A few states had developed departments of welfare as an outcome of the reform movement during the early 1900s to reorganize state governments into more rational, efficient, and responsive operations. However, major responsibility for welfare remained with the localities and private charity.

With the coming of the emergency relief programs of the depression, every state was compelled to develop machinery for working cooperatively with such federal agencies as the Federal Emergency Relief Administration and the Works Progress Administration. Subsequently, the enactment of the Social Security Act marked the establishment of a permanent program of federal grants to the states for public assistance and child welfare and other social services and a clearly discernible and fairly uniform pattern of organization began to emerge among the state programs.

Certain characteristics of the departments of public welfare can be attributed to a number of requirements in federal law that make specified organizational and administrative arrangements a condition of federal financial participation. Among the more significant are the requirements of a "single state agency" to administer or supervise the administration of the programs, a merit system of personnel administration, machinery for handling grievances and appeals, and uniform standards and policies in every jurisdiction in the state. States also must submit required reports and adopt such methods of administration as are necessary for "proper and efficient administration." These and other federal requirements have brought considerable uniformity among the state programs and the state departments.

Because of the original Social Security Act requirement of a single state agency to administer or supervise the administration of federally aided programs, two distinct patterns of organization and administration have emerged, the state administered systems and the county administered–state supervised systems. In the former, the state directly administers the programs through its own local agencies or departments. Thus the County Boards of Assistance in Pennsylvania are units of the state government. In the latter pattern, the county governments administer the programs under state supervision as in Minnesota where the county departments of public welfare are parts of the county governments. Various combinations prevail, however. In Pennsylvania, for example, although public assistance is administered directly by the state government, child welfare services are provided by the child care services of the county governments. The opposite prevails in other states. Titles also vary. Although the term Department of Public Welfare is still common, other titles are: Department of Pensions and Security, Family and Children's Service, Department of Social Services, and Department of Social Welfare. Moreover, there is a trend toward the consolidation of the "human services" such as welfare, corrections, health, and mental health into omnibus or "umbrella" organizations that go by such titles as Human Services Department.

Despite these differences in titles and patterns of organization, the state departments of public welfare have much in common. In all states, they are among the largest of state departments and their budgets are the largest item in state budgets. At the headquarters offices are located the executive and administrative staff and program specialists such as public assistance specialists, social services specialists, and child care consultants. The executive and administrative staff deal with the chief executive of the state, work with the legislature, coordinate the department's programs with those of other departments of the state government, and oversee the operation of the programs in the field, including the local welfare departments and the various institutions and community facilities throughout the state. They and the specialist staff are occupied with policy development, program planning, research and evaluation, training, liaison with their counterparts in the federal agencies, and supervision of and consultation with county staff.

THE LOCAL PUBLIC WELFARE DEPARTMENT

Welfare services must be available in the communities in which people live. Therefore, whether an administrative unit of the state government or a branch of the city or county government, there exists in every locality of the United States a local public welfare department or its equivalent.[8] They range from the huge welfare bureaucracies of New York City and Los Angeles County to the two- or three-person operations in sparsely populated rural counties. Some departments serve geographical areas of thousands of square miles, others serve compact but densely populated urban areas. Nevertheless, although there are enormous variations among the over three thousand county departments, it is possible to identify a general function and a core of programs.

The function of the public welfare agency is to assist certain categories of individuals and families who have insufficient resources to maintain a decent standard of living, provide help to those who have problems in social functioning, and protect and care for those who are unable to care for themselves because of tender age or physical or mental impairment. In general, the programs of the public welfare agency are of two kinds: those having to do with financial aid and those having to do with personal social services. In the former category are AFDC, Medicaid, and general assistance. In the latter category are a wide variety of supportive, therapeutic, family substitute, protective, and facilitative services to families, children, the aged, and the physically and mentally handicapped. Thus, in addition to administering AFDC, Medicaid, and general assistance, the typical public welfare agency may determine eligibility for food stamps, provide child welfare services (including adoption, foster family care, homemaker services, day care, institutional care, as in residential treatment centers, supervision of older children in independent living arrangements, and protective services to neglected or abused children), offer family planning services, provide protective and sup-

---

[8] *The American Public Welfare Directory,* published annually by the American Public Welfare Association, Washington, D.C., contains a list of the state and local departments of public welfare, their addresses, and the programs they administer.

portive services to the aging, and operate services for the mentally ill and retarded and the chemically dependent.

The local department is linked to the voluntary, or private, social welfare and other related public systems in an intricate network of affiliations and relationships. Reference has already been made to the links with the Social Security Administration.

All local welfare agencies operate an information and referral service at which residents of a locality can inquire about services and be referred to appropriate community programs. The public welfare department may refer clients to such community services as the family service agency, private or sectarian child care services, family planning clinics, legal aid, vocational rehabilitation services, the state blind services, and the state employment service. Many cases involving children and youth must be referred to the juvenile court for action. Under present law, most adult recipients of AFDC must be registered with the Work Incentive Program (WIN) for training and job placement. Other agencies with which the department has frequent contacts are the state Workmen's Compensation and Unemployment Insurance offices, the state crippled children's program, child guidance clinics, and community mental health centers. In turn, these agencies are sources of referral for the welfare department as when the juvenile court refers a youth for supervision or a child for care, or when the local family service agency refers a client for financial assistance.

Many departments purchase care or services from other public or private agencies rather than providing them directly. In most localities, the local department has numerous contracts for such services as family planning, foster family and institutional care of children, and day care. Indeed, it is not uncommon for a local department to purchase a great deal of its services and for tax funds through purchase of service contracts to constitute the bulk of a private agency's income. This situation has created considerable concern and controversy in the voluntary sector because of the threat to the autonomy of private agencies. Traditionally, this autonomy has been the basis of the argument in favor of a strong independent private welfare sector separate from the public sector. Regardless of the pros and cons on the issue of tax funds being used to support private agencies, the public-private interrelationship is an important aspect of a local public welfare department's operations and must be seen as part of the public welfare system.

Public welfare departments also perform a number of functions that might be characterized as indirect services in the sense that, while not serving specific clients directly, they do promote their well-being. Thus welfare departments establish and enforce standards and license such services and facilities as foster family homes, nursing homes for the aged, day care centers, and family day care homes, that is, day care for children by private families.

Community education and information activities such as publicity about abused children and services available for them might also be seen as indirect services.

PUBLIC ASSISTANCE

In terms of dollar expenditures, AFDC and Medicaid are by far the two largest programs administered by local welfare departments. Although local departments determine eligibility for food stamps, the recipients purchase the stamps from banks.

AFDC is a federally aided cash payment program for children dependent because of the death, disability, or continued absence of the parent. In about half of the states, children dependent because of the unemployment of the parent also are covered. Thus AFDC serves families who have no or only a marginal attachment to the labor force although a sizable proportion of family heads do have some earnings from employment.

AFDC is a means-tested program. That is, the applicant must demonstrate financial need in addition to meeting the other eligibility requirements. Thus AFDC is for poor families with children. Although AFDC is literally the last line of defense against destitution for the poorest of the nation's children, it has serious inadequacies and is the target of much public criticism. Paradoxically, it is attacked for being too restrictive and punitive at the same time that it is assailed for being too liberal and encouraging dependency and for rewarding the nonworking poor but penalizing the working poor.

The AFDC caseload is made up mostly of female-headed families and increasingly of families broken by divorce, desertion, or unwed parenthood. Racial minorities are disproportionately represented; slightly over half of the families are other than white. To understand the persistence of a major public assistance program in the midst of an affluent industrial society, especially one that serves a population like that of the AFDC caseload, it is necessary to look beyond the program to the larger context within which AFDC operates.

The families who receive AFDC are those who tend not to be covered by the "universal" maintenance programs or who suffer discrimination in the job market. The poverty population is composed largely of the working poor—families headed by fully employed breadwinners whose earnings are still insufficient to bring them over the poverty line—female-headed families, and families of racial minorities. Social insurance such as OASDHI and Unemployment Insurance has limited capacity to deal with the problem of childhood poverty. Eligibility is conditioned on a substantial prior employment record and the amount of benefit is related to the level of earnings. Women and racial minorities suffer discrimination in the job market. Much of their employment is in occupations not covered by social insurance or is irregular and low-paying. Moreover, social insurance does not deal with income inter-ruption caused by family breakup.

While many underlying societal and economic factors help explain why AFDC has not "withered away" as it was hoped when the Social Security Act was enacted, AFDC can be seen as the victim of the "creaming" phenome-non. That is, although total expenditures for income maintenance have grown to an enormous volume and proportion of governmental expenditures as successive groups have been taken out of the "dependent" class, coverage has been very selective and confined to the "deserving poor"—the aged, blind, disabled, survivors, and temporarily unemployed. Generally excluded are the "undeserving poor," mostly poor families with children. Their only recourse is AFDC, and even AFDC excludes the complete family headed by an employed breadwinner whose earnings are insufficient for family needs.

In July, 1976, the average monthly AFDC payment per recipient nationally was only $75.14 but ranged from $132.73 in Rhode Island, $123.87 in New York, and $106.26 in Wisconsin to $10.00 in Puerto Rico, $14.33 in Missis-sippi, and $27.82 in South Carolina.[9] Many AFDC families have other sources of income such as earnings and child support payments and they are eligible for a number of in-kind benefits such as food stamps and Medicaid that can add substantially to a family's total income. Nevertheless, the general picture is of a standard of living that reaches the official poverty line in only a few of the highest paying states and descends to an abysmally low level in the lower paying states. Compared to SSI, AFDC benefit levels are niggardly indeed. Moreover, AFDC "disregards" of income and assets are much less generous than those of SSI.

The generally low payment levels and the violent contrasts among the states in respect to eligibility requirements and payments, plus the fact that AFDC does not assist many of the poor at all, have led to repeated calls for "welfare reform" through a greater federal role, complete federalization, or some new scheme of income supports. An example was the Nixon adminis-tration's proposal for a Family Assistance Plan (FAP) which would have, in effect, guaranteed a minimum income for families with children. Incentive features were built into the benefit formula so that working family heads could retain a proportion of their earnings. Although the minimum guaranteed income was set at a very low level, $1600 per year for a family of four, it would have raised the income of AFDC families in many states, particularly in the South, and extended coverage to thousands of families excluded from AFDC, mainly the working poor. Moreover, state supplementation presum-ably would have continued in the states with AFDC benefits higher than those

---

[9] *Social Security Bulletin* 40, no. 1 (January 1977):69.

provided by FAP, as in SSI. As already noted, FAP failed to pass Congress and SSI was enacted instead.[10]

The Carter administration's plan for "welfare reform" was unveiled in the President's message to Congress of August 6, 1977. It proposes the abolition of the existing AFDC, SSI, and Food Stamp programs and the creation of a new system that would incorporate a program of job creation, preferably in the private sector; a program of income support and work-related benefits for persons able to work, including single individuals, two-parent families, childless couples, and single-parent families with no child under 14; and an income-security program for those not expected to work—namely, the aged, blind, disabled, and single parents with children under age 14. For those required to work, the first $3800 and half of the remainder of earnings would be disregarded up to $8400. To provide an additional work incentive, the earned income tax credit, which presently provides for a 10 percent tax credit on earnings up to $4000, would be expanded and liberalized.

The new system, which would not go into effect until October 1981, would create a single federal system with uniform and simplified eligibility requirements and procedures. A substantial role would remain with the state and local departments, however, in the form of a modest requirement (10 percent) of financial participation in the basic federal benefits program and responsibility for developing the job opportunities program. States could elect to supplement the basic federal benefits, as many do under SSI, with substantial federal sharing in the cost. They could elect to operate the intake function as well.

The Carter administration's proposal would alter the existing public welfare system in fundamental ways: "welfare" in the sense of income maintenance clearly is seen as a direct federal function rather than a responsibility of state or local governments with or without federal aid, and coverage is extended to large groups presently excluded—in particular, complete families and the "working poor." On the other hand, traditional welfare features are retained, such as the strong emphasis on work and work-conditioned benefits, the preference for a "means test" approach rather than change in the social insurance system or a program of "universal" income guarantees based on group membership instead of an individual determination of need, and separate treatment of the "deserving" poor—the aged, blind, and disabled —who receive more generous payments under more liberal conditions than do the "undeserving" poor. Moreover, inequities among the states will continue since state supplementation inevitably will vary widely as it does under SSI.

---

[10]See Vincent J. Burke and Vee Burke, *Nixon's Good Deed: Welfare Reform* (New York: Columbia University Press, 1974), for an interesting account of this episode in the Nixon administration from the viewpoint of a journalist.

Initial reaction to the plan appears to be positive, especially since substantial fiscal relief is promised to the states. However, such a sweeping proposal to reform the welfare system is certain to encounter opposition from interests within and without Congress in respect both to the plan's overall thrust and particular details such as the level of payments provided.[11] Thus, "welfare reform" promises to be one of the most significant and hotly contested issues on the current domestic social policy scene.

MEDICAL ASSISTANCE

The President's message to Congress briefly noted the need for fundamental reform and rationalization of the Medicaid program and indicated that his administration would submit a national health insurance proposal the following year but gave no hints as to the direction such a proposal might take.

In contrast to Medicare, Medicaid is a comprehensive program in the sense that all forms of medical care are covered unless specifically excluded. Thus nursing home care and prescription drugs are covered by Medicaid but not by Medicare. Medicare also is restricted to the aged and beneficiaries of Disability Insurance and requires that the individual pay certain "deductible" and "coinsurance" charges. Medicaid fills some of the gaps in coverage.

Although enacted in 1965 to replace a program of Medical Assistance for the Aged and to supplement Medicare, the Medicaid program has grown at an almost explosive rate. Indeed, Medicaid expenditures now exceed AFDC expenditures. In July, 1976, Medicaid expenditures totaled $1.3 billion as compared with $841.3 million for AFDC.[12] Because of the increasing burden on state finances, there is a growing demand for greater federal sharing of Medicaid expenditures or complete federalization. Concurrently, there is increasing interest in national health insurance.

---

[11]The Carter proposal divides the poor into two categories for eligibility and benefit purposes: an "upper tier" composed of those not required to work, mainly the aged, blind and disabled, and single parents with children under 14; and a "lower tier" composed of those required to work, mainly single individuals not aged or disabled, childless couples, and single parents with no children under age 14.

In the "upper tier," a family of four with no income would receive $4200; aged, blind and disabled individuals would receive $2500 and couples $3750. Single individuals not aged or disabled would get $1100 and a childless couple $2200 if jobs are not available.

In the "lower tier" two-parent families of four and single-parent families of four with children over 14 would receive $2300 unless no job is available in which case they will receive $4200.

For those required to work and who receive a "work benefit" the first $3800 of earnings would be disregarded and the remainder of earnings would reduce the benefit one dollar for each two dollars of earnings, phasing out at $8400 of earnings.

[12]*Social Security Bulletin* 40, no. 1 (January 1977): 68, 70.

In successive Congresses, numerous national health insurance bills have been introduced. The Carter administration is on record as favoring national health insurance. In view of the spiraling costs of health care and the fact that the beneficiaries of national health insurance would include the middle class, the political pressure may be irresistible. National health insurance may be an idea whose time has come. Although the proposals in Congress vary widely as to their coverage, eligibility requirements, means of financing, kinds of health services covered, and administration, the more far-reaching plans would replace or substantially reduce the need for Medicaid.[13] In his "welfare reform" message to Congress August 6, 1977, President Carter briefly noted the need for fundamental reform and rationalization of the Medicaid program and indicated that his administration would submit a national health insurance proposal in the following year, but gave no hints as to the direction that the proposal might take.

SEPARATION OF AID AND SERVICES

Financial aid traditionally has been accompanied by a rehabilitative function of some kind, whether the "moral guidance" of the poor-relief officer or social services in modern public assistance programs. The principle of tying services to aid received congressional sanction with the enactment of the Social Security Amendments of 1962 which authorized federal funds for social services to recipients of public assistance, former recipients, and persons likely to become recipients. The premise of the "services strategy" was that the provision of services by trained staff would lead to the reduction of caseloads and expenditures for public assistance.

The services strategy proved to be a failure. Instead of decreasing, AFDC expenditures continued to increase. The responsibility for administering a massive complicated financial aid program overwhelmed attempts to build up a viable services program. By the late 1960s, social services funding had become what some termed "backdoor revenue sharing," which was brought to an end in 1972 when Congress imposed a $2.5 billion ceiling on federal payments for social services.[14]

Differences of opinion arose over the services strategy. One view held that services were an integral part of financial aid programs. The opposite view

---

[13]For a comparison of national health insurance proposals introduced in Congress as of July, 1974, see U.S. Social Security Administration, *National Health Insurance Proposals* (Washington, D.C.: U.S. Government Printing Office, 1974).

[14]The $2.5 billion ceiling on federal expenditures for social services was imposed by the General Revenue Sharing Act of 1972 and was carried over to Title XX in 1974. For an account of the explosive growth of spending for social services, see Martha Derthick, *Uncontrollable Spending for Social Services Grants* (Washington, D.C.: The Brookings Institution, 1975).

was that determination of eligibility and provision of services were inherently different functions that should be performed by different kinds of staff—the former by nonprofessional workers trained in the specific procedures of eligibility determination, the latter by professionals trained to deal with personal and family problems. Those who favored separation of aid and services also argued that assistance was a right that should not be conditioned by behavioral or service requirements. Consequently, they argued that services should be separate and voluntary. Moreover, they claimed that eligibility determination was an investigative function which introduced an adversary element into the relationship between worker and client and precluded a truly professional relationship. Finally, it was realized that services would have to be disassociated from relief if services were to be made available to a population broader than the public assistance caseloads.[15]

By 1970 sentiment had swung to favor separation and in 1972 separation was mandated by DHEW to include at a minimum (1) separate staff for the two functions of determining eligibility for aid and providing services, (2) separate supervisory and administrative structures, and (3) separate accounting systems. The establishment of SSI in 1974 completed the separation process so far as older recipients are concerned since SSI is administered by the Social Security Administration and responsibility for the adult social services remains with the local welfare departments.

The consequences of separation are clearly evident in local public welfare departments. Applications for financial aid and continuing eligibility are handled by a staff of nonprofessional workers commonly called eligibility technicians. Social services are provided separately by or under the direction of professional staff predominantly trained in social work.

THE PERSONAL SOCIAL SERVICES

On January 4, 1974, Congress enacted Public Law 93-647, its purpose being to "amend the Social Security Act to establish a consolidated program of Federal financial assistance to encourage provision of services by the States." The act abolished the former services provisions of the public assistance titles and created a new Title XX, Grants to the States for Services, in the Social Security Act.[16]

---

[15]George Hoshino, "Separating Maintenance from Social Services," *Public Welfare* 30, no. 2 (Spring 1972):54–61; and "Money and Morality: Income Security and Personal Social Services," *Social Work* 16: no. 2 (April 1971):16–24.

[16]For an account of the development of Title XX and a summary of its provisions, see Paul E. Mott, *Meeting Human Needs: The Social and Political History of Title XX* (Columbus, Ohio: National Conference on Social Welfare, 1976).

Under Title XX, states have wide discretion as to what services will be provided and how they will be organized and delivered. Although still restricted to the lower income population, services can be provided on a fee basis to individuals with incomes up to 115 percent of the state median income.

The personal social services encompass a wide variety of supportive, therapeutic, family substitute, protective, and facilitative services to families and children, the aged, and the physically and mentally handicapped. They include the "soft" or relationship services such as social casework and counseling, and the "hard" or tangible services such as day care, chore services for the aged and disabled, meals on wheels, and residential care. They can be distinguished from the other well-established areas of social welfare—income maintenance, health, housing, education, and employment—and it is clear that they are emerging as a distinct and increasingly important component of social welfare in all industrial countries.[17]

In European countries, the personal social services are more highly developed and universally available and can be readily identified as an essential part of the institutional fabric of social welfare that citizens expect from government. In Britain, for example, a recent reorganization consolidated into a single local-authority Department of Social Services a number of specialized services that had been provided by different agencies, including children and youth services, welfare services, services for the mentally ill and retarded, hospital social services, services for the disabled and aged, and residential care. These departments are now among the largest and most important of local government departments.[18]

A similar development can be anticipated in the United States. The enactment of Title XX can be seen as part of this development.

However, unlike the other established social welfare areas—income maintenance, health, education, housing, and employment—there is as yet no

---

[17]See Alfred J. Kahn, *Social Policy and Social Services (New York: Random House, 1973),* for a description and conceptualization of personal social services. The conceptual framework developed in this book was applied in a cross-national study of U.S. and European social service systems in Sheila B. Kamerman and Alfred J. Kahn, *Social Services in the United States* (Philadelphia: Temple University Press, 1976); and Alfred J. Kahn and Sheila B. Kamerman, *Not for the Poor Alone: European Social Services* (Philadelphia: Temple University Press, 1975). The term personal social services is of British origin and differentiates this constellation of services from the other five "social services": income maintenance, health, housing, education, and employment. In the United States terminology is not yet settled, although "social service" is the most commonly used term and the one used in Title XX.

[18]Robert Morris (Rapporteur), *Toward a Caring Society* (New York: Columbia University School of Social Work, 1974); and Malcolm H. Brown, ed., *Social Issues and the Social Services* (London: Charles Knight and Co., Ltd., 1974). Income maintenance, including National Insurance, Family Allowances, the Family Income Supplement, and Supplementary Benefits (roughly equivalent to SSI and AFDC), are central government responsibilities as is health care which is provided by the National Health Service.

clear unifying intuitive understanding or conceptual definition that can encompass all of the functions and activities that can be grouped under the rubric of the personal social services. Nor is there consensus about their purposes.

Kahn ascribes the following tasks to the personal social services:

1. To strengthen and repair family and individual functioning with reference to ongoing roles.
2. To provide new institutional outlets for socialization, development, and assistance, roles that once were—but are no longer—discharged by the nuclear or extended family.
3. To develop institutional forms for new activities, essential to individuals, families, and groups in the complex urban society even though unknown in a simple society.[19]

Kahn employs a threefold classification of functions: (1) socialization and development; (2) therapy, help, and rehabilitation (including social protection and substitute care); and (3) access, information, and advice.[20]

Despite these attempts at clarification, the personal social services—whether conceived as a system, as discrete programs and services, or as the collective or individual activities of staff—remain broadly and imprecisely defined.[21]

There also is little consensus about the kind of training needed for the social services. Currently, staff providing services includes a wide variety of professional, semiprofessional, and paraprofessional personnel—highly trained family therapists, adoption workers, vocational counselors, homemakers, day care workers, case aides, and residential staff—whose training ranges from graduate professional education to high school and less.

---

[19]Alfred J. Kahn, *Social Policy and Social Services,* p. 16.

[20]Ibid., p. 28.

[21]Title XX defines social services in terms of five goals:
1. Achieving or maintaining economic self-support to prevent, reduce, or eliminate dependency.
2. Achieving or maintaining self-sufficiency, including reduction or prevention of dependency.
3. Preventing or remedying neglect, abuse, or exploitation of children and adults unable to protect their own interests, or preserving, rehabilitating, or reuniting families.
4. Preventing or reducing inappropriate institutional care by providing for community-based care, home-based care, or other forms of less intensive care.
5. Securing referral or admission for institutional care when other forms of care are not appropriate, or providing services to individuals in institutions.

Section 2002 states that the services must be directed to the five goals and "may include, but are not limited to" an illustrative enumeration of ". . . services designed to meet the special needs of children, the aged, the mentally retarded, the blind, the emotionally disturbed, the physically handicapped, and alcoholics and drug addicts."

The recognition by Title XX of the personal social services as a distinct and separate component of a system of social security for all Americans is significant in its immediate consequences for the existing system of social services, in its symbolism and potential for the future development of the services, and in its implications for the social work profession.

Prior to the separation of aid and services and the enactment of Title XX, there was little opportunity to develop a separate viable system of personal social services. The services had been adjunctive to the public assistance programs or to the manpower programs such as WIN, rather than being viewed as needed services in their own right. They were conceived as having primarily an antipoverty function and thus to be provided mainly to recipients of public assistance or those likely to become dependent. Consequently, the establishment of SSI, which separated the money payment program for the aged, blind, and disabled from the adult social services, and the enactment of Title XX can be seen as limited but significant steps toward the goal of a "universal" and "free-standing" system of social services justified in terms of their intrinsic merits and available to the poor and nonpoor alike. If national health insurance becomes a reality and replaces Medicaid, and a guaranteed annual income of some kind for families with children replaces AFDC, local public welfare departments will become social services agencies with a relatively minor assistance function. The provision of social services then will be the primary function of public welfare.

It is startling to note how significant these developments have been for the social work profession. Until a few years ago, public assistance was seen as an important "field of social work practice." Public assistance administration is now seen as a separate career line. The relatively few professionally trained social workers in the AFDC and Medicaid programs are mostly at the policy and administrative levels. In the SSI program there are even fewer professional social workers involved.

The future of social work, therefore, would appear to lie in the personal social services. This area of social welfare is the province of social work; indeed, it may be the only area in which the profession can claim unique competence. Much will depend on the profession's capacity to identify, conceptualize, and train for the personal social services. This will mean systematic description and analysis of the programs that make up the system, a more precise conceptualization of the social service function, delineation of the tasks involved and the generic and specialized knowledge and skill needed for the various service roles, and the development of formal and in-service training programs to impart these knowledges and skills.

It is now clear that the assurance of the basic social welfare services such as income security and health care does not diminish the need for personal individualized social services. Rather, the contrary seems to be the case. The guarantee of income and health care for the older population, for example, has stimulated a need and demand for new and expanded programs of supportive, protective, residential, and socialization services. Social work is not the whole of the social services, of course, any more than is medical practice the whole of health care. Nevertheless, in the emerging and increasingly important field of the personal social services, the social work profession plays a pivotal role.

BIBLIOGRAPHY

Bell, Winifred. *Aid to Dependent Children.* New York: Columbia University Press, 1965.

Brown, Malcolm N., ed. *Social Issues and the Social Services.* London: Charles Knight and Co., 1974.

Bruce, Maurice. *The Coming of the Welfare State.* Rev. ed. New York: Schocken Books, 1966.

Burke, Vincent J., and Vee Burke. *Nixon's Good Deed, Welfare Reform.* New York: Columbia University Press, 1974.

Burns, Eveline M. *Health Services for Tomorrow.* New York: Dunellen Publishing Co., 1973.

———. *Social Security and Public Policy.* New York: McGraw Hill, 1956.

Clarke, Helen I. *Social Legislation.* 2d ed. New York: Appleton-Century-Crofts, 1957.

Coll, Blanche D. *Perspectives in Public Welfare.* Washington, D.C.: U.S. Government Printing Office, 1969.

Derthick, Martha. *The Influence of Federal Grants: Public Assistance in Massachusetts.* Cambridge: Harvard University Press, 1970.

———. *Uncontrollable Spending for Social Services.* Washington, D.C.: The Brookings Institution, 1975.

Elman, Richard M. *The Poorhouse State: The American Way of Life on Public Assistance.* New York: Pantheon Books, 1966.

Friedlander, Walter A., and Robert Z. Apte. *Introduction to Social Welfare.* 4th ed. Englewood Cliffs, N.J.: Prentice-Hall, 1974.

Gilbert, Neil, and Harry Specht, eds. *The Emergence of Social Welfare and Social Work.* Itasca, Ill.: F. E. Peacock, 1976.

Handler, Joel F. *Reforming the Poor.* New York: Basic Books, 1972.

Kadushin, Alfred. *Child Welfare Services.* 2d ed. New York: Macmillan, 1974.

Kahn, Alfred J. *Social Policy and Social Services.* New York: Random House, 1973.

Kahn, Alfred J., and Sheila B. Kamerman. *Not for the Poor Alone: European Social Services.* Philadelphia: Temple University Press, 1975.

Kamerman, Sheila B., and Alfred J. Kahn. *Social Services in the United States: Policies and Programs.* Philadelphia: Temple University Press, 1976.

Mays, John, Anthony Folder, and Olive Keidan, eds. *Penelope Hall's Social Services in England and Wales.* London: Routledge and Kegan Paul, 1974.

Morris, Robert (Rapporteur). *Toward a Caring Society.* New York: Columbia University School of Social Work, 1974.

Mott, Paul E. *Meeting Human Needs: The Social and Political History of Title XX.* Columbus, Ohio: National Conference on Social Welfare, 1976.

Moynihan, Daniel P. *The Politics of a Guaranteed Income: The Nixon Administration and the Family Assistance Plan.* New York: Vintage Books, 1973.

Piven, Frances Fox, and Richard A. Cloward. *Regulating the Poor: The Functions of Public Welfare.* New York: Pantheon Books, 1971.

President's Commission on Income Maintenance Programs. *Poverty Amidst Plenty: The American Paradox.* Washington, D.C.: U. S. Government Printing Office, 1969.

Rossi, P. H., and K. C. Lyall. *Reforming Public Welfare: A Critique of the Negative Income Tax Experiment.* New York: Russell Sage Foundation, 1976.

Schorr, Alvin L. *Poor Kids: A Report on Children in Poverty.* New York: Basic Books, 1966.

————, ed. *Children and Decent People.* New York: Basic Books, 1974.

Schottland, Charles I. *The Social Security Programs in the United States.* 2d ed. Englewood Cliffs, N.J.: Prentice-Hall, 1970.

Steiner, Gilbert Y. *The Children's Cause.* Washington, D.C.: The Brookings Institution, 1976.

————. *Social Insecurity: The Politics of Welfare.* Chicago: Rand McNally, 1966.

————. *The State of Welfare.* Washington, D.C.: The Brookings Institution, 1971.

Stevens, Robert and Rosemary Stevens. *Welfare Medicine in America: A Case Study of Medicaid.* New York: Free Press, 1974.

U.S. Social Security Administration. *Social Security Programs in the United States.* Washington, D. C.: U. S. Government Printing Office, 1973. (Revised occasionally.)

Weinberger, Paul E., ed. *Perspectives on Social Welfare.* 2d ed. New York: Macmillan, 1974.

Wilcox, Clair. *Toward Social Welfare.* Homewood, Ill.: Richard D. Irwin, 1969.

5
RESEARCH IN SOCIAL WORK

H. CARL HENLEY

School of Social Work, University of North Carolina

INTRODUCTION

Social work research began with surveys, and, according to Polansky, many of those connected with the early surveys "began with an awareness that people were suffering, and something was amiss, but what it was and what ought to be done about it were to be clarified through sifting of evidence, painstakingly collected."[1] Among the first such investigators in America, and perhaps the best known of the early reformers, was Dorothea Lynde Dix (1802–1887). She was interested mainly in the mentally ill, and she traveled

---

[1]Norman A. Polansky, "Research in Social Work," in *Encyclopedia of Social Work* (New York: National Association of Social Workers, 1971), p. 1100.

throughout the country for eight years in order to get an accurate estimate of the number of mentally ill and the quality of care they were receiving. After gathering her data, she petitioned the U.S. Congress in 1848 to aid the states in caring for the insane.

Her concern for the welfare of these people is apparent in the following quotation:

> I have myself seen more than nine thousand idiots, epileptics, and insane, in these United States . . . sought out in jails, in poorhouses, and in private dwellings, there have been hundreds, nay rather thousands, bound with galling chains, bowed beneath fetters and heavy iron balls, attached to drag-chains, lacerated with ropes, scourged with rods, and terrified beneath storms of profane execrations and cruel blows . . . I proceed to verify this assertion, commencing with the state of Maine. . . .[2]

Even though Miss Dix's work had a marked impact on the field of social work, large-scale survey research got its real start in the United States with the Pittsburgh Survey, which began in September 1907 under the direction of Paul U. Kellogg, the managing editor of *Charities and the Commons.* This was "the first major attempt in the United States to survey in depth the entire life of a single community by team research," and "the bulk of the financing came through the good offices of the Russell Sage Foundation, which had just been established and chose this project as its first extensive investment in social research."[3] The early surveys were designed to describe economic and social conditions, and among the topics covered by the Pittsburgh Survey were hourly wages; hours worked; conditions of labor, housing, and schools; taxation; the quality of fire and police protection; recreation; and land value.

According to Kellogg, the ultimate aim of the survey was "to reduce conditions in terms of household experience and human life,"[4] but Klein has noted that those connected with the survey thought "that the scientifically impartial organization of collected data would prove persuasive enough to render subsequent action acceptable and inevitable. In this respect, however, the hopes of the Survey Staff were sadly shattered by the reaction of the power structure involved."[5] Nevertheless, "it is fair to say that the Pittsburgh

---

[2]Quoted in Mary E. MacDonald, "Social Work Research: A Perspective," in *Social Work Research,* ed. Norman A. Polansky (Chicago: University of Chicago Press, 1960), p. 9.

[3]Clarke A. Chambers, *Paul U. Kellogg and the Survey* (Minneapolis: University of Minnesota Press, 1971), p. 36.

[4]*Ibid.,* p. 37.

[5]Philip Klein, *From Philanthropy to Social Welfare* (San Francisco: Jossey-Bass, 1968), p. 185.

Survey represents, for better or worse, much of what social work research became during the next three decades,"[6] with the exception that later surveys were narrower in scope and focused upon particular areas of concern.

In the last quarter-century, as Stuart notes, social work research has moved "from early studies based mainly on anecdotal evidence toward increasing reliance on experimental methodology."[7] Even though social work literature is gradually including a larger number of research articles that are of higher quality, a study by Rosenblatt found that "relatively few practitioners make use of research findings or rate them as helpful."[8] Surely, if the field of social work is to progress, it must have not only an increase in the number and quality of research studies conducted by social workers, but also an increase in the consumption and utilization of research by practitioners. As Rosenblatt put it, "Social workers need to make a long-range commitment to research, which means that they must accept the need to support research, to cooperate with researchers, and to pay attention to research findings."[9] Thus the purpose of this chapter is *not* to make social work researchers out of students but to acquaint students with the various research methodologies in order that they might more easily see the usefulness and relevance of research in social work.

DEFINITION OF, AND STEPS IN, SOCIAL WORK RESEARCH

Research in any field is simply the application of the scientific method to the specific material of that field. Thus research in social work is the systematic search for answers that are not yet known, or the systematic testing of assumptions on which practice is based in order to make them certain rather than presumed. Research studies may have purposes ranging from the development of a general theory of human behavior and societal functioning (called "basic research") to the comparison of the effectiveness of two methods of rehabilitating juvenile delinquents (called "applied research"). Since social work is a practice field, more of its research is applied than basic, but the goal of all social work research is the improvement of practice.

It may be true that each researcher has his own method of conducting a research study, but, in general, all researchers who engage in hypothesis-

---

[6]Polansky, "Research in Social Work," p. 1102.

[7]Richard B. Stuart, "Research in Social Work: Casework and Group Work," in *Encyclopedia of Social Work* (New York: National Association of Social Workers, 1971), p. 1106.

[8]Aaron Rosenblatt, "The Practitioner's Use and Evaluation of Research," *Social Work* 13, no. 1 (January 1968):53.

[9]*Ibid.,* p. 59.

testing research will go through the steps included in the following list, although not necessarily in the exact order in which they are presented:[10]

1. *Selection of the problem area.* Suppose the researcher is a school social worker and he has noticed, for example, that some children perform in school at a level equal to or above their intellectual level, while others perform at a level below their intellectual level. Thus the general problem area in which he is interested could be called "pupil performance."

2. *Review of the literature.* In this step, the researcher acquaints himself with the current theory and knowledge in the area. (This is often called "library research.")

3. *Formulation of the exact problem to be studied.* Before the researcher can seek an answer to his problem, he must know exactly what the problem is, and it must be stated in such a way that it permits a solution. The problem usually appears in the form of a question (which may ask the relationship between two or more variables), and it is the answer to the question that is being sought in the research. For example, after reviewing the research that has been done in the area of pupil performance, the researcher may choose the following as his research problem: "What is the relationship between the stability of family life and pupil performance?"

4. *Development of the hypothesis.* The hypothesis is a conjectural statement that provides a possible solution to the research problem by specifying the relationship between the variables in the problem. For example, the hypothesis might be that "if their family life is stable, children will perform at a higher level in school than they will if their family life is unstable." Students should note that in order to test this hypothesis, one must be able to measure the variables included in it. Thus the research must develop "working definitions" for the variables "stability of family life" and "school performance." That is, he must specify exactly how he plans to measure each of these variables.

5. *Development of the formal argument.* The researcher must decide how he will test the hypothesis. That is, he must decide what data to collect and how he will use the data to determine whether his hypothesis is true. If he will use a statistical argument, he would at this point decide what tables he will use. Note that the hypothesis gives direction to the investigation at this point by telling the researcher on which variables he must collect data.

6. *Delineation of the source of the data.* Once the researcher has determined what data to collect, he must decide from whom or from what source

---

[10]Roy G. Francis, "The Nature of Scientific Research," in *An Introduction to Social Research,* ed. John T. Doby (Harrisburg, Pa.: The Stackpole Company, 1954), pp. 12–16.

he will get his data. Obviously, for the research to continue, the data must be obtainable.

7. *Creation of the data-gathering instrument.* The instrument used to gather the data, whether it is a questionnaire, interview schedule, test, etc., must give the researcher the data called for by the hypothesis to be tested.

8. *Pretest of the instrument and possible revision.* If the instrument is a questionnaire, for example, certain questions may be ambiguous and, therefore, give incorrect or misleading answers. The researcher should "try out" his instrument on a small sample of people as nearly like those to be included in the study as possible (but not anyone to be included in the study) before he assumes that no errors exist in it.

9. *Writing a "dummy argument."* After the researcher pretests his data-gathering instrument, he may want to use the data gathered during the pretest to see whether or not he has gathered the *kinds* of data he needs to test his hypothesis. He can accomplish this by writing up his argument in terms of the data he found during the pretest. In this way, he would hope to find out whether other kinds of data were needed or unneeded data were being gathered.

10. *Formal acquisition of the data.* After making any necessary revisions in the instrument, the researcher should apply the instrument to the source of the data identified in step 6.

11. *Analysis of the data.* At this point the researcher performs whatever statistical analyses of the data are necessary for him to test his hypothesis.

12. *Formal write-up and conclusions reached.* After interpreting the analyses performed on the data, the researcher will usually want to convey the results of his study to the public in order to add to the body of knowledge in his field. Making the results public also provides an opportunity for others to challenge his interpretation of the data or to replicate his study at another time.

The rest of this chapter will be spent in discussing research designs and how research studies are classified according to the purpose of the study or the time element involved in the study. There will also be a short section on evaluation research in social work.

THE RESEARCH DESIGN

To the beginning student in social work, the term "research design" may be foreign. However, it really means the blueprint by which the study will be conducted. In other words, the design of the research study includes the rules by which the researcher will proceed. As might be expected, authors differ with respect to how they define the research design. For example, Kahn describes it as "the logical strategy of the study. It deals with the plan developed to answer a question, describe a situation, or test a hypothesis; in other words, it deals with the rationale by which a specific set of procedures, which include data collection and analysis, are expected to meet the particular requirements of a study."[11] Selltiz and co-workers say that "a research design is the arrangement of conditions for collection and analysis of data in a manner that aims to combine relevance to the research purpose with economy in procedure."[12] Riley has stated that "in each inquiry, the investigator selects a particular set of methods that he will follow in obtaining his research findings. We refer to this set of selected methods as the research design."[13]

Choosing a satisfactory research design is of great importance, because it is at this time that the researcher should think through the entire study and try to choose a design that will preclude as many mistakes as possible. In order to choose the most appropriate design, the researcher must repeatedly ask himself exactly what questions he wants to answer, why he wants to answer these questions, and who is most likely to give him the correct answers to these questions. If he can answer these questions clearly and precisely, he has gone a long way toward creating a satisfactory design.

One way of classifying research designs is according to their purpose. The purpose of a research study and the current state of knowledge in the problem area often determine what level of sophistication is needed in a particular research design. In this chapter, three somewhat arbitrary "levels" of designs will be discussed because many researchers find it useful to classify studies as falling in one of these three levels. Students should think of these levels as being points on a research continuum; however, it must be stated that in the real world of research, it is often difficult to indicate exactly at which point on the research continuum a particular study falls.

Exploratory Studies

The least sophisticated research design, that is, the one that falls at the lower end of the continuum, is called an "exploratory" study. Kahn says that an exploratory study has as its objective "the selection of priorities or the specifying of questions and the formulation of preliminary hypotheses."[14] Selltiz

---

[11]Alfred J. Kahn, "The Design of Research," in *Social Work Research,* ed. Norman A. Polansky (Chicago: University of Chicago Press, 1960), p. 48.

[12]Claire Selltiz et al., *Research Methods in Social Relations* (New York: Holt, Rinehart and Winston, 1959), p. 50.

[13]Matilda White Riley, *Sociological Research, A Case Approach* (New York: Harcourt Brace Jovanovich, 1963), p. 5.

[14]Kahn, "Design of Research," p. 50.

and co-workers say that the purpose of this type of study is "to gain familiarity with a phenomenon or to achieve new insights into it, often in order to formulate a more precise research problem or to develop hypotheses."[15] Fellin and co-workers say that exploratory studies have as their purpose "the articulation of concepts and the development of hypotheses."[16] Thus, as the name implies, an exploratory study is called for when a researcher wants to "explore" a problem area in which there has been little or no research performed and consequently there are no precise hypotheses to be tested. For example, if the purpose of the research is to get a better insight into why clients terminate treatment prematurely, the study is exploratory.

Now, if one decides to conduct an exploratory study, what are some methods that are likely to help in the clarification of concepts or the formulation of meaningful hypotheses? One method that is neither terribly costly nor time consuming is a review of the pertinent literature. The researcher may often find helpful suggestions in the work of others, and he may find results that suggest possible solutions to his problem. Not only should the social work researcher review the social work journals and publications, but also he should draw from other social science publications such as those in sociology, psychology, and anthropology.

A second method often used in exploratory studies is that of consulting experts in the problem area. Here, an expert is thought of as being a person who has had a great amount of experience in the problem area, who has competence in the problem area, and who is able to communicate his experiences to others. The point is that only a small proportion of the knowledge gained through experience is ever put into written form and published; hence consultation with experts can prove quite practical. In some instances, it may be quicker and more profitable to talk with experts about a problem than to try to review the relevant literature in a particular problem area. This is especially true when one is interested in an area that has had limited development and in which, therefore, there is a paucity of published information. For example, suppose a researcher is interested in developing behavior modification techniques for emotionally disturbed girls of a particular age. She might consult with the directors of several residential treatment centers for girls about their experience with behavior modification techniques and ask what suggestions they have for techniques that could be tried. A summary of the suggestions might lead to tentative hypotheses that possibly would not have been derivable from the literature. Of course it has to be remembered that the responses given by experts are not necessarily "typical" or "representative" of the whole field.

---

[15]Selltiz et al., *Research Methods,* p. 50.

[16]Phillip Fellin et al., *Exemplars of Social Research* (Itasca, Ill.: F. E. Peacock, 1969), p. 3.

A final method to be discussed here is that of studying selected examples of the phenomenon in which one is interested. If the researcher can study a few well-chosen instances of the phenomenon in question, he may gain almost as much insight into the problem as he would from studying several times as many ordinary cases. But how is one to know just which cases should be studied? Selltiz and co-workers have provided us with a list of eight types of "insight-stimulating" cases, together with the purposes for which they have been found most useful.[17] A review of this list will suggest to the student that for this method to be helpful in leading to insights or hypotheses, the cases chosen must provide sharp contrast to "usual" cases or have striking features of their own.

As an example of an exploratory study, suppose the director of a mental health center notices that a large proportion of the center's clients are terminating their treatment prematurely, and he would like to learn more about the reasons for these premature terminations. One way to gain insight into the nature of the problem is to undertake relatively unstructured interviews with former clients who terminated their relationships with the clinic very shortly after beginning their therapy. The interview schedule could include questions as to why the clients came to the mental health clinic, what they thought their major problem was, what services they expected to receive, whether they liked their therapist, whether the therapist liked them, whether they had transportation problems in getting to the mental health center, whether the cost was prohibitive, what kinds of services they actually received, how well they liked the services they received, and why they decided not to continue with their therapy. The unstructured nature of the interview schedule will provide the interviewer with the opportunity to probe for more information that may lead to insights and/or the development of hypotheses; a tightly structured interview schedule might preclude this possibility.

Descriptive Studies

The kind of research study that is somewhere in the middle range of the research continuum, that is, the kind that is somewhat more sophisticated than the exploratory study, is called a "descriptive" study. According to Kahn, "diagnostic or descriptive" studies have as their aim "the assessment of the characteristics of a population or situation."[18] Selltiz and co-workers say that this type of study is intended "to portray accurately the characteristics of a particular individual, situation, or group (with or without specific

---

[17]Selltiz et al., *Research Methods,* pp. 61–64.

[18]Kahn, "Design of Research," p. 50.

initial hypotheses about the nature of these characteristics) or to determine the frequency with which something occurs or with which it is associated with something else."[19]

Fellin and co-workers go slightly further and say that the "quantitative-descriptive" study has "a range of objectives from the production of facts to the determination of correlation among selected variables and the testing of hypotheses through approximations to rigorous experimental designs."[20] Hence, even though these authors do not use exactly the same names or words to describe this type of study, it seems clear that the study they have described is, by necessity, generally more sophisticated than the exploratory study.

What methods are available to the researcher who wants to conduct a descriptive study? Unlike the researcher who conducts an exploratory study, the one who would engage in descriptive research has precise questions he wants to answer. Since these questions usually involve measuring certain variables, he must have a clear formulation of which variables will be measured and from what source he will get this information. Accuracy is of major importance here; therefore, the research design employed cannot be as flexible as one employed in an exploratory study.

Generally, the researcher conducting descriptive research will have many decisions to make before actually collecting the data. He must first determine exactly what it is he wants to know; that is, he must formulate the precise question to which he seeks an answer. For example, supppose a researcher wants to determine the characteristics of the children in a particular institution that provides twenty-four hour a day care for dependent and neglected children. He must first decide exactly which characteristics he will try to measure on each child. These may include such variables as the date admitted, age at admission, reason for needing placement, who referred the child, why this institution was chosen, the race of the child, the sex of the child, and the academic achievement level of the child. After making this decision, he will have to develop operational definitions of the variables and choose a method by which he will collect the information. That is, will he: (1) conduct personal interviews with children in the institution; (2) have these children complete a questionnaire; (3) have someone extract the information from the institution's records; (4) observe the children through a two-way mirror; or (5) use one of the other methods of data collection available to researchers? Depending upon the particular instrument he plans to use to gather the data, he should pretest this instrument to be sure that all his questions, if it is a questionnaire, are clear to those to whom they will be administered.

---

[19]Selltiz et al., *Research Methods,* p. 50.

[20]Fellin et al., *Exemplars of Social Research,* p. 3.

After determining how he will get the information, he will have to decide from whom he will gather his data. That is, should he gather the data from all children in the institution, or could he "make do" with data from, say, 20 percent of the children? It is usually unnecessary for researchers to study all people in a particular group in order to get accurate information about the members of the group. That is, a sample of the population will often yield the same results as a study of the complete population. However, if the data one gathers from the "sample" are to give fairly accurate and reliable information about the characteristics of all children in the institution, it is obvious that the children who are included in the sample must be "representative" of all children in the institution; that is, they should have approximately the same characteristics as those not included in the sample.

Sampling techniques have been extensively studied by researchers and statisticians, and numerous books on the subject have been written. (See, for example, W. G. Cochran.[21]) One particular kind of sample is a simple random sample. This is the kind of sample one would have if one put the name of each child in the institution on a slip of paper, folded the slips, put them in a hat, and drew out, say, 20 percent of the slips. In this kind of sample, each child in the institution would have an equal chance of being included in the 20 percent sample. Thus, theoretically, the children chosen for the sample should be representative of all children in the institution. However, it should be noted that random sampling does not *guarantee* that those included in the sample will not differ markedly from the rest of the children in the institution, although it does make the occurrence of such an event less likely than if one had just chosen, say, the 20 percent of the children from whom it was the easiest to gather the data. After making the above decisions, the researcher is ready to collect the data according to the plan specified in his design. Depending on the nature of the research and other factors, errors at this point may be impossible to correct at a later date; therefore, at this time he should ensure that the data are being recorded accurately and that they are as complete and comprehensible as possible.

After the data are collected, the researcher will usually want to code them so that the calculations will be much easier. (Coding involves developing categories for each variable and the assignment of scores to the raw data.) Also, he can tabulate frequency distributions for each variable (that is, count the number of times each category, from the largest to the smallest, occurs), which will aid him in computing whatever measure of central tendency he chooses to use to describe the average for each of the variables included in his study. Now that most researchers can gain access to a computer, they usually have their data recorded on punch cards. Having the data on punch

---

[21]W. G. Cochran, *Sampling Techniques* (New York: Wiley, 1953).

cards and using a computer greatly facilitate the calculation of frequency distributions, percentages, measures of central tendency, correlations, and any other statistical computations one might want to use to find the answer to a research question.

Finally, the researcher will want to interpret the results of his data analyses. Simply performing statistical analyses will not tell him what the results mean; rather, he must decide what the various averages, percentages, or correlations tell him about the children in this institution, and he must be able to convey these interpretations either verbally or in writing to others who may want to know the results of his research.

Experimental Studies

At the highest level of the research continuum is experimental design. According to Kahn, this design is "the only design with the potential of providing rigorous testing of hypotheses."[22] Selltiz and co-workers say its purpose is "to test a hypothesis with a causal relationship between variables."[23] Finally, Fellin and co-workers have stated that these studies "have the general purpose of producing empirical generalizations, i.e., verified hypotheses."[24] Thus there is general agreement among researchers that the experimental study is on a higher level of sophistication than either the exploratory or the descriptive study.

A variety of studies that use pseudo-experimental designs will be included under the general heading of experimental designs, but the first to be discussed is the one that many researchers say is the only "true" experimental design. It is usually called a "controlled experiment" in the social sciences, although in the medical sciences it is often referred to as a "clinical trial." In 1950 Samuel Stouffer published an article entitled "Some Observations on Study Design,"[25] and in that article he stressed the importance of always keeping in mind the model of a controlled experiment even though our practice research may have to deviate from it. More and more frequently in social work research we want to talk about the causal relationship between an independent variable, X, and a dependent variable, Y. (Here a causal relationship means that the occurrence of one variable, the cause, makes the occurrence of another variable, the effect, more likely. Also, the cause must

---

[22]Kahn, "Design of Research," p. 50.

[23]Selltiz et al., *Research Methods,* p. 50.

[24]Fellin et al., *Exemplars Social Research,* p. 3.

[25]Samuel Stouffer, "Some Observations on Study Design," *American Journal of Sociology* 55 (January 1950):356–59.

precede the effect in real time.) To do so, we must understand what factors determine the value of the dependent variable (or effect) for any particular subject in the study. First, there are the characteristics that each subject possesses before he is acted upon by the independent variable (or cause), that is, the characteristics he brings to the study with him; second, the amount of the independent variable the subject receives during the study period; and third, the influence on the subject of all other factors that act upon him during the study period, which we might call "confounding" variables. Thus the reason for the importance of the controlled experiment is that it comes closer than any other study design to allowing a researcher to say that any differences between the subjects in the amount of the "effect" that they show after the study were in fact caused by the differences in the amount of the "cause" that they received during the study. That is, the experimental design, or controlled experiment, "controls" more factors than any other design. Hence, it gives us more confidence in being able to say that, all other things being equal, the differences in Y, the dependent variable, were caused by the differences in X, the independent variable. A look at the diagram of a controlled experiment (Figure 1) will make this clearer.

In the simplest controlled experiment, the researcher begins with a pool of people, all of whom are eligible for inclusion in the study, and chooses two groups of subjects that are as nearly alike as possible. He then manipulates the independent variable; that is, to one group, the experimental group, he administers a certain level of the independent variable, and to the other group, the control group, he administers a different level of the independent variable. Some researchers call these two groups "treatment" groups; others call them "study" groups. (Note that the "two levels" of the independent variable often are the presence of the variable in the experimental group and the absence of the variable in the control group.) These two groups are measured to see how much of the dependent variable each subject possesses before receiving the independent variable. After being given the appropriate

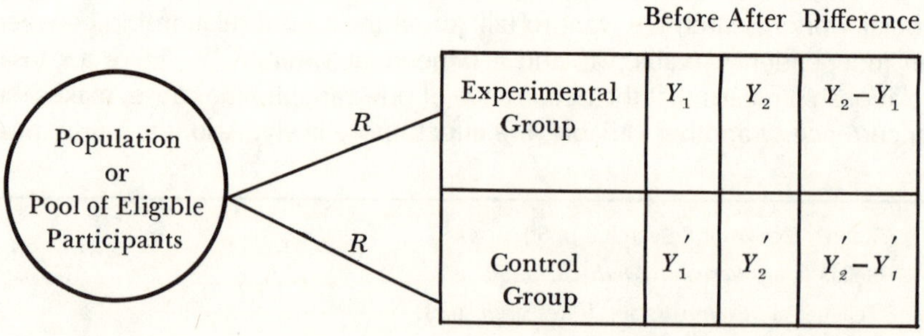

		Before	After	Difference
R	Experimental Group	Y_1	Y_2	$Y_2 - Y_1$
R	Control Group	Y_1'	Y_2'	$Y_2' - Y_1'$

Population or Pool of Eligible Participants

FIGURE 1. Diagram of a controlled experiment.

level of the independent variable, the two groups are followed for a certain period of time and the subjects in each are measured again to see how much of the dependent variable they possess. Usually, an "average difference" between the before and after scores is calculated for each group, and, as long as "all other things are equal," any differences that the two groups show in the "average difference" are assumed to be caused by the differences in the amount of the independent variable they have received.

At this point, the student may ask, "How does a controlled experiment help give the researcher confidence that 'all other things are equal'?" To answer this question, we must recall the discussion earlier about the three factors that determine the value of the dependent variable for any given subject in the study. Now, a technique that is a mandatory component of the controlled experiment is the randomization of the assignment of the subjects to the study groups; hence the R on the lines from the population to the study groups (Figure 1). That is, the subjects are assigned to the experimental group and to the control group in such a way that the subjects in each group form a random sample of the subjects from the population of eligible subjects. If the assignments to the study groups are truly random, and if the number of subjects in each group is large enough, then a result from the mathematical theory of probability (known as the "Law of Large Numbers") assures us that the background characteristics of the subjects in the two groups will not differ significantly.[26] Hence the only difference between the two groups at the beginning of the study period will be that they get different levels of the independent variable.

Factors affecting the subjects during the study period are not so easily handled as the background characteristics, for these can be variables of which the researcher is not aware, but which have a very large influence on the dependent variable. What the researcher would like to do is to assure himself that all subjects in both treatment groups are influenced by equal amounts of the confounding variables during the entire study period. To try to accomplish this, he must identify as many of these confounding variables as he can, and either take care of the effect of each by holding each one constant—in other words, by making sure that all subjects in the two groups are influenced equally by each of the particular confounding variables, or if it is impossible for the researcher to hold constant a particular confounding variable, a fairly effective alternative is to arrange it so that the subjects in the study groups are affected randomly by the variable. If this can be arranged, and if there are large enough numbers in each study group, then the effect of each of these confounding variables in the study groups will be reasonably

[26]Emanuel Parzen, *Modern Probability Theory and Its Applications* (New York: Wiley, 1963), p. 371.

equal. Thus, in the controlled experiment, "all other things are equal" means, at least in theory, that the only way the study groups differ is in the level of the independent variable that they received and in the amount of the dependent variable that they possess. Hence any difference in the amount of the dependent variable that the study groups possess must have been "caused" by the differences in the amount of the independent variable they received.

Let us now give an example of a simple experimental study in which there is no "before" measure taken. Suppose that a researcher is interested in studying the degree of stigma that is exhibited by young children toward another young child who has a mentally retarded sibling. If the researcher could find, say, an eight-year-old child who has a mentally retarded sibling and who is willing to help her conduct a study, and if she could find a group of children, say, eight years old, but none of whom have a mentally retarded sibling, she could proceed as follows:

She could place the child with the mentally retarded sibling in a "waiting room" by himself. The "waiting room" could have a two-way mirror on one side, the floor marked off in three equal rectangles, and a table in each rectangle on top of which would be a box of tinker toys. Billy, the child with the mentally retarded sibling, would be placed at the table in the rectangle at the opposite end of the room from where the other children would enter. He would be told not to move from his table during the time another child is in the room. From her population of eight-year-olds, the researchers could randomly assign half to be in an experimental group and half to be in a control group. One at a time, all of the children could be brought to the building in which she was conducting her experiment on the pretext of taking a test to help her measure a certain variable. To each of the children in the experimental and control groups, she could say that it would be about fifteen minutes before she would be ready for them to take their test, and that she would like for them to wait in the "waiting room" where another child, named Billy, was playing. However, to each of the children in the experimental group, she could say also that Billy is a child who has a mentally retarded brother who has to be in an institution for children who cannot learn as well as normal children. Because she randomly assigned children to the experimental and control groups, she would hope that the only difference in the children in the two groups is that the ones in the experimental group know that Billy has a mentally retarded brother, and those in the control group do not. Thus she would hypothesize that the children who are in the experimental group would show more stigma toward Billy than would the children who are in the control group.

But how should she measure her dependent variable—in other words, the amount of stigma that each child shows toward Billy? If she uses the concept of personal space, she could operationally define this in terms of the total time out of the fifteen minutes that each child spends in each of the three rectangles. Since each child is left in the room with Billy exactly fifteen minutes, a "stigma" score for each subject in the study could be determined, and by calculating the mean scores for the subjects in the experimental group and for those in the control group, she could test whether the average amount of stigma shown by those in the experimental group is significantly greater than the average amount of stigma shown by those in the control group.

In addition to where Billy sits in the room and the total time each subject is left in the room with Billy, an obvious confounding variable that could enter into this study is what Billy says to the other child. If he talks to some of the children more than to others, this could influence unequally those in the experimental and control groups. Thus she could instruct Billy to say, "Hi, my name is Billy. Would you like to play tinker toys with me?" Also, to avoid any bias on Billy's part, she could omit telling him to which of the two groups each of the children has been assigned.

Weaknesses of the Controlled Experiment

Now that we have the design of the controlled experiment clearly in mind, it should not be difficult to understand why Stouffer said that in practice our research design may have to deviate from the ideal. Among the many reasons why a researcher may not be able to conduct a controlled experiment are the following:

1. He may not be able to randomize the assignment of subjects to the study groups. Since in social work it is unethical to withhold treatment from someone who wants and needs it, he may be unable to assign subjects to a group that gets "no treatment." However, to overcome this problem, many studies will have the treatment groups receive different methods of intervention, both of which are thought to be beneficial. For example, a researcher could use an experimental design to compare the benefits received from group counseling versus those received from individual counseling.

2. Even though the controlled experiment is tightly structured, one can generalize the results from the study only to the population that was accurately represented in the study.

3. If the researcher has only a small number of people that he can use as subjects for his study, the numbers in the study groups may be too small for the "Law of Large Numbers" to assure a decent split of the various background characteristics among the two groups. When faced with a small number of study subjects, some researchers will supplement randomization by finding pairs of subjects that are matched as nearly as possible on some key variables that are thought to be associated with the dependent variable (the effect) and then randomly assigning one member of each pair to each

of the study groups. However, it should be noted that matching may be used in conjunction with randomization, not as a substitute for it.

4. In most experimental studies, the researcher must wait a certain length of time after manipulating the independent variable before he can observe the effect. In many situations, he simply may not know how long to wait before attempting to measure the effect. The length of this follow-up period can be quite critical because, if the researcher attempts to measure the effect before it has had time to show up, he may conclude that the "treatment" has had no effect; on the other hand, if he waits too long, the effect may have disappeared. In addition, the longer the follow-up period, the higher the attrition rate of the subjects, because subjects can die, move, or simply drop out of the study.

5. People sometimes change their behavior *because* they are being studied. This phenomenon has become known as the "Hawthorne effect," from a series of studies made at the Hawthorne Works of the Western Electric Company between 1927 and 1932. Researchers found that when management paid attention to workers, no matter what form it took, output increased. Thus the results obtained from a study in which this phenomenon has taken place will probably not be representative of the results that one would have obtained had the subjects not changed their behavior because they were being studied.

Incomplete Controlled Experiments

Often a social work researcher does not have enough money or time to design a completely controlled experiment. Let us now discuss two fairly common situations in which one has something less than the complete design.

Suppose a researcher has the before and after measures of a group of prison inmates, as in the accompanying diagram.

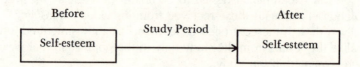

If, through counseling, he is trying to increase the self-esteem of these people, he can certainly measure their self-esteem before they receive the counseling and again after, thereby determining whether their self-esteem actually increased. However, even if their self-esteem did increase, he is not in a position to say that counseling is what caused the increase, because the absence of a control group from his design keeps him from knowing what would have happened if people like the ones he is studying had received no counseling. That is, was the increase in the self-esteem the result of counseling or would it have increased even without counseling during the time that elapsed between the two scores? Now, if the researcher can develop an argument that shows, theoretically at least, that nothing would have changed the self-esteem score if the inmates had received no counseling, then this design is somewhat strengthened. But the fact that there is no control group present means that he really has no strong evidence to tell him what would have happened to the self-esteem scores if the inmates had received no counseling.

As a second example, suppose that a social worker who is employed in a prison in which inmates routinely receive counseling wants to get some idea of how much the counseling has increased the inmates' self-esteem. If he measures the self-esteem of a group of inmates from another prison in which counseling is not provided for the inmates, he would have something like the following diagram:

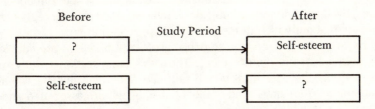

If it happens that the average self-esteem of those who received counseling was ten points higher than the average self-esteem of those who did not, could the researcher attribute the difference to the counseling program? Probably not, unless he can convince himself and others that the two groups of inmates would have had the same self-esteem scores if neither had received counseling, and that there are no other differences between the two groups that could affect their self-esteem.

TIME AS A FACTOR IN RESEARCH STUDIES

We have discussed how research studies can be classified according to the purpose of the study, but there is another way in which they can be classified, and that is according to the "time factor" that is implicitly involved in each. Clark and Hopkins have stated that the "time factor" involved in a study needs to be made explicit because it "imposes limitations on the conclusions that can be drawn" from the study.[27] The names of the studies that will be discussed in this section are not universally accepted; however, students

---

[27]Virginia Clark and Carl Hopkins, "Time Is of the Essence," *Journal of Chronic Diseases* 20, no. 8 (1967):565.

should realize that the name by which a study is called is not so important as the actual design of the study.

"Cross-sectional" is the name given to the first of these studies to be discussed. It is also called a "field survey" by many authors, but the name "cross-sectional" seems to be more appropriate because this study is actually a snapshot of a cross section of a population at one point in time. It usually seeks to establish the characteristics of a population at one point in time and the ways in which the characteristics of that population are related to (or associated with) each other. Another aim of this study is to establish the relative frequency with which a condition occurs in a particular population. Students should note that since all variables are observed simultaneously, there can be no statements made regarding cause and effect relationships. For example, suppose a questionnaire is administered to a sample of children in a junior high school, and it is found that a large proportion of those not doing well academically are also having some emotional problems. One might be tempted to conclude that the students' poor academic performances are caused by their emotional problems; however, since this survey gives no information about which of these variables preceded the other, the reverse might also be true; that is, the students' emotional problems are caused by their poor academic performances. Thus, this cross-sectional study really provides only the data from which one can determine that the variables "academic performance" and "emotional stability" are associated and the frequency with which each occurs.

The second type of study is the controlled experiment, the strengths and weaknesses of which we have discussed previously. This study is necessarily of a prospective nature; that is, it begins in the present and goes forward in time because the researcher administers a treatment, the cause, and looks for the effect at some point in the future. An example of this type of study is Otto Pollak's "Worker Assignment in Casework with Marriage Partners."[28] The basic layout of this study is seen in the following diagram.

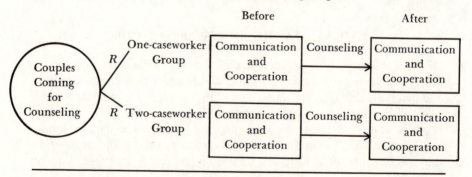

28Otto Pollak, "Worker Assignment in Casework with Marriage Partners," *Social Service Review,* XXXVII (March 1963), 41–53.

Assignment of couples needing a unifying experience was made at random either to treatment 1, the group that was counseled by one caseworker, or treatment 2, the group that was counseled by two caseworkers. That is, the independent variable (or cause) in this study was the number of caseworkers by whom clients were counseled. There were two dependent variables (or effects)—the amount of communication between marital partners and the amount of cooperation between marital partners—that were measured before and after the couples had been in therapy for a given number of sessions. The question to be answered by the study was, "Would one caseworker bring closer together the couples who needed a unifying experience than would two caseworkers?"

The third type of study, called a "cohort" study, is one that appears to be very similar to the controlled study in that it, too, begins in the present and moves forward in time. However, the crucial difference between those two studies is that in the cohort study, the researcher does *not* have at his disposal the random assignment of subjects to the treatment groups. Instead the subjects have placed themselves in one of the treatment groups. (That is, they have self-selected themselves into one of the treatment groups.) In the simple cohort study the researcher observes a group of people who have some characteristic in common (e.g., smoking) that is hypothesized to be the cause of some other characteristic (e.g., lung cancer). Since we usually do not know the motivating factors that cause a person to become a smoker, for example, the problem of self-selection is not easily handled. However, the researcher then tries to find a control group; that is, a group of people who are as nearly like those in the experimental group as possible, except that they do not possess the causal characteristic. This can be accomplished by finding an individual to serve as a control for each individual in the experimental group, or by using as controls a group of people who are "on the average" like those in the experimental group. In matching controls with those in the experimental group, the researcher usually matches on variables that are thought to be associated with the dependent variable. He then follows these two cohorts of people for a certain period of time and determines at what rate each develops the effect for which he is looking. Proof of causality is still very difficult, however, because matching subjects in the control group with those in the experimental group is a very dangerous substitute for random assignment to the two groups, in that one never knows for sure that he has matched on all the important variables. Thus, if the two groups differ with respect to some characteristic that is highly associated with the dependent variable, spurious results can emerge. On the other hand, because the social work profession believes in freedom of choice for every individual, random assignment to treatment groups will be impossible in many studies. Therefore, this design should have considerable appeal for social work researchers.

An example of a cohort study is one by Killian, in which he studied the effects of environmental loss on geriatric psychiatric patients.[29] Killian learned that many of the patients of the north area of Stockton State Hospital were to be transferred to other state hospitals or extramural facilities, and he wanted to study the effect of such transfers on the mortality rate of these patients. Since the patients to be transferred had already been chosen by the hospital administration according to certain criteria, there was no chance for Killian to assign patients randomly to treatment groups, that is, to the experimental group (those to be transferred) or to the control group (those to remain in the hospital). Therefore, from those patients remaining in the hospital he chose a matching control for each patient who was to be transferred. These controls were matched to those in the experimental group on the variables Killian thought would be associated with mortality, the dependent variable, namely, sex, race, age, length of hospitalization, type of diagnosis, and ambulation. After the transfers occurred, Killian followed the study groups for four months and then measured their mortality rates. The following diagram shows the basic layout of this study.

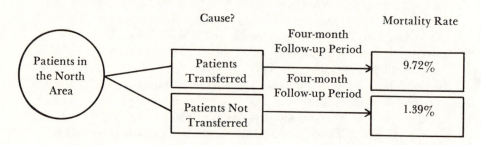

Since random assignment to study groups is not a part of this type of study, it should be clear to students that a major factor in determining the validity of a study such as this is how nearly alike the subjects in the study groups actually are. That is, is there some major difference between the two study groups that could have caused the higher mortality rate for the experimental group?

The fourth type of study to be discussed is one that is probably very familiar to students. It has been given such names as "ex post facto," "retrospective," and "case history," but the latter will be used in this chapter because in this kind of a study one actually takes a group of "cases" and looks at their histories. In other words, the effect has already occurred, the researcher observes it in the present time, and he then looks backward in time to try to

---

[29]Eldon Killian, "Effect of Geriatric Transfers on Mortality Rates," *Social Work* 15, no. 1 (January 1970):19–26.

find the cause. For example, suppose a researcher wants to learn more about the events that possibly cause mental retardation among young children. He can proceed by selecting a group of young, mentally retarded children to compose an experimental group, and by searching their histories since birth, the pregnancy histories of their mothers, and possibly the genetic characteristics of their families. If he can find a control group composed of young, healthy children who are otherwise as nearly like those in the experimental group as possible, he can compare the rates with which certain factors occurred in the histories of both study groups. If he finds one or more factors that occurred at a higher rate in the histories of the experimental group than in those of the control group, he has identified a variable with which mental retardation is associated. It is also possible that this variable is causally related to mental retardation; however, the student should recognize that finding that a high percentage of diseased subjects possess a particular factor is not the same as finding that there is a high percentage of diseased subjects among persons who possess a particular factor.[30] Thus case history studies usually lead to statements about the association between variables rather than statements about cause and effect relationships.

An example of an investigation of this type was conducted several years ago when many children all over the world were being born with "flippers" or other deformities. Since the effect had already occurred, researchers looked backward in time at the pregnancy histories of the mothers and found that the percentage of mothers who had taken the drug Thalidomide during pregnancy was much higher in the group of mothers who had given birth to deformed babies than in a group of mothers who had given birth to normal babies. The accompanying diagram depicts the layout of this study.

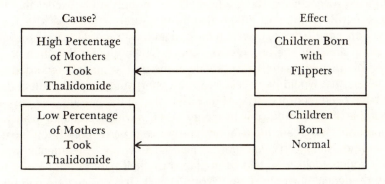

---

[30]Nathan Mantel and W. Haenzel, "Statistical Aspects of the Analysis of Data from Retrospective Studies of Disease," *Journal of the National Cancer Institute* 22 (1959):719–48.

The case history study has much appeal to researchers because it has several advantages over studies that are prospective in nature. Some of these advantages are as follows: (1) the researcher does not have to wait for the effect to show up—it has already occurred. This is a particular advantage when one is studying a condition that occurs rather infrequently, thus precluding the necessity of studying large numbers of people in order to observe a few "cases." Hence case history studies are usually quicker and cheaper than most prospective studies. (2) Probably the biggest advantage they have, however, is the fact that since the effect has already occurred, they pose no danger to the subjects. This is extremely important when an investigator wishes to search for a cause that has produced or may produce a harmful effect.

On the other hand, case history studies are not without their weaknesses, among which the most obvious are the following: (1) inherent in this type of study is the problem of self-selection; in other words, the investigator cannot randomly assign subjects to the treatment groups. Thus, for his results to be valid, the researcher must be able to assert with confidence that the experimental and control groups he is studying were comparable, with the exception of the possession of the causal factor. In other words, "all things are equal." (2) Since this study is dependent on history, records must be available and accurate, and must include information about the causal variable. For example, if, in the Thalidomide study, the records of each drug the mothers took during pregnancy had not been available, the discovery might never have been made. Also, the researcher must decide how far into the past he will go in search of the cause. It is usually true that the further into the past one goes, the poorer the quality of the records becomes.

The fifth and final type of study to be discussed in this section is the "historical-prospective." This study is like the cohort study except that the cause occurred in the past rather than in the present. That is, a researcher begins with a cause that occurred in the past and was recorded, and proceeds forward in time until he observes the effect. Obviously, for this study to be successful, it is necessary that someone in the past accurately recorded the causal data that would be necessary for a cohort study, and the effect data must have been recorded or must be observable in the present. We have as an example of such a study one by Henry Maas, in which he sought to answer the question, "What are the relationships between early (preschool) separation and adjustment in adult life?"[31] He chose as his experimental group twenty young adults who had been placed by their parents in one of three British residential nurseries during World War II. Their placement had been

---

[31]Henry S. Maas, "The Young Adult Adjustment of Twenty Wartime Residential Nursery Children," *Child Welfare* 13, no. 2 (February 1963):57–72.

for their own safety rather than as a result of prior intrafamily trauma and lasted for at least one year. Thus the independent variable was early childhood separation and placement in a wartime residential nursery, and the dependent variable was young adult adjustment (as measured by five different variables). Since the three nurseries in which the children were placed differed greatly from each other, it was also possible to study the effects the "type of nursery" had on the young adult adjustment of the twenty children who were placed.

Maas did not have a control group because he felt that the parents of any young adults who would serve as a control group must have the same orientation as those of the young adults in the experimental group, and he could not find any young adults whose parents had decided to place them for their own safety, but for some reason did not. However, he did use assumed norms for an urban population as comparisons for the experimental group.

Now, this study would not have been possible without excellent records about the nurseries from which Maas could draw inferences concerning their philosophy, staff-child ratios, and children's relationships with their parents. Also, Maas had to locate and interview each of the twenty young adults in the study in order to measure their "young adult adjustment." The accompanying diagram gives the layout of this study.

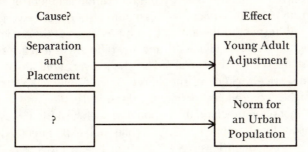

This kind of study has all the strengths and weaknesses of a cohort study, with the added weakness that unless past records are complete and accurate, and include all the information needed on the subjects and causal variables that one would need for a cohort study, there is no way to conduct the study. However, when records are complete and available, the historical-prospective study makes a useful substitute for the cohort study.

EVALUATION RESEARCH IN SOCIAL WORK

In today's world in which there is an almost infinite number of programs to correct specific social problems, the administrator who is seeking supportive funds is faced with stiff competition from other programs, since there are always many proposed solutions for any one problem. In addition, there is a variety of other problems calling for attention and financial support. Thus it becomes important that society be able to learn the answer to the question, "Did a particular program alleviate the problem or not?" Evaluation research seeks to answer questions such as this; for, according to Weiss, "the purpose of evaluation research is to measure the effects of a program against the goals it set out to accomplish as a means of contributing to subsequent decision-making about the program and improving future programming."[32] However, according to Suchman, one of the toughest aspects of evaluative research is trying to answer the question, "What do we mean by a successful result?" He contends that all programs will have some effect, but how we measure these effects and how we determine whether they are the particular effects we are interested in producing are problems that must be faced by every evaluator.[33] In this vein, Fischer has reviewed eleven studies dealing with the effectiveness of professional casework services.[34]

How does one determine how effective any specific innovation has been? Campbell describes the ideal research design as being one in which two groups of subjects are chosen, an experimental and a control, that are similar in every possible way except that they do not get the same program service. The two groups are made similar by the random assignment of subjects to each. After the program service has been administered, the two groups are compared with respect to the amount each possesses of the social problem that the program set out to eliminate, and any differences that are statistically significant (that is, cannot be explained by chance variation) are attributed to the program service.[35] Students should recognize Campbell's description as being that of the "controlled experiment," discussed earlier, and should recall the reasons that often preclude the conduct of such a study. It was for some of these reasons that Campbell added, "While such experimental designs are ideal, they are not often feasible."[36] Even in health program evaluations,

---

[32]Carol H. Weiss, *Evaluation Research* (Englewood Cliffs, N. J.: Prentice-Hall, Inc., 1972), p. 4.

[33]Edward A. Suchman, *Evaluative Research* (New York: Russell Sage Foundation, 1967), p. 109.

[34]Joel Fischer, "Is Casework Effective? A Review," *Social Work* 18, no. 1 (January 1973): 5–20.

[35]Donald T. Campbell, "Measuring the Effects of Social Innovations by Means of Time Series," in *Statistics: A Guide to the Unknown,* ed. Judith M. Tanur et al. (San Francisco: Holden-Day, 1972), pp. 120–21.

[36]Ibid., p. 121.

researchers concur by stating that the controlled experiment is "an optional one . . . deviations and compromises will have to be made."[37]

Now, if one is attempting to evaluate a program's effectiveness and a controlled experiment does not seem to be a feasible design, what alternative designs exist? Any of the designs we discussed in the section on experimental design may serve as a useful substitute as long as the researcher keeps in mind the limitations of each with regard to how well it protects against the effects of outside (confounding) variables. In addition, there is another design, called a "time series" design, which is particularly useful in situations where a new program is applied to all citizens at once. (Campbell provides us with two examples of such an event.[38])

To illustrate the use of a time series design, let us use a hypothetical example. Suppose that a particular city, City X, had been plagued for several years by a rather high number of drug-abuse cases, and the city leaders finally agreed to institute a drug education program. Let us say the program was begun on January 1, 1971, and after it had been in operation for the one year for which it was funded, the mayor reported that "since there were 75 fewer cases of drug abuse reported during 1971 than there were during 1970, we can say that our drug-abuse program was a huge success." In making this statement, the mayor is assuming that, without the introduction of the drug education program, there would have been no decrease in the number of drug-abuse cases. Unfortunately, this assumption may not be valid because it is possible that the decrease observed during the period in which the program was in operation was simply a continuation of a trend that had begun *prior* to the institution of the program.

To get a better idea of the actual impact of the program, one could have used a time series design that involves examining a series of measurements taken at specified intervals before the program began and continuing after the program ended, thus enabling the evaluator to determine whether or not there had been a decisive change in the trend established before the program was instituted. For example, Figure 2 presents three sets of *hypothetical* drug-abuse data for City X, beginning with the data for 1967. In each set of data a fairly clear-cut trend has been established, but the trends are quite different for the three sets. If, as the mayor did, one examined on any one of the trend lines *only* the data for the year immediately preceding the institution of the program (1970), and for the year during which the program

---

[37]Bernard G. Greenberg and B. V. Mattison, "The Whys and Wherefores of Program Evaluation," *Canadian Journal of Public Health* 46 (July 1955):298–99.

[38]Campbell, "Measuring Effects Social Innovations," pp. 121–28.

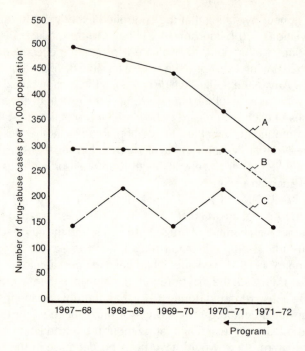

FIGURE 2.   Three hypothetical drug-abuse trends for City X.

was in operation (1971), one could draw the *same* conclusion from each trend line, namely, that the program "caused" a decrease of seventy-five cases of drug abuse. On the other hand, if one uses a time series approach and examines trend line *A* as far back as the 1967 period, it is clear that the number of drug-abuse cases declined each year through 1971, with a sharp decline beginning in the 1969 period. Thus, for trend line *A,* the mayor's implicit assumption that there would not have been a decrease in the number of drug-abuse cases without the introduction of the program was probably wrong and his attributing the seventy-five case decrease to the program seems to be questionable. In the case of the cyclical trend appearing in trend line *C,* again the implicit assumption underlying the mayor's statement appears to be invalid because the decrease observed during the operation of the program is of exactly the same magnitude as the decrease between the 1968 and the 1969 periods—a period in which there was no program in operation to receive credit for the decrease. Only in the case of trend line *B* would the mayor's statement have been justified, since it is the only case in which there was a decisive alteration in the pattern established prior to the introduction of the program. Even in this case, though, the presence of a control group in the study would have added credence to the findings. Greenberg has

128

discussed various alternatives for choosing control groups for evaluation studies such as this.[39]

CONCLUSION

Social work research is the application of the scientific method to problems in the field of social work. Usually, a research study is seeking the answer to a question, and the researcher can enhance the success of his study by choosing an appropriate design, that is, by choosing the appropriate rules by which he will conduct his study. Often the purpose of the study dictates the level of sophistication needed in the design (that is, from one that is loosely structured to one that is tightly controlled), and the level of sophistication of the design determines what kinds of questions can be answered by the study. Another way of classifying research designs is according to the time element involved. The time element is important because it imposes limitations on the conclusions that can be drawn from the study. Thus, when we understand the strengths and weaknesses of each of the designs discussed in this chapter, we have some criteria for judging the validity of the findings from a research study and their applicability in social work practice.

BIBLIOGRAPHY

Campbell, Donald T., and Julian C. Stanley. *Experimental and Quasi-Experimental Designs for Research.* Skokie, Ill.: Rand McNally, 1966.

Chambers, Clarke. *Paul U. Kellogg and the Survey.* Minneapolis: University of Minnesota Press, 1971.

Cochran, W. G. *Sampling Techniques.* New York: John Wiley & Sons, 1953.

Doby, John T., ed. *An Introduction to Social Research.* Harrisburg, Pa.: The Stackpole Co., 1954.

Fellin, Phillip, Tony Tripodi, and Henry Meyer. *Exemplars of Social Research.* Itasca, Ill.: F. E. Peacock Publishers, 1969.

Fischer, Joel. "Is Casework Effective? A Review." *Social Work* 18, no. 1 (January 1973):5–20.

Freeman, Howard E., and Clarence C. Sherwood. *Social Research and Social Policy.* Englewood Cliffs, N. J.: Prentice-Hall, 1970.

[39]Bernard G. Greenberg, "Evaluation of Social Programs," *Review of the International Statistical Institute* 36, no 3 (1968):260–77.

French, David G. *An Approach to Measuring Results in Social Work.* New York: Columbia University Press, 1952.

Goldstein, Harris K. "Criteria for Evaluating Research," *Social Casework* 43, no. 9 (November 1962):474–78.

Greenberg, Bernard G. "Evaluation of Social Programs." *Review of the International Statistical Institute* 36, no 3 (1968):260–77.

Greenberg, Bernard G., and B. V. Mattison. "The Whys and Wherefores of Program Evaluation." *Canadian Journal of Public Health* 46 (July 1955):298–99.

Killian, Eldon. "Effect of Geriatric Transfers on Mortality Rates." *Social Work* 15, no. 1 (January 1970):19–26.

Klein, Philip. *From Philanthropy to Social Welfare.* San Francisco: Jossey-Bass, 1968.

Maas, Henry S., ed. *Research in the Social Services: A Five-Year Review.* New York: National Association of Social Workers, 1971.

————. "The Young Adult Adjustment of Twenty Wartime Residential Nursery Children." *Child Welfare* 13, no. 2 (February 1963):57–72.

Mantel, Nathan, and W. Haenzel. "Statistical Aspects of the Analysis of Data from Retrospective Studies of Disease." *Journal of the National Cancer Institute* 22 (1959):719–48.

Parzen, Emanuel. *Modern Probability Theory and Its Applications.* New York: John Wiley & Sons, 1963.

Polansky, Norman A., ed. *Social Work Research.* Chicago: University of Chicago Press, 1960.

Pollak, Otto. "Worker Assignment in Casework with Marriage Partners." *Social Service Review* 37, no. 1 (March 1963):41–53.

Riley, Matilda White. *Sociological Research, A Case Approach.* New York: Harcourt Brace Jovanovich, 1963.

Selltiz, Claire, Marie Jahoda, Morton Deutsch, and Stuart Cook. *Research Methods in Social Relations.* New York: Holt, Rinehart and Winston, 1959.

Simon, Julian L. *Basic Research Methods in Social Studies: The Art of Empirical Investigation.* New York: Random House, 1969.

Stouffer, Samuel. "Some Observations on Study Design," *The American Journal of Sociology* 55 (January 1950):356–59.

Stuart, Richard B. "Research in Social Work: Casework and Group Work," in *Encyclopedia of Social Work.* New York: National Association of Social Workers, 1971.

Suchman, Edward A. *Evaluative Research.* New York: Russell Sage Foundation, 1967.

Tanur, Judith M., F. Mosteller, W. Kruskal, R. Link, R. Pieters, and G. Rising, eds. *Statistics: A Guide to the Unknown.* San Francisco: Holden-Day, 1972.

Tripodi, Tony, Phillip Fellin, and Irwin Epstein. *Social Program Evaluation.* Itasca, Ill.: F. E. Peacock Publishers, 1971.

Tripodi, Tony, Phillip Fellin, and Henry Meyer. *The Assessment of Social Research.* Itasca, Ill.: F. E. Peacock Publishers, 1969.

Weiss, Carol H. *Evaluation Research.* Englewood Cliffs, N. J.: Prentice-Hall, 1972.

PART TWO

METHODS OF SOCIAL WORK PRACTICE

INTRODUCTION

JANICE H. SCHOPLER AND MAEDA J. GALINSKY

School of Social Work, University of North Carolina

Social workers perform many roles as they work to prevent problems, restore functioning, and provide resources to clients, but the vast majority of social workers are actively involved in direct work with people. The chapters in this section describe the helping methods that have been developed for offering direct services to clients at the individual, family, group, and community levels. Examination of these various helping methods reveals strong similarities. Although the specific methods for dealing with clients differ depending on the size of the client system, all of the methods share a common value base, emphasize skills needed in direct relationships with clients, and provide a sequential approach to problem solving which includes assessing, goal setting, working toward goals, evaluating, and ending.

Because of the many parallels among the various helping methods, in recent years some social work educators have advocated teaching a generic social work method. In the generic apporach, one method is presented which applies to all client systems: the elements of the direct helping process are defined and illustrated with applications to individual, family, group, and, sometimes, community client systems. Many social workers, however, continue to use the specific social work methods which have been developed to meet the needs of different client systems. Although any social worker may be involved, to varying degrees, in helping individuals, families, groups, or communities, the distinct characteristics of the different client systems demand specialized knowledge and skills which are subsumed under the methods of casework, family work, group work, and community organization.

In the chapters which follow, current overviews of the four methods of social work practice are presented. The authors describe the particular needs and characteristics of each client system as well as the knowledge base, practice principles, and techniques that are appropriate for serving individuals, families, groups, and communities. In Chapter 6 on casework, the uniqueness of each client is emphasized as the basis for casework's goal of realizing individual potential. Chapter 7 stresses the the special nature of family systems and role patterns of family members which must be taken into account in providing help to families. Chapter 8 presents the phases of group development and focuses on the social worker's use of group processes to achieve group and individual goals, while Chapter 9 provides a concrete example of group work. Community organization is examined in Chapter 10 in the light of different roles and tasks involved as the community worker contracts with client groups to solve community-based problems.

Diverse schools of thought have contributed to the development of each practice method, and social workers select from a wide range of helping techniques as they provide service to clients. Practicing social workers may use one method to the exclusion of all others or may draw on several methods. When a social worker selects a method for providing help, many factors must be considered: the client's needs and characteristics, the services available within a particular agency, and the worker's own knowledge and skills. Whatever the choice, the social worker's concern is to offer help in a way that is humane, caring, and effective.

6
SOCIAL CASEWORK

LOIS R. TABER
Northwest Community Mental Health/Mental
Retardation Center, Philadelphia, Pennsylvania

and RICHARD H. TABER
Southern Connecticut State State College,
New Haven

Social workers have long held a conviction about the worth of the individual
—that he has a right to find satisfaction in his life, and that society has an
obligation to help him meet his needs when he faces insurmountable problems. Services to individuals, through the professionally disciplined practice
of social casework, have been a commitment accepted by the profession
since its very inception.This commitment is even more crucial today when
the forces operating in society exacerbate the problems people encounter in
everyday living. People are angered by the constraints of poverty in a land
of plenty, particularly in the 1970s with its increase in unemployment and
rising inflation. They are dismayed by the inequalities and discriminatory
practices in a democracy. They are frustrated by the inability to control or
influence the forces affecting them, belittled by the impersonal nature of their
large institutional structures, and bewildered by the disruption of supportive
social networks as the destruction and prolonged delay of rebuilding of
neighborhoods occurs.

Responses to these phenomena have led to feelings of identity confusion and alienation from meaningful relationships with others. This is particularly true of persons living in large cities, cut off from the social networks that once supplied nurture and guidance, and alienated from the social institutions upon which they rely. At the same time, people are satisfying their longings for authenticity in relationships through several channels: encounter and sensitivity groups; religious experience in which they find purpose and meaning; the imperative for controlling some aspects of their lives in the increased participation in action groups; and the search for identity in the supports provided by ethnic groups.

One of the tasks of social workers is to help persons make meaningful connections with these positive sources of strength. However, most persons who come to the attention of social workers are those who have found themselves in the position of needing support and guidance in being able to cope with some particular aspect of their lives or with the inability to negotiate a social system with which they are involved such as school or a marriage. They represent a wide range of differences in cultural backgrounds, in life styles and values, and in coping capacities and incentives. Problems run the gamut of difficulties encountered in living, from childhood through old age. They may relate to such developmental tasks as separation from home to school, finding one's own identity during adolescence, coping with the strains of marriage and parenthood, and dealing with the impact of aging. They often arise out of conflict between personal wishes and social obligations, or when a person is obliged to face society's demands for behavior change, as in a case of child abuse or some form of delinquency. They may be the result of reactions to frustrations in meeting basic human needs such as decent housing, jobs, and recreation. Difficult problems arise when an individual is hospitalized or attempts to find his way back from mental illness or drug use.

ORIENTATION

Settings

Chapter 3 described the development of social work services and their current mode of organization. Whatever the goals and predominant mode of delivery of these services, some part of them involves services to individuals. It is in these settings that worker and client meet and where the purpose of their encounter is determined.

Settings differ, depending on the types of problems encountered and the purpose of the setting. In some settings, such as in family or child placement agencies, social workers carry a major responsibility for the delivery of service. In others, as in large institutional systems such as hospitals, prisons, or schools, the social worker is only one of many persons implementing the institutions' overall purposes. Here her[1] role is primarily one of reaching out to individuals who are having difficulty negotiating that system. At the same time the social worker collaborates with other staff so that together they can effectuate changes which will facilitate the best possible use of the service.

A recent development has seen the emergence of professionally trained private practitioners who, out of their long clinical experience, have attained a degree of competence in their field acceptable to the recently formed National Federation of State Societies for Clinical Social Work. Each private practitioner sets up her own mode of operating and is responsible for her own practice.

Objectives

The purpose of social work with individuals is to offer a means by which a person is enabled to obtain a higher level of social functioning through an interpersonal transaction or face-to-face, person-to-person encounter.

The method utilized by social work in this endeavor, social casework, is an enabling process through which one individual (the caseworker) helps another (the client) to take steps toward achieving some personal or social goal by utilizing the resources available to the client; resources inherent in the strength of his personality, the social system in which he lives or the social provisions supplied by the community, including the agency through which he is receiving help. It is not a method imposed upon an individual but is offered as a means by which he can make use of the caseworker's knowledge and expertise to gain strengths to move more productively in the social situation in which he finds himself having difficulty.

Whatever the problem presented to a caseworker, her objective is to help the person learn how to deal with it and thus to provide a means by which he can increase his capacity for coping with other life stresses. The objective is not toward personality change, although changes in attitudes and feelings may result from this contact. The applicant may become less critical of himself, increase his ability to communicate and relate to others, and learn how to handle hostility and aggression so that they serve him rather than becoming his master. He may feel greater self-confidence and find new values and aims. These gains depend on the quality and substance of the relationship that develops as client and caseworker interact in their joint endeavor, whether the contact is of short or extended duration.

---

[1]For purposes of clarity, the client will be referred to by he or his, the caseworker by she or her.

It is the purpose of casework with individuals to facilitate their engagement in social relationships when their effective participation with others has met an impasse.

Relationship

Whatever factors contribute to the client's increased ability to cope with his problem lie within the framework and quality of the relationship between caseworker and client as they work together. This relationship is based on the concept that all human beings have the capacity for growth and for the realization of their unique personalities through relationships with others, and that they can gain satisfaction through their participation with others as social beings. It is further acknowledged that learning and growth take place through creative interaction with others provided there is a climate of mutual respect and confidence in the participants' integrity and provided the challenges met are related in some measure to their individual capacities. This is especially true of the interaction that takes place between client and caseworker. The caseworker does not manipulate or control but helps the client find his own values and aims through an orderly process that enhances his capacity for self-determination.

Preparation for Practice

For this endeavor to be productive, the caseworker needs to prepare herself by gaining knowledge of the human condition from other disciplines—that is, from the behavioral sciences, psychology, sociology, learning theory, anthropology, and systems theory; by understanding the social forces that affect and are affected by individuals; and by developing the self-discipline and skills necessary to help the client take steps to increase his ability to function more adequately. Her skills are learned through the experiences she encounters in her work and through a training process that includes periodic case conferences with a competent supervisor or teacher. Through this process she learns to understand how she can use her strengths productively and come to terms with attitudes and feelings that color her perceptions or interfere with the client's willingness to use her help. She learns to assess where her own values can strengthen those of the client or where they could jeopardize the attainment of the client's own purposes.

She brings her own unique personality to her work and as she incorporates her professional knowledge she moves more spontaneously and surely in a variety of situations and with a variety of clients.

It is recognized that people have been helped by many different approaches, and by many different individual styles of working. Since there is no one basis for understanding human behavior, nor one theory of casework practice, a worker must choose what is of most value to her. What is of crucial importance is that she have a reliable framework upon which to base her practice. From such a base, she can offer the troubled client a steady source of strength upon which he can rely. In times of stress when people feel confused and vulnerable, they look for support and guidance more than at any other time in life. What a troubled person needs is someone outside of his immediate situation who is strong enough to bear the feelings he expresses without criticism or prejudgment. The helping person needs to be secure enough in her role to interact with the client by means of genuine, honest, and common-sense responses and input.

The necessity for acquiring competence in helping with the complex nature of people in difficulty has led to the professionalization of social work. Like other professions, social work is based on a code of ethics and values, a set of standards for practice, bodies of knowledge and tested principles leading to methods which serve its purposes. As a professional person the social work practitioner is responsible for maintaining standards held by the profession and confirmed in statements of purpose and performance by the National Association of Social Workers which receives sanctions for the implementation of social purposes from society as a whole.

Social casework as a part of the larger social work profession surfaced in response to the problems encountered when social workers attempted to help individuals caught in difficulties resulting from the impact of an industrialized society. The first theoretical exposition of a methodology for casework was formulated by Mary Richmond in 1917. Influenced both by the scientific method and by the medical model of that era, she advocated careful history taking as a means of arriving at a causative factor which would then be the target for effecting change. Her contribution lay in the development of a systematic approach to the study and diagnosis of problems. It was she who set forth some of the principles upon which social casework is based, not only the necessity for a careful appraisal of environmental influences but also an obligation to individualize each client, to recognize his right to determine his own life, and to place great value on the client-caseworker relationship.

In each succeeding era theories and practice reflected a response to human needs within the framework of the value system and scientific knowledge of the day. As in other professions, a variety of theories emerged. Insights from Freud and the ego-psychologists led to a psycho-social diagnostic base for practice, later refined to include problem-solving and crisis-intervention modalities. Differing from these was the functional school which utilized the concepts of Otto Rank in the development of a philosophy and implementation of casework as a service related to specific functions of an agency.

All of these approaches continue to contribute to casework practice today and have been augmented by the adoption of new models such as those based on existential and systems theory. These diversities have served not only to broaden the range of modalities open to caseworkers for their practice but also to enrich the social worker's knowledge of human behavior and understanding of the dynamics of the helping process.

In the 1970s knowledge from philosophers, social scientists, and physicists has introduced a new dimension to social thought; rather than reasoning in a lineal cause-and-effect manner, we now think in terms of action and reaction, a process of constant change within the reciprocal relationship between man and man, and man and his environment. In social work this shift in emphasis to interactional components of behavior has resulted in expansion in the use of multiple interviewing, such as in marital counseling, family therapy, and peer-group counseling. These latter modalities are discussed in separate chapters. In this chapter we concern ourselves with components of social casework as it deals with individuals and their interactions with others and with systems in which they are involved, through the one-to-one relationship of client and caseworker.

Impetus for Service

The impetus for the coming together of client and worker as agency representative occurs when there is a perceived need for service. Perception of need may come from one or more of three sources:

1. The client may come to the agency as a result of his own perception of need for assistance, such as for financial help, adequate housing, foster home placement, or counseling when he experiences feelings of anxiety, depression, or helplessness, often following an incident in which the person feels caught, as in a family quarrel or a threat to job security.

2. The client may come to the agency as a result of perception of need by another person or institution, such as a family member, an employer, the court, a school principal, or a hospital whose staff is concerned about his behavior or his reluctance to use its services.

3. The client and worker may come together as a result of the worker's or the agency's perception of need, such as in outreach services, case finding, or referral within a multiservice agency. For example, a worker in a high-risk

area may perceive a child's need for service by observing the child's behavior in school or in a youth group.

Regardless of the source of impetus toward service, what most clients have in common is that they are having difficulty negotiating a social system. In the case of children, it may be the family or school system. In the case of teen-agers, it may be a peer system or the judicial system. Adults may be having difficulty with a health service system, an employment system, or a social service system, including the system of which the worker herself is a part. In most cases the worker helps the person to participate and contribute more effectively in the system in which he is experiencing difficulty. In some cases her efforts are focused on helping a person extricate himself from a system which is destructive to his social functioning, such as to change his place of employment, to dissolve a marriage relationship, or, in the case of a child, to remove him from his current living situation.

One of the central parts of the helping process is to make a series of decisions in collaboration with a client and/or significant others about the extent to which the social system or the individual will be the target for change. In some cases the most appropriate form of help may be intervention in the social system, such as in changing the interpersonal climate of a classroom or hospital ward or family.

In other situations it may be inappropriate and a violation of client's rights or wishes to intervene in the system, thereby depriving him of the self-enhancing opportunity to handle his own problems. People begin to act differently as they have an opportunity to sort things out, share feelings which may have been unexpressed for years, and gain in understanding of the causes of their own behavior as well as that of others. The flow of energy in the relationship may be the most important—the feeling that one is accepted and acceptable. The relationship may provide the client with an opportunity to model more appropriate behavior. It can provide a feeling of safety and security which is the springboard for the client to risk attempting new and more effective behaviors as he leaves the office and faces the day-to-day world—yet knowing that whatever the results of the new behavior, he can return to discuss it with the worker and find acceptance for his failures as well as his successes.

In any event, it is the individual client who approaches or is approached by the caseworker, and it is their relationship that serves as the milieu in which they will function together. Whether it takes one or more interviews, the process through which they attempt to achieve their purpose depends on an orderly, rational structure which makes problem solving possible and which determines the parameters of their relationship.

We will proceed to outline one possible model for the helping process applied to work with and on behalf of individual clients.

THE CORE HELPING PROCESS

The formulation by Max Siporin (*Introduction to Social Work Practice*) of important elements in the helping process has proven useful. The components include (1) engagement, (2) exploration, (3) planning, (4) intervention, (5) evaluation, and (6) disengagement. These will be discussed as far as possible in sequential order. In actual practice they often overlap.

Engagement

Whatever the circumstances and feelings surrounding the encounter of client and caseworker, each has his unique personality and way of expressing himself, his own outlook on life, and the goals he wishes to achieve. Each has had different life experiences, and since they often have come from quite different backgrounds, each has found different ways of coping with problems. It is partly because of these factors that their coming together holds the promise of new learning and understanding of themselves and others. Its likeness to other relationships encountered in life—such as parent-child, husband-wife, teacher-pupil—lies in its reciprocal nature, each influencing the other as they interact in achieving their individual and social purposes. Its difference from other relationships is that its purpose is to achieve changes through a disciplined process in which one person makes use of another to achieve his goal.

In this respect they meet as equals, each with different roles and responsibilities. The caseworker's role requires that she be professionally responsible and committed to offering what can best be used by the client. The client's role requires that he make the problem understandable to himself as well as to the caseworker and that he take responsibility for whatever steps are required.

When a person arrives at the decision to seek or to accept outside help, the anxiety that the problem itself has produced may be compounded by two feelings: uncertainty of trusting another when he exposes what he perceives as weakness, and the fear of what may result from this new experience. However difficult the circumstances that propelled him to take action and whatever the discomfort he feels in his situation, at least these elements in his situation are familiar. To change his ways and to engage in talk with a strange person are often difficult.

It is the worker's attitude of acceptance and willingness to see a client as a whole person with strengths and weaknesses that enables the building of the interpersonal relationship which is the beginning step of their work together. Relationship happens when there is emotion shared between two people and they come to have ongoing impact in one another's lives. As any two strangers come together and interact, there are feelings and questions.

Will I be accepted by this other person? Will the outcome of our contacts be what I am hoping for? Can this other person be trusted? Will I be "put down," judged, laughed at? In a worker-client interaction these feelings and questions may be intensified.

In situations when people come to social workers for help, the asking for help is an admission that one cannot make it on one's own. In a society which places emphasis on independence and self-reliance, this admission of need for help may be experienced by the person as a step backward toward dependency. Consequently feelings run high. The client may be anxious about the worker's response to his request for help. He may be angry with himself or angry with those who in his perception have caused him to come to the agency. However, he comes too with the hope that he will be helped and with a readiness to mobilize his energy toward a solution and views the worker and the agency in a positive way.

In situations where the contact has been initiated by the worker, or in which the client comes to the agency under pressure from an authority, such as court or school, he may be angry toward the worker, suspicious of the worker's motives or fearful of what she may do. However, frequently he is relieved that someone has been concerned about him and provided him with a means whereby he can obtain some understanding and help in his predicament.

Meanwhile, the caseworker will also be wondering whether she can help the client or whether her personal biases will interfere with her perceptions and responses. Will the client's anger stir her own to such an extent that she will be unable to deal with it, or will the client's distress be so great that she may be overwhelmed and lose perspective? Will the client's problem be so similar to her own that her perception of the client as an individual will be distorted, or will the client's experiences be so different from hers that she cannot identify or empathize with him? However, the caseworker knows that she can rely on the self-discipline she has gained through understanding of herself and she can use the skills she has developed through professional education as well as from her experience. Her greatest assets are her genuine concern and willingness to put herself at the disposal of the client.

Most clients have experienced stressful relationships in their growing-up years or have been embittered by circumstances over which they have had no control. It may take some time before a person can trust the worker, since these experiences have not been conducive to trust in others. However, until he learns to trust the worker, there can be no benefit derived from their contact. No amount of good intentions can take the place of the client's belief and trust in the worker. This basic ingredient provides the greatest incentive for change.

It is the worker's skill in "tuning in" to the heightened feelings of the client that is essential to the development of their relationship. It is often useful to help a client verbalize what his feelings are about coming to or being approached by the agency. This can be done by a direct question or by commenting on one's perceptions of his nonverbal communications. The client may respond and talk about feelings, thus giving him an opportunity to reduce his anxiety or vent his anger or frustration. The client may deny the emotion perceived by the worker. In either event the worker sets the stage in terms of making it clear that the interview situation is a place where there is concern for feelings as well as for facts. While it is true that feelings need to be expressed, overindulgence in their expression may cause a client to react by feeling he has opened up too much of himself, and he may then feel guilty and exposed. Or he may release feelings that he cannot manage. The caseworker's task is to keep these expressions within bounds by focusing on the reality of the situation and by dealing with the specific problem facing the client. A full description about what happened can help lessen the client's anxiety and enable him to proceed with what, if anything, he wants to do about it.

The first step has to do with the worker's skill in listening and the ways by which she elicits information. She needs, first of all, to be receptive to the client's telling his story in his own way, being sensitive to both verbal and nonverbal communications that reflect feelings, anxieties, and tensions. If the client is unassuming and tentative in his presentation, the worker will want to encourage him by introducing leading questions, at the same time permitting him time to organize his thoughts. If he comes across strong, with anger and vituperation, the worker must accept his blowup to a point, but know when to cut into his harangue by playing back the content of the client's outburst. Throughout, the worker communicates her strength by her own composure and willingness to wait until the client is ready to go on.

By whatever means the client manages to tell what troubles him, the very telling brings a new sense of himself as a person able to communicate and share with another.

Most people present their problems as caused by external circumstances. If the "other" were different, he would be different. The perceptive worker understands that people find it difficult to see their part in a problem situation, let alone share their knowledge of it with someone else. At the other extreme is the client who blames himself entirely, as if he were the sole perpetrator of all that has happened. In either case, if these attitudes persist, the worker cannot be of immediate help. Overcoming the impasse is dependent upon her skill in helping the client see something of the relationship between what has happened to him and what he has done to contribute to his dilemma.

When she listens and asks questions, the worker has no stake in the rightness or wrongness of the issue. She accepts the client's view of the situation and does not belittle its meaning or importance, however bizarre or superficial it may sound. She knows that when a person asks for help, even though he is motivated to do something about it, he will have ambivalent feelings about accepting that help; that he both wants and does not want to meet the challenge it represents and to take on the responsibility for its solution. The client's resistance can be expressed in a variety of ways. He may block in answering a simple question, argue about some point that is brought up, or treat his situation in an offhand or humorous manner when in reality it is serious. Recognizing that people need their defenses for purposes of stability and integrity, the worker does not try to cut through at once but continues to listen and to provide the means by which he can deal with his ambivalence. She may want to know, for instance, how it happened that the client decided to do something about his problem at this time and what he hopes the worker can do to help him. Before the end of their first interview, there needs to be some expression on the part of the client that he is willing to do his part in working on the problem. It is his, not the worker's, problem that is at stake.

The question that both worker and client must address at this point is whether there is a resource in the agency services which is usable and useful to the client. It is a process of clarification of client needs and agency resources. The consequence of this phase of the engagement process is a decision that ongoing service is or is not appropriate. Often when the agency does not have the resource that is needed, the applicant is referred elsewhere. Thus the worker needs to have not only a thorough familiarity with her agency's resources, but also with other sources of assistance in the community. The worker must also be clear about the restraints imposed on her by the policies and procedures of the agency and by the resources available. She must help to make them understandable to the client in down-to-earth language. When the agency cannot provide service because of eligibility standards or waiting lists or lack of money, the resultant discussion can be a difficult responsibility, as workers want to respond to need.

As the agency representative the worker also makes clear to the client what responsibilities are his in this undertaking. Thus in an agency which gives financial assistance, the client will need to produce evidence of need; or in a foster placement agency, the prospective foster family will need to reveal facts and attitudes which make it possible to determine whether it can offer an appropriate home for a foster child.

When worker and client come to an agreement on goals for work together, plans can be made for ongoing service. The agreement should stipulate the frequency and duration of further contacts and the immediate tasks to be undertaken by both worker and client. A client should leave the initial interview with more than a casual "See you next week" on the worker's part, which leaves the client wondering why and what he should do in the meantime. For instance, the purpose of an encounter may be stated in broad terms, such as a mother's desire to improve her relationship with her child; the mother's task in this regard might then be that she write down the details of a disturbing incident for discussion in the following interview, and the worker's task that she contact the child's school to learn how the school views the child. Having definite objectives, however immediate and tentative, and tasks to be accomplished, both persons leave the transaction with a sense that positive movement will take place and both have assumed some accountability for what is to happen. The very articulation of the problem and the decision toward action in themselves comprise the beginning means of mastery and heighten motivation for continuing work together.

Exploration

In any responsible professional enterprise the first step needs to be the gathering of facts which define the parameters of the problem; thus it is important to explore any attempts the client has already made to solve the problem or answer the question. Consequently the worker focuses the interaction on understanding how the difficulty first surfaced and respects the fact that solutions have been tried and have failed. In addition, she explores those areas in which the client has been successful and in what ways he has learned to handle other problems. Thus they can understand what coping capacities the client has at his disposal. It gives both client and worker clues as to the nature of his personality strengths and how he takes advantage of opportunities open to him. The problem facing him at this point is one for which his usual ways of coping have not proved adequate to handle either internal or external stresses.

Social workers tend to believe that behavior is motivated and that its precipitants can be understood. Interventions made on the basis of limited facts and faulty judgments can be a disservice to the client and sabotage any effective help that may be given. The emphasis on the facts to be gathered varies widely according to the theoretical framework of the worker. Psychotherapeutically oriented workers may tend to emphasize historical data, whereas existentially oriented workers may focus much more on the "here and now."

The worker gathers facts through skilled interviewing techniques, and by her responses she guides the client in offering appropriate data. Simple responses such as nods let the client know that the information is understood and related to the topic under discussion. Rephrasing a statement may encourage a client to think through what he is sharing. Feelings as well as facts are important to understanding behavior. If the client is not verbalizing feelings, the worker may wish to reach for feelings with statements such as, "How did you feel when that happened?" or "From what you are saying, I'm wondering if you're not angry about that." Reflections may also be made about nonverbal communication such as muscle tensions or facial expressions. In so doing the worker transmits not only her acceptance of the client as a feeling person but also her respect for his autonomy in the problem-solving relationship.

The extent of exploring and confronting must be judged in relation to the strength of the relationship and the resilience of the client. It is often important to "reach for the opposite." If the client is talking primarily on a rational, intellectual plane, the worker may encourage verbalization of feelings, or if the client is caught up in emotional expressions she may want to ask questions that focus on the client's thinking on the issues being discussed.

As a result of this exploration the worker can make an assessment for purposes of judging what can be offered to the client for further work on his problem. Her assessment consists of determining the strengths the client has at his disposal as well as the environmental supports and opportunities available to him, including his family.

To determine the client's strengths, worker and client need to judge how pervasive and inhibiting the problem is to other areas of his life. As the client talks, the worker will be thinking about whether his anxiety is heightened or lessened through discussion of reality issues and whether the feelings surrounding his predicament are appropriate, keeping in mind that anxiety is always present in a new undertaking. In this, she will be sensitive as to whether the client's responses to her questions are appropriate and logical or whether there is an inordinate amount of emotional overlay. She will be thinking about whether or not the client's actions seem to be in tune with his values and intellect. She will be aware of the stresses operating from environmental conditions and how they affect the client, how he relates to friends and family and group associations, and whether he takes advantage of the resources available to him. This helps in understanding the supports the client has at his disposal and gives a clue as to his ability to interact socially. How he uses others and how he takes hold of what the caseworker offers indicate where his potential ability lies in being able to cope with the present problem. The worker can therby assess the severity of the problem, its relation to the client's total life experience, and the appropriateness of its being dealt with in the particular agency or institution in which she functions. She can discuss her assessment with the client and thus have a basis for making plans about what seems most appropriate to do in tackling the problem.

In this whole process it is hoped that what helps the client most is that the caseworker engages him in a discussion of his hopes and expectations and encourages his full participation. By revealing the feelings and attitudes that surround his problem he is able to see the problem more realistically. By exploring related facets, he gains a better perspective on how the problem relates to his present and past life, and he begins to face the problem with a greater degree of objectivity. He begins to feel that the worker understands and accepts him and he senses he can rely on the worker's expertise—"She knows what she is about." At the same time it conserves and strengthens his feelings of self-worth and mastery. Its intent is to free the client so that the choices he makes will lead to actions that take him a step forward in fulfilling his aims.

Planning

When the worker and client have gained a shared understanding of the problem and have identified factors which have impeded the client's ability to cope with it, they will need to explore what resources can be of assistance and formulate a plan of action. The plan should identify specific goals agreed upon by both worker and client. The worker must be genuinely convinced about the right of a client to choose a course of action freely. She will give an explanation about what the agency has to offer and what would be entailed in working together on the problem that has been presented.

Resources outside of the agency may be considered as more appropriate to meeting client needs, in which case the worker would suggest alternative sources of help. The selection of resource would be dependent on an evaluation as to whether the resource is one that will indeed further the client's aims and purposes.

Often workers can help clients find needed resources from their own social context. A client may determine with a worker that he needs experiences in which he can achieve success in order to help him feel more positively about himself. She may then work with his teacher or parent or recreation leader to help them set up, or help him set up, such activities. There may be a neighbor or friend who can supply immediate needs or stand by as a stabilizing influence for a very troubled person.

In many instances the resource needed is not present in either the client's current social context or in the agency to which the client is looking for help. In this case the worker may want to help the client link up with sources of such help. In addition to established health and welfare agencies, there are a variety of mutual aid organizations such as Alcoholics Anonymous, Parents Without Partners, fraternal organizations, and political clubs.

When worker and client agree on an appropriate external resource, a referral is made. The way the referral is made depends on the nature of the problem and the capacity of the client to carry through with it. The referral may be made on one level by a simple suggestion on the part of the worker, which is easily followed through by the client. At another level the worker may need to take time to prepare the client by talking through fears, apprehensions, and lack of knowledge. The worker may "pave the way" by contacting the other agency and sharing information so the work can be done more expeditiously. A highly agitated or depressed client may need to be escorted to a psychiatric facility. The principle here is that the client be encouraged to do as much as is feasible for himself.

The influence that the worker has with the client comes largely from her knowledge and expertise about community resources and from the authority of her position as agency representative, especially in crisis situations. The worker's effectiveness in helping the client take stock, sort out alternatives, and choose a course of action is critical in providing linkage services. In doing this she is aware of the possibility that the client may have feelings of frustration which need to be expressed. Often clients have gone from agency to agency in attempts to find a solution. The handling of feelings can free a client so there is positive motivation for seeking help elsewhere.

In making a determination for plans to utilize the agency, particularly with a multipurpose agency or institution, there will be a number of resources from which to make a selection. The worker's responsibility in these situations is not only to determine if, when, and how much of the agency's resources can be offered but also to help the client make the best possible use of them. To do this the worker must gather appropriate data and give clear information about available resources, policies, and procedures. Her attitude should convey to the client that he has a right to avail himself of these resources. She will use her casework skills in helping him overcome barriers to the use of the resource (e.g., in meeting eligibility standards or in overcoming doubts, fears, or feelings of shame) while at the same time making clear to him what resonsibilities he must assume. Her success in obtaining the needed resource will be dependent on their maintaining positive working relationships with other staff, or, in some settings, on her ability and skill in confronting those in authority.

When the client-worker relationship is the important resource, planning may involve setting priorities. The worker may, for instance, see deficits in patterns of child rearing or household management, while the client is focused on more specific goals, like getting the electricity turned back on or having his child's classroom changed. Realistically, these are of crucial concern and the worker will help him attempt to meet those needs which require immediate attention. Whether or not these needs can be met depends on the realities of the other social systems. The outcome of these endeavors may be successful or unsuccessful, but the sharing of mutual tasks in the effort gives worker and client a beginning sense of value in each other's contributions to their undertaking. Through the experience of coping with these realities they may later wish to move toward dealing with some of the underlying factors which brought about the client's predicament.

In another context, if worker and client decide to focus first on marital problems, the worker can use this agreed upon plan to pull the client back into this focus if he should begin to spend a lot of time talking about his relationship with his employer. Here flexibility, of course, is important. If the employment situation has become increasingly stressful and the verbalization is not an effort to avoid the focus on the marriage, then it may be appropriate to alter the plan since this may in reality be putting stress upon the marriage. The important thing is that the work is purposeful and both worker and client are clear about the goal toward which they are working.

As they progress, each of the parties should know what is expected in behavioral terms, since it is through behavior, whether by the spoken word or by action, that persons give expression to their aims and move toward achieving them.

Because of the increased awareness of the importance of accountability and clearer goal definition, many social workers have found it useful to set forth a plan in the form of a contract. The contract is the result of negotiation between worker and client and spells out goals and tasks to be performed. Such a contract can help to make clear to the client that change in social functioning does not take place within the interview situation. Change takes place as the client takes steps to interact with others in new ways, or to alter his patterns of negotiating with the systems which he faces day to day, or as systems are altered in ways which enhance his functioning. The contract itself gives a base for talking about what has and hasn't been done and why and serves as a vehicle for making choices, including choices as to what mode or modes of intervention to take.

Intervention

Intervention is activity on the part of the worker to bring about change so that the client can participate more effectively in the social system in which he is involved. In addition to the actions taken by the worker in obtaining resources and setting the stage for future working on a client's problem, intervention may be undertaken (1) with significant others, (2) in advocacy for change, or (3) within the client-worker relationship itself.

1. *Intervention with significant others.* The nature of the influence process when a worker intervenes with significant others within the client's social system is usually dependent on the extent to which she can find common ground with them so that together they can enlarge their understanding of the needs and/or problems confronting the client and can find ways of helping to alleviate the attendant stresses.

It is important that a worker respect the feelings, attitudes, and beliefs of those involved in this endeavor. A common mistake of caseworkers, particularly of beginning workers, is to overidentify with their clients to the extent that they have little tolerance for what are perceived as "uncooperative" persons such as parents, teachers, and neighbors. Time may be needed to establish good working relationships so that goals and outcomes may be clarified in the change effort.

When a caseworker serves in a "host" setting, such as in a school or hospital, she is one of many staff members who are committed to rendering an overall service. In such a setting she may serve as interpreter, mediator, or facilitator in situations where there is a breakdown in communication between a client and a staff member or when there is some obstacle in the effective functioning in carrying out the purposes of the setting. By intervening, the worker hopes to ease attitudes so that responsibilities will be understood and taken by both the client and significant others in order to meet their common purposes.

In collaborative undertakings, such as when a teacher seeks the help of a caseworker because she is concerned about a pupil's behavior, the success of their combined efforts is dependent on the extent to which they can trust and respect each other's expertise in their common task. For both teacher and caseworker there is a reduction in anxiety when a responsibility is shared. Likewise, there is an opportunity to enlarge their knowledge about the pupil's behavior and the problems with which he is attempting to cope. The teacher may be encouraged to experiment with alternate ways in which she can help the pupil to feel that he is achieving, which in turn may lessen the pupil's need to compensate for failure by negative behavior. At the same time the pupil is encouraged to come to grips with what he is doing and to take positive steps to avoid the pitfalls that are defeating his purposes. Thus, in this, as in other collaborative undertakings, the worker uses her skills to help both participants increase their effectiveness in reaching their goals.

2. *Intervention as advocacy for change.* When there is evidence that the needs of a client or group of clients are not being met, a caseworker has an obligation to take an advocacy role in pressing for changes, either within the setting itself or in the larger community. She may elect to do this independently or in participation with the client when appropriate.

Within the setting itself, because she has the meaningful contacts with clients and understands their needs from firsthand knowledge, she can bring to staff or administration whatever changes she sees as desirable to provide the best possible service. These may concern such simple matters as providing appropriate reading material in a waiting room or such complex matters as doing away with outmoded procedures that interfere with flexibility in practice or outreach to clients. They should be given full consideration by all staff members involved in the effort. Changes so implemented require judgment as to their effectiveness and their influence on other services.

The changes that a worker perceives as necessary within the wider community can be related to housing codes, institutional arrangements, lack of municipal services, and the like. Here the worker may participate with other groups who have the same concerns, such as a Welfare Rights organization, or she may work through her professional association, the National Association of Social Workers. The overall purposes of any such changes are to help service delivery systems become more responsive to clients and their needs.

3. *Intervention within the client-caseworker relationship.* Within the client-caseworker relationship the inputs of the worker are forms of intervention which are designed to result in movement toward the desired goal. These inputs represent those responsibilities which a worker assumes for guiding, motivating, and educating in the client-caseworker relationship. The worker may become a truly important person in the client's eyes. Her verbal and nonverbal messages are studied by the client for signs of approval and disapproval. The worker must be aware of her own values, attitudes, and feelings so that she can be clear that she is helping the client to change as he wants, rather than as she wants.

Each interview should take a client one step forward in mitigating or resolving his problem. The worker's responsibility is to keep the client focused at the task he is embarked on without fostering his dependency but rather strengthening his sense of autonomy.

How a worker can intervene depends on her perceptions of the client's way of dealing with life situations. Some act without giving much thought beforehand; others reflect before taking a step until they are sure it will work. Still others are so introspective that they are unable to get beyond self-analysis to take action. Others are so highly emotional that they need considerable venting of their feelings before they can act. What the worker attempts to do is to help each client build on or modify his usual coping abilities so that he can integrate thought and feeling sufficiently to be able to take the action which will further his aims.

The worker keeps in mind that no one finds change easy, even when it is desired, and least of all when it requires changing oneself and one's ways of relating to others. Since change represents the unknown, there are strong tendencies to maintain the status quo or to see problems as being caused by factors outside of one's own control. There are resistances to accepting one's own responsibilities. Therefore, both client and worker respect the fact that progress is not even and that there will be ups and downs.

Most people mobilize their energies to take specific actions when they result in tangible rewards. In the casework effort, a client may be motivated by the attainment of immediate needs, such as financial assistance or benefits received from undertaking a new approach with spouse or child. Another client may find benefit in understanding aspects of his personality that he has not understood before. Moreover, the client may be benefited by the lessening of anxiety or the assurance of the worker's continued support. This is true particularly when a client has experienced severe emotional deprivation or has low self-esteem. Motivation may result as well from being challenged, or from increased competence gained through making choices that lead to productive actions. Whatever the means by which a client's motivation is stimulated, it is the caseworker's responsibility to use this knowledge of the client by bringing into the helping process those techniques of intervention that will increase the client's competence.

The worker's skills revolve around her ability to know when to be supportive, to empathize, to relieve anxiety; when to question, to stimulate, to confront; when to clarify a point or to interpret behavior. She will need to know when it is important to provide information and knowledge or to share her own experience and point of view, and how to reward the client's efforts and competence. The undertaking they are embarked on is a new and different experience from others in which the client has engaged. It is one that offers a means by which the client can learn to take more responsibility for his actions and anticipate or learn to deal with the consequences of the choices he makes.

Each client needs to proceed at his own pace. For some, it is important to set time limits for the accomplishment of a specific task. For others, a time limit can impose undue anxiety so that the client is immobilized. No amount of pressure can substitute for a client's own motivation and readiness to progress; nor can a client be prompted to develop his own capacities by a caseworker's desire to provide a prescription that the client should follow. A worker may point out realities or suggest alternatives, but the client's own view of what he can do is the primary motivating force, and it should be respected as such. The worker encourages him to experiment or to take risks, but she must be ready to support and help him bear the consequences of his efforts. Both can review what has happened and think about alternatives. The important element is that the client participate in discussion and make the decisions as to what he can do and/or think about in the interim between appointments. The worker stands by to handle the feelings and attitudes that accompany any change.

Evaluation

As worker and client approach the completion of their contract, the worker initiates an evaluation process. Evaluation involves reexamination of the objectives set out in the plan and a review of the progress which has been made toward those objectives. The advantage of having objectives which were limited and definable in behavioral terms during the planning is clear here. This look at the history of the helping process is often useful in helping the client to realize how far he has come. He can take pride in what he has been able to accomplish and thereby feel more confident in himself and his capacity to participate effectively in the systems in which he lives.

It is important that the evaluation include a review not only of what progress was made, but also of how the movement took place. Progress did not take place through magic. Worker and client together need to evaluate what happened. What activities of client or worker seemed most helpful? Which ones failed? Why? What might have been done differently? Dealing with such questions will, it is hoped (1) reinforce client gains, (2) help the client to be more conscious of the problem-solving process so that he can apply it again when new difficulties arise, and (3) provide the worker with important feedback so that she can grow in her own effectiveness as a helping person.

Failures as well as successes in reaching objectives must be reviewed, though this is often painful for worker and client. Why were attempts at problem-solving blocked? How might it have been done differently? Were objectives realistic? Their expectations may have been too high or the needed supports inadequate. Whatever the reasons, the worker must have the courage to face the full impact of the meaning this has for them both, since both have invested themselves in the effort. For the client, in particular, the feeling of failure can compound the sense of inadequacy that prompted him to seek help. A review of the realities that made their endeavor unproductive can serve to place the problem in perspective without undermining the client's feeling of self-worth or of adequacy in other areas of his life. A sharing of their disappointment and the worker's emotional support for the strengths that are required for the client to "live in his circumstances" must not be overlooked; indeed this in itself can be a strengthening experience.

The evaluation process often leads to discussion of problems which were not the focus of the initial contract. The client may have had concerns which could not be expressed in the beginning—perhaps because it was too risky to share them with a stranger at that time. The worker may have perceived problems which the client was not ready to deal with because other concerns were more pressing to him. If they have been involved in a process which has led to movement in a desired direction and if trust has been developed, then it is only natural that these other concerns be raised. In this instance worker and client will reinitiate the process of problem definition, exploration, and assessment, and establish a new contract. Otherwise the helping process moves into the stage of disengagement.

Disengagement (Termination)

Disengagement occurs when (1) the objectives set out in the contract have been accomplished, (2) further progress does not seem possible, or (3) external reasons such as the worker's leaving the agency intervene. In the disengagement process client and worker withdraw from their relationship.

This does not mean that the change process ends. If they have been successful, the client and/or significant others in his life have developed their problem-solving resources to the point where continuing progress can be made in the client's efforts to negotiate the significant social systems in his life.

Disengagement needs the worker's careful attention since the ending of a relationship can bring with it feelings of loss which may reactivate other feelings of loss which the client (or worker) may have encountered at other times in his life. Feelings of anger, uncertainty, and insecurity are common, particularly if the contact has been intense or has lasted over a period of months. In these situations it is important that the client be prepared early for disengagement. By bringing up ending several weeks before the actual date of their last contact, worker and client have an opportunity to talk over feelings. Referral to another resource in the community may be appropriate, or reassurance that the client may return at a later time. If the client is one who has had difficulty trusting people and has come to trust the worker, it may be necessary for the worker to help him to find others whom he might trust. Workers have also found it useful to increase the interval between contacts as the end approaches, so that the client can feel increasingly confident of his problem-solving capacities as he moves away from dependence on the relationship.

Conclusion

In this chapter we have discussed some of the objectives and components of the casework process as well as the roles which caseworkers generally assume to be necessary in working with and on behalf of clients so that they can utilize the opportunities available to them when there have been breakdowns in their abilities to function adequately in the systems in which they are involved. In so doing, we hope that these considerations can serve as basic principles upon which casework practice can be implemented in the various settings in which caseworkers function. Although each setting differs in its purposes and requires certain specialized knowledge to achieve those purposes, the worker's essential skills and knowledge can be enlarged or refined according to the needs of each setting.

The presentations in the following chapters cannot hope to cover the full gamut of services but will introduce important areas of practice, pointing out some of the changes that are taking place in the 1970s. There is considerable overlapping in the delivery of these services, with a variety of agencies performing similar functions. However, the fields of practice considered here revolve around services to families and children, adolescents and aging persons, as well as to those in the specialized areas of schools, corrections, health, and mental health. The changes that are taking place present a challenge to the social worker to keep an open mind and develop flexibility in the uses she makes of her practice, as well as to experiment with and incorporate new concepts and methods as they emerge and are tested for their reliability and serviceability.

BIBLIOGRAPHY

Aptekar, Herbert H. *Basic Concepts in Social Casework.* Chapel Hill: University of North Carolina Press, 1941.

Bartlett, Harriet H. *The Common Base of Social Work Practice.* New York: National Association of School Workers, 1970.

Benjamin, Alfred. *The Helping Interview.* Boston: Houghton Mifflin Co., 1969.

Briar, Scott, and Henry Miller. *Problems and Issues in Social Casework.* New York: Columbia University Press, 1971.

Faatz, Anita J. *The Nature of Choice in Casework Process.* Chapel Hill: University of North Carolina Press, 1953.

Hamilton, Gordon. *Theory and Practice of Social Work.* New York: Columbia University Press, 1951.

Hollis, Florence. *Social Casework: A Psycho-Social Therapy.* New York: Randon House, 1964.

Kadushin, Alfred. *The Social Work Interview.* New York: Columbia University Press, 1972.

Kanfer, F. H., and H. Phillips. *Learning Foundations of Behavior Therapy.* New York: John Wiley & Sons, 1970.

Keith-Lucas, Alan. *Giving and Taking Help.* Chapel Hill: University of North Carolina Press, 1972.

Lowe, C. Marshall. *Value Orientations in Counseling and Psychotherapy: The Meaning of Mental Health.* San Francisco: Chandler Publishing Co., 1969.

Meyer, Carol H. *Social Work Practice: A Response to the Urban Crisis.* Glencoe, Ill.: Free Press, 1970.

Parad, Howard J., ed. *Crisis Intervention: Selected Readings.* New York Family Service Association of America, 1965.

Perlman, Helen Harris. *Perspectives in Social Casework.* Philadelphia: Temple University Press, 1971.

Pincus, A., and A. Minahan. *Social Work Practice: Model and Method.* Itasca, Ill.: Peacock Publishers, 1973.

Reid, William, and Laura Epstein. *Task-Centered Casework.* New York: Columbia University Press, 1972.

Reid, William, and Ann Shyne. *Brief and Extended Casework.* New York: Columbia University Press, 1972.

Rich, Margaret E. *A Belief in People.* New York: Family Service Association of America, 1956.

Richmond, Mary E. *Social Diagnosis.* New York: Russell Sage Foundation, 1917.

Roberts, Robert W., and Robert H. Nee. *Theories of Social Casework.* Chicago: University of Chicago Press, 1970.

Robinson, Virginia. *A Changing Psychology in Social Casework.* Chapel Hill: University of North Carolina Press, 1930.

Rokeach, Milton. *The Open and Closed Mind: Investigations into the Nature of Belief Systems and Personality Systems.* New York: Basic Books, 1960.

Siporin, Max. *Introduction to Social Work Practice.* New York: Macmillan, 1975.

Smalley, Ruth E. *Theory for Social Work Practice.* New York: Columbia University Press, 1967.

Timms, Noel. *Social Casework, Principles and Practice.* London: Routledge and Kegan Paul, 1964.

Towle, Charlotte. *Common Human Needs.* New York: American Association of Social Workers, 1952.

Whittaker, James K. *Social Treatment.* Chicago: Aldine Publishing Co., 1974.

7
SOCIAL WORK WITH FAMILIES

JANE H. PFOUTS

**School of Social Work,
University of North Carolina**

The United States is currently experiencing a revolution in family life. Although a trend toward greater flexibility in this area has been evident for half a century or more, it was during the turbulent 1960s that the family, along with other societal institutions, came under serious attack, particularly among middle-class young people. Since that time, sweeping changes in male-female relations, sex norms, birth rates, and divorce rates have been occurring at an accelerating rate among all segments of the population, and the end is not in view. People today become sexually active earlier, marry later, have fewer children, and divorce more frequently than in the past. Nontraditional alternatives to marriage such as living together, communal families, and one-parent families by choice have emerged along with a confusing variety of other experimental arrangements. Within traditional marriage, couples are attempting to maximize self-actualization through open marriages, shared roles, and new approaches to child rearing. These dramatic changes in family life reflect equally dramatic changes in the American culture. Between 1965 and 1977, the society has been characterized by fierce power struggles between the sexes and the generations, rising relationship expectations, widespread access to effective birth control methods and therapeutic abortion, and the movement of almost half of the women in the population into the labor force—all of which have profoundly altered the nature of male-female relationships in every major social institution, and especially within the family.

It is important to remember, however, that successful social revolutions do not occur until the society is ready for dramatic change. The family revolution was not "caused" in any basic sense by such recent harbingers of the times as the new feminism, permissive child rearing, or the self-actualization movement. The true causes can be found in the vast social and economic changes brought about by industrialization which have given us a new kind of society which demands a new kind of family. Child psychiatrist Bruno Bettelheim belives that

> ...the conditions which gave substance to the earlier family and made for its cohesion—or forced such cohesion on what, even then, may have been a reluctant or disappointed partnership in a common enterprise—are no longer present. In the past, companionship—under the most desirable circumstances, intimacy—was based on and the consequence of dire necessity. Now companionship is expected to hold the family as successfully together, when the necessity of living together as a group has been replaced by other social and economic conditions. Today it is quite feasible for males and females to succeed in life as well when they are single as when they are married, and often a single parent can readily afford to raise children. No longer does survival command that all family members stay and work together in order to avoid extreme emotional, social, and economic deprivation. Choice became available only when affluence no longer required the coordinated labor of all family members to guarantee their survival. . . . With so many reasons for its existence removed, marriage necessarily became more problematic.[1]

Whether one views present trends with approval or alarm, it is obvious that we are living in a period in which traditional family norms have become blurred, and new guidelines for courtship and marriage have not yet been clarified. Nor has a satisfactory substitute for the family been found to take responsibility for the socialization of children. In this time of ambivalence and flux, social workers face the formidable challenge of ensuring that in their

---

[1]Bruno Bettelheim, "Untying the Family," *The Center Magazine,* September–October 1976, pp. 5–9.

practice they will be relevant and effective in helping troubled families cope with the old and the new dilemmas inherent in family life today.

FAMILY THERAPY: A NEW APPROACH TO PRACTICE WITH FAMILIES

During the second half of the twentieth century, a challenging new approach to practice with families has gained a secure foothold within social work. It is an approach which focuses on the total family system, rather than on the individual as the unit of study and treatment. This approach is based on the belief that within the family unit can be found both the source and the solution for a wide range of problems of individual maladjustment. The target of intervention is the existing family system, and the therapist joins the system in order to facilitate change from within. The goal of intervention is not so much to help family members find reasons for current difficulties in past mistakes as it is to assist them in restructuring their present family life in new and better ways. Because this orientation focuses mainly on observable problems in the here and now rather than on tracing the tangled threads of causation, it is applicable to types of clients and problems considered inappropriate for individual insight therapy. Family units need not be middle class, highly verbal, or introspective in order to be able to work together to solve their relationship problems with one another. They only need to want to be a family and to improve life within the group for all its members. Although casework and group work with families are still indicated in many cases, family therapy is the treatment of choice, either alone or in conjunction with casework, in those situations in which it appears that overall family patterns are detrimental to the functioning of one or more of the members.

The assumptions and methods of family therapy highlight dynamics of family life which are familiar to social work practitioners. Caseworkers have always been aware that, in many instances, the individual client has failed to solidify gains made in treatment because the family system has sabotaged his efforts to change. It has been equally apparent that when a family system is functioning badly, all members suffer, although in differing degrees. Vulnerability to particular family problems varies among members depending on such factors as age, sex, temperament, and role differences.

While only a minority of social workers are engaged primarily in family therapy practice, the principles which therapists and clinicians in this group have generated are highly relevant for social work practitioners in a wide variety of settings. This is not to say that the family therapy method as practiced in a relatively small number of mental health clinics and family agencies, where entire family groups are seen over a period of time, will ever be either appropriate or feasible for most social work practitioners. Nor is it true that all human problems originate within the family. In some cases, the principle locus of difficulty is within the individual himself, and, in others, the problem has its origin in the larger society. Nevertheless, the structure of family relationships must be taken into account by all practitioners because, in most instances, it plays a part, either central or peripheral, in the creation or solution of client problems.

DIFFERENCES BETWEEN FAMILY THERAPY AND CASEWORK WITH FAMILIES

Casework is primarily oriented toward change in an individual client while family therapy focuses on changing the organization of the family. Family therapists believe that if the structure of the family group is altered, all members, including the client, will also change because individual personality is, in large part, formed and modified in interaction with significant others. Thus while caseworkers tend to see the individual as the site of pathology, family therapists are apt to look for the roots of individual malfunctioning in the emotional relationship system of his family unit.

In comparing the two methods, a leading family therapist, Salvador Minuchin, likens the therapist who works with individuals to "a technician using a magnifying glass. The details of the field are clear, but the field is severely circumscribed. A therapist working within the framework of structural family therapy, however, can be compared to a technician with a zoom lens. He can zoom in for a closeup whenever he wishes to study the intrapsychic field, but he can also observe with a broader focus."[2] For instance, a young housewife, with three preschool children, comes to a mental health clinic with complaints of anxiety and depression. In working with this kind of case, a worker with an individual orientation would be likely to concentrate on the client's feelings about herself and her family. In addition, the worker would almost certainly hold individual interviews with the client's husband and perhaps other family members as well. In contrast, a family therapist would meet with husband, wife, children, and other significant household members *together* in order to discover, by direct observation, why the family has a member who is symptomatic. Perhaps the husband, who earlier appeared highly solicitous and reasonable in an individual interview with the worker, will reveal by manner, gesture, tone, or words in interaction with wife and children that in actual practice he is neither helpful nor supportive. Indeed, it may be clearly demonstrated that he is not even fully aware of the heavy domestic burden carried by his wife. The worker may also see that, because

---

[2]Salvador Minuchin, *Families and Family Therapy* (Cambridge: Harvard University Press, 1974), p. 3.

of low self-esteem, the wife actively encourages her husband and children to make ceaseless demands on her time and energy while she makes none on theirs. This is a group problem with responsibility scattered among individual members, although only one member is seeking help for the problem. For this reason, the family therapist would work with the total group toward changing family structure in the direction of greater equity in domestic responsibilities and rewards. In the same situation, a caseworker would probably work primarily with the wife to help her shift her position in the family structure. However, it is likely that the wife would find it very difficult to restructure the system if other members had not also been helped to work with her to effect the desired change.

DIFFERENCES BETWEEN FAMILY THERAPY AND GROUP WORK

Family therapy uses many of the concepts of group work (e.g. values, norms, roles, structure, process) because the family is a small group. However, small group theory cannot be applied to families without modifications because the family is a unique small group. Social group workers generally deal with artificially constructed groups of unrelated children, adolescents, or adults who meet for a specified length of time to deal with an agreed upon set of problems and to achieve specified goals.

In contrast, a family is a group of individuals united by bonds of blood in a relationship which, far more than any other, is central to the emotional development and life chances of all its members. Unlike other small groups which tend to be homogeneous, the family is composed of members of differing ages and sexes and is heavily weighted with dependents. Other small groups are time-limited while families have a past and a future. Membership in most small groups is a voluntary commitment. This is not true of the family group. One does not choose his family members (except for a mate) and kinship is a permanent condition, whether the individual wishes it or not, and regardless of separation in time, space, or life circumstances.

Therefore, the group worker who does family therapy must change some techniques and modify others in order to deal with the qualitative differences between family groups and groups of nonrelated individuals.

OLD CONCERNS AND A NEW FOCUS IN FAMILY SOCIAL WORK PRACTICE

What is it that is new about family therapy? Certainly social work involvement with families is not new. Social work has always acknowledged the critical importance of the family to the development and functioning of the individual, and practice has traditionally emphasized problems of husband-wife and parent-child interaction.

The family-centered focus of social work was made explicit long ago in Mary Richmond's classic, *Social Diagnosis,* published in 1917. In this book, which guided practice in its time, major attention was given to the importance of the family unit, interpersonal relationships within the family, and cultural, social, and economic forces impinging on the family. However, beginning in the 1920s, social work became absorbed in the essential task of incorporating psychoanalytic theory into casework practice. Unfortunately, as psychological knowledge increased, social factors began to assume less importance in social work theory. As a result, for almost forty years, from the 1920s through the 1950s, the psychosocial balance which is the hallmark of social work remained tilted in favor of the inner life of the individual at the expense of the social reality of his environment.

In 1958, Robert Gomberg, an outstanding family theorist in social work, pointed out that ''our conceptualization has been primarily in relation to individual personality, growth, pathology, adjustment, and so on. All of us are aware that in our practice we have worked with families, have planned with and for them, and were helpful to them. Yet there is no doubt that our diagnostic formulations have been framed in terms only of the individual and lack any crystalized conceptual system of family dynamics and family interaction which dealt with the family as a unitary organism.''[3]

Family treatment, then, is not a new concern in social work. Indeed, long before the present development of family therapy theory and practice, there were a minority of workers in family agencies who were doing something very similar to what today would be called family therapy.[4] In addition, social workers in all settings have traditionally taken family histories, interviewed the client's family members, and given help to families in crisis. However, in most social work settings the focus has been almost exclusively on the individual client and his perception of the family rather than on direct clinical observation and treatment of the complex interaction of the individual and the total family system. Indeed, significant influences of family-system level variables on all members, including the client, were often missed entirely because they were outside the consciousness of both worker and client.

What is new in family therapy is that it gives primary emphasis to the family as a system of patterned activities which shapes the behavior of all family members in important and often unintended ways. By clarifying the psy-

---

[3]M. Robert Gomberg, "Family Diagnosis: Trends in Theory and Practice," *Social Casework* 39, nos. 2–3 (February-March 1958): 74

[4]Morton D. Schumann, "The Social Work Relationship to Family Therapy in Perspective: Past and Future," *The Family* 2, no. 2 (Spring-Summer 1975): 4–10.

chosocial linkages between the individual personality system and the family social system, family therapists have made available to all social workers a highly useful set of concepts and techniques which, like psychoanalysis in the 1920s, add a new dimension to practice. According to family therapist Sanford Sherman, family therapy has raised its clinical eye one notch in the social organizational continuum and in so doing has demonstrated the clinical advantage of moving back and forth between the atomized level of the individual and the nuclear level of the family.[5] As a result social workers in all settings are becoming better able to chart their course in the dimly understood terrain of the client's family world and to use this knowledge to help both client and family achieve higher levels of functioning.

FAMILY THERAPY THEORY AND PATTERNS OF PRACTICE

The body of theory on which family therapy is based is drawn from psychiatry, psychology, and the social sciences. Among the theoretical contributions which have helped shape practice are general systems theory, the ego-psychology of such neo-Freudians as Hartmann and Erickson, Parsonian theories of socialization and interaction within the family, role theory, small group theory, and the clinical research of the Bateson,[6] Lidz,[7] and Wynne[8] groups with families of schizophrenic children.

Family therapy practice reflects a similar professional diversity with representation among psychiatrists, psychologists, social workers, and a variety of other therapeutically oriented groups. Along with a high tolerance for professional difference within their ranks, practitioners from different disciplines frequently collaborate as treatment co-therapists, carrying joint responsibility for conducting family sessions. Interdisciplinary co-therapy most frequently involves a social worker teamed with a psychiatrist or a psychologist, but family therapists also engage in a wide range of less traditional collaborative arrangements. In general, co-therapists are selected on the basis of such considerations as the problem presented by a particular family, the complementarity of the personalities and skills of the two therapists, and their

[5]Sanford N. Sherman, "Family Therapy," in *Social Work Treatment—Interlocking Theoretical Approaches,* ed. Francis J. Turner (New York: Macmillan, 1974), p. 459.

[6]Gregory Bateson et al., "Toward a Theory of Schizophrenia," *Behaviorial Science* 1 (October 1956): 251–64.

[7]See Theodore Lidz, *The Family and Human Adaptation* (New York: International Universities Press, 1963).

[8]Lyman Wynne, "The Study of Intrafamilial Alignments and Splits in Exploratory Family Therapy," in *Exploring the Base for Family Therapy,* ed. Nathan W. Ackerman et al. (New York: Family Service Association of America, 1961).

ability to work together. For example, a marriage counselor and a psychiatric nurse with skills in the parent-child area might be selected as the members of a clinic team best suited to work with a family characterized by marital strife and inadequate parenting.

One reason for the widespread use of co-therapists in family therapy is that the therapeutic complexity of working simultaneously with multiple family members can be shared. In addition, in some family situations, it is considered clinically useful to have a male and female therapist working together because in their interactions with one another and with family members, they can serve as spousal or parental role models. For example, for a family in which the husband and wife cannot allow any expression of difference, it can be very instructive to see that the co-therapists can differ openly and even angrily at times and still maintain a good relationship.

Given the traditional interest of social workers in the family, it is not surprising that of all professions, social work is the one most highly involved in the practice of family therapy. According to a 1970 survey conducted by the Group for the Advancement of Psychiatry,[9] 40 percent of family therapists are social workers. A growing body of social work practice literature devoted to family therapy reflects this high professional involvement.

Because family therapy is still in its infancy, and because a wide range of helping professions are actively engaged in formulating its practice principles, there are many differences of opinion concerning the specifics of treatment. Nevertheless, consensus about certain basic principles has been established. It is these principles which the social work profession is beginning to incorporate in its own way to meet its own needs in such varied settings as social service departments, health agencies, correctional institutions, retirement homes, and day care centers.

CHARACTERISTICS OF THE FAMILY SYSTEM

What is meant when the family is described as a social system? According to Grace Coyle, social group work theorist, a social system is "a set of interacting relationships which has a life of its own, a relation to the larger social and physical environment, a differentiation among its interacting parts, and a constant interaction with individual personalities."[10] Because family systems are highly complex and intensely personal, they do not yield the nature of their transactions easily to outside observers—even when that observation is sought. It takes time, a trusting relationship, a clinical ability to

---

[9] *The Field of Family Therapy* (New York: Group for the Advancement of Psychiatry, 1970).

[10] Grace Coyle, "Concepts Relevant to Helping the Family as a Group," *Social Casework* 43, no. 7 (July 1962): 350.

move back and forth between the family system level and the individual level, and considerable diagnostic skill for the therapist to unravel the complexities of group interaction and begin to discern patterns of behavior.

Family System Membership

The first problem the therapist faces is the definition of family boundaries. Who are the members who constitute the primary family system, and who are the significant relatives outside the nuclear family who influence its functioning? The matter is more complicated than simply widening the circle to include extended family members who live with or in close proximity to the nuclear family treatment group. Sometimes, a close family friend serves as an honorary kinsman with great influence on the family system. In other instances, ghosts from the parents' families of origin haunt family interaction. In still others, a dead grandparent, an absent son, or a former spouse continues to influence family functioning. It is essential for the therapist to take account of all members, present and absent, who are included by the family in its psychological world, even though the actual treatment group is necessarily much smaller.

Family System Boundary Maintenance

A family maintains its boundaries by erecting barriers between the family system and the environment. Boundary maintenance is necessary in order to preserve the integrity of the system. Outsiders must gain membership at the boundaries before they are admitted, and the culture of the nonfamily world must be evaluated before it is accepted. In a well-functioning family system, the screening process is neither so restrictive that the system becomes isolated nor so nondiscriminating that the system disintegrates. Social workers frequently deal with families whose boundaries are so diffuse that the family system has begun to dissolve. Such families are often seen as a result of problems stemming from a weak relationship system such as child neglect, truancy, marital conflict, or desertion. Social workers also work with families who guard their boundaries so vigilantly that the members are virtually sealed in and the rest of the world sealed out. Usually it is not the family itself, but someone from the community, such as a neighbor or a teacher, who becomes alarmed at the inappropriate behavior of individual family members and refers them to a mental health clinic or social agency. Because closed family systems are deprived of both inputs and corrective feedback from the environment, they develop rigid maladaptive social systems which are particularly vulnerable in times of stress which demand new behaviors. Such closed family systems are, in extreme cases, fertile breeding grounds for such problems as neurosis, psychosis, or child abuse.

Family System Goals

An important reason that family systems vary is that individual families differ in what they want to accomplish. Briar has pointed out that only by examining the goals of a particular family can the social worker determine the criteria by which it structures its member interactions and evaluates its performance.[11] While all families share roughly similar goals (i.e., the socialization of children and the meeting of adult needs) there are wide differences among families in the relative importance they attach to competing goals. One family may consider the occupational advancement of the father to be paramount, another may center its activities around the parenting function, a third may put the mother's career ahead of her homemaking role, while a fourth may favor expressive husband-wife activities at the expense of parent-child interactions. An understanding of the group goals that motivate the family of the client gives the social worker a valuable diagnostic key to the puzzle of why family power, communications, tasks, and feelings are sometimes structured in ways which on the surface appear to be irrational. Such an understanding also enables the social worker to work directly with the total family system to find more effective ways to meet group goals.

It is also important to determine the extent to which consensus exists among family members concerning the ranking of group goals. Lack of consensus may pass virtually unnoticed so long as the family system has the resources to meet the preferred objectives of all members. In times of crisis, however, when some goals must be abandoned or modified if others are to be accomplished, families are often torn by conflict or indecision in deciding among competing goals. For example, a young father may want to go back to school in order to get the academic qualifications which are needed for a desired promotion. Such a move would require the family to live on a drastically reduced budget for a year or two, and would also involve the temporary absence of the father from the home except on weekends. In such a situation, if the husband considers his career advancement the most important priority for the family and if his wife puts family "togetherness" first, conflict over goals is likely to ensue.

Structure of the Family System

One of the best ways to gain understanding of a particular family system is to analyze its structure. Family structure refers to patterned interaction among family members. All families, no matter how disorganized they may appear to the outside observer, operate under some set of stated or unstated norms.

---

[11]Scott Briar, "The Family as an Organization; An Approach to Family Diagnosis and Treatment," *Social Service Review* 38, no. 3 (September 1964): 248.

Because the family is a unity of interacting personalities the interdependence of the members must be coordinated by a set of rules, however primitive or ill-defined, which specify member relationships and roles and the allocation of resources.

According to Briar,[12] structure tends to develop in each of the major areas of family life.

1. *Division of labor.* To what extent are adult male and female roles segregated or shared? Is the division of labor equitable? Is too much or too little responsibility given to children? Is there agreement among members concerning task allocation? Are tasks performed poorly or well? Are some tasks overemphasized at the expense of others? Is family life orderly and predictable or chaotic on a day-to-day basis?

2. *Distribution of power and authority.* Can this family be characterized as patriarchal, matriarchal, democratic, or anarchic? Is the use of power and authority reasonable, consistent, and nonpunitive? Do all family members accept the distribution and use of power and authority as legitimate?

3. *Assignment of roles.* What are the roles that the family has implicitly or explicitly assigned to individual members (e.g., the good child, the bad child, the drudge, the scholar, the scapegoat)? What behaviors do these roles involve? What family needs are met by specific role assignments? What is the effect on members of their role assignments?

4. *Patterns of communication.* Who speaks to whom, who is left out, and who speaks for whom? What types of communication are not permitted? Is the communication network open and direct or blocked by distortion and ambiguity? Do members communicate their feelings of sadness, anger, tenderness, or delight appropriately or is the manner of speaking at variance with the words spoken? How are differences of opinion handled?

5. *Relationships outside the nuclear family.* How close and extensive are family ties to kin? Is the family estranged from one or more close relatives? Do relatives help the family when it is undergoing stress? To what extent are family members involved in community affairs? What are the family patterns of entertaining and visiting?

6. *Handling of feelings.* Do family norms encourage or discourage spontaneity and the open expression of both positive and negative feelings among members? Under what conditions will nurturance and praise be given and by whom? Is the family characterized by excessive displays of anger, hatred, or physical abuse? What is the role of the family pet in the emotional life of the family?

---

[12]Ibid., 251–54.

7. *Family rituals.* How does the family celebrate birthdays, anniversaries, and national holidays? What are family meals like? What leisure time activities does the family share? Does the family have its own private terminology, jokes, rituals, and symbols? Are all members included in family rituals?

Just as there is variation among total family structures in their effectiveness in meeting member needs, so do different areas within the family show variation. Some families are very well organized in certain areas and poorly organized in others. For example, the affectional substructure may be strong but the performance of housekeeping tasks weak. The distribution of power and authority may be unclear but the communication among family members direct and unambiguous. Or the division of labor may result in a very smoothly run household which does not include warm and loving interactions among family members.

It is also important to remember that family structures vary in the degree to which the needs of all members are met. For example, the division of labor may be completely satisfactory from the point of view of the husband who is exempt from chores but much less satisfying for his overburdened wife. Or the family may be structured around the needs and wishes of the children at the expense of the marital relationship of their parents.

Caseworkers and group workers, as well as family therapists, must look closely at the family structure of their clients in cases where family structure appears to be operating in such a way as to distort or inhibit the client's growth. In order to do this, it is often necessary to arrange one or more home or office appointments with the entire family. Only by direct observation can the social worker hope to get a clear diagnostic picture of the strengths and weaknesses of a particular family structure. Because a family which is not in family therapy is unlikely to view itself as a client, there are limits to what the worker can do to effect extensive structural change, and it is unlikely in the few interviews that can be arranged that the family will shift its label of "problem" from the client to its own structure. However, at the very least, the worker has the opportunity to assess the strengths and weaknesses of the family structure, and to enlist the help of the family in making specific structural changes which appear essential to the welfare of the client.

In addition, seeing the interaction of the client with other family members provides diagnostic and treatment clues which can be obtained in no other way. Family sessions bring out aspects of the client's behavior that are less evident in individual treatment sessions. For example, it is in the interaction of family members that the worker can observe, perhaps for the first time, the manipulative techniques of the family martyr, the provocative behavior of the family scapegoat, or the emotional coldness of the dutiful parent—all of whom may be unaware of their part in creating their own problems.

Variations in the complexity of family systems   Individual families differ greatly in the extent to which the behavior of members is structured. At one exteme are overorganized families which inhibit spontaneity and restrict the development of personal autonomy. In these families, members adhere to a tight schedule of duties which allows scant opportunity for self-directed leisure. At the opposite extreme are underorganized chaotic families which fail to provide the secure and nurturant environment which is essential for socialization and emotional well-being. All members in such an unpredictable environment, adults as well as children, suffer losses which can be directly attributed to the malfunctioning of the family system.

Variations in Member Participation in Shaping the Family system   Families also vary in the degree to which individual members have a role in shaping the system within which they live. In some cases, it is the patriarchal father or the matriarchal mother who sets all the rules, in others, parents divide or share this responsibility, and in still others, the children also have a voice, sometimes a very powerful one, in affecting modifications of the system. None of these ways of distributing family power has shown itself to be markedly superior to the others in terms of family happiness or the performance of the members; however, the American middle-class cultural bias tends to favor equalitarian norms which may prejudice a worker against family systems of her clients when they do not conform to this model. It is easy to forget that, contrary to popular myth, there are countless well-adjusted happy families in which husband and wife do not share interests, roles, or power to any appreciable extent, and in which little weight is given to opinions voiced by children in shaping family policy. What is important is not whether the family system of the client fits some preconceived model in the worker's head, but whether it appears to suit the needs of its members and the social norms of their group.

Variations in Member Consensus Concerning the Family System   It is also important to determine the extent to which the family system represents consensus among family members. In every family, no matter how well integrated, almost all aspects of the structure inevitably elicit a certain amount of member discontent and rebellion. Unfortunately the "perfect" family doesn't exist except in children's books, in television dramas, in advertisements aimed at the family market, and in the minds of millions of members of real-life imperfect families. Conflict is as integral a part of family life as is consensus. However, in families in which consensus about basic family values, norms, and routines is very weak or nonexistent, the survival of the group as a family unit is in jeopardy.

Variations in the Efficiency of Family Systems   Family systems also differ in the extent to which they display overall efficiency and rationality. Regardless of income and regardless of other family system characteristics, some families, for a variety of reasons, make better use of the resources available to them and are more effective in meeting their goals than others. Many highly inefficient families manage to rock along quite well until a crisis occurs in which efficiency is essential because resources are sharply diminished or member needs greatly increased. At this point, unless new coping abilities are learned, the family system begins to break down and a once marginally functional unit becomes dysfunctional. Poor families, of this type, are particularly vulnerable in times of crisis because they live close to the edge of disaster at all times and have no financial margin to allow for meeting the crisis in customary ways. Affluent families, too, are sometimes characterized by family systems which lack the efficiency to cope with serious problems. Help for such floundering families, on all economic levels, might well include short-term material and emotional support to deal with the crisis, but a family therapy focus would suggest that the long-range social work goal would be to work with the family as a unit to decrease dependency on outside resources and to increase competency in family system management and membership behaviors.

Subsystems of the Family System   Within the general family system there are three distinct subsystems—husband-wife, parent-child, and sibling. Each of these subsystems has a life of its own in the sense that it meets needs of members not satisfied elsewhere in the system. Husband and wife meet one another's adult needs in the sexual, affectional, social, economic, and home-making spheres. Parents satisfy the needs of children for nurture, protection and guidance, and children, in return, satisfy powerful parental needs. Siblings serve as near-in-age companions, rivals, models, and teachers, and in their relationship with one another first learn the costs and rewards of interacting with peers.

Ideally, all subsystems in the family operate equally well and are coordinated into a smoothly functioning whole. In the real world this is usually not the case. Few families are totally competent just as few are totally incompetent. A highly satisfactory husband-wife relationship does not ensure good performance in parent-child relationships. A very satisfactory son or daughter is sometimes an unloving sibling. An exemplary parent may be a deficient spouse. One might assume, in view of the strengths which are exhibited by family members who need help because of uneven role performance, that the modification or elimination of dysfunctional relationship patterns would be a relatively straightforward therapeutic task. Professional practitioners have learned from bitter experience that, too often, this is not the case. Now, family therapy is helping social workers to see more clearly why families, even when they appear to welcome therapeutic intervention, often find ways to sabotage the help that is given. Family therapists, by carefully observing

171

family systems in action, have been able to monitor the chain reaction which is experienced throughout the entire family system when any part of that system alters its interactional patterns. They have observed that therapeutic gains in one subsystem may cause unexpected and painful losses in another, and that family systems have powerful resources which they can mobilize to defeat efforts of outside change agents to disturb their pathological equilibrium. On the basis of these observations, family therapists are convinced that the only therapeutic strategy that can successfully effect permanent change in a client's family relationship is one which involves the total family system in the change process.

Both the family therapy literature and the direct experience of practitioners provide numerous examples of specific ways in which pathology originating in each of the three subsystems can spread throughout the entire family system. Family therapists believe that the most important and far-reaching system effects are those which originate in the husband-wife subsystem. It is in this adult relationship that the family has its beginnings and it is here that the greatest power to shape parent-child and sibling interactions resides. For example, it is not uncommon for parents who are unhappy in their marriages either to overidentify with their children in an effort to gain the love and approval not available in the adult relationship or to include the presence and behavior of the children as part of their general dissatisfaction with family life. Sometimes one or both parents will actively or covertly draw the children into the marital struggles as scapegoats, pawns, or allies. When this occurs, the sibling group is forced to take sides in an adult conflict which they neither understand nor want, and in so doing become divided from one another in their loyalties. If the marital conflict persists over an extended period of time, a new equilibrium will become established. No longer will the family system be composed of three interdependent subsystems working together in the service of family well-being but will have been replaced by a system characterized by polarized hostile coalitions and isolates functioning in the service of family pathology.

It is also common for transactions within the parent-child subsystem to enhance or diminish both the spousal relationship and the sibling relationship. For example, marital difficulties can result from the resentment of a husband toward both spouse and children when he feels that his wife is overinvolved in the role of mother and underinvolved in the role of wife. A wife may also feel deprived by her husband's greater interest in the children but, in our culture, it is more likely that her rival for her husband's attention will be his job rather than his absorption in the parental role. The parent-child subsystem can also adversely affect the sibling subsystem in cases where parental favoritism and differential treatment greatly exacerbate sibling rivalry and jealousy.

Finally, transactions within the sibling subsystem, although often overlooked by both researchers and practitioners, can contaminate the entire family system if marked by hostility and can block the flow of essential information from children to parents if marked by solidarity.

In summary, family therapists believe that disequilibrium in any of the subsystems leads to disequilibrium throughout the entire system. Families themselves, however, do not make this assumption and seldom seek help for system level problems. Indeed, they strongly resist the therapist's contention, however tactfully stated, that the family system may be part of the client's problem. The family seeks treatment, not for itself, but for a problem member who needs to be straightened out so they can all get back to normal. Therefore when a family comes for social work help with a subsystem problem that, in the worker's view, is causing or is caused by problems elsewhere in the family system, the worker must help the family to see that within the family system itself can be found both the cause and the cure of subsystem dysfunction.

Effects of the Helping Process on Family Systems   When therapists intervene in family systems in order to effect change, they sometimes underestimate the impact of the helping process itself on the family system. Social work has traditionally been the most active of all professions in helping families in situations of stress and adversity. Systems theory sharpens the conviction that practitioners have always held that unless the effect of the helping process on the entire family is taken into account, the family unit may be further weakened. Social work intervention may solve one problem only to create another. For example, an unemployed father may feel his authority has been seriously undermined when publicly funded training and job opportunities are available for his wife and teen-age children but not for him. A family may be broken by desertion because needed welfare assistance is less apt to be forthcoming with a marginally employed father in the home. Outpatient care for a mentally ill family member will enable him to remain with his family but a high price may be paid in the disruption of family routines.

The social worker whose clinical eye is focused on the total family system is more likely than one who thinks mainly in terms of individuals to recognize that help, even when it is essential, may be a mixed blessing for the family unit. As a result the family-focused worker is more apt to arrange sessions with the entire family to help them deal with the dysfunctional aspects of change in the family system so that the functional aspects will not be undermined.

The Family Life Cycle   The nuclear family, like the individual, moves through a progression of developmental stages. The family life cycle begins with a marriage, it expands as new members are added, it contracts as members leave the group, and it disappears as a unit when the founders die.

Each stage in family development involves both losses and gains for the individual members, and each transitional stress point contains the potential for family crisis. For example, the newly married couple must be able to break

173

infantile ties to parents and to establish an adult heterosexual relationship as husband and wife. When the family adds a new member, the dyadic marital relationship must be drastically altered and a new balance achieved between spousal and parental roles. As the years pass, parents must be flexible enough to give infants and growing children nurture they need, and, at the same time, to encourage age-appropriate independence, while the children must be willing to accept the responsibility of increasing maturity. Inevitably, if the life cycle progresses normally, parents are faced with the task of letting their grown children go, and the children must find the courage to reject dependency and to accept autonomy. As the family cycle of the parental marriage enters its final stages and the new family cycle of the children and their spouses begins, both parents and children have the task of accepting a new kind of closeness and a new kind of difference unencumbered by feelings toward one another of anger, guilt, or dependency.

Families often seek social work help when the members are experiencing problems in moving out of one stage of development and into another. Sometimes the very strengths which have made an earlier stage successful become liabilities when new behaviors are required. For instance, a highly nurturing mother may cope very well with the needs of babies and small children but find herself unable to accept the emerging sexuality and independence of the early adolescent period. Or a man may be a loving and supportive spouse but an impatient or disinterested new father.

Transitional stress, if not successfully resolved, can result in permanent family dysfunction since the tasks of each stage of family development must be successfully mastered in order for the family to move on to the next. Sometimes, for this to occur, the social worker must work with all family members to help them resolve their ambivalence about change, and to accept new tasks and new roles.

The Multigenerational Transmission Process   Although parents die and siblings scatter, adult children continue to carry their families of origin with them as long as they live. Thus there is a strong thread of continuity from generation to generation as children socialized in one family become spouses and parents in another, bringing to the family of procreation patterns of behavior learned in the family of origin. Most clients are initially unable to see the clinical relevance of the extended family to their specific problems, but family therapists are convinced that difficulties within the current family are often best understood as reflections or extensions of unfinished relationship struggles in the family of origin. Murray Bowen, an eminent family therapy theorist, believes that the family projection process continues to operate through many generations. In this process the weakest members of each generation are most vulnerable to pathological patterns of family behavior while stronger members are less affected. In extreme cases, a downward spiral can occur in which the most impaired members of a family transmit ever more virulent family pathology from generation to generation. Bowen believes that a downward spiral continuing over eight to ten generations is required to produce a schizophrenic child.[13]

The strength of the multigenerational transmission process lies in its obscurity. Clients do not know that they are being crippled in their present family relationships by the burden of unfinished emotional business with parents, siblings, and other relatives.

Many family therapists help troubled nuclear families to reestablish contact with kin in order to reevaluate the past with adult eyes and to establish a new basis for mutual support and understanding within the extended family. In short, a viable emotional relationship with kin appears to family therapists to be a very important factor in the well-being of the nuclear family.

Family Interaction   Patterns of family interaction reflect a basic dilemma of human existence—the desire for both closeness and independence in relationship with others. The never-ending struggle between the "I" and "We" can be seen in the shifting balance of family alliances. Members vacillate along an emotional continuum between the ever present dangers of total fusion and total detachment in one-to-one relationships between husband-wife, parent-child, and brother-sister. Most families are able to avoid the extremes, but a minority of troubled families can be characterized as either enmeshed or detached. Murray Bowen describes the highly enmeshed family as an undifferentiated ego mass in which the boundaries between the individual members are blurred and in which the unique characteristics of members are submerged in order to eliminate the possibility of difference or conflict. In contrast, a detached family is characterized by the extreme individualism of members and the emotional distance which separates one from another.[14] In either case, the focus of a social worker using a family systems approach would be primarily on restructuring dysfunctional relationships between family members and only secondarily on treating individual pathology.

Triangles   Inevitably, when any two-person relationship system becomes too threatening, too demanding, or too intense, one of the members moves to create distance between the two by bringing a third person, object, or issue into the system. By converting an unstable twosome into a triangle, the need to deal directly with one another is avoided. All people regulate their dyadic relationships through the use of triangles, and in most cases triangles serve

---

[13]Murray Bowen, "Theory in the Practice of Psychotherapy," in *Family Therapy-Theory and Practice,* ed. Philip J. Guerin (New York: Wiley, 1976), p. 86.

[14]Ibid., pp. 65–75.

the very useful purpose of defusing the inevitable tensions of day-to-day interactions. However, in some situations, triangles are harmful because they are used to evade serious interpersonal problems which demand solutions. For example, a husband and wife may avoid marital strife by making their child a scapegoat for their frustrations with one another. Or the wife may bring a sympathetic friend into the relationship to listen to confidences about marital problems which cannot be openly confronted. Or the unwary social worker may find himself absorbed in a triangle where he is pressured to take sides of both husband and wife. Or the third component of the triangle may be political differences of the couple, or a mutual enemy, or the high involvement of one of the spouses with television, golf, or gardening. In fact, anything or anybody that allows the couple to avoid the real issues between them can serve as the stabilizing factor in their relationship. Unfortunately as long as a triangle persists, it prevents any straightforward resolution of dyadic problems.

The aim of the family therapist, when he finds dysfunctional triangles operating within a family, is to help the individuals involved to move back into one-to-one interactions in order to work out their relationship problems. A family functions best when each member is able to relate to every other member openly and responsibly, even though in the short run conflict may increase.

The Family Treatment Process   According to Freeman,[15] family treatment consists of three stages—definition, working through, and termination. In the first stage, the social worker has the difficult task of reassigning the role of client from the individual member to the total family unit. This is a new and frightening approach and initially family members will resist changing their definition of the problem. Carl Whitaker calls this stage the "struggle for structure."

If the view of the social worker prevails, treatment moves into the middle stage in which family interaction processes constitute the most crucial part of the treatment process. In this stage, the family no longer concentrates on the shortcomings of the original client, but works on problems and issues affecting the entire group. During this often painful process of self-examination, the family itself does most of the therapeutic work and it comes to know that it is its own best treatment resource. The worker, however, is also very much involved in the ongoing interactions. He helps the family members define the issues, he encourages them to deal directly with one another, he insists that each member take responsibility for his own actions and his own

---

[15]David Freeman, "Phases of Family Treatment," *The Family Coordinator* 25, no. 3 (July 1976):265–70.

statements, and he works with them in extending their family boundaries to include kin and community resources in their support system.

The ending stage is reached when the family sees that it has acquired sufficient internal and external resources to deal with its problems alone. Because the relationship between the worker and the group is usually much less intense than is the case in individual treatment, dependency problems are less likely to hinder termination. Indeed, it has been demonstrated that many families can successfully complete treatment within the relatively short span of eight to twelve sessions.

In all stages of the treatment process, the family therapist tends to be more active, more spontaneous, more present-oriented, and more task-centered than the therapist working with an individual client. In his dual role of participant and observer, the therapist faces the ever-present danger of becoming caught in the family pathology because of unresolved conflicts from his own past. For this reason, it is essential that he come to terms with his personal family history so that it does not handicap him in his efforts to help other families solve their problems.

CONCLUSION

In this chapter, the emphasis has been on concepts which describe the functioning of the family as a small social system. These concepts are currently being translated into practice by social workers in a wide range of settings. While most social workers will continue to work primarily with individuals, the family therapy orientation adds a new and exciting dimension to both diagnosis and treatment. However, because the family therapy method is still in an early stage of development, many questions about its use remain unanswered. Therefore, each worker must rely to some extent on his own judgment in choosing among a variety of theoretical emphases and practice principles. Is a particular family best served by using a family approach alone, a combined family and individual approach, or individual treatment only? Are these instances in which open communication among family members is more harmful than helpful? To what extent should sexual concerns of parents be discussed with children present? Should young children be included in the treatment group at all? Should family treatment be refused to families if one of the members refuses to participate? Should past family relationships with parents and grandparents be emphasized or should the focus be mainly on current family functioning? As yet there are no definitive answers to questions such as these. It is hoped that social work practitioners and researchers will continue to learn more about the specific ways in which a family systems orientation can be used to enhance service to all client groups.

BIBLIOGRAPHY

Ackerman, Nathan, W. *Treating the Troubled Family.* New York: Basic Books, 1966.

Beels, C. C., and A. S. Ferber. "Family Therapy: A View." *Family Process* 8 (1969): 280–310.

Haley, Jay. *Problem Solving Therapy.* San Francisco: Jossey-Bass, 1976.

Jackson, D. D., and W. I. Lederer. *Mirages of Marriage.* New York: Norton, 1969.

Macgregor, R., et al. *Multiple Impact Therapy with Families.* New York: McGraw-Hill, 1964.

Minuchin, Salvador, et al. *Families of the Slums: An Exploration of Their Structure and Treatment.* New York: Basic Books, 1967.

————. *Families and Family Therapy.* Cambridge: Harvard University Press, 1974.

Satir, Virginia. *Conjoint Family Therapy.* Palo Alto: Science and Behavior, 1964.

8
SOCIAL GROUP WORK

JANICE H. SCHOPLER AND MAEDA J. GALINSKY

School of Social Work, University of North
Carolina

Social group work is perhaps best characterized today by its diversity, a diversity that spans client populations, client problems, and social work settings. Consider, for example, the group experiences described by several social workers at a recent meeting. One had just begun meeting with residents in a housing project to help them organize so they could have more voice in housing authority policies. A social worker from the state mental hospital was conducting sessions with a group of patients in relation to their individual discharge plans. A school social worker had been consulted about grouping problems within the sixth-grade classroom. A social worker from the YWCA was arranging a series of workshops for women on changing sex roles.

Another "Y" worker was acting as a co-leader with a colleague from the community mental health center at weekly encounter sessions.[1]

These experiences are representative of the direct and consultative work that social workers are doing to meet client needs as they use groups for many purposes, including treatment, education, recreation, growth, and environmental or social action. At one time, social group work was a narrowly defined specialty that could be most easily described by designating the activities of a small number of "group workers." They worked in selected settings such as settlement houses, "Ys," and camps where groups were the core of the program. Today, social group work has become a method whose theory and techniques may be applied to a wide range of situations, problems, and questions.[2] We define social group work as one of the methods of social work practice, based on the values and ethics of the social work profession, using groups as the primary means to provide services to clients, to help them enhance their individual functioning, or to help them deal with personal, group, or community problems.[3]

While we will stress the use of groups for the purpose of meeting client needs, it should be noted that groups are also widely used within the profession of social work for training, supervision, and program development as well as for enhancing the personal growth of social workers. In addition, there are many group models used by professionals in social work, psychology, education, and psychiatry. Although social group work can be differentiated as a social work method for helping clients, many techniques from other models and from other professions have been usefully applied within the framework of the social work profession. Why this burgeoning interest in groups in all of the helping professions?

The proliferation in the use of groups can be attributed to a variety of developments in our society and within the profession of social work. Social scientists have long recognized the importance of groups in the socialization

---

[1]The group examples presented throughout this chapter to illustrate the range of group work services available today are composites created from our own field experience and from group experiences that have been shared with us. We respect the confidentiality of these experiences and stress that any resemblance to an actual group or individual is purely coincidental. We express our appreciation to our colleagues and especially to our students for helping us keep our perspective current with respect to social group work.

[2]This definitional change over the years is apparent in the *Social Work Year Book,* now referred to as the *Encyclopedia of Social Work.*

[3]This definition is in basic agreement with the generalizations reached about social group work in the 1959 Curriculum Study and encompasses the current conceptions of social group work reported in the most recent *Encyclopedia of Social Work.* See Marjorie Murphy, "The Social Group Work Method in Social Work Education," in *A Project Report of Curriculum Study,* XI, Werner W. Boehm, Director and Coordinator (New York: Council on Social Work Education, 1959), p. 78; and *Encyclopedia of Social Work,* Vol. II (New York: National Association of Social Workers, 1971), pp. 1251, 1256, 1265

process.[4] We grow within basic family units and learn to be social beings as we relate to others in groups at play, in friendship, in the classroom, and at work. It is in these groups that we learn to feel secure or insecure, become effective or ineffective in relating to others, gain a sense of mastery or of failure. We spend a large portion of our daily lives in groups, and these associations are crucial in determining the ways we think and act and feel. In recent years, our understanding of these social units has become more sophisticated. Thus part of the current group vogue can be attributed to the knowledge explosion. We have an ever-increasing number of group theories and techniques to apply in understanding and meeting the needs of our clients. Perhaps more importantly, however, the increasing demands of our complex society have led us to a renewed search for meaning and the mutual support of our fellow man. This search may well underlie the popular movement toward group associations, such as encounter weekends, consciousness-raising sessions, theme-centered workshops, and human potential experiences.[5] As a result of the prominent use of groups in our culture, both social workers and clients are likely to see groups as a viable means for meeting needs.

Effective use of the group requires a social worker to have an understanding of how small groups operate, how they affect their members, and how they relate to the environment. While it is true that there are a number of different social group work models or approaches to meeting client needs, all models build on this knowledge base concerning small groups. Social workers have gained their practice wisdom and their experience about groups from a variety of sources. They work in settings with a wide range of functions and meet with clients who have very different problems, needs, and concerns. Social group work training thus reflects the common base of knowledge about groups, common elements of working with groups, and the differing perspectives for viewing groups.

The present chapter provides a framework for understanding the diverse use of groups in social work. An examination of group work history reveals some of the theories, techniques, and practice principles that social workers have drawn on and developed to meet the varied demands for service over the years; and a brief overview of current group work practice illustrates the

---

[4]The socialization process is defined even by reference to our group relationships. See Secord and Backman, who state, "Currently, socialization is thought of as an interaction process whereby a person's behavior is modified to conform with expectations held by members of the groups to which he belongs." Paul F. Secord and Carl W. Backman, *Social Psychology* (New York: McGraw-Hill, 1964), pp. 525–26.

[5]Back points out that today's group movement in many ways parallels the events of an earlier day when huge numbers sought spiritual meaning in pilgrimages. See Kurt W. Back, *Beyond Words* (New York: Russell Sage Foundation, 1972), p. 26.

range of group services, some of the reasons for using the group method today, and the typical course of a group. In the next chapter we present excerpts from the record of a social work group in a junior high school.

HISTORICAL PERSPECTIVE

The history of social group work has been very much intertwined with the needs and the mood of the times. Its beginnings were in the settlement houses, which were part of the social reform movement of the late nineteenth century.[6] Social workers of this period were outraged at the impossible living and working conditions of the poor and immigrant city dwellers who were crammed into slum housing, working long hours seven days a week. These people had no social or recreational outlets and no effective political voice. Overworked and frequently separated from the society around them by language and cultural barriers, they had neither time, energy, nor resources to change their situation.

In 1889 Jane Addams founded Hull House in Chicago to serve this population, and similar organizations soon followed in New York and other urban areas. Settlement houses provided a center for neighborhood activity—places where people were able to become acquainted, form relationships in small interest groups, share in recreational and cultural offerings, and begin to learn how to live in the cities of America. At the settlements, neighbors met each other through dances, clubs, and recreational activities, and found much needed services such as health clinics, legal and housing counseling, and nurseries. Citizenship classes were a particularly prominent part of these early settlement programs. Here, many adults for the first time gained some understanding of their rights under a democratic form of government; in addition, immigrants learned English and prepared for citizenship tests. Around the turn of the century, settlement workers and the poor they had helped organize fought for improved housing, better working conditions, child labor laws, and recreational facilities. Until the end of World War I, group work was identified as part of the settlement house movement. This early action-oriented concept of group work, emphasizing the value of social and recreational activities and the power of group associations for political purposes, continues in the present day to influence aspects of social work with groups.

As the rate of immigration decreased and as America became more prosperous in the 1920s, attention turned from the poor to the growing middle class. Agencies such as the Young Men's and Young Women's Christian

---

[6]For an excellent overview of the history of social group work, see Ruth R. Middleman, *The Non-Verbal Method in Working with Groups* (New York: Association Press, 1968), chap. 1.

Associations, Boy Scouts and Girl Scourts, 4-H Clubs, and Community Centers were organized to provide socialization for the young and wholesome leisure-time activities for all age groups. The concern with societal problems was still alive as "Y" workers helped members in their struggles for women's rights, voting rights, union participation, and an eight-hour working day; similarly, many of the children's organizations grew out of a belief in every child's right to fresh air and recreation. Increasingly, however, group services, influenced by the writings of Eduard C. Lindeman and John Dewey, were directed toward providing educative experiences for average, normal citizens.[7] Group involvement for recreation or action provided individuals with an opportunity to gain new interests and knowledge, as well as skills in democratic functioning.

The marked increase in the use of groups led to beginning efforts to formulate group work as a professional approach in the 1930s. Since group workers came from many different fields, there was much disagreement about the definition of the method and the professional identification of group workers. Grace Coyle played a major part in guiding group work toward the profession of social work through her activities in the 1930s.[8] In general, however, the informal activity-oriented group work approach for normal people and social reform seemed alien to caseworkers of the day who were developing a formalized, problem-based method with a focus on treating the individual.[9] Thus the movement of group work into social work was slow.

Toward the end of the 1930s, group workers had begun to extend their efforts to a new area—the treatment of individuals in and through the group. Therapeutic groups had been attempted in the past; in fact, youthful drug addicts at Hull House had met in groups in 1909 and experimental groups were first tried with the emotionally disturbed at Chicago State Hospital in 1918. In these and other early efforts, however, group workers had been viewed as recreational adjuncts to the "real" treatment programs conducted by caseworkers, psychiatrists, and psychologists. The new perspective on group work, in contrast, advocated that treatment needs could be met in groups and that group workers could be treatment specialists.

During the decade of the 1940s, group workers became established in child guidance clinics, hospitals, correctional institutions, and other mental

---

[7]Eduard C. Lindeman, "The Roots of Democratic Culture," in *Group Work, Foundations and Frontiers,* ed. Harleigh B. Trecker (New York: Whiteside, and William Morrow Co., 1955), pp. 13–25; and Middleman, *Non-Verbal Method,* p. 27.

[8]Gisela Konopka, *Social Group Work: A Helping Process* (Englewood Cliffs, N. J.: Prentice-Hall, 1963), pp. 11–13.

[9]Paul Simon, ed., *Play and Game Theory in Group Work, A Collection of Papers by Neva Leona Boyd* (Chicago: The Jane Addams Graduate School of Social Work at the University of Illinois, 1971, p. 12.

health settings. Here, their focus was on personal adjustment, insight, and self-understanding rather than on social reform, citizenship training, and recreation. By the end of the 1940s, following much debate, group work had achieved a professional identity and was closely aligned with social work. The American Association of Group Workers, formed in 1946, had a place within the National Conference on Social Work [10] and published a statement defining the function of the group worker as an enabler who used both group interaction and program activities to contribute to individual growth and the achievement of desirable goals.[11]

Events during the 1950s completed group work's union with social work. Group workers continued to clarify their methodology and moved into even more traditional casework settings, such as welfare departments and public schools, where they focused on individual change through the group method. Schools of social work now not only offered courses in group work but also gave it the status of a major. Finally, in 1955, group workers joined with other parts of the social work profession—the caseworkers, policy makers, administrators, and community organizers—to form the National Association of Social Workers.[12]

This completed group work's entry into the profession of social work and led to other influences on the development of group work purposes and methodology. As the group method became accepted, caseworkers began to meet with their clients in groups and had new ideas about the use of groups. Supervised training opportunities within social work were not expanding as rapidly as interest in groups, so social workers often apprenticed themselves to group psychotherapists and brought the perspective of group therapy into social work. Some social workers returned from personal group experiences, such as summer laboratory training sessions, and applied their new insights about groups in their work with clients. In still other situations, social workers were the first to form groups as they recognized the natural ties between clients who were from the same community or who lived together in an institution. Thus group work was no longer practiced only by "group workers" but was becoming one of several methods social workers could use in serving their clients.

Out of the experience and discussion that followed during the 1950s and 1960s, a written methodology developed which identifies common elements of the group method and serves as a guide to social work practitioners. This methodology is built upon the professional values of social work and the practice wisdom that has developed over the years. In the tradition of group work, it relies heavily on the growing body of social science knowledge,

---

[10]Grace L. Coyle, "Group Work in Psychiatric Settings: Its Roots and Branches," *Social Work* 6, no. 1 (January 1959): 74.

[11]Middleman, *Non-Verbal Method,* p. 36.

[12]Ibid., p. 39.

especially in the areas of social psychology, sociology, and personality theory. Some of the more prominent theorists include Gisela Konopka, Helen Phillips, Robert Vinter, William Schwartz, Alan Klein, and Helen Northen. Although these writers agree that social workers face common tasks as they work with groups, they view these tasks with varying perspectives. In their writings, they emphasize different facets of group operation and have proposed a number of somewhat different strategies and principles for working with groups. Social workers also utilize many other group approaches, such as T-group, encounter, gestalt, behavior modification, and transactional analysis, when these seem useful to the clients they are serving and compatible with the ethics of the profession. Of course, practitioners who use these additional approaches need to obtain specialized training and supervision.[13]

The current scene in group work reflects a continuing diversity in keeping with the historical development of the method. There is a concern with the social environment and with effecting change in social institutions, a concern present at the inception of group work in the nineteenth century. There is an emphasis on democratic traditions in group functioning, planful use of activities, and the enhancement of normal growth and development, which was characteristic of the 1920s and 1930s. There is also a thrust toward treatment of individuals, which has been prominent since the 1940s. These various historical influences will become evident as we look at some of the situations where social workers use the group work method today.

THE SOCIAL WORKER IN THE GROUP

The following case vignettes represent a limited array of social workers' activities with groups. While the range of social group work purposes and skills is much wider than indicated below, these illustrations should provide the reader with some "feel" for the current scene in social group work.

In an elementary school, four first-grade children have been referred to the school social worker because they can't sit still in class, disrupt the work of other children, and can't be controlled by the teacher. The social worker plans a series of group sessions to help them learn more appropriate classroom behavior. Meetings include activities such as playing school, baking, and listening to stories.

A social worker at a community mental health center has been seeing several women who are expressing frustration about handling the behavior of their pre-

[13]For a summary of a variety of current group techniques, see John B. P. Shaffer and M. David Galinsky, *Models of Group Therapy and Sensitivity Training* (Englewood Cliffs, N.J.: Prentice-Hall, 1974).

school-age children. She begins meeting with these mothers as a group. Much of the meeting time is spent discussing the problems of toilet training and eating behavior. The mothers share ideas on handling themselves and their children's behavior. Members gain insight and feel relief as they recognize their commonalities, find solutions, and, at times, relate their current difficulties to their own childhood experiences.

Several inmates at a state prison complain to the social worker about the restrictions and boredom of prison life. The social worker begins to meet with these men to explore their concerns. As a result of their discussion, they become involved in planning a Christmas party. Their responsible behavior during this and other activities is noted by the warden. Somewhat later, he authorizes the formation of an Inmate Council, with the social worker as a sponsor.

An adoption agency is looking for a more effective way to respond to inquiries during the initial phase of application. After considering several alternatives, two of the social workers form an orientation group, which meets once a month. All couples who have applied for adoption during that month are invited to attend an evening meeting. During the meeting, the workers explain agency and legal procedures that will be followed, the requirements for adoption, and the kinds of experiences the applicants may anticipate. Questions are encouraged to clarify concerns, and a movie about a couple involved in adoption is shown to stimulate discussion. The sessions help the prospective parents gain information, share concerns, and more fully consider whether they want to continue the adoption process.

Several elderly women who live near a community center discuss with the social worker in charge of the program some of the difficulties they face in living alone. She helps them plan a number of sessions related to their concerns. The first few meetings include practical presentations by resource people such as a public health nurse and a home economist, discussion, and socializing. The people who attend share useful ideas and have an enjoyable outing. Some of the regular participants form a club and become active in recruiting other elderly people to join.

WHY USE GROUPS?

In each of the situations described above, the clients brought very different problems to the social worker. Why was group work the method of choice? The first-graders might have been seen alone in conferences and engaged there in play therapy; each of the mothers had already established a relationship with the social worker and could have gained insight and expert advice from her; the complaints of the prison inmates, the questions of the adoption applicants, and the concerns of the elderly could have been handled individually. To provide a basis for justifying group work as the appropriate method in each of these situations, we need first address ourselves to the more basic question: What is there about the nature of groups that is potentially effective? or *Why use groups?*

Small Group Forces

As we mentioned earlier, groups are a natural and, currently, very popular context for many of our daily activities. They also exert a tremendous influence on the way we think and feel and act.

For the first-graders, the mothers, and the prison inmates, the selection of the group method meant that the social workers could draw on the power of the group to help these clients achieve their goals. When the first-graders make their own rules about hand raising and being quiet while others talk, the group will enforce these behaviors more fiercely than any adult. Members tend to accept and abide by group rules they have helped formulate much more readily than they follow the directives of a leader or authority figure.

Small group forces do not, however, automatically produce beneficial results for their members. All of us can recall "bad" as well as "good" group experiences. A social worker who uses the group method productively for clients must have some understanding of how groups are structured, how they operate, and how these forces can be guided or redirected.

The same small group forces present in a delinquent gang are also present in a successful treatment group such as the one for mothers of preschoolers; yet, in the gang, group pressures move members toward destructive behavior, while in the mothers' group, positive changes are encouraged and supported. To ensure that the treatment group would be helpful to its members, the social worker had to actively affect the group's structures and processes. Initially, in composing the group, she selected mothers who were compatible, who were facing similar difficulties, and who had a range of experience to share; she helped members select realistic goals in relation to their child-management problems; she directed the group in establishing norms that would require the mothers to attend meetings, to participate in discussion, and to try out new behaviors; and she encouraged relationships among members so that the group would become cohesive and members would help each other. When forming a group, a social worker takes responsibility for creating and maintaining group conditions. In contrast, a social worker who begins work with a natural group, such as a gang, may need to change existing group patterns. Before the powerful ties among members can become a positive influence, gang members would need to be motivated to set different, more socially acceptable goals and would need to modify their norms to support the new goals.

In any case, groups can be a potent force for change. This quality makes groups an effective means for helping many clients but also calls for caution in their use. The social worker who selects the group approach needs to

187

ensure that the group is operating to help, not hinder, the attainment of its members' goals.

Commonality of Members

In discussing small group forces, our focus was primarily on groups as an aid to the worker in meeting client needs. We are also concerned with the viewpoints of the members and what groups have to offer them. For many people, it is a tremendous relief to know that there are others like themselves, people who have similar interests or who share similar burdens. Whenever it seems that clients can benefit from recognizing the commonalities of their situation, group service should be considered.

With the mothers of the preschoolers, for example, the social worker recognized the mothers' pressing need for relief from their frustrations. Although she could empathize with each of them individually, she could only indirectly experience with them the fury of a two-year-old's tantrum or the tyranny of a three-year-old's absolute refusal to eat. Only other mothers who had been overwhelmed by the same feelings of inadequacy in the face of a toddler's defiance could fully share in the meaning of these experiences. The social worker could clarify the problems, point out strengths, help identify weaknesses, provide consultation, and be a source of support, but the mothers were living testimony to each other that they were not alone in their difficulties. Knowing that "it's not just me, others have this problem too," can be the greatest reassurance of one's ability to handle a problem.

The support provided by other members can go beyond the confines of a meeting. Whereas a social worker is often restricted to giving help during a conference or over the phone, members may see each other outside the agency. Through the club formed as a result of the sessions at the community center, many of the elderly people made new friends in the neighborhood and gained continuing support from these relationships. In many situations, the help members can give each other between meetings is crucial in helping them attain their goals. For example, mental patients who meet weekly in a socialization group can give each other daily encouragement as they try out new behaviors on the ward. Without this constant reinforcement, new social skills might be forgotten before the next meeting.

At times, age and cultural differences create barriers to communication between social workers and their clients. To a black mother on welfare, it may well seem impossible that her white middle-class social worker can accept or help someone who is poor and black and uneducated. Even when the social worker makes direct inquiries about her problems, she smiles and reports that things are fine. In circumstances like these, clients may be more comfortable when discussing their difficulties with others who have had similar experiences. The welfare mother, for example, is used to going to her neighbors for help and gives them a hand when she can. "Mutual aid" is a part of her life style. Thus when the social worker invites her to a meeting with other mothers from her area, she unloads her troubles and asks for the group's help. She also becomes active in giving suggestions to other members. In another instance, Sam, a teen-ager with a retarded sister, has never admitted to the social worker in individual or family conferences that his handicapped sibling is frequently a source of embarrassment to him. Although he bitterly resents his sister on these occasions, he feels this attitude isn't "right." In a group with other teen-agers, he hears a girl his own age describe how "mortified" she is when strangers stare at her retarded sister; suddenly, it seems "okay" to feel this way, and Sam is free to express his own feelings.

As these cases illustrate, sharing a common frame of reference can help clients feel more easy and is an important factor in considering whether group service would be beneficial for particular clients. In fact, one reason the adoption agency decided to use a group approach for handling the inquiries of prospective parents was to create a more comfortable atmosphere. Couples attending an orientation session relaxed as they learned that others had similar anxieties about adopting a child. With this reassurance, they "opened up" and were able to ask the questions that had been troubling them.

The common nature of the group members' roles as clients is one means of overcoming or avoiding group members' possible resistance to the social worker. No matter how benign, the social worker is often seen as an authority figure by virtue of his or her professional status and agency position, and thus members may be unwilling or unable to engage themselves with the worker. This is particularly true in situations where the client is a resident of an institution that governs his life twenty-fours hours a day and makes vital decisions that affect his freedom and movements. When group members can feel the support of the group and know they are not alone and powerless, they may be able to respond positively to the worker. In the prison situation, the social worker's willingness to meet with the inmates as a group, and his encouragement of group action, prevented the inmates from labeling him as a stooge for the administration—someone whose role is to uphold prison rules and pacify prisoners.

Members can also gain a more realistic view of their situations through a group experience. It is easy to deny the severity of a problem until we see someone in a similar position. Putting off any serious study for yet another day will work until a roommate comes back from class with a failing quiz grade; suddenly, all rationalizations collapse and the books come out. In like fashion, group members may alter their perceptions as they hear accounts from other members' lives. For instance, in a parents' group meeting with a child guidance worker, Mrs. Smith describes her son's aggressive, and sometimes sadistic, behavior toward other children as typical boyish behavior. At a later meeting she hears another parent express deep concern about his son's activity. This father relates an incident that ended in another child's trip to the emergency room. Mrs. Smith sees a resemblance to her own son's behavior and recognizes that she has been denying the severity of his problems.

Sharing does not always have to be problem-focused. Meeting with others who have the same interests can be a very fulfilling experience, and groups may be formed to help clients develop these interests. For instance, adolescent girls in an institution may ask for help in learning personal grooming habits. Several men in a halfway house may inquire about pursuing their woodworking skills. Mental patients may want to learn soccer and form teams. Parents of handicapped children may become interested in organizing to gain more effective special education facilities. In all these situations, groups would be an appropriate means for helping clients pursue their common interests and develop their potential.

From the client's point of view, a group experience may be desirable for several reasons. In a group, clients may find relief in knowing they face the same difficulties or fulfillment in sharing experiences and interests. For some, it is easier to talk about concerns with those whose lives are similar; sometimes, their support means more and may be more enduring. Despite these advantages, groups are not for everyone. Some clients resent the lack of privacy in a group; others are terrified at having their lives on display before so many; and still others may think that a group is a waste of time—they want to hear solutions to their own problems, not accounts of the mistakes of others. Every client must be evaluated individually to determine whether a group experience will be a benefit or a burden.

Creative and Problem-solving Potential

Groups provide an arena where members exchange their ideas and opinions, act out their problems, engage in novel experiences, and stimulate each other to new ideas. The varied perspectives and range of experiences members bring to the group are a rich resource as members begin to work together. Further, as they form relationships with each other, members recreate aspects of the world outside the group; in this way the group provides a realistic proving ground for new behaviors, attitudes, and ideas. It is fallacious, of course, to argue that groups are always superior for problem-solving efforts or that group "brainstorming" produces more creative ideas than individual thought.[14] Groups can, however, work out solutions that might never de-

---

[14]For a comparision of group versus individual problem solving, with a review of current research, see Harold H. Kelley and John W. Thibaut, "Group Problem Solving," in *The Handbook of Social Psychology*, ed. Gardner Lindzey and Elliot Aronson (Reading, Mass.: Addison-Wesley, 1969), IV, pp. 61–88.

velop from an individual conference or might never be accepted if offered by a social worker alone.

The creative potential of groups derives from member differences as well as from their similarities. As they meet with the worker, they bring together a far broader base of experience and ideas than any individual would have. The game a mother has developed for feeding her toddler, the techniques a prisoner uses to keep his "cool" when provoked by guards, or the way adoptive parents reveal to their child the story of his adoption may never occur to the members (or to the social worker) who are also wrestling with these difficulties.

As a group draws on the resources of its members, creative solutions often emerge. For instance, in the prison inmates' group, the idea of an Inmate Council grew from the complaints of the members about prison life and their work together to relieve some of these pressures. In a group of welfare mothers interested in affecting employment opportunities, the members find avenues for opening up job training for unskilled workers in a new shopping center. Such solutions would not be possible without a pooling of member potential.

Besides enabling members to find solutions to their problems and to develop their interests, groups allow the ready identification of member problems through the members' interactions in the group. Many of the difficulties that brought clients to the group appear spontaneously as members relate to each other and to the worker. Husbands who dominate their wives, children who hit classmates, and clients who dress inappropriately for job interviews are likely to act in a similar fashion in group meetings. When such behaviors occur, the group has an opportunity to identify problems and discuss the consequences of these actions. Positive behaviors can also be pointed out and supported.

Because people often manifest their strengths and weaknesses in group interaction, groups are useful for diagnostic purposes. Many agencies, such as child guidance clinics, group homes, and treatment institutions, have required that applicants participate in a diagnostic group prior to acceptance so that their interaction with the current population can be observed. Data gathered from such diagnostic sessions provide the treatment staff with an additional basis for assessing whether or not the applicant's needs can be met by the agency's current program.

Since client problems are sometimes confined to their performance in specific roles, it may be helpful to purposefully re-create problem situations in the group. A mother who becomes livid when dealing with her defiant daughter may appear very controlled in other situations. In cases like this, groups provide a useful context for evoking problem behavior and for experimenting with new behaviors through the use of role playing or other programming techniques. As the mother role-plays a typical scene with her daughter, the group can see problematic responses and, during the discussion, can make suggestions about different ways for the mother to behave. The mother may even reenact the scene and try to implement the hints from the group.

The school social worker who was referred to the first-graders used activities as well as role playing to help the children learn more acceptable classroom behavior. Activities can be planned to provide clients with an opportunity to develop skills in problem areas. Girls in a YWCA group who have trouble working together may be motivated to cooperate with each other by engaging them in a brownie-baking project. Adult groups may use nonverbal exercises to understand and deal with problems. A group of alcoholics, habitually jailed for public drunkenness, continually deny that drinking is a problem for them. As one member, Mr. B., puts it, he could "walk away from the bottle" any time he wants. The social worker capitalizes on this declaration by involving the group in acting out Mr. B.'s statement. The social worker designates himself as the "bottle," grasps Mr. B. firmly around the middle, and then directs him to "walk away." After this demonstration, the other group members pair off and participate in the exercise. The discussion that follows indicates that this is an insightful experience.

As members meet together, they can draw on their collective resources to achieve their goals. Not only do they bring ideas from their past experiences to share in the group, but they also discover that the group itself can stimulate new ways of thinking and acting. Group techniques such as role playing, activities, exercises, and games combine with discussion and group interaction to generate ideas and action, promote member growth, and resolve problems.

Convenience

In addition to the factors already discussed, it is important to note that the group approach is at times the most "convenient" way to provide much-needed services. Clients may already be in a natural group in a neighborhood or in a work group; they may make the same requests for service; or the agency may identify similar needs. For instance, at a medical out-patient clinic, arthritic patients awaiting their appointments are encouraged to meet with a social worker in one section of the lounge to discuss questions and problems related to their arthritis. The social worker discusses general information about their disease and indicates resources such as places for purchasing discount drugs and special household equipment; patients have an opportunity to exchange practical suggestions about furniture arrangements, shortcuts to shopping, and gadgets to make household tasks easier. Seeing each of these patients individually would be impossible for the hospital's present social service staff, and without this informal group, waiting time would be wasted and questions unanswered.

Whenever a number of people need information, a group should be considered. Groups are generally as time consuming as seeing people singly. They require planning, follow-up on meetings, special individual conferences, and worker interventions in the client's environment, in addition to group meetings. Frequently, however, facts can be presented and questions answered more efficiently in a group. This was one rationale for the orientation sessions planned by the adoption agency. Groups similar to this one may prove useful when clients are facing any new experience. Examples include people entering a mental hospital or prison, disabled persons applying for financial aid, and adolescent girls experiencing their first pregnancy. Although the group may serve as an appropriate vehicle for conveying information and stimulating questions, the importance of individualizing during crucial times such as these should not be forgotten. The group may not be the only service needed and is not always the best approach for all clients.

An Answer

We have explored the power of small group forces, the benefits derived from the commonality of members, the creative and problem-solving potential of groups, and the convenience of the group method. Many reasons have emerged for using social group work, but as yet there is no single answer to the question, "Why use groups?" At present, we have no definitive criteria for determining whether individual, group, or family methods are indicated in a specific case. Thus whenever a client seeks help, the costs and benefits of various methods of service must be weighed. When it is determined that social group work is an appropriate service, groups are formed to meet the special needs of clients. The diversity of social group work is apparent from our illustrations; yet all of these approaches to group work share common patterns of group development.

HOW GROUPS DEVELOP

The development of any group will reflect the unique characteristics of its members and their situations. A friendship group that develops in a dormitory over the course of a year may appear to have a very different type of beginning, middle, and ending then a weekend encounter group. Nevertheless, the members in both groups will need to handle similar problems during the course of their group's life. These groups must find a reason for being and a way of operating; relationships must be maintained and tasks must be completed; and, at some point, associations must be terminated. It is these common elements of group life that provide social workers with a basis for understanding and guiding group development.

There are many ways to chart group movement.[15] The number of phases reported and the elements described vary with the perspective of the observer. Because social workers deal more frequently with relatively short-term groups, many features of group development noted over longer periods of times may never materialize.[16] Thus our discussion is limited to the central issues that confront the members and the social worker as they work together during three broad phases of group development: the beginning, the middle, and the ending.

Beginning Phase

The first phase of any group's life revolves around selecting the members of the group, determining a common aim or purpose, establishing member and worker roles, assigning tasks, and developing a climate conducive to achieving the group's purpose. In essence, every group must answer the questions: What is our reason for meeting? How are we going to work together? For some groups, the answers come easy and "beginning" may take only a single session or part of a session; for other groups, this may be a long and involved process.

Students who have been together in a course for a semester may have little difficulty in forming a study group for a final exam. The purpose that brings the group together is self-evident, and its urgency may facilitate a swift division of labor. In other situations, where groups are meeting for education or orientation, the nature of the group may be predetermined. A public health nurse who visits a home for unwed mothers to provide teen-agers with birth control information, or a social worker responsible for orienting newly admitted patients to a psychiatric ward, may not involve members in discussing procedural matters. Interpersonal relations are secondary to the purpose of providing information or of beginning the patient's involvement with the hospital. In these examples, beginning is a rapid process.

The members of most of the groups served by social workers, however, require more time and consideration as they move through the beginning

---

[15]Numerous descriptions of group development based on both practice observation and experimental studies are available in the small group literature. For a review of several current models as they are applied to social work, see James K. Whittaker, "Models of Group Development: Implications for Social Group Work Practice," *Social Service Review* 44 (September 1970): 308–22.

[16]At present, there is no single satisfactory definition of a "short-term group." We do not intend to prescribe a certain number of sessions for a specific time period; rather, we are thinking in relative terms. We realize that some therapy groups and many open-ended groups meet for a year or more. We would estimate, on the basis of our experience, however, that the majority of groups currently served by social workers meet for periods ranging from several sessions to several months. This we would describe as "short-term" service.

phase. Members need to become acquainted; even when they know each other, they may be unsure about how to relate within the context of this group. In many groups, members have little notion of their common interests, and gaining some consensus on goals may be a lengthy process. Further, when members have had little experience in organized groups, they may need to be involved in learning about group operation—how groups proceed and how members work together. For instance, in a group formed at a juvenile court to help parents prepare for the return of a son or daughter from one of the state training schools, the social worker may find parents very hesitant about discussing plans. Until they trust each other and recognize their common concerns, the group will not be able to set goals and move forward. In similar fashion, several AFDC mothers may take considerable time to begin operating as a group. Even though they know each other and share an interest in gaining employment, they may initially feel uncomfortable in a group situation.

For a group to be effective, the worker must ensure that certain conditions are met in the beginning phase of group development. Care must be given to selecting members who will be compatible and helpful to each other. A basis of commonality must be established: the members must know each other and understand what brought them to the group. The members and social worker must come to an agreement about the goals of the group: what the group members will work together and what the members expect to achieve individually. Members must consider ways of reaching these goals: what activities they will use and how they will be expected to participate in these activities. There should be an initial sense of cohesion and commitment to the group. Members must begin to trust one another, to relate around their common concerns, and to understand their responsibilities as group members. Finally, there must be a climate that will support the work of the group and the members' contributions. Rules, or norms, about how members should behave need to be set and the group must find ways to enforce these norms. Although these norms differ from group to group, norms characteristic of social work groups might include rules about confidentiality, attending meetings, listening while others are talking, and being understanding of fellow members. The beginning phase is thus one of finding common aims and ways to pursue them so the group can proceed with its work.

Middle Phase

By the time they reach the middle phase, groups are characterized by more stable patterns of behavior. Members know each other, have shared expectations, and are ready to work together. The central functions of any group during this phase are to work toward agreed-upon goals and to maintain member relationships.[17] The relative emphasis placed on group tasks versus the emotional and interpersonal aspects of group life varies from group to group, depending on the needs and abilities of the members. Groups whose members have known each other or whose members have a particularly strong basis of commonality may need to spend little time on maintaining relationships. Mothers who are meeting to share ideas about dealing with their handicapped children and to keep informed about their children's treatment may focus almost exclusively on programs related to achieving these goals and may rarely discuss relationships with other members. In other groups, where members are less compatible or lack interpersonal skills, the worker and members may need to devote more attention to member relationships; in fact, the goals of the group may revolve around problems in interpersonal relationships. This focus on members' interpersonal needs may be equally necessary with a group of aggressive delinquent girls who are constantly bickering during meetings and with a group of withdrawn mental patients. The important consideration during this phase is to achieve a balance, satisfactory to each group, between goal-directed activity and group maintenenace.

Although groups become more stable during the course of their existence, it is important to note that the patterns formed in the beginning phase do not remain static. Frequently, the middle phase is marked by one or more periods of upheaval when members challenge the existing structure, question their goals, and seek revisions in their rules and responsibilities. When this first occurs, it may be referred to as "the end of the honeymoon." The quest for change may occur as less secure members become more comfortable in the group and attempt to assert their ideas; or it may spring from general dissatisfaction if members feel the group is no longer adequate for their needs. In a group organized to obtain neighborhood improvements, for instance, the more successful, aggressive members of the community may "take over" at first, assuming responsibility for making group decisions. Later, other members who feel "left out," or who realize their interests have been ignored, may openly seek more important roles or may try to undermine the acting leaders. Whether efforts toward internal change result in revision or reaffirmation of previous structures and commitments, the worker can expect some strife in the middle phase.

---

[17]For further discussion of group maintenance and goal achievement functions, refer to Robert F. Bales, "Task Roles and Social Roles in Problem-Solving Groups," in *Readings in Social Psychology,* ed. Eleanor E. Maccoby, Theodore M. Newcomb, and Eugene L. Hartley (New York: Holt, Rinehart and Winston, 1958), pp. 437–47; and Dorwin Cartwright and Alvin Zander, "Leadership and the Performance of Group Functions," in *Group Dynamics* (3d ed.), ed. Dorwin Cartwright and Alvin Zander (New York: Harper & Row, 1968), pp. 301–17.

Certain long-term groups reach a mature, highly developed state and can function independently prior to termination. Effective work groups or committees could be described in this way but these characteristics rarely typify groups served by social workers. Because of their shorter duration and the fact that client problems may be in the areas of interpersonal relationships and self-direction, social work groups usually need continuous guidance throughout the middle phase. In response to group needs in the areas of group maintenance and goal achievement during the middle phase, social workers intervene at the individual, group, and environmental levels. Ongoing evaluation of group progress during this phase provides the social worker with a basis for determining how and when to act. No matter what approach is used, social workers must be responsive to both feelings and activities of members if the group is to move effectively toward its goals.

Ending Phase

Groups terminate for a variety of reasons. In successful groups, all or a number of the group's goals may be achieved. Less effective groups may end because their members have been unable to define common goals, handle interpersonal relations, or deal with pressures from the group's environment. In other groups, members may have agreed to meet for a certain number of sessions and simply disband at the designated time. Whatever the reason for termination, the central tasks of the ending phase include evaluating the group's activities and dealing with member feelings about leaving the group.

The way in which groups deal with ending is related to the cause of termination as well as to the needs and desires of the members. A group designed to teach a new approach to child training, and limited to four sessions, may spend only a brief period at the final meeting in evaluating what parents have learned. Unless personal relationships have developed among members, there may be little emotional content to the ending process. In contrast, a group of couples that meets for a number of months to discuss marital problems may have strong emotional ties and find it difficult to face termination when several of their members decide to leave town. They may spend several sessions evaluating their progress, expressing their feelings about separation, and discussing new sources of emotional support. Although these "endings" differ in form and content, both serve to complete the group experience.

The social worker should promote evaluation and examination of feelings in this phase. Evaluation not only should serve to highlight gains but also should lead to discussion of the group's shortcomings. Thus, during the evaluative process, the social worker encourages members to express and to examine both positive and negative reactions. In order to deal with their feelings and learn from their experiences, the members need to understand the reasons for both their successes and their failures. Involving the group in this process and eliciting member feelings help members reaffirm their progress and provide closure to the group experience.

Whether or not the group has been successful, the social worker's major tasks during the ending phase are to involve members in evaluating their group experience and to prepare members for leaving the group. Throughout this phase, the social worker must be sensitive to member reactions related to the group's impending termination. With the social worker's reassurance that ambivalence is a natural part of ending, and with support for their achievements as well as understanding of their failures, members can use termination as a base for new experiences.

It may appear from our discussion of the developmental process in groups that members move through the various phases in orderly, sequential fashion. Actually, groups rarely develop this systematically. In every group, the members and the social worker establish their own patterns of beginning, working together, and ending. The way any social work group operates is unique and is related to the characteristics of its members, the style of the social worker, and the nature of its environment. There are, however, common elements in all groups: their members interact, set goals, make rules, decide on tasks, and work together to achieve their aims. When we understand how groups grow and change in relation to these elements, we have a basis for evaluating group progress and for helping groups become an effective means for serving client needs.

WHERE AND WHEN GROUPS ARE USED

As we followed the history of group work, surveyed the ways in which groups can be helpful to clients in the present day, and reviewed the process of group development, many settings for group services were mentioned. Examples have been cited of the use of groups in mental health, corrections, education, recreation, and child welfare. In any agency or institution where social workers practice, social group work may be one of the methods for providing service. Groups are currently used more extensively in urban agencies because there is a greater number of trained workers, opportunities for gaining group work skills are more likely to be available, and larger agencies lend themselves to specialization. Group services in rural areas such as county welfare departments and mountain health clinics should not be ignored merely because of their lower frequency. If the present trend toward training for generic practice with individuals, groups, and families continues, more social workers will be prepared to work with groups, and group services can be expected to increase.

Social workers use the group method for diagnosis, education, orientation, problem solving, individual treatment, recreation, promotion of individual growth, and social or environmental action. Historically we have seen that as our interpretations of client needs change, the purposes for which we use groups vary. We have emphasized the range of purposes for which groups have been and are used. Now our attention turns to an illustration of social group work. In Chapter 9, we have selected a short-term school group as the basis of our description of the process of a "typical" group's development. We will consider the social worker's basic tasks and the members' experience as the group begins, as members work together, and as the group terminates.

BIBLIOGRAPHY

American Association of Group Workers. "Definition of the Function of the Group Worker." *The Group* 11 (May 1949): 11–12.

Aronowitz, E. "Ulterior Motives in Games: Implications for Group Work with Children." *Social Work* 13 (October 1968): 50–55.

Back, Kurt W. *Beyond Words.* New York: Russell Sage Foundation, 1972.

Bernstein, Saul, ed. *Explorations in Group Work.* Boston: Boston University School of Social Work, 1965.

———ed. *Further Explorations in Group Work.* Boston: Boston University School of Social Work, 1970.

Briar, Scott. "Social Casework and Social Group Work: Historical and Social Science Foundations," in *Encyclopedia of Social Work.* Vol. II. New York: National Association of Social Workers, 1971, pp. 1237–45.

Coyle, Grace L. *Social Process in Organized Groups.* Peterborough, N. H.: The Richard R. Smith Co., 1930.

———. *Group Work with American Youth.* New York: Harper & Row, 1948.

———. "Group Work in Psychiatric Settings: Its Roots and Branches." *Social Work* 6, No. 1 (January 1959): 74–81.

Follett, Mary Parker. *The New State.* 4th ed. New York: Longmans, Green & Co., 1934.

Galper, Jeffry. "Non-Verbal Communication Exercises in Groups." *Social Work* 15 (April 1970): 71–78.

Garvin, Charles D., and Paul H. Glasser. "Social Group Work: The Preventive and Rehabilitative Approach," in *Encyclopedia of Social Work.* Vol. II. New York: National Association of Social Workers, 1971, pp. 1263–73.

Garvin, Charles D., Rosemary C. Sarri, and Robert D. Vintner, eds. *Individual Change through Small Groups.* New York: Crowell-Collier and Macmillan, 1974.

Hendry, Charles E., ed. *A Decade of Group Work.* New York: Association Press, 1948.

Klein, Alan F. *Social Work through Group Process.* New York: School of Social Welfare, State University of New York at Albany, 1970.

Konopka, Gisela. *Therapeutic Group Work with Children.* Minneapolis: The University of Minnesota Press, 1949.

———. *Social Group Work: A Helping Process.* Englewood Cliffs, N. J.: Prentice-Hall, 1963.

Lieberman, Joshua, ed. *New Trends in Group Work.* New York: Association Press, 1939.

Middleman, Ruth R. *The Non-Verbal Method in Working with Groups.* New York: Association Press, 1968.

Murphy, Marjorie. "The Social Group Work Method in Social Work Education," in *A Project Report of the Curriculum Study,* XI, Werner W. Boehm, Director and Coordinator. New York: Council on Social Work Education, 1959.

Northen, Helen. *Social Work with Groups.* New York: Columbia University Press, 1969.

Papell, Catherine P., and Beulah Rothman. "Social Group Work Models: Possession and Heritage." *Journal of Education for Social Work* 2 (Fall 1966): 66–77.

Phillips, Helen U. *Essentials of Social Group Work Skill.* New York: Association Press, 1957.

Redl, Fritz. *When We Deal with Children.* New York: Crowell-Collier and Macmillan, 1972.

Rose, Sheldon. *Treating Children in Groups.* San Francisco: Jossey-Bass, 1972.

Schwartz, William. "Group Work and the Social Scene," in *Issues in American Social Work,* ed. Alfred J. Kahn. New York: Columbia University Press, 1959.

———. "The Social Worker in the Group," in *The Social Welfare Forum.* New York: Columbia University Press, 1961, pp. 146–77.

———. "Toward a Strategy of Group Work Practice." *Social Service Review* 36 (September 1962): 268–79.

———. "Social Group Work: The Interactionist Approach," in *Encyclopedia of Social Work.* Vol. I. New York: National Association of Social Workers, 1971, pp. 1252–62.

Schwartz, William, and Serapio R. Zalba, eds. *The Practice of Group Work.* New York: Columbia University Press, 1971.

Shaffer, John B. P., and M. David Galinsky. *Models of Group Therapy and Sensitivity Training.* Englewood Cliffs, N. J.: Prentice-Hall, 1974.

Shulman, Lawrence. *A Casebook of Social Work with Groups: The Mediating Model.* New York: Council on Social Work Education, 1968.

Simon, Paul, ed. *Play and Game Theory in Group Work, A Collection of Papers by Neva Leona Boyd.* Chicago: The Jane Addams Graduate School of Social Work at the University of Illinois at Chicago Circle, 1971.

Spergel, Irving A. *Street Gang Work, Theory and Practice.* Reading, Mass.: Addison-Wesley, 1966.

Trecker, Harleigh B. *Social Group Work, Principles and Practices.* New York: The Woman's Press, 1948.

————, ed. *Group Work, Foundations and Frontiers.* New York: Whiteside, and William Morrow & Company, 1955.

Tropp, Emmanuel. *A Humanistic Foundation for Group Work Practice.* New York: Associated Educational Services Corporation, 1969.

————. "Social Group Work: The Developmental Approach," in *Encyclopedia of Social Work.* Vol. II. New York: National Association of Social Workers, 1971, pp. 1246–52.

Tuckman, Bruce W. "Developmental Sequence in Small Groups." *Psychological Bulletin* 63 (1965): 384–99.

Vinter, Robert D. "Group Work: Perspectives and Prospects," in *Social Work with Groups, 1959.* New York: National Association of Social Workers, 1959, pp. 128–48.

Whittaker, James K. "Models of Group Development: Implications for Social Group Work Practice." *Social Service Review* 44 (September 1970): 308–22.

Wilson, Gertrude, and Gladys Ryland. *Social Group Work Practice.* Boston: Houghton Mifflin, 1949.

9
GUIDING GROUP DEVELOPMENT: AN ILLUSTRATION

JANICE H. SCHOPLER AND MAEDA J. GALINSKY
School of Social Work, University of North Carolina

An overview of the developmental process is illustrated through an account of a group of six girls who share a mutual dissatisfaction with school. Excerpts are given from the records of the social worker who meets with these junior high school students for twelve sessions. This case material can serve as a basis for a closer examination of member experiences and social worker tasks that should be considered as any group develops.

A social worker from the Jenson Mental Health Center is assigned to work directly in Crosswell, one of the local junior high schools, as the fall semester begins. Crosswell Junior High is located across town from the center in a rundown section of Jenson, a midwestern community of about 60,000. Although the composition of Crosswell's student body is mixed in terms of both race and economic status, many of the students referred to the center are from the low-income families living near the junior high. The staff at Jenson Mental Health Center previously has had trouble involving students and their parents and has decided that part of their difficulty in serving this population has been related to their distance from the Crosswell neighborhood and the middle-class nature of the center itself. The director suggested to the principal at Crosswell that students and their families might feel more comfortable and find it more convenient to meet with a social worker located in their own neighborhood school. He also expressed the hope that the center and Crosswell Junior High might develop a close working relationship. The principal and his faculty are dubious about this plan but cooperate to the extent of providing a conference room for the social worker, Ms. E., to use three days each week.

From her observations in several classrooms and the limited referrals she has received, Ms. E. identifies a number of ninth-grade girls who appear to share a basic similarity. In the classroom, these girls range from noisy aggressors to dreamy nonparticipants, but all seem uninterested in learning. They do just enough to "get by." Teachers have mentioned they "can't reach" these particular girls, hint at family problems, and expect them to drop out of school within the next year or two. After consulting with several teachers about the dropout problem, Ms. E. decides that a group might serve as an effective means to involve some of these girls in school and help them resolve any individual problems they might be having. She arranges appointments with ten of the girls to explore their interest in having a group. One of these interviews proceeds as follows.

EXPLORATORY INTERVIEW

Diane stalks into the room, slumps immediately into a chair, and glares at the social worker. Ms. E. smiles, introduces herself as a social worker from Jenson Center, and asks for Diane's name. Ms. E. says she hopes getting a note from a social worker didn't trouble Diane, but she has some ideas she thinks might interest her. Since Diane maintains a stony silence, Ms. E. gives Diane some examples of the things the Jenson Center is interested in doing in the school "to make things better for students, teachers, principal, and parents." Diane comments that Ms. E. has a good line but wonders, "What's all that got to do with me being sent down?" Ms. E. responds that she's been especially interested in finding out what people think about the school and she's learned that there are a number of students who are unhappy or just plain bored. When she was in one of Diane's classes, Ms. E. continues, she noticed that Diane didn't seem too pleased with the way things were going. Ms. E. then asks Diane, "Am I off base, or was I reading you right?" Diane responds with, "What's it to you?" Ms. E. explains that she has been talking to several ninth-grade girls who are "turned off" by school. She tells Diane that she's trying to find out if they'd like to form a group to see if they can improve their lives at school, since they have to attend anyway.

At this point, Diane begins to show interest. She wants to know who would be in the group, what the group could do, and where and when it would meet. Ms. E. answers these questions as best she can, indicating that if this seems to be a good idea, the members would be ninth-grade girls who aren't getting much out of school. They would meet during the activity period to look at why the school wasn't doing them any good, to rap about other things that might trouble them, and to work on some solutions. Ms. E. inquires whether Diane would have anything to share in this type of group. Diane, by this time, has become more responsive and begins to explain how ''impossible'' everything seems to her. At home her mother nags her, at school the teachers are after her, she's always behind on her work and usually ''in trouble.'' As Diane talks on, her concerns about the future and her inability to cope with her present emerge. She sums it all up by saying, ''In a year or so I'll be on my own and what's going to happen to me then? Folks around here couldn't care less.'' In many ways, Diane appears to be a frightened little girl. Ms. E. reassures Diane of her interest. She adds that other girls may share Diane's concerns and that, from her own experience, people can do a lot when they are working together.

Diane has more questions about what a group experience might be like but generally seems in favor of one and says, ''It can't make things worse, no way!'' Since Diane seems willing to try out the group, Ms. E. tells her she can probably get the best answers to her questions by coming to a meeting if they can get a group started. Diane agrees to come to one session, at least, to see what the group can do. Before ending the interview, Ms. E. mentions that if the group is formed and Diane wants to be a member, Ms. E. will need to explain the group to Diane's mother and get her agreement for Diane to come. Diane groans but seems to understand why this is necessary and decides it would be okay for Ms. E. to call her mother or send a note. Ms. E. also gains Diane's permission to look at her school record after pointing out that this is one way she can find out what the school thinks about Diane and that this information might be helpful to them. Then Ms. E. thanks Diane for coming and for helping her learn more about the school. She tells Diane that she will be in touch with her about the group and, if it doesn't work out, she would always be glad to talk further with Diane.

Although the girls' reactions vary, similar content is covered in Ms. E.'s other exploratory interviews. In all, Ms. E. sees eight of the ten potential candidates, and of these, six are definitely interested in forming a group. Two girls never show up for their appointments, one girl seems much too apprehensive to be a part of the group, and another girl says frankly, ''It's a dumb idea.'' After phoning or sending notes to the girls' families, as well as reading the girls' files and reviewing her individual interviews, Ms. E. forms tentative impressions about each of the prospective members.

DIANE: Pert, pretty, often defiant, fifteen-year old black girl. Her mother works to support Diane and her four younger children; is eager to have Diane go to work. Diane seems to do a fair amount to help out, but her Mom has only criticism and thinks Diane will never grow up. Records show steady decline in Diane's performance, from a kindergarten comment, "bright, interested in everything," to eighth-grade notation, "academic work generally unsatisfactory, lacks basic skills, recommend social promotion." Diane feels everyone is pushing her but no one is giving her help in preparing for her future.

TONI: Pudgy, rather plain, fourteen-year-old white girl. Mother finally returned permission slip after two notes. Toni says parents are busy doing their own thing; evidently, they aren't home much. Her older sister dropped out of school to get married. Toni gets mostly C's and D's, but school records indicate she has the ability to do better. Teachers have described her for years as "quiet, passive, hard to get to know." Toni says no one cares about her; she wants to find herself a husband but thinks she's too ugly.

JOYCE: Gentle, stocky, fifteen-year-old black girl with dreamy quality. Mother "ran off" when she was eight; father agreed to her participating in the group because "she's alone a lot." From records, Joyce appeared to be an average student until her mother left; then her grades dropped to the level of borderline failures. Teachers comment that Joyce "stares off into space, daydreams, shows no interest." Joyce seemed mildly surprised that there might be other girls "like her"; says she has no friends; wonders "what's to become of me?"

LUCIA: Bouncy, witty, fourteen-year-old black girl. Mother was never home when worker called but returned permission slip promptly; both parents work and Lucia helps her older sister care for four younger children. Her older sister and brother left school as soon as they were sixteen and now work occasionally. Teachers say Lucia is a bright girl who isn't trying. She gets mostly C's and has numerous "behavior incident" reports in her record. Lucia states she is bored, has no respect for teachers; only good part of school to her is "seeing friends and making things happen."

JULIE: Cute, sassy, fifteen-year-old white girl. Parents live in another state; couldn't control her, so sent her to live with her grandmother who views her as a typical boy-crazy teen-ager. Julie's record has little information. She's been in this school for only a year, has barely passing grades, is often absent. Julie put on a "tough" front for most of the interview; hates school but seemed uncertain what was going to happen to her.

DARLENE: Pretty, mild-mannered, fifteen-year-old black girl. Her family lives in the housing project and receives financial assistance for her father's disability. Darlene's mother sounds worn out from the care of her four children and depends heavily on Darlene, whom she describes as a "good girl." According to Darlene's records, she has low average ability. Teachers see her as hard-working but lacking basic skills. Absences have increased in the last year and Darlene's grades have dropped from mostly C's to frequent D's. Darlene is discouraged about school, doesn't think she can "make it" and has no ideas about what she can do.

Although she has had little choice in composition of the group, Ms. E. thinks it will be a compatible one. All of the girls are approximately the same age, have similar backgrounds, and are expected to be pretty much "on their own" as far as their families are concerned. The membership will include both black and white girls who have a range of abilities and differences in personality and behavior. The girls come from the same relatively stable neighborhood, so Ms. E. doesn't expect the mixed racial composition to cause any tension; and because each of the girls shares some characteristics with other members, Ms. E. anticipates that no one will be "left out," although some girls may participate more actively than others. As Ms. E. reviews the girls' needs, she notes the following: their home situations are all problematic, they have doubts about their futures, they feel school is not relevant, and their current school performance is poor.

With school and parental approval and expressed interest from each of the girls, Ms. E. proceeds with plans for the group. She decides to limit it to twelve sessions so that the group's termination will coincide with the end of the fall semester. Ms. E. also thinks the time limit may serve as an incentive to get the group moving and will keep these girls from getting impatient. Given the girls' overwhelming needs, she anticipates her greatest difficulty will be to help the group focus on some limited, realistic goals that can be achieved in twelve meetings.

Recognizing that none of the girls selected for the group are close friends and that they had no previous experience with any type of organized group outside the classroom, Ms. E. makes careful preparation for the first meeting. She arranges to have the girls excused from activity period (an hour and a half, set aside for school meetings and activities, which the members spend in study hall because they are not involved in any "activities") and sends them notes informing them of the meeting in her conference room. She has cokes ready to lessen the formality of the occasion and has arranged chairs in a circle. She expects to spend some time just getting acquainted, to review the girls' common interests, and to discuss plans and "ground rules" for the group.

First Meeting

The girls straggle in after the first bell rings. Darlene is first and slips unobtrusively into a chair. Lucia and Diane arrive together in a rather boisterous mood and make straight for the cokes. Toni and Joyce come in quietly. The girls begin to settle down as Ms. E. passes out cokes. Several minutes after the second bell, Julie makes a grand entrance, stirring up everything with some loud comments about this looking like a "prayer meeting." Ms. E. welcomes Julie warmly; then, mildly but firmly, points out that even though the girls will have a lot of freedom to do what they want in the group, they need to follow school rules about not wandering in the halls after the last bell and keeping noise down. Ms. E. asks each girl to make a tag to wear on which is printed her name and one thing she's interested in talking about in the group.

After Lucia, Diane, and Joyce exchange a few smart remarks and everyone finishes her tag, the girls lapse into an uneasy silence. Ms. E. comments that it's always a bit awkward when people don't know each other well and don't know exactly what's going to happen. She shows her tag which reads, "Ms. E., Social Work Snoop." As the girls laugh, Ms. E. says she's only gotten the reputation of being a "snoop" since she's been at Crosswell. The girls relax a little and Ms. E. continues: "Well, I'm not really an undercover agent for Mr. P., but I am interested in getting to know each of you!" She points out that in talking about problems, people sometimes say some very personal things and, far from reporting to Mr. P., she intends to keep everything they say confidential unless she has their permission to talk about their business to someone. She stresses that people can get hurt if others gossip about them and wonders if the girls would agree to keep group business in the group. All of the girls think this is a good idea.

Ms. E. then reminds the girls that in her individual appointments with each of them she had explained that as a social worker she helps individuals and groups work on problems and on improving their lives. She adds, "And I've found out groups can work together only when everyone knows each other and what they want to do. Why don't we finish going around, introducing ourselves, and explaining our tags?" The girls read their tags in the following order: "Joyce, life; Lucia, trouble; Diane, jobs; Toni, men; Julie, getting out; Darlene, work." The girls mostly just read off what they've written, but there is quite a bit of giggling and some comments about the "interests" stated by Lucia, Toni, and Julie.

As they finish, Ms. E. indicates that even though they put down very different things, these words all make her think about their futures. She wonders what they want to do in the future and if the school is helping them "get ready for life." This sparks a flurry of comments about the school, directed at the teachers, the classes, the other students. Lucia and Diane take a particularly active part in this discussion, but all of the girls join in, even Joyce and Toni. At times, the whole group seems to be talking at once as they share their common feelings and join in putting down the school. Ms. E. only gets into the discussion to suggest that they talk one at a time. Among their comments are "teachers don't care; classes aren't no use to anybody that's going to have to hustle for a living; nobody has time for you unless you're on the 'college track'; you can't do nothing unless you've got grades and who can get grades when the stuff don't make sense." Several of the girls share their feelings of being "shut out" and being stuck in study hall during activity period because they don't "qualify" for any of the clubs or activities. Darlene says at that point, "This group is the first thing I've ever got to join." Diane laughs and replies, "Well, maybe having problems does pay off!"

Ms. E. finally interjects, "Whew! It sounds as if you're all finding things really bad here at Crosswell." She then supports Darlene's comment, adding, "Since the school is letting us meet, maybe there is some hope that things could be improved." Julie laughs and says sarcastically, "Yah, like what could we do? Fire P.? Burn down the building?" Ms. E. replies that Julie's ideas do seem a bit "far out." She explains that before you can make life better, usually you have to decide what you want to do; then you can figure out how to do it. She points out that they all seem to agree that the school isn't helping them get ready for "life," but they still haven't shared any ideas about what they want to know or what they want to do in the future. Diane answers, "Every-thing!" Ms. E. smiles, saying, "That's a big order," and asks for other ideas. The girls generally seem interested in jobs: how to get them; how to know what there is to do "besides sweep somebody's floor or wash the crap off their dishes"; and how to "get qualified." Julie and Toni both agree they'd rather get themselves a man than go to work, but Diane retorts, "You'd end up supporting any man that would have you," and Darlene agrees with her.

Ms. E. notices they have only about fifteen minutes left and sees that she needs to help the group agree on some focus and ground rules. After briefly summarizing the discussion, she inquires whether the girls would like to spend their time finding some answers to questions about jobs. All members are enthusiastic about this idea but wonder how they'll go about this. Ms. E. indicates she can find out what the school can do to help them and points out there is a counseling office. Julie comments, "It's about time they did something for us and not just their college pets." Ms. E. agrees but says, "We'll all have to work if we're going to get anything done. Perhaps we'd better talk about how long we're going to meet and who's going to do what." The group discusses meeting until the end of the semester and agrees this is okay. Ms. E. points out that they won't be able to work as fast unless everyone comes, and the girls chime in to say, "Don't worry. As long as we can get out of study hall, we'll be here!" Ms. E. says she hopes the meetings will be enjoyable and helpful, but forewarns the girls that when people are working together, they sometimes get upset with each other. She adds, "We can get through those times if we stick together and talk about things honestly and face-to-face." Lucia comments, "Yeah, and not behind people's backs! Like you said, stuff should stay in the group."

Just before the bell rings, Ms. E. compliments the group, saying they've accomplished a lot for one meeting: they've gotten to know each other a little, have expressed some of their feelings about the school, and have decided at least one thing—they want to work on as a group. She says she looks forward to seeing them next week and will have some information about jobs. In the meantime, she asks them all to think about things they like to do and things they are good at doing.

Summary of Second Meeting

The second meeting proceeds smoothly. The girls are especially interested in the information Ms. E. has found out about the vocational training program at the high school. In order to learn more about this program, the group selects Darlene to call the director of the program. They discuss what they want to find out, and Darlene practices making the phone call, with the worker playing the role of the vocational director. Toward the end of the meeting, the girls share some of the individual interests that Ms. E. asked them to think about at the first meeting. Several of the girls like taking care of children and think they are good at this.

Summary of Third Meeting

At the third meeting, Darlene reports that the director of the vocational program can come and talk to the group in two weeks. The girls begin to discuss immediate job possibilities like baby sitting, and Diane says she's so busy at home she never gets to do anything for money. She complains at length about her mother. Then Julie makes some derogatory remarks about Diane's mother. This leads to a heated verbal battle between Julie and Diane in which Diane threatens to leave the group. Darlene plays a central role as "mediator" and reminds the adversaries that the group agreed at the beginning to talk things out. The girls finally calm down and the group decides it might be helpful for Ms. E. to talk with Diane and her mother together.

Home Visit

The following day, after school and by prior arrangement, Ms. E. goes home with Diane so they can talk together with Diane's mother. In this conference, Ms. E. stresses Diane's interest in working, which surprises and pleases her mother. They discuss the possibility of Diane doing some baby sitting. Although the mother begins to see the conflict between her pushing Diane to get a job and then not letting her have time for work, she says Diane is needed at home. She does agree to try to let Diane off some evenings to earn money by baby sitting. Even though little is changed by this conference, Diane seems pleased to hear her mother talk in a positive way about her "being needed" at home.

Program for Fourth Meeting

Ms. E. is concerned that the girls link their future plans and enthusiasm to their present school situation. She particularly wants to help the more aggressive girls "tone down" some of their annoying behavior, to encourage the quieter girls to speak up occasionally, and to help all the girls learn to participate in classes in a more productive fashion. For the fourth meeting, she devises a role-playing game, which she hopes will help them prepare for the visit of the director of the vocational training program and have some impact on their classroom behavior. She calls the game "Participation."

Each of the girls will have a turn being the discussion leader; the leader gets to choose the topic for discussion but must pick something related to jobs. Then the rest of the girls will discuss the topic for five minutes. Each time a girl contributes an idea or asks an appropriate question, she is awarded one positive point. For each smart remark or distracting comment, a negative point will be earned. Ms. E. plans to keep account of the time and points. After each girl has had a chance to be leader, the girl with the most points gets a prize (a candy bar) and the other members will get consolation awards (pieces of candy). Ms. E. allows time after the game for discussion about how this relates to classroom behavior and to the group's conduct when their guest speaker will be present. She plans to support appropriate participation during this discussion.

Summary of Fourth Meeting

At the meeting, Ms. E. introduces her game after the girls have settled down and exchanged comments about how things are going. She recalls the practicing the group did for Darlene's phone call and says this will be a similar kind of experience except that they can all "play" and they will earn points. The girls quickly grasp the idea of the game and play with enthusiasm. For a while, Lucia and Julie seem to be in contest for negative points but curb their smart remarks when Ms. E. points out they are only hurting themselves. Darlene and Diane tie for first place and split the candy bar. The discussion following the game is the most productive and orderly talk the group has had. Joyce and Toni are able to share some of the difficulties they have in speaking up in class, and the group decides on some of the questions they want to ask the vocational program director.

Summary of Fifth, Sixth, and Seventh Meetings

The girls continue to attend regularly. They are very excited about the program of vocational training at the high school and accept the director's invitation to visit the high school and "see the program in action." At the sixth meeting, they plan for their visit and go to the high school for the seventh meeting, after getting special permission from the principal to be absent one morning. The trip is a success and all of the girls begin to talk about going on to high school.

Summary of Eighth Meeting

After some initial discussion about the trip to the high school, the group falls into disgruntled silence. Ms. E. asks if the girls are feeling a let down after all the excitement of the last few meetings. This seems to hit home, and a few members also indicate they are feeling down because "there's so little time left." Ms. E. is finally able to help the group focus on what they want to accomplish in the remaining four meetings. Darlene says what they need to do is find some ways to stay in school if they want to have a chance at the vocational program at the high school. Diane gloomily reflects they may as well "drop out" before they "flunk out." Joyce, in an unusual burst of feeling, says, "That's not true. We can make it if we get to work." Toni, surprisingly, supports Joyce. Ms. E. helps the girls explore the problem of staying in school. All of them need to get much better grades but aren't too sure where to start, since they are doing poorly in everything. The girls end their discussion by deciding to try studying something every night for at least fifteen minutes and to come to the next meeting prepared to figure out some goals. They also agree to have Ms. E. consult with their teachers and get any suggestions that could help "save them."

Teacher Conferences

Ms. E. makes appointments with all of the girls' teachers during the following week. The teachers seem interested in hearing about the group and most of them express surprise and pleasure that the girls want to do better work. Some even comment that they have noticed minor improvements already. Darlene seems to be making the most progress, and Joyce has contributed to class discussions for the first time all year. For each of the girls, Ms. E. is able to identify with the teachers one or two central things that would help her performance. For instance, Diane needs to stop talking out of turn and begin handing in her homework; Toni can rewrite her last English paper and start bringing her book, paper, and pencils to class. Ms. E. is pleased to learn that these teachers, who earlier had written off these particular girls as hopeless, can involve themselves in making positive suggestions. One teacher also informed her about a new tutoring program that may be helpful for some of the girls.

Summary of Ninth, Tenth, and Eleventh Meetings

Ms. E. provides the girls with feedback from her teacher conferences. The group realistically discusses the fact that they are just getting by, but with the teachers' suggestions the members are able to set some individual goals. Their individual goals are mainly related to improving academic performance so that they will be able to complete the ninth grade successfully and go on to the vocational program at the high school. Diane plans to start working on controlling her smart remarks in class, completing her daily assignments, and improving her writing skills. Julie aims to attend all of her classes unless she's sick enough to stay home, to try to do her homework, and to be polite to her teachers. Darlene wants to improve her attendance (she says she has been using baby sitting with her brothers and sisters as an excuse to stay home), do her homework every day, and begin to participate in class. Toni is going to start doing her work and wants to "get enough nerve" to talk in class, especially when asked questions. Lucia vows to start showing some "respect" and wants to work on staying out of arguments with teachers and other students; she also plans to start doing her homework. Joyce admits she's shy and feels funny about not having a mother but wants to learn to make some friends and find some ways to keep busy and around people after school. She is interested in school now and thinks she can improve her grades if she gets help from her teachers.

These three meetings center around discussions and role playing related to each member's goals. Several of the girls (including Diane, Julie, and Darlene) enroll in the tutoring program. The others plan their study time more appropriately, and Joyce goes to some of her teachers for help. Frequently, members refer to how little time is left. They talk about how much they will miss the group but are concentrating more and more on individual goals.

Final Meeting

For the last session, Ms. E. plans to have the members review and evaluate the group's progress, discuss plans in relation to individual goals, and allow time for reminiscing and having a last good chat together. To celebrate their achievements, she bakes brownies and brings chips and cokes.

The girls drag slowly into the meeting. Julie is late and Diane reminds her she was late for the first meeting. This leads naturally into a discussion of many of the things the girls have done in the group. They have lots of memories about the role playing and recall their nervousness as well as funny incidents. The discovery of the vocational program at the high school has the most meaning for everyone. As each girl talks about how this may affect her future, the girls express their disgust that they didn't know about the program sooner. Comments like "that's just typical of this dump, they never tell you anything" pepper the discussion, and soon the girls are once again busy running down the school.

After a few minutes, Ms. E. smiles and interrupts, asking, "Does this remind you of any talks we've had before?" The girls laugh as they recall the first meeting. Ms. E. comments that it's usually rather sad to be ending something, especially if you've enjoyed it, and that one way to make things last is to go back and start over. She wonders, however, if the group hasn't moved beyond just complaining about things to doing something about things and reminds them briefly of some of the group and individual accomplishments they mentioned earlier in the meeting. Diane picks this up, saying, "That's right. What can we do about the school not letting us in on this program over at the high school?" Darlene replies they've already done something about themselves and "there's no use crying about the past." She wonders then how many other kids in the junior high school would like to find out about the high school's vocational program. Gradually, as the girls discuss this, an idea forms. They decide to go to the counselor and explain what this knowledge has meant to them and ask that this be included as a regular homeroom counseling session, just like the ones on college information. They also decide to volunteer to come back and help her, if she wants them, to explain the program after they have gone on to the high school. They select Darlene as their chief spokesman and ask Ms. E. to make an appointment for them and to send them notes telling them when to meet with the counselor. As the girls discuss this final project, Darlene laughingly comments, "Guess we just can't give up this group!" Ms. E. responds, saying, "The group really does seem to mean a lot to each of you and you've been a lot of help to each other." She then helps the girls talk about some of the problems they'll continue to encounter and what they can do when they can no longer turn to the group.

As they reach some conclusions about how to handle future difficulties, Ms. E. asks them to complete a brief evaluation to help her in planning for future groups. She gives them each a sheet with the following questions: Did this group help you? If it did help, how did it help? What suggestions do you have for other groups like this one? Since all of the girls have difficulty with writing, it takes them about ten minutes to fill out the evaluation forms, but they work seriously and steadily. As they finish this task, Ms. E. asks if they would like to talk about their answers. Each of the girls is eager to find out what others have put down. The girls all found the group helpful and their answers to "how" range from "made me shape up" to "gave me some interest in high school." Suggestions for future groups include "meet oftener and longer, have teachers come to meetings, and keep things just the same."

After the girls exchange their comments, Ms. E. brings out the refreshments. The girls are delighted to finish off with a "party" and end the meeting with much chatter and protestations of undying loyalty to each other. Before the bell rings, Ms. E. reminds the girls she will be sending them notes about their appointment with the counselor. She tells then again how much they have done together and reminds them she'll still be around in the spring semester if any of them want to come in and talk. The girls leave as slowly as they arrived and wish Ms. E. many fond goodbyes.

In every group, the members and the social worker establish their own patterns of beginning, working together, and ending. The group development framework discussed in the preceding chapter indicates the member experiences and worker tasks that are characteristic of any social work group. The record provides a basis for examining the social worker's activity and member responses as Ms. E. guided this particular group's development. In analyzing this short-term group, certain facets of the beginning, middle, and ending phases are apparent. As Ms. E. began in this group, she was concerned with focusing members on appropriate goals, clarifying members' responsibilities and group rules necessary for group operation, and developing bonds of trust and mutual interest among members. During the middle phase, group members took on more responsibility and Ms. E. altered her role to correspond with increasing member abilities. Ms. E.'s program plannning, use of collateral contacts, attention to member relationships, and assignments for individual members reflect her continuing assessment and facilitation of group and individual progress. Finally, in the ending phase, Ms. E. helped the group members evaluate their achievements, express and understand their feelings about termination, and plan for the future.

SUMMARY

The way any social work group operates is unique and is related to the characteristics and aims of its members, the style of the social worker, and the nature of its environment. There are, however, common elements in all groups: their members interact, set goals, make rules, decide on tasks, and work together to achieve their aims. An understanding of how groups grow and change provides a means for evaluating group progress and for helping groups become an effective means for serving client needs.

10
COMMUNITY ORGANIZATION AND ILLUSTRATION OF PRACTICE

MORRIS H. COHEN

School of Social Work, University of North Carolina

Community organization in social work is a growing and changing area of work whose boundaries overlap those of a number of other professions. This work is carried out under many names and a variety of auspices and is characterized by several distinctive modes of practice. As is appropriate for a human service profession, community organization responds to changing needs. The work has been defined at different times in terms of the realities currently applicable to prevailing social conditions, community problems, and the tools and resources available for solving community problems. Community organization practice includes planning and coordination of social welfare services, citizen organizing and action, and community development. The present emphasis in practice today is directed to problem-solving methods and strategies.

PROFESSIONAL PRACTICE IN THE COMMUNITY

The practice of community organization in social work builds upon specialized knowledge and particular skills in organizing and planning. A community organization social worker not uncommonly finds that he works with individuals and groups as well as with community agencies, institutional structures, and government agencies. Frequently, in actual practice, distinctions between different practice modes do not have clearcut boundaries. The distinguishing feature that differentiates community practice from casework or group work modes is the locus for the change and the type of change desired.

Micro and Macro Perspectives

From its earliest beginnings, social work addressed itself to both "micro" and "macro" perspectives—the needs of individuals and groups for help, and the need or wish to change conditions in the community so that these needs might be eliminated. On one hand, there is the pain, hurt, hunger and deprivation of individuals to be ameliorated, and on the other hand, the need for community change, reform, and reconstruction of the social environment. The micro thrust in social work has been geared to providing direct assistance and support so that clients, individuals, and families might move from dependence and need to independence and self-direction.

Macro work—the work with and in the community—is comprised of two parts. One part concerns itself with the need for improved provision of social services, and the other part deals with the pervasive influence and force of social conditions in creating and perpetuating conditions of need and injustice for various population groups. The most important aspects of community organization practice have been characterized by efforts to achieve social change and social justice. Poverty as a social problem, inadequate housing, poor nutrition, lack of health and medical services, unemployment, and so on have been principal concerns of social workers from the earliest beginnings of the profession. In responding to these problems, community social workers strive to change or reform social conditions and to achieve better organization and coordination of the community systems for meeting needs.

Values

A commitment to democratic process and goals is of central importance to community practice as well as of importance to social work practice in general. Certain other basic social work values—such as belief in the right of client self-determination, in the worth and dignity of individuals, in the ability of people to change, and in the commitment to seek social justice—are shared in the social work profession.

Community practice in particular stresses certain values that focus on the social context. Principally, these are:

1. The responsibility of society to organize itself in such ways as to permit the fullest possible meeting of the basic needs of its members.
2. The responsibility of society to create conditions that permit opportunity and self-fulfillment for individuals.
3. The responsibility of society to provide opportunities for mutual assistance and common action through which individuals may work in their own behalf.
4. The belief that cooperation and collaboration should in general be promoted among individuals, groups, and institutions.
5. The recognition that tension and conflict will be part of resolving differences among individuals, groups, and institutions.
6. The belief that institutions and organizations must be flexible and changing in order to adapt to changing conditions, needs, and problems.

Knowledge Base

Community organization practice is based primarily upon social science foundations. Research and theory building in these sciences have expanded greatly in recent years. The responsibility of social workers in community organization practice has been to apply this knowledge effectively. Practice in different agency settings and/or in relation to different intervention approaches serves to particularize the knowledge utilized.

Final answers to effective practice, to the "how to do it" questions, do not exist. Practitioners are called upon constantly to reexamine their theoretical and practical approaches. New research findings frequently call into question older established "truths." For example, the efficacy of collaboration and coordination as a strategy or means for successful problem solving in American cities is called into question in a recent research report by Roland Warren.[1] Warren suggests that the collaboration-coordination "model" applied first in social welfare planning and organization, and then adapted in such current programs as those sponsored by the Economic Opportunity Act and Model Cities legislation, serves not so much to solve problems as to serve certain "latent functions" such as (1) strengthening and reinforcing agencies,

---

[1]Roland L. Warren, "Comprehensive Planning and Coordination: Some Functional Aspects," *Social Problems* 20, no. 3 (Winter 1973):355–64.

(2) providing an aura of change without affecting the causes of the problem or the basic injustices in the social system, and (3) providing employment for social scientists and professional practitioners.

Among broad categories of knowledge in the social sciences, at least six identifiable content areas are fundamental to successful community practice. These are:

1. The characteristics of populations worked with and being served.

2. The characteristics and functions of the community and its constituent groups, organizations, and institutional systems, including the systemic relationship of economic, social, political, and human factors.

3. The behavior of people in relation to social systems, including such subjects as role theory, group dynamics, small group behavior, organizational behavior, communication, and decision making.

4. The indicators and causes of community dysfunction, problems, and breakdowns.

5. The contributions (present and potential) social welfare and related institutional policies, programs, and actions can make toward the control, alleviation, and prevention of problems and needs.

6. The roles, strategies, techniques, and modes of practice which the practitioner uses selectively in carrying out his profession.

Occupational Roles and Practice Settings

The skills of the social worker, such as the ability to work with people and to carry out analytical, planning, and implementing tasks, are necessary in a wide variety of occupations and fields of endeavor. Community organizers are employed in citizen self-interest and self-help groups, and in both private and public service agencies; in social welfare planning, coordinating, and fund-raising organizations; and in a variety of positions in governmental agencies and educational institutions, research organizations, professional groups, and business organizations.

Most educational programs for the preparation of professional practitioners in community organization build upon "core" knowledge for helping and working with people and communities. Curricula in individual schools frequently are particularized or specialized in relation to a variety of manpower needs in service delivery systems, social policy development, planning and programming tasks, and social change activities. Growth and change in community organization practice are reflected in the development of the specialized roles and functions for workers, and in the increasingly more diverse contexts and settings for practice. The earlier traditional model of an essen-

tially process-oriented worker staffing a welfare council committee or organizing a local self-help effort continues to have meaning and validity, and a
number of community social workers continue to be employed by agencies
requiring the fulfillment of those kinds of services. However, many of the new
community workers have job titles and job descriptions unknown in social
work not so long ago. A typical roster of the positions to be filled in meeting
current manpower needs for community organization includes:

1. Social planners within local, regional, state, and federal governmental
    agencies.
2. Managers and administrators in public welfare and voluntary agencies.
3. Systems analyzers in the human service fields.
4. Researchers to evaluate program needs and service effectiveness and
    to undertake cost-benefit studies.
5. Coordinators in all areas of the public sector to foster efficient and
    effective working relationships among various governmental levels.
6. Community organizers and developers to enhance further the concept
    of consumer input and citizen participation in governmental and pri-
    vate agency policy making and programming.
7. Educators for the rapidly growing human service disciplines on junior
    college, B. A., and graduate levels.
8. Staff developers and trainers to upgrade the skills and techniques of
    professionals already in the field and to train paraprofessionals, de-
    velop "new careers" programs, etc.
9. Specialists in the areas related to planning, coordinating legislation,
    and governmental reform.
10. Special staff for social problem-solving efforts in the private sector and
    business communities.
11. Advocates to protect and strengthen the community's role in govern-
    mental decision making and to assure appropriate services for con-
    sumers in a variety of public and private settings.
12. Organizers and staff workers for citizen self-help organizations, civil
    rights organizations, and other change-oriented groups.

AN EVOLVING PROFESSIONAL PERSPECTIVE
FOR PRACTICE

Certain major ideas can be identified in evolving definitions of community
organization and community organization practice beginning in the 1920s
and up to the present time. These principal ideas are:

1. Commitment to enhancing widespread participation and democratic process.

2. Notions of cooperation, collaboration, coordination, and integration.

3. The idea of meeting needs and bringing about a balance between needs and resources.

4. The focus on relationships among agencies, programs, and services as contrasted to direct service to individual clients or client groups.

5. The idea of specific intervention by a professional worker engaged in "problem solving" to help a community meet its needs and prevent social problems.

6. The importance of carrying out both analytical and interactional tasks.

7. The relevance of practice settings (voluntary organizations, service agencies, planning organizations) in determining the nature of practice.

8. Community development, social planning, and social action as major overall strategies for community intervention.

9. Altering resource allocation patterns, service functions, or decision-making power in effecting community change.

10. The utilization of direct action, confrontation, and other "contest" approaches when agreement on issues is not possible between competing interests.

Early Definitions

A review of the literature indicates that social work authors began in the 1920s to formulate specific definitions of community organizations. In 1921, Eduard C. Lindeman stressed "Democratic Process" and "Specialism," stating that community organization was concerned with the "conscious effort on the part of a community to control its affairs democratically, and to secure the highest services from its specialists, organizations, agencies and institutions by means of recognized interrelations."[2] In 1922, Edward T. Devine linked community organization directly to chests and councils, writing of "coordination and harmonizing of existing agencies" and "the kind of planning for future development of a community's social work which is done by the budget committee of some of the financial federations."[3] In 1930, Jesse F. Steiner described community organization as being concerned "with problems of accommodation and social adjustment, . . . concerned with the interrelationships of groups within communities, their integration and coordination in the interest of efficiency and unity of action," and as a

---

[2]Eduard C. Lindeman, *The Community* (New York: Association Press, 1921), p. 173.

[3]Edward T. Devine, *Social Work* (New York: Macmillan, 1922), p. 68.

"continuous process in which adjustments are being made and remade to keep pace with changing conditions."[4]

These three definitions, and others subsequently developed by different writers and social work leaders (and, in two important instances, by committees), reflect efforts to conceptualize community organization in relation to the principal contexts for practice and the nature of the work being carried out at the particular time. Thus Lindeman, Devine, and Steiner reflect the historical period of the development of chests, councils, and federations. As new definitions were developed in successive years, they continued to be influenced by the changes in agencies and auspices for community practice as well as existing social realities with respect to social conditions, problems, and needs and the resources available. As more sophisticated and more explicit social theory developed in the social sciences, especially in sociology, social psychology, and political science, it was possible for the more recent definitions and conceptualizations of community practice to define much more explicitly the strategies and techniques for practice.

The Lane Reports

The first overall view of community organization as a field of practice and as a process was presented in the Lane reports of 1939 and 1940 at the National Conference of Social Work.[5] A committee headed by Robert P. Lane, then executive director of the Welfare Council of New York City, produced the first group effort by social work community organization leaders and practitioners to define what in fact were the nature and characteristics of community organizations. Lane's 1939 report moved the practice field beyond chests and councils, emphasizing community organization as a generic, pervasive process with which all social work is concerned. Although as many questions were raised as were answered, the report articulated a number of practice concepts and set up a framework for the examination of community organization practice. No explicit definition of community organization practice was provided, but the report did indicate that the general aim of community organization practice was to bring about and maintain a progressively more effective adjustment between social welfare needs and resources. The

---

[4]Jesse F. Steiner, *Community Organization* (New York: The Century Company, 1930), p. 323.

[5]Robert P. Lane, "The Field of Community Organization," in *Proceedings of the National Conference of Social Work* (New York: Columbia University Press, 1939), pp. 495–511, and "Report of Groups Studying the Community Organization Process," *Proceedings of the National Conference of Social Work* (New York: Columbia University Press, 1940), pp. 456–73.

1939 report stated that "community organization is concerned with (a) the discovery and definition of needs; (b) the elimination and prevention of social needs and disabilities, so far as possible; and (c) the articulation of resources and needs, and the constant readjustment of resources in order better to meet changing needs."

Community Organization as Process

The Lane reports and other earlier formulations of community organization practice viewed the practitioner primarily as an enabler in carrying out a process. The practitioner was seen not as an expert in a specific substantive field, but as an expert in carrying out a process that helps to bring people together to clarify their problems, identify their needs, and help them to develop their capacity to deal with their own problems more effectively.

The Lane reports served to stimulate considerable discussion and efforts at refinement over subsequent years. Articles appeared in the *Social Work Yearbook* (now the *Encyclopedia of Social Work*); a number of papers were presented at national meetings; and several important textbooks were published.

The first of these textbooks was Wayne McMillen's *Community Organization for Social Welfare*, in 1945, which carried forward the process perspective of the Lane reports.[6] McMillen's book was specifically oriented to social welfare agencies dealing with the provision of services by both public and voluntary agencies; with matters of interpretation of social welfare programs and needs; and with social welfare coordination, joint financing, and planning by agencies.

A second book, *Community Organization: Theory and Principles,* 1955, was authored by Murray Ross, School of Social Work, University of Toronto. Ross, whose experience was primarily in the community development field, agreed with Lane on the importance of process but placed his emphasis on integration of the group. Ross viewed the community organization process as not limited to social welfare problems, programs, and agencies. In describing the process, he identified a series of principles that could be utilized in a variety of community programs and with respect to a variety of community problems and needs:

Community organization, as the term is to be used in this book, is to mean a process by which a community identifies its needs or objectives, orders (or ranks) these

---

[6]Wayne McMillen, *Community Organization for Social Welfare* (Chicago: University of Chicago Press, 1945).

needs or objectives, finds the resources (internal and/or external) to deal with these needs or objectives, takes action in respect to them, and in so doing extends and develops cooperative and collaborative attitudes and practices in the community.[7]

The 1962 National Association of Social Workers (NASW) Report

The NASW report, "Defining Community Organization Practice," identified community organization concepts following categories used in the earlier document prepared in 1956 for the NASW Commission of Social Work Practice entitled "Working Definition of Social Work Practice."[8] These categories were values, purpose, sanction, method, and techniques. For the purposes of this chapter, it is important to note that the report makes explicit for the first time the concepts of intervention and problem solving. The report restates the importance of the worker's facilitating this process and enhancing relationships among individuals, groups, and institutions, but it stresses equally the importance of attaining selected goals and influencing public social policies and decisions.

With respect to method, the report stated: "The focus of community organization method is upon ways of helping communities or segments thereof to become more effective and efficient in moving from the point of community problem identification to problem solution, i.e., the community organization problem solving method."

DEVELOPMENT OF COMMUNITY ORGANIZATION AS PROBLEM SOLVING

The thrust of contemporary practice was largely shaped by attention to social change and reform brought about by the catastrophic conditions of unemployment and poverty that followed the Great Depression of 1929. This period was marked by the shift of basic responsibility for social welfare from the voluntary sector to the government sector. Federal actions, such as the establishment in 1933 of the Federal Emergency Relief Administration and in 1935 the social security legislation, were the beginnings of expanded developments at all levels of government in the social welfare field. The responsibility for study, fact finding, experimentation and innovation, program development, improvement of standards, interpretation, as well as other aspects of community organization, which formerly were principally a re-

---

[7]Murray G. Ross, *Community Organization: Theory and Principles* (New York: Harper & Row, 1955), p. 39.

[8]"Working Definition of Social Work Practice," *Social Work* 3, no. 2 (April 1958):5–9.

sponsibility of the private voluntary agencies, also became a governmental concern. This growth of governmental financing of services and programming continues.

Further impetus to new community organization problem-solving activities and roles for community workers developed after World War II, as it became clear that although the United States was reaching higher and higher levels of economic productivity and prosperity, a variety of legal, physical, psychological, and social problems continued to plague large numbers of people. Groups with multiproblems were recognized as using up a large share of the direct services available, with very little evidence that the services provided were effective. New pressures were being felt to deal with such problems as slum housing and urban decay, high unemployment rates (particularly among minority ethnic groups and young people), health and educational problems, discrimination and segregation, and the problem of poverty itself.

In the post–World War II years and thereafter many new federal programs, services, and resources were made available for dealing with community needs and problems. These federal program "interventions" included financial aid in the form of grants, loans, and loan guarantees; shared revenues; support for research and demonstration projects; technical assistance, counseling, and so on. For example, in the field of housing, the 1946 Housing Act contained, in addition to an authorization for low-income housing, the first comprehensive urban renewal programs for slum clearance and land redevelopment, and the first federal requirements for participation of citizens in advisory roles. Subsequent legislation added such features as nonprofit housing programs for moderate-income families, low-income demonstration grants, rent supplement programs, social services in public housing, and provisions for nondiscriminatory "fair" housing.[9]

Civil Rights

The 1954 decision by the Supreme Court, outlawing segregation in the public schools, paved the way for greatly expanded civil rights activities and a variety of organizational developments that are identified collectively as the Civil Rights Movement. The refusal of Mrs. Rose Parks in Montgomery, Alabama, on December 1, 1955, to move to the Negro section at the back of the bus, where there were no seats, led to the establishment of the Southern Christian Leadership Conference and the emergence of the Reverend Martin Luther King, Jr., as a principal leader of the movement. Dr. King's

---

[9]See Nathaniel Keith, *Housing America's Low and Moderate Income Families* (Washington, D. C.: National Commission on Urban Problems, 1968), pp. 12–30.

leadership, his philosophy, and his advocacy of nonviolent mass resistance greatly influenced community-change tactics and strategies used in the civil rights struggle. These change tactics were also used in other community-change efforts which were designed to weaken the morale of the opposition and to win allies and sympathizers to the cause.[10]

Issue Organizing

The writings of Saul Alinsky and the work of the Industrial Areas Foundation (IAF), which Alinsky founded as the operational arm of his approach to community organization, also greatly influenced community practice. Alinsky advocated a more aggressive approach than the nonviolent, passive resistance or selective civil disobedience that characterized much of the early civil rights struggle. He believed in building mass organization by making certain issues the focus of constant daily activity, through which participants developed a sense of purpose that led to action and victory. The mass organization was built by grass-roots organizing efforts and by trading off on issues to gain widespread support for the action program. The key element in the change process, for Alinsky, was altering power arrangements—a thesis that power can be altered only by power. Agitation, "rubbing raw the sores of discontent," was to be used for organizational building that would lead to meaningful confrontations. IAF projects in the 1950s and early 1960s—such as the Chelsea Project in New York City, the Woodlawn Project in Chicago (TWO, The Woodlawn Organization), and Project FIGHT (Freedom, Integration, God, Honor, Today) in Rochester, New York—served to further elaborate choices the community worker–change agent could make to effect community change.

The passage of the Economic Opportunity Act in 1964, which commenced the War on Poverty, provided further impetus to the development of problem solvers and community change agents. The original legislation was conceived by President Kennedy and, following his assassination, forcefully pushed through Congress by President Johnson. The legislation provided for a variety of new programs to be administered by the Office of Economic Opportunity (OEO): Job Corps; Work Training for Youth and Adults; Domestic Volunteer Service Programs (VISTA); Community Action Programs, to be administered by "community action boards" with "maximum feasible citizen participation"; special programs such as Upward Bound, Head Start, and Follow Through; Family Planning Programs; special programs for migrant and

---

[10]See Martin Luther King, Jr., *Stride Toward Freedom* (New York: Harper & Row, 1958), pp. 190–201, for the story of the Montgomery bus boycott and for a description of nonviolent resistance.

seasonal workers; Legal Assistance; as well as others.[11] Many of the original OEO programs, in the years that followed 1964, were shifted to other operating arms of the federal government. Citizen action and citizen participation became controversial (in OEO programs and in Model Cities programs established in 1967). Much of the social-change thrust of the War on Poverty became diluted, and many OEO programs emerged more as service and/or research demonstration projects. Today limited community action programs continue, funded through the Department of Health, Education, and Welfare.

Thus social workers and others engaged in organizing, planning, and programming activities began, by the beginning of the 1960s, to see themselves more clearly as professional workers engaged in the discipline of problem solving. These community workers consciously attempted to utilize existing knowledge and social planning theory; they frequently view themselves as social engineers attacking problems with "expert" knowledge and using explicit strategies to influence decision making and social policy.

COMMUNITY ORGANIZATION PRACTICE

The practice field consists of workers who use a problem-solving focus as organizers and planners. Working out of different settings, they carry forward particular strategies or approaches for change. The work requires the ability to perform analytic and interactional tasks, that is, to determine what should be done and to interact with others to get it done. Practitioners must be able to function in multiple roles and must be able to execute a number of tasks and use a variety of techniques.

The application of the problem-solving process is central to effective community practice. Many problem-solving models, which are similar to planning models, are found in the literature and are used in practice. Although these models may differ in detail, all are essentially orderly, sequential ways of dealing with problem situations. An example of a basic problem-solving model may be presented in this way:

1. Define the problem situation clearly.
2. Obtain, study, and analyze all important facts related to the problem: causes, history, scope, effects, previous and current efforts to deal with it, etc.
3. Explore and detail possible solutions.

---

[11]There is available today a substantial literature concerning the War on Poverty. Sar A. Levitan, *The Great Society's Poor Law: A New Approach to Poverty* (Baltimore: The Johns Hopkins Press, 1968), is especially recommended to students who wish to have more information concerning theoretical aspects of this program.

4. Determine the practicality of each solution from the standpoint of facts, experience, time, organizational purpose, outcomes desired, resources, policies, etc.

5. Select the best solution.

6. Develop an appropriate structure for action.

7. Evaluate the results.

Inasmuch as no two community situations are exactly alike, the model we use at a given time must be adapted to the problem situation, to the agency or group sponsoring the action, and to the type of outcome desired. For example, if we are engaged in problem solving as part of a citizen-based community project, increasing the capacity of the community to deal with problems is an important goal. The involvement of the community, and keeping everyone informed, is an important addition to the basic model.[12] Each step in the problem-solving process is important. The first step, how we define the problem, is the most crucial step of all. Perlman and Gurin pointed out that "the way in which a problem is formulated will strongly influence how it will be handled in successive phases of solving.[13]

PRACTICE SETTINGS

How practice is carried out is very much influenced by characteristics of the practice setting. Just as no two problem situations are alike, so also no two settings for practice are the same. We can identify in a general way the types of settings or agencies that employ community organization practitioners, and we can also identify aspects of these settings or agencies that make for differences among similarly classified settings.

For the most part, community organization practice is carried out in one of three types of settings:

1. *Voluntary associations.* These are usually membership organizations designed to accomplish particular objectives, frequently "self help" or social action projects. Examples are block clubs, neighborhood improvement associations, tenant organizations, consumer groups, PTAs, civil rights organizations, and professional organizations.

---

[12]A useful model for examining broad social problems can be found in Nathan E. Cohen, ed. *Social Work and Social Problems* (New York: National Association of Social Workers, 1962).

[13]Robert Perlman and Arnold Gurin, *Community Organization and Social Planning* (New York: Wiley, 1972), p. 61. For Perlman and Gurin's full discussion of "A Social Problem Solving Model," see pp. 61–75.

2. *Service agencies.* This category includes those under both public and private auspices. Typically they are bureaucratic organizations with clients, service providers, sources of support, and designated policy makers. These agencies are established primarily to provide a direct service. Examples are public social service agencies, family counseling agencies, protective services, agencies providing direct service to particular groups such as older persons or children, and agencies providing particular kinds of services such as health and education.

3. *Planning, coordinating, and allocating organizations.* These organizations usually are involved in interorganizational relationships and are concerned with institutional arrangements and service delivery patterns. Examples are health and welfare planning councils, municipal planning bodies, regional planning organizations, central fund-raising organizations, private foundations, and sections or departments in public and private agencies.

A practitioner's role in two settings of similar type may vary as much as one classification of setting varies from another. Each setting will provide an opportunity for the practitioner to make some choices as to what he will do and how he will carry out his duties. At the same time, each setting will also have its special constraints, depending on who the sponsoring body is, the funding of the program, the purposes of the organization, its intervention targets, and the internal structure of the organization.

STRATEGIES FOR CHANGE

When one examines the many different activities and tasks in which practitioners actually engage and the different goals and objectives pursued, it becomes apparent that there is more than one method of community organization practice. Jack Rothman has suggested a useful typology of three strategies, or models, which serves to classify the major approaches used in practice. These models are locality development, social planning, and social action.[14]

Locality development may be described as community change that involves widespread citizen participation at the local community levels in determining goals and implementing action. As far as possible it utilizes local leadership and resources and emphasizes democratic procedures, voluntary

---

[14]Jack Rothman, "Three Models of Community Organization Practice," in National Conference on Social Welfare, *Social Work Practice, 1968* (New York: Columbia University Press, 1968), pp. 16–47.

cooperation, self-help, leadership development, and educational objectives. The community development model referred to by other writers involves similar methods and procedures.

Social planning centers chiefly on the technical process of problem solving and emphasizes rational, planned, and controlled change, especially in relation to the planning and delivery of needed services or in relation to substantial social problems.

Social action seeks to achieve basic changes in major institutions, law, or community practices by taking action and applying pressure through a variety of contest and confrontation techniques. Social action is usually carried out by groups who are concerned with social injustice or who perceive themselves as being disadvantaged with respect to some situation.

Different "mixes" of strategy will be characteristic of different practice settings. For example, allocating and planning organizations will chiefly use a social planning approach, but they may well have a citizen participation component in their planning and policy determination processes, which could be identified as an aspect of locality development. A voluntary association may be primarily organized for community self-help, but it may also be involved in planning. The community organization component of direct service agencies will very likely consist of both social planning and locality development approaches. All three general types of settings are very likely to engage in social action, but the particulars of the settings will influence the kinds of social action tactics employed. Voluntary associations would be freer to take more aggressive direct action than would service agencies or planning organizations because the latter two inherently have more constraints in their structures.

PRACTICE ROLES

Current practice as carried out in a variety of contemporary settings commonly identifies three typical roles: enabler, planner, and advocate.[15]

The enabler brings people's discontent and concerns into a conscious focus so that through discussion, exploration, and interaction with others they can begin to recognize their needs and aspirations and find ways of taking action. The practitioner, as an enabler, helps to set goals and priorities in a realistic way and helps to identify appropriate action techniques. In carrying out this role, the practitioner does not have his own set of priorities but rather

---

[15]See Perlman and Gurin, *Community Organization*, pp. 87–88.

responds to the people with whom he is working. Some theoreticians refer to this role as catalyst.

The planner is concerned with both short- and long-range problems. The practitioner, as a planner, has both knowledge of basic planning techniques and substantive command of the subject matter with which he is dealing. This role requires analytical ability to define the problem and ability to grasp its scope, recognize alternative solutions, and estimate expected outcomes from different courses of action. The planner serves to help clients and/or community make their own program and policy decisions by providing them with the necessary know-how and the feasibility of various solutions.

The advocate usually is closely and personally identified with the problem situation; he is openly partisan and works actively to further the interests of the community or groups with which he works. The advocate may initiate action on behalf of an apathetic community; or other times he may respond to the community's request for help. This practitioner tends to achieve his goals through organized action on the part of the "victims" of injustice and/or those who share the concern and are committed to the action goals.

In addition to what have been termed these "typical" roles, we find described in current practice such specialized roles as administrator (an "old" role, primarily involving the management of a program and personnel); broker (someone who serves as an intermediary, between those in need and the service provider, to expedite delivery of the service); coordinator (someone who coordinates various program elements); consultant (someone who provides expert help with respect to process tasks or goal tasks in a specific, delimited situation or project); researcher (someone who helps to secure information, quantify data, and/or evaluate effectiveness of program or approach); and trainer (someone who can help to impart necessary knowledge and skill to participants involved in community problem solving).

PRACTICE TASKS

The activities carried out in practice by the community organization practitioner have been defined as practice tasks. These practice tasks include aspects of methods and particulars of techniques. The list that follows is not inclusive but is rather an attempt to make as concrete and realistic as possible a range of activities that is representative of what practitioners actually do.

1. Defining the client system. The community worker operates with various kinds of communities. Definition of the client system depends on the nature of the problem, the degree of sanction available, the mandate given the worker, and the readiness of the community to engage in problem solving. The client may be a total metropolitan community, a group of communities,

or only subparts of a community. The worker may involve all residents of a geographic area, only certain interest groups, only the most deprived members or segments of a community, or a combination of these.

2. Getting to know the local community structure, relevant population groups, and significant individuals.

3. Securing agreement from clients to participate in change and securing acceptance for themselves as persons willing and able to help in a change process.

4. Assessing motivation and capacity of the client system to undertake problem solving.

5. Helping the community and its leaders to recognize discrepancies between their perception of reality and the actual environment, through exposure to problem areas. This may be a lengthy or a rapid process, depending on the depth of the problems facing the community, its present capacity for problem solving, the nature of community relationships, and urgency.

6. Sharpening the community's perception of problems through fact finding, study, and research, which may be done by experts, self-study, or a combination of both. This process may include gathering not only factual data (e.g., census) but also less tangible information about community values, customs, rituals, leadership patterns, and group relationships.

7. Mobilizing energies to deal with community problems by utilizing one or more of these steps:

a. Encouraging discontent with current conditions and the expression of this discontent, and spreading these feelings more widely throughout the community.

b. Building up confidence by partializing and clarifying the nature of these problems; selecting and dealing with situations that are clearly perceived as problems that are subject to relatively simple solutions and from which satisfactions can be gained.

c. Developing capacity (knowledge, skills, perseverance, optimism, etc.) to work on more complex problems requiring greater expenditure of time and energy.

d. Fostering and facilitating interdisciplinary and interprofessional collaboration to bring to bear on community concerns a wide array of skills and knowledge.

ILLUSTRATIONS OF PRACTICE

Voluntary Organizations and Grass-roots Organizing

In many communities in all parts of the United States voluntary grass-roots organizations are successfully dealing with a variety of neighborhood, community, and statewide issues confronting lower- and middle-class people.

These groups organize neighborhood residents or a particular concerned group (i. e., the aged), research the issues, and use education, lobbying, publicity, public hearings, law suits, and any other means of influencing change they can find. ACORN (Association of Community Organizations for Reform Now), headquartered in Little Rock, Arkansas, a collection of 120 neighborhood and community organizations in six states,[16] and Carolina Action with groups in Durham, Raleigh, Greensboro, and Charlotte, N. C., are examples of such organizations.[17]

The illustrations that follow are from field work reports of two graduate students working as community organizers for an organization similar to ACORN and Carolina Action. The two reports reflect the *inside* job of research and planning and the *outside* job of working the streets.

Worker 1 My first task was to develop familiarity with the organization's goals and objectives, and I perceived these to be organizing citizens so that they might have significant influence over the organizations that affect their lives. Tactics used vary with objectives sought. In the past such strategies as publicizing voting positions of elected officials, forcing night hearings, mobilizing large numbers of citizens to appear at hearing meetings, picketing, and distributing leaflets have been used.

My principal assignment has been to do research for city budget hearings. This has involved surveying neighborhoods and developing maps depicting areas in which citizens wanted more tax dollars spent and compiling status sheets on recreation facilities, street conditions, police protection, and sanitation services.

It was necessary for me to familiarize myself with the tax office, check what information was open to the public and what was closed, and why. I checked at the Institute of Government to determine the legality of certain industrial exemptions and to gain information on criteria used for assessments. I developed a scenario of tax issues to be followed in working with the neighborhood groups. The development of the necessary information from reluctant officials and voluminous files is a slow and laborious process. It requires cross checking of sources, detailed recordings, following leads that may lead nowhere, and knowledge of where to look and what questions to ask.

Worker 2 My activities have consisted almost entirely of "door knocking" in the neighborhoods. In connection with the questions asked and issues raised, I often have to go to city officials for information. I also have been

---

[16]See "Lobby of Have-Nots Nettles the Southern Establishment," *New York Times*, October 6, 1976.

[17]See *Action Power* 4, no. 1 (January 1977), Durham, N. C., Carolina Action.

setting up house meetings to discuss neighborhood priorities in advance of the city budget hearings.

My organization operates primarily by going into neighborhoods and digging up issues around which people can be organized. Some of the issues that have come up are a blocked drainage ditch resulting in flooding in several yards, loose dogs scaring children and responsible for biting at least one person, and dumping trash at the end of one dead-end street. On the first problem we were able to get action after several calls, finally talking to the city engineer. On the second, although some pushed for a leash law, we dropped the issue because of its potential destructive qualities in terms of the organization (many people were against a leash law). And on the third problem we organized a phone campaign, calling city officials with twelve to fifteen families participating until we could get a commitment that something would be done about the problem.

Service Agencies

Service agencies provide a variety of direct services to individuals, families, and groups. Today, much current practice is directed to specialized concerns and particular groups. The segment from a worker's report provided below illustrates the work of a community organizer in an agency providing for the specialized needs of women.

The Women's Center is a nonprofit group, open to all races, all classes, and all life styles. It is feminist in orientation. Activities and services of the center include a women's health cooperative, a referral service, counseling, and an educational program relevant to women and their interests.

I have worked to augment the existing doctor and clinic referral information file by developing a unit concerning general practitioners. Members have expressed the need for access to better and more complete information relevant to the general practitioners in the area. The development of the new information was accomplished by the efforts of the health cooperative members. My role has been to organize the project, be a facilitator, and guide the project to a successful end.

I have also undertaken the assignment of helping to develop a proposal for funding the existing health cooperative program. Both public and private sources of support are being explored. Funds are needed for expanding the outreach program, for the self-help clinic, for patient advocacy training programs, and for equipment. My role is to involve the Women's Center members and to organize and coordinate the effort to complete the funding proposals.

Other service agencies strive to meet a variety of needs and provide services to diverse groups. Community Action Agencies operating today with a mix of federal and local funds, and frequently developing projects to tap particular state or federal programs, are examples of such agencies. The case material that follows is excerpted from a worker's monthly report and illustrates the variety of tasks undertaken by community organizers in such settings.

ACTIVITIES:

1. Met with various agency representatives and community leaders among older persons to determine what transportation problems and services existed for the elderly poor in the two-county area.

2. Began planning for the Summer Lunch Program (SLP). I familiarized myself with SLP guidelines, reviewed problems with past SLPs, and developed a flow chart depicting the events, activities, and time allowances for proposal submission. I attended community meetings in connection with SLP at the Multipurpose Center and at the Community Church to determine the amount of support for SLP.

3. Met with staff, neighborhood leaders, and local farmers at the Multipurpose Center to discuss feasibility of a farmer's market there this summer.

4. Began working on reorganizing the Head-start Advisory Committee and developing a plan for evaluation of the current program. Will be meeting with staff of the six Head-start centers.

Planning and Coordinating Agencies

The final segment illustrating community organization practice is drawn from a report of a student in second-year field placement with a voluntary agency responsible for planning and coordinating services for senior citizens. The material in the report illustrates planning and interorganizational tasks in working to achieve coordination and cooperation among several agencies in carrying forth a particular project.

My project was to head up a planning effort in the county which would focus on developing a long-range plan for the boarding homes to carry out activity programming with the residents. This particular project was based on the need for activity programming in the boarding homes and on the anticipated new licensing regulations which would mandate such programming. The initial planning effort began with a meeting of representatives from the Coordinating Council, Department of Social Services (DSS), and Area Mental Health Center. We met three times to discuss tasks of the agency representatives, composition of the planning group, and to establish interagency sanction for my coordinating this project. At the final meeting DSS agreed to gather some data to bring back to the group within one month. When that data was still not available by the next month I began my own independent efforts. I initiated contacts with the Division of Facility Services and the State Division of Social Services and got a copy of the draft of the proposed regulations. I talked with staff at Facility Services several times, and they put me in contact with the Adult Foster Care Consultant from whom I received a copy of the draft of the proposed regulations.

In the proposal (which was passed by the Social Services Commission on November 9 and will be effective January 1, 1977), a state-wide training mechanism was designated for boarding home staff to be trained in activity programming. This mechanism is the Department of Community Colleges and specifically the course entitled "The Activity Coordinator Program." That course was developed in 1973 for nursing home staff, and at this time does not address the training needs of the boarding home staff population for whom it is now mandated.

Through my supervisor I got a copy of the curriculum and a copy of the modifications she had developed for the curriculum. I was instructed to follow this project in its natural course even though at that point it was clearly larger than just this county. During the next month I obtained more information, had regular meetings with the Division of Social Services staff, and secured their cooperation and sanction to investigate how revision of the curriculum could be done. I met with staff from Department of Community Colleges and we determined the need for an advisory committee to do the revision. I set up this committee with agency representatives and we met several times. Consensus was reached about the need for revision. A community college staff member was assigned to coordinate this revision process. The Department of Community Colleges now has stated their wish to have a "grass-roots" advisory committee (representatives from the boarding homes). I am now in the process of setting this committee up.

BIBLIOGRAPHY

Abrahamson, Julia, *A Neighborhood Finds Itself*. New York: Harper & Row, 1959.

Alinsky, Saul D. *Reveille for Radicals*. New York: Random House, 1969. (First Vintage Books edition; published previously by University of Chicago Press, 1946.)

———. *Rules for Radicals*. New York: Vintage Books, 1972.

Arnstein, Sherry R. "A Ladder of Citizen Participation." *American Institute of Planners Journal* 35 (July 1969):216–24.

Biddle, William W., and Loureide J. Biddle. *The Community Development Process: The Rediscovery of Local Initiative*. New York: Holt, Rinehart and Winston, 1965.

Brager, George A., and Francis P. Purcell, eds. *Community Action against Poverty*. New Haven, Conn.: College and University Press, 1967.

Brager, George A., and Harry Specht. *Community Organization*. New York: Columbia University Press, 1973.

Cary, Lee J., ed. *Community Development as a Process*. Columbia, Mo.: University of Missouri Press, 1970.

Clinard, Marshall B. *Slums and Community Development*. New York: Free Press, 1970.

Cox, Fred M., John L. Erlich, Jack Rothman, and John E. Tropman, eds. *Strategies of Community Organization: A Book of Readings*. Itasca, Ill.: F. E. Peacock, 1970.

Cunningham, James V. *The Resurgent Neighborhood*. Notre Dame, Ind.: Fides Publishers, 1965.

Dunham, Arthur. *The New Community Organization*. New York: Thomas Y. Crowell Company, 1970.

Ecklein, Joan, and Armand Lauffer. *Community Organizers and Social Planners: A Volume of Case and Illustrative Materials*. New York: John Wiley & Sons, and Council on Social Work Education, 1971.

Gurin, Arnold. *Report and Recommendations: Community Organization Curriculum in Graduate Social Work Education*. New York: Council on Social Work Education, 1970.

Kadushin, Alfred. "The Knowledge Base of Social Work," in *Issues in American Social Work*, ed. Alfred J. Kahn. New York: Columbia University Press, 1959.

Kahn, Si. *Community Organizing*. New York: Doubleday, 1973.

Khinduka, S. K. "Community Development: Potentials and Limitations," in *Social Work Practice*, 1969 (published for the National Conference on Social Welfare). New York: Columbia University Press, 1969, pp. 15–28.

Khinduka, S. K., and Barnard J. Coughlin. "A Conceptualization of Social Action." *Social Service Review* 49, no. 1 (March 1975):1–4.

King, Clarence, *Working with People in Community Action*. New York: Association Press, 1965.

Koch, William H., Jr. *Dignity of Their Own*. New York: Friendship Press, 1966.

Kotler, Milton. *Neighborhood Government*. Indianapolis, Ill.: The Bobbs-Merrill Co., 1969.

Kramer, Ralph M., and Harry Specht, eds. *Readings in Community Organization Practice*. Englewood Cliffs, N. J.: Prentice-Hall, 1975.

Lane, Robert P. "The Field of Community Organization," in *Proceedings of the National Conference of Social Work*. New York: Columbia University Press, 1939.

Levitan, Sar A. *The Great Society's Poor Law: A New Approach to Poverty*. Baltimore, Md.: The Johns Hopkins Press, 1968.

Marris, Peter, and Martin Rein. *Dilemmas of Social Reform: Poverty and Community Action in the United States*. New York: Atherton Press, 1967.

National Association of Social Workers. *Community Development and Community Organization*. New York: NASW, 1961.

Perlman, Robert, and Arnold Gurin. *Community Organization and Social Planning*. New York: John Wiley & Sons, and Council on Social Work Education, 1972.

Oppenheimer, Martin, and George Lakey. *A Manual for Direct Action*. New York: Quadrangle Books, 1965.

Ross, Murray G., and Ben Lappin. *Community Organization: Theory, Principles and Practice*. New York: Harper & Row, 1967.

Rothman, Jack. "Three Models of Community Organization Practice," in National Conference on Social Welfare, *Social Work Practice,* 1968. New York: Columbia University Press, 1968, pp. 16–47.

Rothman, Jack, John L. Erlich, and Joseph G. Teresa. *Promoting Innovation and Change in Organizations & Communities*. New York: John Wiley & Sons, 1976.

Schaller, Lyle E. *Community Organization: Conflict and Reconciliation.* Nashville, Tenn.: Abingdon Press, 1966.

Spergel, Irving A., ed. *Community Organization Studies in Constraints.* Beverly Hills, Calif.: Sage Publications, 1972.

Taber, Merlin A., et al. *Handbook for Community Professionals.* Springfield, Ill.: Charles C Thomas, 1972.

Turner, John B., ed. *Neighborhood Organization for Community Action.* New York: National Association of Social Workers, 1968.

Warren, Roland L. "Application of Social Science Knowledge to the Community Organization Field." *Journal of Education for Social Work* 3 no. 1 (Spring 1967): 60–72.

Weissman, Harold H., ed. *Community Development.* New York: Association Press, 1969.

Zald, Mayer N., ed. *Organizing for Community Welfare.* Chicago, Ill.: Quadrangle Books, 1967.

PART THREE
SETTINGS FOR SERVICES

INTRODUCTION

JANE H. PFOUTS

School of Social Work, University of North Carolina

In this section, the emphasis shifts from a theoretical discussion of casework, group work, family treatment, and community organization to a description of the actual practice of social workers with clients in a variety of settings. It is important that the student remember that great as the differences are among programs in such varied settings as public welfare departments, family service agencies, schools, hospitals, community mental health clinics, correctional institutions, and centers for the aging, the similarities of social work practice across settings are even greater. The professional social worker brings to the employing agency practice competency in working with individuals, groups, families, or communities as well as a knowledge base and value system shared by social workers in all settings. However, while the profession, not the setting, is the source of the generic skills, knowledge, and values of the worker, it is the setting which determines the conditions of practice. The role of a social worker in any specific setting is, to a large extent, shaped by the structure and function of the agency and the characteristics and needs of its client population.

There is a division of labor among agencies and each directs its principal efforts toward helping a particular client group. Some agencies deal mainly with economically disadvantaged clients, and others with middle-class clients, but most have a social mix because problems of living, such as financial reverses, family breakup, child neglect and abuse, wife abuse, and physical and mental illness, do not respect social class boundaries.

Superimposed on the common knowledge base of social work, there is also a division of specialized expertise among social workers in different settings. For example, a child welfare worker must know a great deal about child growth and development, parent-child relationships, and the psychological, social, and legal implications of foster care and adoption. It is necessary for a psychiatric social worker to have a grounding in behavioral dynamics and the techniques of psychotherapy. A medical social worker must have an understanding of the meaning of illness to a patient and his family. There is no setting which does not demand of the social worker a fund of highly specialized knowledge, some of which is gained in academic courses prior to employment and some of which is learned on the job.

The selections which follow illustrate the similarities and differences in practice among social workers in a variety of settings. Descriptions of the agencies highlight the differences among them but the social work case material reflects the similarities. Regardless of the type of problem or client characteristics, these workers in quite different settings exhibit a common concern for the welfare of the client, a belief in his ability to solve his own problems, and a commitment to using their professional skills to help him achieve his goals. This paradox of agency difference and professional similarity results in a creative tension which is both divisive and enriching and which never can be completely resolved within the field of social work.

Finally, a word of warning to the student. The selections which follow do not describe perfectly run agencies, totally satisfactory outcomes for clients, or infallible practitioners. Rather, they accurately reflect the real-life limitations and frustrations of practice as well as the satisfactions and successes. What these selections show is the dedication, patience, and practice skill of practitioners in a field where resources are often lacking, where knowledge is still far from complete, and where small as well as large successes are valued as new beginnings for troubled clients.

11
SOCIAL SERVICES IN A PUBLIC WELFARE AGENCY[1]

GEORGE HOSHINO
School of Social Work, University of Minnesota

It may be trite but it is true to say that there is no "typical" public welfare case. The services of the local public welfare department run the gamut from cash assistance to highly specialized professional services. Some involve groups, rather than individuals, as with group services for older adults, and many activities of the department are concerned with whole communities and neighborhoods, as in community or neighborhood work. Although the clientele is predominantly poor or from lower income groups some services such as adoption and day care are utilized by middle and upper income groups. Child abuse and mental retardation occur at all income levels. The

[1]The author is indebted to Al Kohl, Director, Family Services Division, and Carol Murphy, Principal Social Worker, Child Protection Services, Hennepin County, Minnesota, Department of Public Welfare, and Margaret Malloy, student, Graduate School of Social Work, University of Minnesota, Minneapolis, for assisting with the case material used in this chapter. All names and identifying information have been disguised.

cases handled by the staff may range from the relatively routine review of continuing eligibility for assistance, to intensive counseling with a child temporarily in a foster home and with his or her family, to the crisis situation of a severely abused child that makes news headlines.

The case of Mrs. Smith and her two children presented here is neither mundane nor particularly unusual for a local welfare department. As a reported case of suspected child neglect, it does illustrate the functions of a typical department, the role of the social worker, and the interaction of various services within the department and in the community as the worker brings her knowledge and skill to bear on the family's problems.

The agency is a large multifunction public welfare department in a major midwestern metropolitan area of about a million population. It is typical of departments of its size. The two functions of income maintenance and social services had earlier been separated so that there are now two separate program divisions, the Income Maintenance Division and the Social and Rehabilitation Service. The former administers AFDC, Medicaid, the SSI State Supplement, general assistance, and food stamp eligibility. The latter includes two subdivisions, the Adult Social Services and the Family and Children's Service. The Family and Children's Service offers the full range of child welfare services either directly or through purchase from other community agencies. The Smith case involves the Child Protective Services unit of the Family and Children's Service. This unit is typical of such units in larger welfare departments. It is highly professionalized and staffed by social workers most of whom have graduate social work training. Several students from schools of social work are placed in the unit for their field instruction.

The offices of the department are located in the downtown area of the city and occupy several floors of the new county government building and several nearby buildings, including one devoted entirely to income maintenance staff.

In the spring of 1976, relatives of Mrs. Smith called the department to complain about Mrs. Smith's care of her two children, Julie, age four, and Johnny, age two, alleging physical and medical neglect of the two children. The call was taken by the department's Central Application and Intake Unit, which takes and screens all referrals whether made in person or by mail or phone. After a brief exploration of the situation on the phone with Mrs. Smith's relatives to get identifying information, addresses, and phone numbers, and a picture of the problem, the assessment worker quickly concluded that the case warranted a prompt and complete investigation by the outreach staff of the Child Protective Service and immediately initiated a referral to that unit.

A report of suspected child neglect or abuse brings a welfare department into immediate action. Children of Julie's and Johnny's age are extremely vulnerable as they cannot defend themselves or readily bring their plight to the attention of other adults. Moreover, the public welfare agency is charged under the state Child Abuse and Neglect Reporting Law to receive and investigate any reported case of suspected child neglect or abuse and to take any steps necessary to protect and care for the child.

The Smith case illustrates a fundamental characteristic of a public welfare department. It operates under statutory authority. Within the limits of its resources, the agency must offer or provide services to all who qualify for or require authorized services. In a case of suspected child neglect or abuse, the agency operates under a specific statutory mandate. Reports of suspected neglect and abuse come from various referral sources: the police, hospitals and medical personnel, schoolteachers, neighbors, and parents themselves. In discharging its responsibility to protect and care for a child, the agency may be in touch with the hospital, physicians and other medical personnel, the school, and the police. If removal of the child from the home is indicated, the worker may initiate action in the juvenile court and utilize foster family or institutional care. In a case of a severely battered child, the law enforcement agencies may be involved. Thus the department may be in contact with a number of community organizations and resources.

The worker's first step was to clear with the department's central register. Although this step ordinarily is routinely taken, in neglect and abuse cases it takes on an added significance. Child abuse involves nonaccidental harm or injury. Often it is ascertained only after a pattern is identified through a child's repeated contacts with several medical and social service agencies.

Mrs. Smith was known to the department as a recent applicant for AFDC. Her application had been approved on the basis of her separation and because her income and assets were below state standards for AFDC. The record indicated that divorce action was pending and would include the matter of child support for the two children. In the meantime, the worker called Mrs. Smith, explained that information had come to the department that was cause for concern about the children, and arranged for a home visit.

The complaint from the relatives alleged that Mrs. Smith, age twenty-three, was not giving Julie and Johnny balanced meals, had no consistent bedtime routine for the children, did not properly discipline them, and was not seeing to their medical needs. They referred to a breakdown in parent-child relationships and Mrs. Smith's recent separation from her husband.

The worker visited the home. She briefly reviewed the information the department had received and made it clear that the agency was required by law to look into all situations in which a child might not be receiving proper care. At the same time, the worker emphasized that the department was more concerned with seeing how it could be of help to Mrs. Smith in caring for her children.

Mrs. Smith hotly denied that she was neglecting her children. She acknowledged that she was having some problems but insisted that she had them in hand as she was filing divorce papers, had moved into an apartment with her children, and was now receiving AFDC and food stamps.

In opening the interview, the worker focuses sharply on her reason for being in Mrs. Smith's home, a concern about the children. She makes it clear that she has a legal obligation to intervene.

A primary purpose of the initial interview is to establish a helping relationship with the client. Concern for the children is a point on which the worker's interests and Mrs. Smith's interests converge. It is this mutuality of interests that forms the basis of the casework relationship. However, the children's problems are part of a larger family system. Mrs. Smith has already moved in that direction as she shifts the discussion to her own problems as they relate to those of the children.

The interview situation is colored by the fact that protective services involve nonvoluntary interventions to protect an individual who cannot care for himself. In the case of children, the intervention arises from the unwillingness or inability of the "natural guardian," the parent, to properly care for the children. Thus the worker's presence is inherently threatening. Indeed, it implies a potential adversary relationship should it become necessary for the worker to seek court action to remove the child from the home over the parent's objections. Since child abuse involves bodily harm, the case can even be handled under the criminal law.

The worker is sensitive to the threat that her presence poses to Mrs. Smith. Mrs. Smith's denial of neglect is to be expected. One does not readily admit to being an inadequate parent, whatever the causes. The worker senses that Mrs. Smith is aware of her problems, however, and may be receptive to an offer of help. Moreover, the worker notes that Mrs. Smith has already taken several steps to cope with her situation. By clarifying her own role and responsibilities, the worker has also recognized Mrs. Smith's rights and role as the adult responsible for the children. Thus the worker has begun to develop the basis for the relationship, the respective expectations of the worker as helper and Mrs. Smith as client and parent.

Mrs. Smith has had her fill of criticisms and accusations. With the worker she is encountering a different kind of relationship. Another person is intervening in her life—indeed, irrespective of her wishes—has a clear and valid reason for doing so, is unhesitant about it, and yet, unlike the others, is not reacting in an accusatory fashion. Rather, the emphasis is on understanding and helping. Mrs. Smith has less need to defend herself and has begun to use the casework relationship constructively.

The worker's next task is to get the facts about the children and Mrs. Smith's perception of her situation. A simple question, "How do you see your situation?" is enough to enable Mrs. Smith to explain things as she sees them.

She states that although she has problems enough, she is happy to be separated from her husband and on her own. She wants a new life for herself and her children and eventually to find employment. The worker, in effect, is a neutral but concerned and knowledgeable person with whom Mrs. Smith can test out her assessment of her situation and discuss how she has coped with her problems and her plans, however vague at this time, for the future.

While in the home, the worker is able to observe the two children and chat briefly with them. The worker ends the interview by recognizing the steps Mrs. Smith herself has already taken to deal with her problems and suggests that now that she has an idea of what the situation is, at the next visit the two should try to work out a plan by which the agency could be of specific help. Mrs. Smith agrees and an appointment is scheduled for the next week.

In assessing the case, the worker concludes that the children are in no immediate danger. Mrs. Smith is hardly the best of homemakers but she seems concerned about her children. On the other hand, marital conflict, separation, and the need to apply for financial assistance introduce severe stresses with which she needs help in coping. At the same time, the worker recognizes that Mrs. Smith is coping with her problems in her own way, and it seems reasonable. The worker is still responsible for the children, however. In her judgment, the family is on the borderline of potential neglect and further work will have to be done to prevent neglect. This will be the focus of the next interview.

At the second interview, Mrs. Smith reiterated her determination to go ahead with the divorce and to make a new life for herself. The worker suggested that what they needed to work on was a more specific plan. Together the worker and Mrs. Smith discussed the needs of the children in relation to her own plans. As a result, the following plan emerged and was agreed to:

1. To investigate available preschool programs for Julie and Johnny in order to (1) encourage the early growth and development of the children and (b) involve Mrs. Smith in her children's growth and development.

2. To put Mrs. Smith in touch with the public health nurse so that she could get a better understanding of the nutritional needs of the children and herself.

3. To get the children to a public dental program where they could get some badly needed dental work done.

4. To provide for ongoing counseling in respect to child development and coping as a single parent.

The worker felt that the above could be accomplished in thirty to sixty days, and this time frame was agreeable to Mrs. Smith.

In jointly developing the service plan, Mrs. Smith is able to participate in planning for herself and her children. Her role and responsibilities as a parent are respected. The plan emphasizes specific achievable objectives within a limited time frame focused on problems that Mrs. Smith is able to acknowledge and for which she can accept help.

The worker's primary responsibility is still to the children and the services are tangible ones that Mrs. Smith understands. The worker's role is to provide support, make available to Mrs. Smith her knowledge of community resources, and help Mrs. Smith face up to and deal with the reality of being a single parent.

During the subsequent period, the goals of the service plan were essentially achieved. Julie and Johnny were enrolled in a child guidance clinic program that tests children with symptoms of developmental problems and works with both child and parent. Mrs. Smith attended classes regularly at the clinic; the children attended three times a week. A referral was made to the public health nurse and a nurse is available on a weekly basis. Mrs. Smith discussed with the nurse the nutritional problems of the family and together they worked on how they could be dealt with on the AFDC budget and food stamps. The public health nurse and the social worker together referred Mrs. Smith to a dental program, and Mrs. Smith was put on a regular six-month dental program for herself and the children.

During the visits, Mrs. Smith discussed the innumerable problems that she was encountering as a single parent. In fact, she was even considering attending a therapy group, had attended once to see if it was what she wanted, and was debating whether to continue.

In view of this progress, the worker suggested that her visits were no longer necessary. Mrs. Smith agreed, and the case was closed with the understanding that Mrs. Smith could call the worker if anything serious developed.

Many cases in a public welfare agency involve disorganized "multi-problem" families known for years to a succession of workers. Mrs. Smith was a mother caught in a crisis situation that had the potential of developing into a serious child welfare problem. In a time-limited but intensive relationship with the worker focused on specific reality problems that were dealt with through the provision of tangible assistance and services for herself and her children, Mrs. Smith was able to assume a more responsible and adequate role as a parent.

12
INNOVATIONS IN FAMILY CASEWORK SERVICES

ARTHUR L. LEADER
Jewish Family Services, New York City

Along with traditional casework services offered to individuals, couples, and families through a variety of modalities including conjoint marital, family, and group therapy, a number of agencies, including ours, have embarked in the past few years upon innovative approaches and programs. These are designed to reach people in new and more effective ways and to reach out to special groups such as alienated youth, the very submerged aged, and the invisible poor who, without such intervention, would not be likely to apply for help.

Our agency has, for example, developed a crisis-intervention unit for an inner-city catchment area, which offers help in a variety of crises on the spot and will stay with the crisis until it is resolved. At times this involves visits to the home, hospital, jail, or other centers, and in complex cases requires more than one caseworker.

We have tranformed a basically one-interview intake process into an up-to-six-interview crisis-intervention model for all applicants. We call this a

"Quick-Response Unit." Emphasis on realistic goals, agreed upon by worker and client, and the constructive use of time limits are proving helpful in most situations. Criteria governing suitability for a six-interview limit have still not emerged. Our experience indicates that the greater the conviction of the caseworker in the value of short-term treatment, the greater the benefit to the client. If additional service is needed beyond the six interviews, the case is transferred to the "assigned service" worker. From the beginning, the emphasis is on understanding the presenting problem within the context of the whole family, and the effort is to involve all family members early for a comprehensive family diagnosis and then a consideration of whom and what to focus on.

Beyond the initial "Quick-Response" model of a series of interviews up to six, the professional field in the last few years has also experimented with various additional periods of planned short-term treatment ranging in the number of interviews anywhere from eight to twenty-four. As in the Quick-Response work, the underlying belief is that more people can be given effective help in a shorter period of time with less cost to themselves and a quicker sense of mastery of their problems. There is continuing responsibility on the caseworker to adhere to realistic and shared goals, to hold to a consistent focus, and, near the ending phase, to be flexible about the possible real need of continued treatment.

In line with the increased concern of most of the helping professions to be related and available to people in their neighborhoods, we have developed a number of satellite offices in old and new neighborhoods. We have also opened more and more "outposts" in schools, community centers, and similar community areas so that personnel can spot an incipient problem and immediately bring it to the attention of the caseworker. The caseworker then helps the personnel deal with the problem by involving, when necessary, the child and then the parent at the critical moment of emerging trouble.

Our agency has developed a series of programs to reach youths, ranging in age from the early teens to late adolescence, who are by and large in a variety of conflicts with their families. Some of these are dropouts from school, and some are depressed and functioning in school and at home on a marginal level. Others are in open defiance against their parents and society, and some have run away from home; some are into drugs, promiscuous behavior, and live "on the streets." To reach these youths, most of whom are alienated from family and the establishment and are "turned off" from any social agency, we have developed a number of youth service centers in several parts of the city. We try to reach them through mixing with them where they congregate, in the street, schools, shopping centers. We have a walk-in center where they can drop in at any time for almost any purpose. We have a 27-foot mobile van that serves as an initial magnet for "rapping" with children. These informal ways are often "safer" for many children who can chat in the safe presence of peers but can use the experience to seek out professional help later if indicated. These informal ways are proving very effective in reaching many children, who do begin to reveal their sense of boredom, restlessness, and emptiness, then begin discussing family problems, and who in some instances become involved with their families in a more formal, helping relationship. At times one of these youths makes a connection with one of our professionals which leads to a meaningful encounter, some opening up of his troubled state and feelings, and some subsequent accommodation to family unity. We have reached many youngsters, including runaways of both sexes, sometimes literally picking them up in the street.

In a new large area, Co-Op City (in a sense a new, self-contained city created almost overnight, with a population of 60,000), in addition to opening a family-counseling branch office there from the beginning, we have also set up a program to reach out to a large group of teen-agers who were suddenly transplanted to a new area and found themselves rootless and restless (some on drugs), aimlessly wandering in a central mall. A small group of young professional workers began mixing and informally "rapping" with these youths. Once having won their trust and having reached them on an emotional level, these workers were able to form groups that were designed to probe the youths' feelings and family conflicts. This resulted in cooperative action that led to a more productive and socially satisfying life. A number of these children were stimulated to seek out individual help, and this often was a first step toward family involvement; at other times, referrals were made to the regular counseling unit. Since the beginning we have also had a part in operating a "Hot Line," manned by volunteers whom we train. A wide variety of problems from both adults and (especially) children, involving sex, drugs, and family conflict, keeps surfacing.

In another newer but not so large area, Starrett City, we have developed a similar service designed in the same way to be available to youths and families in a completely new community.

A number of family agencies have developed an "advocacy" service. With increasing bureaucratization and the hardships of negotiating the medical and particularly the welfare system, caseworkers (or sometimes case aides or paraprofessionals) find it necessary to pursue benefits vigorously on behalf of their clients, sometimes actually accompanying the client to speak in his behalf. It is at times necessary to apply considerable pressure through repeated telephone calls to supervisory personnel or to help the client in person present himself strongly and loudly. In our agency, which has a legal aid service, we sometimes call upon our legal staff for supplementary pressure and assistance.

Group therapy is a well-established modality in the professional fields. Agencies utilize this service with various kinds of groups, from young children to the aged, including parents and children, young single adults, married couples, single parents, and so forth. In line with heightened interest in coping with death in many spheres, including the communication media, our agency has begun a series of groups for the widowed.

Multifamily groups are relatively new but expanding. Here, generally three families, including all parents and children, meet regularly, often with two caseworkers serving as co-therapists, to work out and help each other out with a variety of child-parent and marital problems.

Sex therapy has become quite popular. In the last few years, under the direction of our psychiatric director, we have developed a training and a clinical program for the treatment of a variety of sexual problems, usually in conjunction with casework treatment of psychological problems in the marriage.

The following summaries of case material are examples basically of innovative ventures. Names of participant clients have been eliminated. The first case described was handled by our Quick-Response Unit.

Mr. and Mrs. L. (both forty-seven years old) and their two children, Mary age seven and a half, and Jane, age six and a half, were seen six times. The family was seen initially together. Mr. and Mrs. L. were seen alone for the second interview, the third session was split, first with parents, then with the children, the fourth and fifth sessions were held in the playroom with the whole family, the sixth interview was in my office with the whole family.

Mr. and Mrs. L. applied to the agency upon recommendation of the children's school psychologist. Jane was disruptive in class, at least twice a week—temper tantrums, kicking other students. This behavior was unlike her behavior the previous year, first grade, during which time her testing showed her to be in the 99th percentile of her class; this year, she was not reading up to grade level. Mary was, according to the psychologist, a "model child" —bright, hard worker, many friends, and no problems with teacher or other classmates. What broke down in the family's usual style of operating was Jane's new disruptive behavior, and the school was pressing to obtain family counseling.

Mr. L. had a steady work history with the City of New York. He was a bright, articulate, overweight, appealing man who expressed in the first interview much concern about Jane's behavior and appeared highly motivated to work as a family to help Jane. Mrs. L. was also overweight and worked as a travel agent part-time. She was bright and articulate but was extremely resistive to exploring the family situation, insisting Jane's behavior was a mystery, unrelated to events in the family. She was extremely rigid and controlled in acting as spokesman for the family, using denial as a primary defense. Mary, the 7½-year-old, was a very bright, extremely verbal, pretty child. Jane, the 6½-year-old, was a plump, nice-looking little girl who was also extremely bright and verbal. Both children were able to articulate what they were feeling, with prodding, when the feelings were "appropriate" in their family system—i.e., happy. Jane could say she was "upset-nervous" and "I don't know why," but it was evident that expression of feeling was taboo, as everyone, especially the children, would change the subject, or the girls would become disruptive (run in and out of the room).

In exploring a precipitant to Jane's disruptive behavior in school, I inquired about any shifts in the family recently. Mrs. L. stated that the only thing she could think of was that the girls' "nanny," Dora, died in August and they had not told the children, for fear that it might upset them. Dora, a Dominican woman, had been with the family as a live-in nanny since Jane was born. In June, she was hit by a car and was hospitalized for a week, but returned then to the family until August. She went to visit relatives in Canada for vacation, during which time she suffered a brain hemorrhage and died within a week. Dora's cousin called Mrs. L. to let her know and the message from Mrs. L. was clearly "don't talk about it." The girls were told that Dora was in Canada that she was sick and that's why she was not with them. During the first interview in talking about Dora, the girls became noticeably anxious, went for water, etc., during which time Mrs. L. quickly and quietly let me know that Dora was dead, but the girls didn't know, knowing this to be a critical issue to be dealt with. I asked to see Mr. and Mrs. L. alone for the second interview. The girls both expressed delight that they wouldn't have to come, possibly relieved that the spotlight was taken from them. Jane was the major scape-goat, but Mary was also troubled; she would provoke Jane at home into physical fights, was jealous and competitive. Mary was only a year old when Jane was born and was reacting to this family addition.

At the end of the first session I decided to focus on how the family was reacting to Dora's absence as it was evident that no one had mourned her death and in light of how the family patterns and roles had shifted since then. Jane was able to say how very worried she was about Dora and how she missed her. Mary said she didn't miss her really, "only that she brought us candy and my mother doesn't, she's mean."

The second interview was focused on evaluating the family's strengths, weaknesses, and coping abilities as well as discussing Dora's death. Mr. and Mrs. L. are a couple who like and love each other very much, who are free to talk to each other, and who consider their relationship a special one; they both love their children, deny favoritism. In talking about Dora's death Mr. L. stated that he felt it was time to tell the children, but that Mrs. L. always has a problem with "death." Pursuing this, I discovered that Mrs. L.'s own mother died when she was three and I geared the session toward helping Mrs. L. accept her feelings of sadness and abandonment, rather than maintain her rigid denial of this having had any affect on her. Mr. L. was supportive of hearing Mrs. L. speak—"she's never talked about it"—with Mrs. L. originally responding, "I don't think there's anything to talk about," to "I don't like sharing my problems." With his interest and my support, Mrs. L. was able to vent her feelings of being alone as a child and sad. Her father had remarried to an apparently rejecting woman and she and her sister were left to themselves. Mrs. L. left home after high school graduation, moved to New York from Detroit, worked in travel agencies, and met and married Mr. L. in 1961. She was able to connect her own rejection of Dora's death with the trouble she has in dealing with death in general. I was extremely supportive to Mrs. L. as she expressed her feelings as well as giving credit to her. Also, I encouraged Mrs. L. to talk about her feelings about giving up her work to shift to the full-time mother role. She was initially resentful of it and still was, though she denied it.

I stated that I believed Jane's misbehavior was a reaction to her feelings about Dora's absence—that I felt the children knew that Dora was dead and needed to be told, that their fantasies could be of their being responsible in some way, etc. Both Mr. and Mrs. L. agreed and agreed to tell the children in the coming week. The L.'s experienced the death of Mr. L.'s mother two years previously, so we reviewed how they coped with that death, which was of great benefit to their present task of coping with this present event.

The third session Mr. and Mrs. L. first came in alone, at my request, to let me know that Mr. L. had told the girls that Dora had died in August as a result of her car accident and that she was in heaven and would not be returning to them. I gave much credit to the L.'s for doing this particularly difficult task. Jane began to cry and Mrs. L. was able to cradle her through the tears. Mary had no visible reaction. I encouraged Mr. and Mrs. L. along with the girls to talk about their feelings and all along, I was supportive. What then came out was from Mary: since Dora had left, mother had been working only part-time and was not as good to them as Dora had been. Apparently Dora spoiled the children, something that Mrs. L. disliked, and she was planning to let Dora go in a year once she was able to collect social security. So Mrs. L. felt guilty now that Dora was dead; she really was jealous of the girls' affection for Dora and resented their misbehavior when with her.

So the task at hand was dual: to continue helping them mourn as well as to help the family shift to having Mrs. L. assume and carry out more effectively the role of mother. Mr. L. was able to be drawn on as a resource for helping Mrs. L. parent two bright, precocious, and many times energy-draining children. They split the responsibility (taking them to school, cooking, etc.), thereby alleviating some strains from Mrs. L. Mr. L. seemed pleased.

My assessment of this family was basically that their equilibrium had been disrupted by Dora's death. The disruption had continued because of the family's ongoing message that expression of feelings was not to be tolerated, compounded by the shifts of roles for the mother (from out of home to full-time mother) and the resulting strain for all involved (though the parents rigidly adhered to their marriage being a solid one without major disagreements), giving rise to anxiety, being acted out by Jane primarily, though sometimes spurred on by Mary. Discussion of the origin of the anxiety among all family members with the girls hearing their mother talk about her own childhood began the restoration of equilibrium to the family. I also encouraged Mr. and Mrs. L. to talk about themselves, their history of meeting, marriage, and desire for children. The girls made a play in the fourth session.

Mary's puppet was a mother and she carved out a baby, stating that the play was about a little baby being thrown out of the house. I said that it seemed that she felt left out in the family and that it must be hard to have to share her parents with her sister. My evidence about this came from Mr. and Mrs. L.'s stating that Mary always had to be on stage, to have the attention of all, and was extremely demanding and difficult when she did not get her way. In the office, Mr. and Mrs. L. were able to show Mary their love and concern for her as well as add that she wasn't going to be left out of the family.

Specific interventions used in treatment were play therapy with the girls and allowing them to express their feelings as well as to help their parents see, through the girls' play, what the girls were experiencing. The plays primarily consisted of Mary's fear of being left out and Jane's gradual learning to say what she felt and having the parents feel okay about it, rather than exploding in tantrums at school. Also, encouraging Mr. and Mrs. L. themselves to talk about their past disappointments as well as joys helped bring Mr. and Mrs. L. closer.

I spoke with the school psychologist periodically during our six-week contract, and reports on Jane improved. There had been no tantrums and her grades were improving.

Termination was met by both worker and family as having successfully begun to master the two tasks set out in the beginning: mourning and role shifting with both agreeing that the family needed to continue the work on their own. I believe that short-term counseling was beneficial to this family, and they also expressed their satisfaction at the girls' improved behavior. Mr. L. also stated that he never really acknowledged out loud what a difficult job it was raising a family and felt good that he and his wife were beginning to pat each other on the back "like me."

The girls, especially Jane, stated that they were angry at ending, that they liked playing in the playroom. I encouraged this expression of anger and then said that separations were always sad and that I would miss them. I explained that their mother and dad and I believed that their family could continue on their own now and talk among themselves on their own without me, in their house. I asked if they agreed. Jane said "maybe"; Mary kept playing. I hugged both and explained the follow-up date.

Follow-up two months later showed continued improvement in the grades and behavior of Jane, though Mrs. L. was still concerned with their competition and fights. The family in general was very pleased with their continued improvement. On exploring the possibility of continued service (my concern primarily being Mary's behavior—feelings of abandonment, etc.), both Mr. and Mrs. L. felt they could work things out themselves, but if not, they would call.

The following material is the recording of the first session of a Multifamily Therapy Group. Here generally three to four families meet weekly, usually with two therapists to help them deal with common problems in family living. In this group of three families (X, Y, and Z) there were three married couples, two of whom had three children and one of whom had two. The children ranged in age from five to eighteen.

The group began with the usual uneasiness, although several people asserted themselves and came in to make introductions and tell something about themselves. Joan (Mrs. X) was particularly gushy about her symptoms, Laura (Mrs. Z) fairly straightforward about some marital discontent and difficulties around menopause with her feelings, and Paul (Mr. Y) open about his alcoholism. It helped them to air these issues, but there was a great deal of beginning time spent on the fact that families can have problems and that this is not the end of the world, and also that the existence of problems is not particularly unique. After talking about this at some length, people were more willing to jump in and at least share on the surface what it was they were struggling with. They were very reassuring to each other in terms of the acceptability of making mistakes and Gail Z (seventeen) also talked about her flight from home at too early an age, which was not successful. Toward the middle and end of the group, Jody Z (thirteen) confronted her mother around some very strong feelings that she had which she thought would either kill or injure the mother or in some way cause Laura great uncomfortable pain. The theme of wounding a parent who easily cries or is hurt was a big one, and while most of the children did not participate, it obviously had meaning even to those who were silent. We talked about the flip side of this then for Jody, who holds her feelings in, and tried to draw Gary (Mr. X) out on all that he holds in which results in physical symptoms which cause him great pain. Jody's openness in the group had an element of anger and certainly received a push from Gail who sat conferring with her privately and egging her on. I believed that Gail, in this family, felt that she was a bad influence on the other girls because mother put it in these terms, and I thought Gail would have liked to see other sisters assert themselves on their own without having it associated with her badness. Laura was floored by the attack but did get some good feedback from other group members and some eye-openers about her relationship with this particular daughter.

256

Another theme was parents wanting to escape from the pressures of children and the children's reactions as shared by Gail that the word "escape" had a terrible negative connotation and that it was quite hard to take in that a parent would have such a need. There was much discussion around this reality of both parenthood and childhood, with most people participating. We made the point that all feelings can exist and that there is no right or wrong with regard to this. The issue of people's fears was brought up around Joan's fears of riding the trains and Doris's (Mrs. Y's) fears of letting go. In both of these families we highlighted the difficulty of separating from children. The co-therapist and I discussed ground rules about what would and would not be and tried to encourage the equal participation of all in the group without regard to age, role, or status in life. We actively intervened where one person tried to speak for the other or reveal something about the other person that might have been prematurely embarrassing to them.

We felt that for a first meeting it went well, with a great deal of risking and openness on the part of both parents and children. There was recognition that the younger children had not participated very fully but some faith that they would come to do so when they were more comfortable within the group. The X family tended to emerge here as rather lively but with a great many platitudes that were vaguely familiar from AA. At some point we would have to help them go deeper in their talking so that more real feeling would come out rather than the openness disguised under vague cliches.

The following material is extracted from a record of group therapy with ten widows who met for twenty sessions. Their ages ranged from fifty to seventy. Except for one woman who was widowed for fourteen months when the group began, all the others were widowed between one and three months. This was the first such group, and there are now plans to form groups of widows and widowers of all ages and to serve their family members too.

The group process went through several stages: first, the impact of death and reactions including emptiness, loneliness, depression, insomnia, and guilt; then, in session six, some tentative anger at the dead husband and some indication for the first time that the marriage had not been all positive; then a series of sessions on anger at and conflict with grown children who by and large do not show enough concern for them; then a lifting of this sadness; then interest in socialization and a new life for themselves.

In the first session, tales of utter loneliness and the misery of sleeping alone were almost unbearable. At times there was such a depression and such behavior in the room that Rose was prompted to say she was feeling worse and Betty, at another time, to question whether it was good to talk things out —"We're all going to go home and feel worse!" Several others, however, responded that they were beginning to feel relief.

A few women dared to mention their interest in meeting men at the second session, but the rest of the group was not ready for such a consideration. They were still too bogged down in depression and guilt. In the third session, after again talking about the trauma of death, the group turned to guilt. I commented on the emphasis on doing the right thing. What did it mean? Most said that they wanted to do the right thing for their husband and their memory; several said they felt bad about something they had said or done and if they had a chance, they would do things differently.

In session six, as the group was congealing and feeling less sorry for themselves, a few began expressing some dissatisfaction with their past marital relationship and began to talk more of their need for a male relationship and to express a renewed interest in sex. However, not all were this ready.

In sessions eight and nine there was still some resistance to looking at themselves as women in their own right and to feel entitled to enjoy themselves. But in the next session one member stated, "I feel a little guilty," and then went on to say how she was beginning to enjoy the feeling of being responsible only for herself: she didn't have to prepare meals, her husband used to complain if she talked on the telephone or if she didn't give her full attention to a TV program with him, and now she could do what she wanted. Then another member said that the group had made her think. She was seeing things differently now. Her husband had not liked to go out or entertain much; he always wanted to rest in the evening. Now she was aware that she had resented it and was aware for the first time it wasn't "nasty" to be angry.

In session fourteen, a recurrent theme of the uncaring children surfaced and old family conflicts also emerged. Fannie launched into a hurt and angry attack on her children. They were not attentive enough, her daughter didn't visit enough, refused to accompany her to the doctor, and she was going to draw up a new will leaving her children out. Rose and Fannie apparently had had a fight over this on the phone and Rose now again told Fannie she was wrong. Pam also joined in vigorously, accusing Fannie of being a martyr, driving her children away and not letting them lead their own lives. Fannie was shocked and hurt and the dialogue escalated with Pam saying that was exactly what her own mother had done to her. She had always given in to her mother and it had ruined her life. Fannie felt that Rose and Pam were attacking her. I helped Fannie see that they had a different point of view even if they were perhaps presenting it too forcefully. Then Fannie shifted a little and said, "How can they go out and enjoy themselves? They show no respect for their father." Then there was a heated discussion on how they reacted to their own parents when they were children and still carried some resentment toward their own mothers.

In the following session there was a continuation of the discussion. Getting into the area of complex feelings toward mothers, Fannie intellectually understood that Pam and Rose last week had been basically trying to help her see that she was in danger of turning her children against her, in line with their experience. There were also several complaints about how their married daughters did not side with their mothers or against their husbands. But Evelyn said that was wrong: it would only create trouble between the daughters and their husbands. Others agreed and Ruth commented how in retrospect this created a problem in her own marriage. For example, her mother had always insisted in a daily phone call from Ruth, and this infuriated her husband because Ruth really didn't want to but did so just to placate her mother. She had even defended her mother, but now she saw that her husband had had a point.

In the next session, sixteen, there was a beginning discussion of ending, but it was almost too painful to talk in full about another loss. However, Pam indicated that she wanted to end but was finding it difficult. She said that in part she really wanted to be helpful to Fannie, and Fannie responded warmly saying that she had been helped, she no longer felt criticized. Pam now was ready to terminate. Rose shook her head sadly and tried to enlist the others to persuade Pam to continue. However, Pam gave a touching account of her need to pursue her own life and the pressure to continue immediately stopped. Now all were feeling ready to move on to acting differently, to putting the stamp of widowhood behind them, and to pursuing their own life styles. Some talked about visits, others about new friends, new jobs, etc.

The remaining sessions focused on how most of the group were functioning with more freedom, comfort, confidence, and independence. Fannie was still bogged down with very little confidence in herself. The group, rather than I, challenged Fannie to do something for herself rather than just complain; they accurately pointed out, but supportively, that Fannie should try to get attention in a more positive way than by trying to make people feel sorry for her. Fannie and a few others, too, appropriately asked for, and arrangements were made for, additional individual help with the ending of the group. At the final session each member accurately reported her own progress.

A 27-foot mobile van is used in several parts of the city, as described above, to make contact with rootless, aimless youths; some of these are troubled, and a few are delinquent. The discussions are by and large informal and the intent is to help them begin to look at themselves seriously and, for some, to establish a first step toward a therapeutic encounter that will result in a formal contact with the youth and eventually his family. The following excerpts are from two successive "rap" sessions with a mixed "drop-in" group of about twenty-five boys and girls from fifteen to eighteen years old.

The kids were all drinking in the park. Jim (co-therapist) and I got off the van and went into the playground area to talk with them since we did not want them on the van. They already knew that this violated our ground rules and they did not make an attempt to come on the van. Some kids were drinking pints of liquor while others were just drinking beer. A few were not drinking.

As Jim and I talked with the kids and walked around among them, it became clear that the girls were somewhat separated from them. The girls were not drinking and were in their own group. Older kids, driving age, were stopping and talking to the girls. Some of the girls would get into the cars and go for a ride.

The boys in this group were depressed about this. Joe said that the girls were going for older guys. He said in three years they'll be back "kissing our asses and we won't want them then." Others also expressed anger and depression over the girls' interest in older guys—or at least guys that could offer them more.

After spending an hour with the kids in the park, we were able to understand the reason for the drinking this evening. The boys were strongly reacting to the girls' pulling away from them. They were angry and depressed over this. We did help them express their frustration and anger, but our efforts to connect this to their drinking were not very productive, as there was too much chaos and horseplay. We made it clear that we would be back next week with the van and hoped they would be there ready to talk and not drink.

The next week all came to the van. None of them was high and none had been drinking. Gary had two six packs of beer with him but left them in the bushes outside the van.

After everyone came on the van, Jim and I initiated a discussion around the past week in the park and our observation as to why all the guys were drinking. This opened a hot conversation about the girls dating and looking for older guys and leaving them. Most of the guys blamed it on the cars the older guys could drive. They were asking the girls how they would like this done to them. The girls felt somewhat attacked but expressed their right to do what they wanted. They should be able to go out with the person they chose, etc. Feelings slowly emerged about the importance to the group as a whole to be running around together and now the girls seemed to be moving away. The boys were upset about this and expressed their anger. The girls maintained their position but also explained that they were not moving totally away. Jim and I moved the discussion into the area of choice—for them as well as for the girls—observing that choices are hard for everyone but they are a part of life.

All agreed that cars, money, looks, etc., influenced their decisions as to whom they were going to go out with. Some of the girls pointed out that the guys had choices and often would drop one girl for another. Thus there were similarities operating for boys and girls. This led to a good discussion on feelings that are in operation when someone is dropped or when someone goes out with another person. The air was definitely cleared and there was a new sense of relaxation.

BIBLIOGRAPHY

Ackerman, Nathan W. *The Psychodynamics of Family Life.* New York: Basic Books, 1958.

The Field of Family Therapy. New York: Group for the Advancement of Psychiatry, 1970.

Hoffman, David L., and Mary L. Remmel. "Uncovering the Precipitant in Crisis Intervention." *Social Casework,* May 1975.

Lang, Judith. "Planned Short-term Treatment in a Family Agency." *Social Casework,* June 1974.

Leichter, Elsa, and Gerda L. Schulman. "Multi-Family Group Therapy: A Multidimensional Approach." *Family Process* 13, no. 1 (March 1974).

Minuchin, Salvador. *Families and Family Therapy.* Cambridge, Mass.: Harvard University Press, 1974.

Parad, Howard J., ed. *Crisis Intervention: Selected Readings.* New York: Family Service Association of America, 1965.

Pellman, Renee, Rory McDonald and Susan Anson. "The Van: An Innovative Mobile Approach to the Delivery of Mental Health Services for the Adolescent." *Social Casework,* May 1977.

Sunley, Robert. "Family Advocacy from Case to Cause." *Social Casework,* June 1970.

Yalom, Irvin. *The Theory and Practice of Group Psychotherapy.* New York: Basic Books, 1975.

13

SERVICES FOR CHILDREN

BARBARA L. GLASER

Division of Social Services, Department of
Human Resources, Arlington, Virginia

A quality child welfare program should protect children's welfare and their rights by offering broad-based services accessible to all children; its goals those of supporting and strengthening family life whenever possible, and of providing adequate substitute living arrangements for children whenever necessary. Although both public and private agencies have long provided services to children, an effect of the 1975 federal legislation, Title XX of the Social Security Act, has been to induce a more coordinated fiscal and programmatic relationship than heretofore. Closer working relationships have fostered a variety of supportive services, such as those with a health-related, legal, institutional, or psychiatric focus. In large urban areas, where well-established private agencies coexist with public agencies, flexibility to provide the broadest range of services to most of the population in need is possible. In localities which must depend upon a few service providers who may not even be located within the specific geographic area to be served, many children will continue to remain at risk. It is in the quantity and the quality of available services that a community's commitment to the welfare of children is reflected. Accessible to the entire child population should be the primary services of adoption, day care, day treatment, foster family and institutional care, emergency shelter, services to children in their own homes, preventive and protective services, counseling to unmarried parents, and treatment services. A description of some of the most basic of those services follows.

Foster Care services, which include the provision of emergency shelter, foster family, group homes, and institutional treatment must be available to children who cannot live in their own homes. In addition, specialized foster homes for handicapped or disturbed children who might otherwise be institutionalized need to be available. While some children who have been neglected or abused or who come from disturbed families can be helped by a skilled social worker to remain in their own homes, for others, removal and at least temporary placement in a foster home are necessary. The social worker must be very sensitive to the effects on the child of separation from his home and parents, and must weigh potential benefits against the perceived necessity for removal. Because of emotional damage to the child, foster care should not be considered a long-term solution.

When removal from the home is necessary, the social worker helps the parents understand why the child is being placed in a foster home and what will be necessary before the child can be returned. Emphasizing the necessity for permanence for the child, the worker establishes a contract with the parents with the goal of return of the child and the reestablishment of the family unit. If the parents are unable or unwilling to work toward this goal, the worker makes clear to them the potential necessity for a consideration of termination of parental rights so that the child may become available for adoption. Helping the child understand why he has been placed in foster care and assisting him in coping with his feelings of rejection and possible worthlessness are difficult tasks which the worker must handle. The worker also provides support and counseling to the foster parents who are often poorly trained and inadequately compensated.

Adoption has altered significantly in the past few years. From a service primarily designed to provide permanent homes for relinquished infants it has changed to a service actively seeking homes for older and/or handicapped and otherwise hard-to-place children. Childless couples desiring the experience of parenting their own infants still come to agencies requesting babies. Unfortunately, the scarcity of infants for adoption results in such couples being placed on long waiting lists. Adoption workers attempt to help couples face and resolve their feelings about their childlessness. They may help the would-be parents stretch their thinking to include parenting a child who is not an infant, or one who has physical or other serious problems. Studies have shown that careful selection, preparation, and continuing support of parents who accept hard-to-place children can assist in the creation of a healthy, corrective environment. Adoption of such children can be a mutually fulfilling experience, but the worker must carefully consider such factors as the effects of moving the child from a familiar foster home to a new adoptive one, the age of the child, and the ability of the adoptive parents to cope with the stresses and problems the child may bring with him.

Institutionalization of children can bring many of the same as well as additional problems that placement in foster homes may cause. Children who are a danger to themselves or the community, who are seriously emotionally disturbed, who act out their conflicts in an antisocial manner, or who are delinquent are children for whom residential treatment may provide the structure and therapy requisite to resolution of problems and return to the community. However, the institution may be located far from the child's home, thus making monitoring of his progress with regard to the standards of the institution difficult. Home, community, school, and social work relationships may be so disrupted by the distance of the placement that potential benefit is negated. Expense of such institutionalization may be prohibitive. Versatile, relatively small, and less expensive community-based facilities are seen by many agencies as solutions to some of these problems. If the child remains in the community, the social worker can continue to help both child and family. He may be able to continue to attend school, if he is not too disturbed. Thus he remains at least peripherally part of his community, so that later reentry problems are minimized. While some communities have been successful in establishing a range of such facilities, in others, the fears held by potential neighbors and funding problems have prevented development of placement alternatives.

Protective Services are receiving strong financial and legislative support on the federal and state levels. On the local level, both public and private agencies have therefore been enabled to provide intensive services to families who have abused and/or neglected their children. Many states have enacted laws designating one agency in the community as the sole agency to receive and act on complaints regarding child protection. A requirement for twenty-four hour availability of service workers and back-up services also exists in many communities. Mandatory reporting laws for professionals, and concentrated community education efforts have contributed to considerable increases in protective service caseloads.

The social worker who counsels with abusive and/or neglectful parents must have as her focus the protection of the child or children. While utilizing her skills as well as the agency's resources to help keep the family together, she must be prepared at any time to remove children in imminent danger. She may face parental disbelief and extreme hostility, but she must remain nonjudgmental, empathetic but firm, and able to use the authority of her position and of the courts as well as the agency's mandate in a constructive manner. The ideal protective service caseload is specialized and low. The worker is well trained and able to call upon medical, psychiatric, and foster care consultants, as well as homemaker services, to assist in assessment and treatment. Placement of a child at risk may often be averted by the provision of day care services to an overwhelmed mother, or the placement in the home of a homemaker who can help the parents learn new ways of caring for their children and of managing the budgeting, meal planning, cleaning, and other essential housekeeping functions.

The case presentations that follow show how sensitive professionals can draw upon their skills and the broad range of services offered by an agency to protect children in need while strengthening family life.

THE DEPARTMENT OF HUMAN RESOURCES: AN UMBRELLA AGENCY REACHES OUT

The agency which extended itself to the Browns and the Drivers whose cases are described below is the Department of Human Resources of Arlington County, Virginia. It was formed in 1968 as a consolidation of the county's health, mental health, and social service programs. Now encompassing special programs such as drug and alcohol counseling, parent-infant education, a diagnostic and evaluation clinic, and integrated multifunction service delivery teams, its goal is to promote and improve the health and welfare of the citizens of Arlington county.

The Child Welfare Section, under the Division of Social Services, includes the Work Incentive Program (WIN), Family Services, Day Care Services, the Adoption and Foster Care unit, and an institutional referral program. The largest unit in the Child Welfare Section is Protective Services, which, since receiving a three-year Department of Health, Education, and Welfare demonstration grant in 1974, has been known as Pro-Child. Pro-Child offers diverse services to actual or potential cases of child abuse and neglect, including emotional neglect. Such services include multidisciplinary team case planning and review, individual counseling and casework, group therapy for parents and adolescents, family therapy, art therapy for children, homemaking services, medical and psychiatric diagnosis, legal counseling, psychological testing, and emergency and ongoing day care. Since 1975 when a new law was passed in Virginia, the Division of Social Services has been the single county agency mandated, on a twenty-four hour basis, to receive reports and carry out treatment planning and offer services to abuse and neglect cases.

Tommy and Jerry

Mr. and Mrs. Brown were referred to Pro-Child in April, 1975, by a public health nurse who had been alerted to potential family problems by the local hospital where three-year-old Tommy Brown, a victim of cerebral palsy, had been operated on for a broken leg. The nurse reported that Mrs. Brown had a very hard time understanding her son's disability, was complaining of being "at her wit's end," and had difficulty controlling her anger. Tommy, who had attended a special school, would soon be home recuperating. Mrs. Brown, also the mother of sixteen-month-old Jerry, expressed fears of what she might do to her children if left alone with them all day.

The Pro-Child intake worker made several attempts to effect a home visit, but was told firmly by Mrs. Brown that she did not want services. She therefore closed the case. Eight months later, Mrs. Brown called the worker and appeared to be desperate. The worker then visited the home and met the Browns, two very needy parents whose own parents had neglected them and who had little to give to each other or their children. Mrs. Brown, the elder by several years, was an overworked, bitter woman who had listened quietly when the public health nurse had discussed with her the possibility of placing Tommy in an institution. Hysterical at first, because of her feelings of being overwhelmed, she responded to the nurse's suggestion with increasing calm and allowed her to make the referral without interference. Mr. Brown, less educated and far warmer toward his children than his wife, denied his son's handicap, talked wistfully of "college someday" for him, but showed no feeling for his wife.

At a joint conference between Pro-Child staff and staff of the local training school, a plan was developed whereby Tommy could visit the local training school occasionally, both on a respite care basis and for possible preplacement visits. The nurse and the Pro-Child worker coordinated their efforts: the nurse was to gather information for the social history, and the social worker was to drive Mrs. Brown to and from the training school, as needed. Mr. Brown remained adamantly opposed to complete institutionalization and showed his disapproval by refusing to become involved in any of the appointments at the school. However, when the Pro-Child worker discussed with them their need to become involved in group sessions, he did not refuse. Shortly thereafter, the ongoing group worker visited Mrs. Brown and was refused permission to see Tommy. When she insisted, she was distressed to observe an emaciated five-year-old who appeared to weigh less than twenty pounds and who rocked spastically. Jerry appeared to be small but within normal developmental limits. Mrs. Brown told the worker that she was angry at the family's lack of money and her husband's drinking and nonsupportive attitude. Although she attempted to find excuses not to become involved in the group sessions, she reluctantly agreed, but refused to allow her husband to participate. She seemed to resent him bitterly and noted that "he can't give me anything."

The worker then presented the Brown case at the weekly staffing at which other members of the team were present. Institutionalization seemed to be the best plan for Tommy, who could not be prepared because of his inability to understand speech or to speak himself. The Pro-Child staff supported the use of group therapy to enable the mother to accept placement and work through her feelings of loss, and to assist her in functioning more effectively within the family unit. However, the psychiatrist expressed concern for the welfare of both Tommy and his younger brother. She observed that when one child requires excessive attention, as did Tommy because of his handicap, a needy mother becomes even more angry and may reject both children still further.

A coordinated plan was then developed, focusing on the protection of both children. The worker would transport Mrs. Brown to the weekly group meetings and use the time in the car for discussions to develop a trusting relationship. She would also attempt to involve Mr. Brown in the group and the couple in marital counseling. Individual therapy with the mother was planned, which would focus on her feelings of loss and separation, and on the need to provide her with nurturing experiences as compensation for her early and continuing severe deprivation. Plans would continue for pre-institutional evaluation of Tommy and close observation of him in his special class when he was well enough to return to school. The public health nurse would make home visits to observe Jerry on a continuing basis in order to detect any deterioration in his care and well-being. Attempts would be made to expedite the acceptance of Tommy into the training school.

During the next several months, Mrs. Brown became involved in the parent group. She was extremely verbal and cried out frequently that she had a child who would not do anything and a husband who would not help her. The group members were supportive of her frustrations but urged her to accept the relief that institutionalizing Tommy would bring, pointing out to her the destructive effect that her rejection to Tommy was having on her husband and other child. Facing reality was so painful for Mrs. Brown that she began to withdraw from the group. When she did come to meetings, she remained silent with her eyes downcast. Realizing Mrs. Brown was depressed, the worker initiated an immediate placement at the training school, stating that she feared for Tommy's life. She had noted, in her individual sessions with Mrs. Brown, that the slightest effort seemed to be too much for her and that she was sleeping most of the day. Mrs. Brown herself realized that she was becoming immobilized and asked the worker to find a day care home for Jerry so that his needs would be met. She knew that she could not physically handle two children and had begun to develop a phobia about driving the car.

An intensive watch and close communication by all the involved professionals culminated in a twenty-four-hour crisis period. Almost simultaneously, the nurse reported to the worker that Jerry had lost two pounds in ten days and suffered from a bruise near his ear, and the day care provider called the worker and also reported bruises. Convinced that Jerry was a victim of the failure-to-thrive syndrome, the worker confronted both parents with the seriousness of his condition and took him to the local hospital where the physician confirmed the diagnosis.

The hospital staff noted that Jerry needed a great deal of encouragement in order to eat solid food and that he did not know how to chew. They theorized that his eating problems may have been partially due to his mother's harsh and inconsistent feeding practices, the fact that she had not taught him how to eat, and mourning for his brother who had been placed in the training school a few weeks before. It was observed that when others suffer loss and separation, a possible consequence—especially in pathological families—is the inability of the mother to continue parenting because of resultant grief and anger. Jerry seemed to be suffering because his mother could no longer cope with multiple blows to her self-esteem and separation from her first-born child.

It was agreed that the social worker would petition the court for temporary custody in order to place Jerry in foster care, the aggressive treatment of choice in such cases. After discharge from the hospital, Jerry was placed in foster care, accompanied by his mother and by a foster care worker who had already established a relationship with Mrs. Brown. She had been the co-leader of the group in which Mrs. Brown had participated. Because the hospital had given insufficient notice of the timing of Jerry's discharge, careful preparation and preplacement visits were not possible. However, Jerry's favorite toys joined him in his new home where he began to respond immediately to the warmth and attention he received.

Immediately after Jerry's placement, the foster care worker sat down with both Mr. and Mrs. Brown and discussed the impending plans. Although Mr. Brown was at first somewhat remote, Mrs. Brown responded well to the worker whom she had learned to trust in the group meetings in which she had participated. It was the worker's plan to establish a contract with the parents which emphasized the creative use of foster care both for the protection of the child and for the educating of the parents. She explained her plan factually, and described the setting of a contract as new and innovative, a way to ensure a quick return of the child if the parents were to agree and cooperate. Both Mr. and Mrs. Brown agreed that they wanted Jerry to return home as soon as possible and stated that the contract was acceptable to them. Although initially dubious, Mr. Brown felt under pressure to agree to weekend involvement in visits, while Mrs. Brown was to visit and participate in Jerry's care during the week.

During the thirty-day planned duration of the placement, the parents visited each weekend together, and the mother visited at mealtime twice a week in order to accustom Jerry to her presence and to be reeducated about feeding needs and practices. In addition, the foster mother, the mother, and

Jerry attended the Parent Education program of the Department of Human Resources, whose objective is to train parents to be effective teachers of their own children. Mrs. Brown continued to attend the group meetings and engaged in a casework relationship with the protective services worker, while the foster care worker supervised the placement and worked with the foster parents and Jerry.

Foster care was terminated in thirty days, as planned. Mrs. Brown continued in individual and group therapy. Afraid that she would lose Jerry again and more able to trust the worker, she began to express her dependency needs more cogently. The daughter of an abusive mother, she seemed to be unaware of how to parent. The mother of a handicapped child and the wife of an unresponsive man, she felt unloved and worthless. The resources of the agency had mobilized to assist and support her as she attempted, without quite knowing how, to give to her remaining child at home what her parents had never given her: tender loving care. Continued involvement of the foster mother on a day care basis, and genuine concern on the part of the director of the Infant Stimulation program, helped her identify her continuing difficulties in functioning adequately as a mother.

Mr. Brown, encouraged by Jerry's return as promised, had become newly involved in his son's care and welfare during the foster placement. When the Pro-Child worker suggested marital counseling, his feelings of trust enabled him to respond positively. For nine weekly sessions the worker arrived at the Brown home at 7 A.M., so that she could meet with the Browns before he left for work. His eagerness to participate was evidenced by his warm welcome, complete with steaming cup of coffee when she arrived! During these weeks, husband and wife talked about previously forbidden topics. Mrs. Brown cried a good deal as she spoke of her feelings of being unloved and worthless, of her need for her husband to help and support her. Mr. Brown seemed surprised at the intensity of her feelings and responded warmly to the needs his wife expressed. The worker helped him verbalize his concerns about his children and his distress when his wife drove him away with her hysteria. As the sessions ended, he was able to say how much he loved his wife and that he enjoyed her and Jerry and wanted them to remain a family. Mrs. Brown had calmed down considerably, and seemed to realize anew that her husband really cared for her and wanted to help her.

Several months have passed since Jerry returned home and the Browns completed their marital counseling. Tommy remains at the state training center and will continue in placement for his protection as well as to maximize whatever potential he may have. Jerry's weight and physical condition have been under the close surveillance of Pro-Child's public health nurse, who now reports that he is blossoming! Mrs. Brown remains in group and individual therapy, and she and Jerry attend Parent Education classes. The communication between Mr. and Mrs. Brown has improved considerably, and each seems to be both giving and receiving more from the marriage than ever before. Mr. Brown has not wanted to become involved in the group sessions, but stays at home to care for Jerry when Mrs. Brown attends, thus solidifying his caring relationship with his son. As Mrs. Brown's sense of self-esteem has grown in the warm environment of acceptance and empathy she has found in both group and individual counseling, her anger and sense of being overwhelmed have dissipated, and Jerry's welfare is no longer in jeopardy. Because of this, and because the marital relationship no longer seems to pose a threat of conflict, mutual plans are now being made by Pro-Child and the Brown family to close their case to protective service.

Ralph Driver

Child Welfare services encompass far more than placement, as the Brown case illustrates, and extend to working with adolescents who may be simultaneously in a period of conflict and crisis at several different levels. Struggling to resolve dichotomous pulls of dependence and independence, the adolescent often harbors within himself an ambivalent anger toward his family. If he attempts to resolve his problems by running from them, he denies himself and his family the opportunity for self-understanding and for joint and individual growth from which can emerge a stronger family and a young adult with a firm sense of self.

Ralph Driver was referred to the agency in early December, 1974, by a guidance counselor at his high school who reported that he had left home and had found shelter in a runaway house in a nearby community. A handsome sixteen-year-old and an excellent student, Ralph was contacted at the shelter by the agency intake worker. He told her that because of communication problems within his family, he had run away before and had gone to live with relatives in Texas. When he returned home, the family situation had not improved and he had therefore left home "permanently." The worker then spoke with a counselor at the shelter who stated that she had met once with Ralph's parents who seemed unaware of the existence of serious family difficulties but were passively willing to accept a foster home placement for Ralph, if that was what he wanted. Although the counselor urged immediate placement, the intake worker decided that an evaluation of the family unit with emphasis on determining the feasibility of family therapy would be a less drastic alternative to pursue initially. Accordingly, she transferred the case to Pro-Child.

The Pro-Child worker contacted Ralph's family immediately. Bewildered and confused, the Drivers came to the agency and expressed to the worker their concerns about Ralph. A simply dressed, middle-aged couple, they told her that they had had difficulty in reaching him for some time. They had realized that there had been a breakdown in communication and stated that they would welcome help. As they spoke of their son and their pride in his accomplishments at school, the worker observed two basically loving parents whose somewhat austere exterior may have been incorrectly interpreted by their son as rejection. They and the younger daughter of whom they also spoke appeared to comprise a relatively healthy family unit. The worker supported their concerns and their desire for help and told them that she would contact them again after speaking with Ralph.

In her interview with Ralph, she was impressed with his articulateness and with the warmth with which Ralph spoke of his feeling for his father, who, he felt, did not really care for him. He described Mr. Driver as "an O.K. guy," but one who yelled too much and who did not spend enough time with him. Less important to him seemed to be the favoritism he felt his mother showed for his younger sister. He expressed surprise and pleasure when the worker told him that his parents had stated how much they wanted him to come home, and agreed to return as soon as possible, and to use whatever help the agency could extend to assist the family in improving its communication.

In determining the appropriate intervention in the Driver case, it was necessary to assess the strengths and weaknesses of the family unit. To the worker, it seemed that the Drivers had sufficient strength and solidity to be able to benefit from short-term family therapy. The goals of such therapy would be to bring the family together again and, within the therapeutic milieu, to offer sufficient interpretation of behavior to facilitate the open communication that parents and son agreed was missing. Interpersonal problems and conflicts and individual stresses could be identified and clarified with healthy, open struggles and resolution substituted for repression and avoidance. It was hoped that the family environment would be improved as children and parents, with the aid of the therapist, would begin to express their feelings, to hear each other, and to gain new respect for the individuality of each family member.

At the Pro-Child staffing, the psychiatrist and other team members were in agreement that family therapy be offered to the reunited Drivers. In therapy, a fine balance would have to be struck between Ralph's dual needs for self-determination and for belonging to the family unit. He would need to be given support within his family to solve his problems rather than to run away from them, thus establishing a self-defeating pattern.

At their first meeting the two Pro-Child social workers who function as family therapists established a contract for eight sessions with the family. It was agreed by all that improving communication within the family would be the main goal for these sessions. During the first few sessions, the parents projected all the blame for poor communication on Ralph, who passively listened and offered no comments. The therapists, noting that the parents were defensive and intellectualized about such concrete barriers to family unity as differing work schedules, attempted to create within the sessions an accepting atmosphere in which each would feel the freedom to risk vulnerability and to express deep-seated feelings. While no problems of consequence seemed to exist between Ralph or his parents and his sister, it gradually became apparent that while parents and son cared very much for each other, each held long-standing resentments which had never surfaced before.

Within the safe confines of the therapeutic sessions, they began to share expectations and feelings. Mr. Driver noted that he wanted to be closer to his son, while Ralph began to relate positively to his father's interest in sports, rather than continuing to expect Mr. Driver to show interest in his school work. He was able to complain that his father was never spontaneous in his feelings or expression. Rather than fight this, Ralph had preferred to withdraw. Mr. Driver had recognized this, was puzzled at his son's silence, and resented the fact that Ralph never shared his feelings. As the therapists clarified for the family the behavioral patterns that had emerged in the sessions, a rigid man who wanted to reach out but did not know how and a son who felt unloved and could not say why had tentatively begun to form a new relationship. While Mrs. Driver continued to relate somewhat harshly and impatiently to Ralph, it was clear that a new family atmosphere was being created. Defensiveness gradually dissipated as each felt free to say what he or she really felt. Ralph was able to admit that he had always thought that his parents should understand him even when he remained quiet. In his own way, he may have been testing them, but this need disappeared in the new, open climate of problem recognition and resolution.

At the eighth and final session, accomplishments were discussed and the family's current status was reviewed. As Ralph noted that his family seemed to understand him better, the therapists, parents, and children agreed that the goal of the family therapy, the opening of communication, had been reached. Mr. Driver expressed his appreciation to the agency for its concern and help, and the Pro-Child social workers offered the future services of the agency should the need arise. The case was then closed, a brief three months after the referral for placement was rejected. It remains closed. The family knows that it can return to the agency should further problems develop. It is hoped that the new ways of relating to one another and the direct method of dealing with problems rather than running away have reinforced the Drivers' latent strengths and coping mechanisms. A family that was enabled by the agency to reunite may now depend upon itself to remain together and thus supply Ralph with the necessary stability to be able to cope adaptively with later crises.

CONCLUSION

The social worker of the 1970s who provides child welfare services in a public agency has to cope with unprecedented demands. The recent recession has caused unemployment and a resultant increase in caseloads. Decreased tax revenues and funding have coincided with growing need, and Title XX's eligibility and reporting requirements have served to erode the time a worker is able to spend in direct service provision. Private agencies, while benefiting from newly expanded purchase of service agreements available from public agencies, have also suffered from budget and staff cuts and client inability to pay for services. Concrete resources such as emergency shelters for families and adequate transportation often do not exist in the communities where the need is the greatest.

Yet social workers continue to enter the field. They are workers who know that children who cannot speak for themselves need strong advocates who are prepared by experience and exposure to alert citizens and legislators to emerging and expanding needs. They are workers whose personal qualities of self-awareness, warmth, and empathy, as well as the ability to combine sympathy with confrontation, enable them to use authority wisely and their skills purposefully, always with the best interests of the children uppermost. Today's child welfare social worker must respect and be able to collaborate with professionals in other disciplines, whether as part of a structured team or in consultation. He or she must be able to recognize the need for and be able to help develop previously nonexistent resources on behalf of children and families.

Well-trained in child development and human behavior, the social worker should also possess treatment skills enabling him or her to communicate with children and understand their deepest feelings. In the individualized service plans for each child and family, as well as in the public advocacy positions he or she assertively assumes, the effective child welfare social worker will reflect a personal commitment to an active belief that each child has the right to a safe and healthy environment in which he can grow to reach his maximum potential.

BIBLIOGRAPHY

Anthony, E. James, and Therese Benedek, eds. *Parenthood: Its Psychology and Psychopathology.* Boston: Little Brown and Co., 1970.

Child Welfare in 25 States—An Overview. Washington, D.C.: U.S. Department of Health, Education, and Welfare, 1976.

Children Today 4, no. 3 (May–June 1975) (Entire issue devoted to issues of child care.)

Dinnage, Rosemary, and M. L. Kellmer. *Foster Home Care: Facts and Fallacies.* New York: Pringle Humanities Press, 1967.

Evans, Sue L., John G. Reinhart, and Ruth A. Succop. "Failure To Thrive: A Study of 45 Children and Their Families." *Journal of the American Academy of Child Psychiatry* 11, no. 3 (July 1972):440–57.

Felker, Evelyn H. *Foster Parenting Young Children.* New York: Child Welfare League of America, 1975.

Geiser, Robert L. *The Illusion of Caring: Children in Foster Care.* Boston: Beacon Press, 1973.

Jenkins, Richard L., and Galen Stahle. "The Runaway Reaction: A Case Study." *Journal of the American Academy of Child Psychiatry* 11, no. 2 (1963):294–313.

Jenkins, Shirley, and Elaine Norman. *Filial Deprivation and Foster Care.* New York: Columbia University Press, 1972.

Kadushin, Alfred. *Adopting Older Children.* New York: Columbia University Press, 1970.

Kline, Draza, and Helen-Mary Forbush Overstreet. *Foster Care of Children: Nurture and Treatment.* New York and London: Columbia University Press, 1972.

Sugar, Max. *The Adolescent in Group and Family Therapy.* New York: Brunner/Mazel, 1975.

14
SCHOOL SOCIAL WORK

EDITH C. WOODARD

Social Work Department, Hamden Public
Schools, Hamden, Connecticut

School social work is carried out in partnership with education. The goals of school social work are closely related to those of education. Social work emphasis is on maximum development of all children with particular attention to those who have been deprived or disadvantaged. Educators too stress the fostering of the growth of each individual so as to fulfill his or her potential. Both agree on the task of socialization of the young for future place in society. The target population as defined by each is all of the children in the school. In order to serve this population the school social worker must look at those dysfunctional elements which hinder the development of clusters of children as well as at the individual child. The social worker gives direct service to children but must also confront general school practices and policies, curriculum, classroom management problems, and social interaction patterns. The social worker must look at the child as part of an interacting social system which includes the family, peer group, and community as well as the school.

Community problems which impede student progress and growth or which create problems must receive the attention of the worker but other concerns —sometimes brought to the attention of the community by the school social worker—must be addressed by coalitions or agencies within the school district.

Let us look briefly at some ways in which the goals of education do support and offer sanction for the role of school social work.

There is an interesting affinity between the discussion among social workers of an ecological stance which portrays the human being in the environment as a system and that being carried on by educators around confluent education. Historically, affective education is seen as being influenced by the mental hygiene movement, as was social work. Just as the social work practitioner (in the 1930s) was encouraged to look deeper into psychological variables of human behavior (leading to the refinement of casework), so were educators exhorted to look more deeply into these psychological factors in understanding the affective component of learning. Just as some social workers in the 1960s and 1970s are questioning the abstraction of the person from his total environment (such as taking children out of classrooms for individual treatment), educators are wondering if cognition and emotion are as separated as they have believed. Colleges have set up departments of humanistic education; papers are written on the use of cognitive insights to change behavior and values; and many programs and techniques, such as Class Meetings, Magic Circle, and Values Clarification, are standard classroom procedure. There is much evidence that confluent education has gained ground. Based on the ideas of perceptual psychology which view behavior as a result of the way in which an individual sees himself and his situation and the interrelations between them, confluent education is compatible with the ecological approach taken by many school social workers.

In helping change attitudes to support curriculum changes which are based on the development of problem-solving and value-clarifying skills, social workers can make an impact on thousands of children. By learning techniques which will help classroom teachers to implement these ideas and sharing them in classrooms and workshops, social workers will be enormously helpful to those colleagues. There is no doubt that workers who are prepared to be flexible, innovative, and risk taking have a secure place in the partnership between social worker and education. Indeed, it is possible that the giant tasks of restructuring schools, creating viable alternative programs, and building humanistic curriculums require the unique contribution of social work in order to "happen."

During the 1960s school social work was in transition between what had been primarily a casework service and the current view of the school as a social system. Other methods, such as group work, were beginning to be considered valid interventions, and many innovative ideas were introduced.

276

Society's confrontation with social reality in the 1960s also brought school social work closer to an understanding of the person-in-the-situation and the consequent need to bring knowledge and skill to bear upon the total system as well as in help to individual children and/or their families. Many leaders in the profession at large as well as in school social work tend to support the ideas expressed by systems theorists.

"It is in school social work that one effective worker can have an enormous impact. It is in schools that the otherwise hard-to-reach population abounds. It is in school that children can be crippled psychologically for life or aroused to do great things."[1] Schools, in the 1970s, are seen by many as being places where "the action is" and therefore a primary target for creative, energetic social work.

CURRENT PRACTICE

Social workers in the schools provide direct services which include casework and group work to children and their families. Indirect services include consultation with teachers and administrators, coordination of services in the school and community on behalf of a child or children, and organization and supervision of programs to meet special needs, that is, volunteer service, small group activities, tutoring, special education, etc.

The way in which these services are organized in a particular school district varies. Some of the current models of practice are the following:

1. *The Traditional clinical* model focuses on the individual student identified as having social and emotional difficulties which block attainment of his potential in school. The goal is the adjustment of the student to the school program. The target population is the student and/or his family. The worker strategy is casework. Although under considerable attack, this method is probably more widely followed than the literature would indicate.

2. *School change,* which can also be called a change-agent model, focuses mainly on altering dysfunctional conditions of the school which pose barriers to learning or create pupil difficulties. All persons within the school constitute the target population. The worker must have knowledge of organizational behavior and skills in effective negotiation to work within this model. This model is espoused by many social activists among social workers, but it is unlikely that it exists by itself in many school systems. This way of work would be arduous. The worker who is able to function within this model

---

[1]Norma Radin, "A Personal Perspective on School Social Work," *Social Casework,* December 1975.

might have spent many hours in direct service to gain sanction and credibility within the school community.

3. *The community-school* model focuses on deprived or disadvantaged communities or school systems. A product of the 1960s, this model attempts to develop community understanding of and support for school programs, especially from parents. Emphasis is placed on program development to assist disadvantaged students and the alleviation of conditions which affect the child's functioning within the school. The workers must have skills in mediation and advocacy and face the problems involved in both advocating for pupils and attempting to bring about collaboration between educators, parents, and students. Many workers have foundered on this extremely difficult task, as administrators are likely to feel very threatened by the implied or real criticism which the advocate for the disadvantaged child must communicate to the school.

4. *The social-interaction* model primarily focuses on a concept of mediation and negotiation. The major goal is to help the child and the school recognize their common ground and work it out together. The social worker's role is that of linking or mediating among the various systems, which are school, family, community, teacher, and child. These systems constitute the target population. Specific methods are deemphasized and the mandate is for worker involvement and intervention with systems interacting with the target system. The problem-centered approach, using all social work modalities, would be useful to this model.

No model is used exclusively. The social worker must assess the situation, the specific needs, and the resources to meet those needs; then he must make a plan to deliver the necessary services in collaboration with appropriate colleagues and community resources.

HOW SCHOOL SOCIAL WORKERS OPERATE

Social workers in schools are usually organized into departments within a larger complex, often called pupil services. They function as members of teams which include speech and language, psychological, special education and, sometimes, nursing services. The worker often functions as facilitator or coordinator of these teams.

Referrals are made to the school social worker by teachers, administrators, parents, community agencies, and students themselves. Teachers constitute the largest resource since they are closest to the pupils while self-referrals occur mainly at the secondary level. Referrals are increasing. The impact of major social changes such as the emergence of the single-parent family or social problems such as unemployment, inflation, child abuse, drug abuse, and family disorganization on children is enormous. More sophisticated methods of diagnosing learning and emotional problems have identified large populations (often as high as 20 percent of school enrollment) with special needs. The number of children in trouble seems to be beyond the capacity of one caseworker to affect. While casework services must be available as a treatment choice, increasingly the worker calls on local agencies to provide the in-depth therapy required by some children and families. Work with teachers and parents may take place without the child being seen individually by the worker. The social worker may meet with children in a problem-centered group or go into a classroom to help the teacher with a problem in pupil relationships among class members.

Children meet with social workers *with the sanction of teachers* to discuss their feelings and problems in relation to school. The worker, therefore, cannot function without a good working relationship with the teacher and must be viewed as a practical, supportive colleague. The worker must understand the pressure of the classroom and the demands made upon the teacher. The worker must acknowledge the demoralizing effect of public criticism of schools upon school staff. The building of a partnership with teachers is of the utmost importance to the school social worker. Discussions with teachers must be jargon-free and focus on the needs of children and not on the attitudes of the teacher. A very exciting force can be liberated on behalf of children when social worker and teacher constitute a working team.

EXAMPLES FROM PRACTICE

Worker W. received a referral from a second-grade teacher on a child exhibiting serious control and peer problems. The child appeared desperate for attention from her classmates and the teacher and she succeeded in obtaining it. Unfortunately the kind of reaction she received reinforced her feelings of inadequacy and worthlessness since the children were angered by her way of relating to them. She gave orders, hit, spat, pushed, talked incessantly, and moved excessively around the room and the building. Mary was a very bright child and able to achieve academically although not up to her potential. She began to take things from other rooms and the children's desks, which brought her to the attention of other staff and children. It was clear that the rejection she was experiencing was causing greater anxiety and, as the teacher described her, "her motor was running all the time."

The worker made several attempts to bring the mother to the school. Each time an appointment was set it was broken. Finally the teacher called and insisted that the mother appear. A joint conference was held in which it became very evident that many serious family problems were keeping this very caring mother from being able to move on Mary's behalf. A remarriage, twin babies, an angry adolescent and Mary's overactivity kept the family upset and in turmoil. Discussion of the child's predicament in school and the suggestion of referral to a community mental health agency led to the disclosure that the stepfather was adamantly opposed to "outside interference" in his home. The mother promised to talk to him and try to persuade him to cooperate in seeking some help for this troubled child. The worker and the mother met alone following the joint conference and the mother revealed the seriousness of the family difficulties. An agreement was reached for the mother to contact the worker within a two-week period.

Again, the mother proved difficult to contact. Calls were interrupted because of illness, offers of home visits were rejected, and school conferences never materialized. After three weeks of this, a telephone conversation was held in which the mother counterattacked, saying that she felt the school was not doing its part in helping the other children to accept Mary. The worker acknowledged the justice of this and agreed to work on the relationships within the class. The worker also reiterated her belief that the child needed help too since her feelings about herself were so negative. The mother reminded the worker of the bind she was in, saying that she was still trying to work out things at home.

Worker W. approached the teacher with the idea of trying some class meetings. The teacher, once assured that such activities were purposive, goal-oriented, and teacher-led, acknowledged that other pupils exhibited some variations on Mary's behavior and that it might help many pupils. Accordingly, a plan was worked out whereby meetings were to be held at least weekly and more often if possible. The worker and teacher met to prepare for each session, to choose materials and activities, and to evaluate the previous week's meeting.

In the meantime, Mary's situation remained critical. After she took many things from the desk of the kindergarten teacher, another meeting was held with related school staff. The kindergarten teacher suggested that Mary come into her room each week for two hours, ostensibly to "work off" the things she had taken. This was agreed to by the principal, who suggested that either he or the worker look in and chat with Mary each day while he would reward her for especially good days. These seemed like good ideas, but the worker was not wholly satisfied, believing that the child needed casework help as well.

Another crisis between Mary and a number of children led the principal to demand that the mother come in. She arrived saying she had to "get right back" and immediately began to accuse the other children and the school of labeling Mary, saying that she knew other children were not perfect either. Seeing that the mother was responding to the situation defensively and knowing the fix she was in, the worker played the role of trying to help the principal, the mother, and the teacher communicate. It helped all three to have the worker remind them that they had to look at the special needs of

Mary as well as the needs of the group to accept children with special problems. The mother began to work *with* the group of school staff and seemed less threatened as they focused more on the child in a positive way. The mother needed to receive credit for the actions she had taken in order not to feel the situation was hopeless and to feel that she, in spite of her serious problems, was a working member of the helping team on Mary's behalf. Both the teacher and the mother needed the special skills of the worker to help them communicate. This time the mother agreed to support casework with Mary. She indicated that she understood that the child had to be able to express her concerns freely to some adult. The worker had acted as an intermediary for the mother which in turn allowed the mother to trust the worker.

The plan for this child was only evolved after the worker played a mediating role within the school and between the home and the school. Group work and casework were subsequently chosen as part of the treatment plan but neither would have been possible without the intervention of the worker in the total system first. A long-term goal is to involve the stepfather as part of the helping team. However, since this worker views the child as part of an interacting system, the family configuration will be a vital part of the treatment process. The plan also called for other elements within the school system to be mobilized on behalf of the child. It is very clear in this case that the plan for Mary will benefit other children as well, as it has brought about a regularly scheduled opportunity for all pupils to discuss their feelings about school and to work on their relationships.

As a follow-up to this case, Worker W. set up a two-hour workshop for a group of classroom teachers in this building in which affective education was discussed. The workshop included group exercises and simulations and was very well received by the faculty. Materials and ideas in many areas of affect and emotion were shared and the teachers asked for a follow-up after they had tried some of the ideas.

This is school social work in the late 1970s. The worker who is willing to be innovative, creative, and risk-taking has a real contribution to make to the education of the total child.

Briefer examples from practice follow:

Worker L., assigned to special education self-contained classes, perceived a connection between student success and parent involvement. Individual experiences frequently showed that student behavior and learning improved after families visited school or had been visited by the worker. Many parents had worked hard to find the proper placement for their children, only to feel unnecessary after it was made. These parents often felt that they were failures and these feelings were reflected in the children.

With the help of social work graduate students for one year and adding a social worker in the following year, a complete parent program was established. Each self-contained class had a parent group with its own goals and program. Some families received casework and referral services as needed, but many were helped to become more secure and adequate parents through the group experience. Other professionals were asked to carry responsibility for group work—a psychologist, a teacher, and other social workers. An ability to establish collaborative relationships is essential to carry out such a task.

The groups fed into a parent-teacher group which gained new strength from them. This group constituted a powerful voice for the interests of special education children, one which was raised whenever they perceived their children's programs to be in jeopardy.

This required special skill on the part of the worker. The dual identification problem existed since the target of the parents was not always the state legislature but often became the school system. Expertise in mediating and negotiating was of prime importance.

Worker A., at the high school level, was approached (very tentatively) by three teachers in the language department about a problem they had identified. They felt their goals for a group of students who were first-generation immigrants, and for whom English was a second language, were different from those of their parents. They thought this confronted the students with a value conflict which interfered with their learning. They wondered what a social worker could do for these students. After some discussion, she suggested the formation of a group in which these problems could be discussed. The worker met weekly with the students to help them formulate their own goals for the future, to deal with the issues in communicating these goals to their parents, and to discuss some of their immediate social concerns. She tried to see each family, although this was not always possible since all adults were usually working. At the end of the year the teachers indicated satisfaction with the program and asked that it be continued. Both students and teachers felt that not only had students clarified their goals but also some parents were more favorably disposed to continuing their children's education after sixteen years of age. Some students became more free to learn. An unplanned side-effect was a heightened level of comfort and interest in the high school on the part of the students, many of whom felt it was their school for the first time.

Worker K., in talking to students in an urban-suburban high school, in casework relationships, recognized a commonality of problems from those students who raised serious questions about the relevancy of their education to their lives. Many concerned teachers and administrators believed this to be part of the general social unrest and a problem impervious to solution by the school. This worker had discussed the idea of involvement in helping disadvantaged children with some of these students and found them receptive to the idea. With an interested counselor the worker approached the principal with the idea of beginning a volunteer program at the high school. He gave support to the idea and the two adults began to work with the students as leaders to organize such a program. Teachers, reading consultants, social workers, and community agencies were contacted by both staff and students, and a list of jobs was compiled. A corps of "turned-off" students took leadership in this project and many became reinvolved in school life, once again making academic progress. Students who had never enjoyed school and who were academically unsuccessful found a sense of achievement and competence in becoming club leaders or academic tutors. Teachers were very excited by having high school students in their classrooms and working with small groups, while children were stimulated by the presence of these youths, some of whom became models to them.

Many social work modalities were useful in this effort: casework, community organization, group work with the students, and supervision and consultation with them and their "field supervisors."

CONCLUSION

In spite of the profession's tendency to swing between overemphasis on external factors and exclusive concern with inner factors, perhaps we are ready to arrive at the appropriate relationship between the two. One cannot fail to point out the many insightful analyses of Bertha Reynolds which took our profession some thirty years to incorporate and which still challenge us to consider the social control elements of our work. This is *the* critical issue of school social work, in the opinion of this writer. The extent to which we can see the reciprocal nature of person-interacting-with-environment determines the extent to which we seek to help effect changes in the environment as well as in the person.

There is impetus for change in both social work and education as exemplified by the many creative, innovative programs which have appeared in the 1970s as they have been implemented by social workers in Connecticut. These include changes in curriculum, development of parent organizations, and the implementation of school-community-family liaison functions.

In these efforts social workers can make a contribution to the development of schools so that the present experience of the child and his life-space is valued and nurtured. This is the challenge of the future. Young people now in school will have to take us in to the next decade, building on the past while creatively finding new solutions.

BIBLIOGRAPHY

Alderson, John. "Models of School Social Work Practice," in *The School in the Community,* ed. Rosemary Sarri and Frank Maple. Washington, D.C.: National Association of Social Workers, 1972.

Costin, Leila B. "Adaptations in the Delivery of School Social Work Services." *Social Casework,* June 1972.

―――. "A Historical Review of School Social Work," in *Social Services and the Public Schools,* ed. Dewayne J. Kurpius and Irene Thomas. (A final report of a project from Jane Addams School of Social Work, University of Illinois, Urbana, 1975.)

Ellis, Jack A. N., and Vernon E. Bryant. "Competency-based Certification for School Social Workers." *Social Work,* September 1976.

Gallant, Claire B. "Innovative School Social Work Programs." *Social Work Monograph #2.* Connecticut State Department of Education, 1973.

Glasser, William. *Schools without Failure.* New York: Harper & Row, 1969.

Radin, Norma. "A Personal Perspective on School Social Work." *Social Casework,* December 1975.

Reynolds, Bertha C. *An Uncharted Journey.* New York: Citadel Press, 1963.

Sarason, Seymour E. *The Culture of the School and the Problem of Change.* New York: Allyn & Bacon, 1972.

Sarri, Rosemary, and Frank Maple, eds. *The School in the Community.* Washington, D.C.: National Association of Social Workers, 1973.

Simon, Sidney B., et al. *Values Clarification Handbook.* New York: Hart Publishing Co., 1972.

15
SOCIAL WORK PRACTICE IN A GENERAL HOSPITAL SETTING

GERTRUDE I. COHEN

Social Service Department, Beth Israel Hospital,
Boston, Massachusetts

Social work in health care settings is a specialty that is growing and broadening its parameters as scientific knowledge advances and both the practice and philosophy of medicine undergo changes. By definition, social work practice in the health field reflects the goals and functions of the institution in which it exists, and hence can best be described by looking closely at a social work department in a specific institution.

Beth Israel Hospital, Boston, Massachusetts, is a 450-bed general nonsectarian hospital. It offers care unlimited by geographic boundaries, patients' income levels, ethnic or racial backgrounds. Supported mainly by voluntary contributions, grant funds, and third-party payments, it is a major teaching facility of Harvard Medical School. The hospital provides postgraduate training for interns, residents, and clinical fellows in medicine, surgery, and a variety of specialties. It has training programs, too, for postgraduate dieticians, laboratory technicians, and dental hygienists. It is affiliated with two graduate schools of nursing, and with two graduate schools of social work, Simmons College and Smith College.

The wide scope of its educational program and its many ongoing scientific research activities combine to help the hospital in its service goal. This institution provides patient care in a variety of ways—in-hospital care for acutely ill patients, ambulatory care both at the hospital site and in a satellite clinic in the community, emergency care through its Emergency Ward, and a Home Care program. The latter provides multidiscipline care to those who need it and are too ill to go to a private physician's office or to use the hospital's ambulatory services but are not ill enough to require in-patient hospitalization. The hospital has a psychiatric ward for adult patients, and the large and active Psychiatry Service provides out-patient psychiatric consultation and treatment for adults and children. Its approved child guidance clinic within the hospital setting further extends the services of the hospital by accepting referrals from social agencies, schools, and parents in the community.

From the time of the hospital's inception, the Social Service Department has been considered an integral, professional part of the institution. As such, it is actively involved in all of the hospital's patient care programs as well as in education and research. Its broad goals are those of the institution, namely, the promotion of the optimum health of its patient population. More specifically, the Department's focus is multifaceted—to contribute to the total understanding of the patient by determining the social, emotional, and cultural factors which may be impeding his health and/or his ability to make the best use of medical care; to intervene when such factors exist; to recommend and implement the use of those community resources which would be useful to the patient and his family; and to help medical and paramedical staff utilize the social worker's special knowledge in carrying out a total treatment plan.

To achieve these service goals the professional social work staff must be skilled in applying the generic knowledge, methods, and techniques learned in their graduate education and developed in their subsequent professional practice. Further, they must integrate with these the added specific knowledge of the implications of acute, chronic, and terminal illness and preventive health concepts. They must be able to interpret their profession skillfully to medical and paramedical personnel and to work collaboratively with them in order to function effectively as part of the total treatment team.

Because of the importance of the team concept in patient care, the social work staff in this hospital is assigned to specific services. For example, workers are assigned to the In-Patient Medical Service, the Obstetrics-Gynecology Service, Home Care, the various ambulatory services, and special medical care programs such as kidney dialysis and transplant, and open heart surgery. Illness can create overwhelming problems for patients and families, regardless of their financial status. Personal and family stresses, and problems in social milieu, can likewise create illness for people at all income levels. Since the hospital, as well as the Social Service Department, believes in one class care for all patients, social work services are provided to both private patients and those cared for by the resident physician staff. The social worker's function remains essentially the same, whatever the assignment—namely, to provide those social work services necessary to help patients and their families to function optimally.

Referrals to the Social Service Department originate from many sources: patients themselves, their families, hospital personnel, and community agencies. The largest proportion by far, however, comes from physicians, and frequently these referrals are made at weekly patient care conferences. These regularly scheduled meetings are often called Social Service Rounds, when they occur on an in-patient service. They are led by a social worker and usually entail a discussion of each patient currently hospitalized in a particular area of the hospital. All of the people involved with the care of these patients contribute to the discussion. The social worker's role is twofold—to teach the physicians, nurses, and other personnel what the indices are for social work services and to accept referrals on the basis of information given to the social worker.

The following illustration demonstrates how a typical referral is made in the Medical Service and describes the social worker's role once she accepts the referral.

Mrs. M., a fifty-nine-year-old married woman, was hospitalized on the Medical Service because of a massive myocardial infarction (heart attack). At the weekly patient care conference, the intern expressed concern about her future medical care after discharge from the hospital, which he anticipated would be in another four weeks. He felt that neither Mrs. M. nor her husband seemed to be coping well with her illness and pointed out that her past medical history had included a diagnosis of "psychoneurosis." He wondered about her ability to adjust to her present illness. The social worker asked how Mrs. M. was relating to the intern and other hospital staff, and he, the head nurse, and the dietician all described their contacts as frustrating, since the patient did not respond to their reassurance. In addition, they felt that Mr. M. was demanding and manipulative. Considerable discussion, with interpretation by the social worker as to possible reasons for the couple's reaction, led the group to begin to think about patients' varying reactions to heart disease, and the acknowledgment that Mr. and Mrs. M.'s behavior was the result of fear and anxiety. The social worker recommended possible ways the staff might handle this situation, such as allowing Mrs. M. to express her fears, initiating frequent discussions of her care and treatment plans with Mr. M., and enlisting him as an ally rather than an adversary. The social worker raised the possibility of the use of the hospital's Home Care program. This might allow Mrs. M. to go directly home from the hospital and would provide a physician to make home visits. The Home Care physician was on call twenty-four hours a day, seven days a week, and could give needed reassurance to both Mr. and Mrs. M. If necessary, a home health aide could offer part-time nursing care under the supervision of the Home Care nurse-coordinator. The Home Care social worker could provide ongoing casework treatment. It was agreed that the social worker would see both Mr. and Mrs. M. to evaluate the situation further and would discuss her findings with the intern and nurse who had primary responsibility for Mrs. M.'s care.

The conference discussion was helpful to both the social worker and the staff, giving the worker important diagnostic clues about both Mr. and Mrs. M. and at the same time providing an opportunity to educate the interdisciplinary staff in terms of resources available to them and methods of dealing with patients' reactions to illness. A further help prior to her first interview with the patient was the medical record itself.

It is essential that a social worker read the patient's medical record thoroughly and frequently, in order to keep abreast of the current thinking and treatment plans for him. In addition, the past medical history can offer significant information about the patient as a person, about his family background, and about the effect of any previous illness on him or his family.

In reviewing Mrs. M.'s medical record, the social workers learned that she had had symptoms through the years, due to relatively minor health problems but apparently causing her to view herself as a "very sick woman." She was indeed quite ill now, and the worker could speculate that she would have difficulty in adjusting to this new diagnosis. Also noted in the medical record was the fact that Mrs. M. had two married children. Yet no one on the staff had mentioned visits by the children.

In her initial interview with Mr. and Mrs. M., the social worker focused on two interrelated areas: the appropriate continuing care plan for this patient and her family, and the formulation of diagnostic impressions of Mrs. M. and her husband to determine the need for future social work treatment.

When Mrs. M. was first seen, she presented herself as a somewhat depressed and very apprehensive person. She verbalized quickly her fear of further damaging her heart by any movement whatsoever. She saw the future as a bleak one, was concerned about what would happen when she returned home and no doctor or nurse was available. She talked about not wanting to be a burden to her husband, of the frustration of not being able to do her own housework and cooking. She had always received much satisfaction from household activities. The possibility of Home Care following her discharge from the hospital was most reassuring. Despite the worker's efforts to gain an understanding from her of the family relationships, she could talk of her husband and children only in terms of the care they could or could not give her. She could not discuss them as individuals with whom she had positive relationships.

Mr. M., in contrast, was able to discuss easily and openly the problems he saw in terms of the future. He felt he had endured "a lot of trouble" since his wife's surgery twenty years ago, and now there was more, with inactivity forced upon his wife who had always been nervous but active despite her long-standing heart condition. He felt it was his duty to care for her himself, although he was afraid of this responsibility. He could not allow himself to consider assistance from his children ("a parent should give, not take") or from a housekeeper ("I can do it myself if my wife gives me instructions"). Of added concern was their financial situation, as he had planned to apply for part-time work to supplement his limited income. Now this option was no longer feasible. Mr. M. saw Home Care as reassuring to him both emotionally and financially.

It was the social worker's impression that there were indications of several problems in this situation. Mrs. M.'s fear of further cardiac damage and the implied subsequent death were literally immobilizing her. Her apprehension and discouragement about the future as well as her verbalized need for activity and "independence" would require casework treatment, in view of the limits her medical condition would place on her lifestyle. In terms of Mr. M., the worker felt that his overemphasis on having to assume responsibility for his wife's care without assistance from anyone indicated some difficulties in family relationships and the existence of guilt over his underlying hostility toward Mrs. M. and/or the situation in which he found himself. If Mrs. M.'s medical condition continued to require his full-time presence at home, the social worker wondered how long he could cope with the situation without having his defenses break down with resultant open hostility. Again, social work intervention was clearly indicated. In considering the total situation in terms of the best plan for continuing care for Mrs. M., the social worker, the intern, and the nurse decided together that the hospital's Home Care program would best meet the needs of this patient, providing coordinated care at home by a multidisciplined team to whom both Mr. and Mrs. M. could relate on an ongoing basis.

The reactions of this couple during Mrs. M.'s hospitalization demonstrate some of the impact of a life-threatening illness on patients and their families. Fear of impending death arouses anxiety in most people. Old conflicts are aroused frequently and may become overwhelming, impeding recovery, as in the case of Mrs. M. The dependency caused by illness is another important factor to which patients react according to their individual personality structures. While Mrs. M.'s conflict was such that she could not tolerate the thought of dependency, another patient might have reacted in the opposite way, prolonging the dependency state unnecessarily. In both instances, the patient's optimum recovery would be inhibited.

Perhaps the most striking impact of Mrs. M.'s illness was its effect on the equilibrium of her relationship with Mr. M. Prior to this illness the couple had been able to function relatively comfortably despite underlying marital conflict. Mrs. M.'s heart attack and the limitations it imposed upon her activity brought this conflict to a fore, disturbing the existing balance. The task of the social worker in this situation, as in many others, was to define the underlying problems of both the patient and her family, set immediate and long-term goals, and implement them within the context of an appropriate medical care plan.

As mentioned earlier, the hospital's social work staff is assigned to each service of the institution, and the function of the worker reflects the practice of the specific medical care program. When hospital social work practice is directly associated with the drama of new scientific medical advancements, it becomes even more complex. Organ transplants, open heart surgery, new methods of population control, and new means of controlling chronic disease have all led to greater demands for social work participation, not only in terms of direct services to patients but also in resolving the ethical, social, and emotional issues involved.

The social worker assigned to the hospital's hemodialysis (an artificial means of cleansing the blood, normally done by the kidneys) and kidney transplant program must consider issues such as the cost to patients and their families of chronic hemodialysis—both emotionally and financially. This form of treatment is essential to the life of the patient whose two kidneys have ceased to function. It often involves changes in the family's life style and in accustomed family roles, since the procedure itself takes several hours and must be done three times a week—either at home or in a dialysis center. This may mean loss of employment for the patient, or a change of job or job status. For those to whom chronic dialysis is the only life-saving treatment, however, these strains on themselves and their families may well be worth the costs. It is the social worker's role to help them to live as comfortably and productively as possible in the prolonged course of treatment. She must provide the needed concrete services to maintain family functioning, and work with both patient and family to help them to redefine their roles when necessary. She must enable them to express their sadness and perhaps anger at the situation the illness has created. The social worker must also help other staff members recognize and accept the feelings of patient and family, interpreting, for example, the real meaning of behavior that might appear to them to be uncooperative but in fact is an expression of depression.

For the patient for whom a kidney transplant is a possibility, a donor must be found, and members of the family may be asked if they are willing to be tested to determine their potential as a donor. Medical staff and social workers must recognize the implications which exist for the donor. If he gives up one of his kidneys, what will happen if the other one becomes diseased? Does he feel he "has to" do this? How will his saying "yes" or "no" affect his own emotional functioning? How will it affect his relationship with the patient?

What if the transplant doesn't work? How can the medical staff decide whether to accept the donor's offer to give a kidney? Should the donor be someone outside of the family? All of these questions must be dealt with, and the use of the social worker's expertise is an enormous contribution to the decision-making process for donor, patient, and medical staff. If transplant is the decision, the team continues to work together to enable patient and family to face the risks of surgery, the possibility of failure of a transplant, and to cope with the postoperative period, with its emotional trauma, whatever the outcome of the surgery.

When considering new medical advances such as this one, it is well to bear in mind that despite the difficulties involved for everyone, the prime concern is the life of an individual. Research, methodology of treatment, and the ongoing team work invested in each situation are aimed at enabling people to function as optimally as possible for as long as possible.

AMBULATORY CARE

Perhaps because of the dramatic advancements in the treatment of many diseases, one major area of health care has been neglected until recently, namely, the daily ongoing services given to ambulatory patients who do not require hospitalization. The prevention of serious illness by regular check-up examinations and early treatment has only recently claimed the attention of professional health personnel, the public, and the legislature. The passage by Congress of Title XVIII (Medicare) and Title XIX (Medicaid) began to focus national interest on enabling people of all ages and income levels to obtain quality out-patient care. We are just beginning to see, ten years later, a proliferation of ambulatory care centers, some providing health care through enrollment in a plan which is prepaid annually, others using a fee-for-service basis as a means of financing. The current consideration of a variety of national health insurance plans indicates the country's recognition of the fact that even today many people are unable to obtain adequate continuous medical care.

Concern about improving ambulatory care resulted in the establishment of two new programs at Beth Israel Hospital, the first of which began in 1964 as a small pediatrics program in the Out-Patient Department and a year later expanded and relocated as a satellite clinic of the hospital in the Roxbury area of Boston in order better to meet the needs of most of its patients. Currently the clinic functions as a center of health care for families (and individuals) from birth through old age, using the hospital to provide in-patient and specialized care as needed. Emphasizing prevention of illness as much as therapeutic medical care, the program has always presupposed the need for multidisciplined teams which can contribute expertise in many areas. Its staff includes physicians, nurses, social workers, psychiatrists, psychologists, and a nutritionist.

The role of the social work staff assigned to this clinic is a multiple one, encompassing both problem-solving techniques and educational programs focused on prevention of illness—physical or emotional. The staff works with all age groups, using a variety of methods—individual casework, couples therapy, family and group treatment. Since the greatest number of the population attending this clinic have marginal incomes or less, the social work staff frequently is called upon also to use community resources imaginatively in order to obtain necessary services for patients.

Many of the families coming to this clinic have used it for their health care for several years and are well known to the clinic staff. Some have used the skills of a social worker periodically. The T. family represents this kind of situation and illustrates how the social worker, having known them before, was able to intervene quickly in a new crisis.

Mr. and Mrs. T., ages forty-three and thirty-nine, were the parents of two children, a daughter, sixteen, and a son, ten. Mr. T. worked as a skilled laborer for a large firm which provided excellent fringe benefits such as major health insurance, extensive sick leave, and a retirement plan. The family was a close-knit one. Five years ago Mrs. T. became ill and was hospitalized at Beth Israel for several weeks. She was found to have a chronic lung condition which periodically caused her to become acutely ill. Between bouts, however, she was able to function fully as a housewife and mother. Prior to Mrs. T.'s hospitalization, the clinic social worker had been able to obtain a housekeeper to care for the children and to assume other household duties. Mrs. T. and the social worker had developed a strong relationship, discussing at length the meaning of Mrs. T.'s illness to her and to her family, and meeting with her physician and her family regularly. The children expressed fear that they might lose their mother, concern that they had been "bad" and her illness was their punishment. Mr. T. was worried that his wife would overwork when she returned home and fearful that this would kill her. Mrs. T. felt she was letting her family down by being ill.

The social worker enabled the family to talk openly together about their feelings: and after several discussions they could recognize that Mrs. T.'s illness was no one's fault and that they had the strength to cope with it together. After the doctor's detailed explanations and clear responses to their many questions, they understood the disease itself and could help comfortably in caring for Mrs. T. whenever she might need this.

For five years the situation remained stable. The T. family attended clinic regularly for treatment of minor illnesses, and it was a "stomach virus that won't get better" that brought Mr. T. to see his physician now. Following his evaluation, x-rays and laboratory studies were recommended, and when Mr. T. returned to clinic to hear the results, he was told that he had a mass in his abdomen which had to be removed immediately. His physician explained that without prompt surgery Mr. T. would require emergency care in a week, and further told him that until the tumor was removed there was no way of knowing whether or not it was cancerous. Mr. T. became angry, said that he would make up his own mind about surgery, and prepared to leave the clinic. At this point his physician suggested that Mr. T. discuss the pros and cons of the operation with the clinic social worker before going home. Because of his past experience, the patient agreed.

When she approached Mr. T., the social worker noted that he was gripping the sides of his chair with both hands and appeared almost rigid. Her verbal recognition of his distress allowed him immediately to express his shock at the news he had just received. "It's what you read about in magazines and never believe will happen to you." He went on to say that he wasn't afriad of the operation so much as what the doctors might find—that the tumor had spread and they could do nothing for him. He knew they couldn't tell without seeing the mass. He felt helpless not knowing; it was like being in the dark. He was afraid of the dark—it made him feel defenseless and afraid. He was pleased that the doctor had told him everything so far, had even given him the results of each test they had taken. When the social worker asked him what these results were, he replied that there were no signs of the tumor having spread. There was a good chance of the operation being successful. He guessed he should have the surgery. When the social worker commented that he still seemed unsure and wondered if there was something else worrying him, he nodded and went on to tell her about his brother who had had a similar operation seven years ago and "did not come out." They discussed the differences between Mr. T. and his brother—the latter had been ill for a year and had refused to see a doctor until he could no longer function. By the time he had surgery it was too late. Mr. T. acknowledged that perhaps he could prevent this from happening to him. He began to talk in terms of wanting to live, to care for his wife and children. As he talked of his family he began to think in terms of the strengths he had, and of his ability to cope with his wife's illness. "If I can do it for her, I can do it for myself." The interview ended with Mr. T.'s comment, "I can see things more clearly now. I don't feel so much in the dark."

In this situation the family's past relationship with the social worker enabled Mr. T. to immediately share his feelings with her. He knew she was part of the medical team, yet sufficiently removed from the authority of the physician in relation to his care so that he could discuss any of his feelings with her. She, in turn, approached him by using the social work tenet of "starting where the patient is," allowing him to face what he could, giving him permission to avoid the threatening areas. Using the social work value that an individual has the right to self-determination, she was able to identify with his feeling of frustration at having his mind made up for him. In short, she gave Mr. T. permission to be himself, to feel accepted as he was, and ultimately to use essential medical care.

This illustration from an ambulatory setting demonstrates the two basic requirements of multidiscipline practice—unity of purpose (the provision of care to the patient) and differences in knowledge and function. In the T. situation the interweaving of professional activity is seen clearly.

Another form of ambulatory care at Beth Israel Hospital, begun in October, 1972, uses group discussions extensively. This is called Beth Israel Ambulatory Center (BIAC) and is based on the premise that primary medical care must be separated from specialty care. It provides an opportunity for patients to have a "home base" and a health care team that will be the focal point for their total health care. It uses the hospital's thirty-six specialty clinics for consultant services. BIAC has five basic goals: (1) quality care, (2) education to several professions and paraprofessions as a result of quality care, (3) accurate measurement and evaluation of its services and their cost, (4) dissemination of information to other health care providers, and (5) consumer involvement in health care. Patients are offered twenty-four-hour availability of physicians or other appropriate members of the health care team and continuity of care by them, including during hospitalization, should this be necessary. Personalization of care is emphasized.

Because BIAC recognizes that the life situations of patients are of crucial importance to their health, social work services play important roles in providing treatment. Social work staff alerts other staff members to the kinds of repeated medical problems and patterns of medical care that might be indicative of serious emotional stress in patients' life situations. They offer social work intervention in these situations, both through direct counseling to patients and their families and through consultation with other team members. Social workers are very actively involved in group discussions with patients. Some are educational in focus, some therapeutically oriented. For example, a group of patients with chronic lung disease meet regularly with a social worker to share the problems and pain which have resulted from their illness. A nurse and social worker conduct an educationally oriented group for teen-age pregnant girls, to help them understand the physical changes they are undergoing and to prepare them for delivery and parenthood.

Group discussions among the staff themselves are helpful in sorting out their own feelings about illness, aging, and the stress of working with patients with particular kinds of illness (e.g., cancer). As vital as any of the aforementioned are the teams' discussions geared toward helping themselves work together as a true health care team.

It is hoped that this chapter has given the reader a basic understanding of current social work practice in a hospital and health setting and its alliance with the philosophy, goals, and practices of the institution in which it exists. The illustrations included have emphasized the strengths of the profession based upon its own body of knowledge, its skills, and its values, all applied to a specific setting and geared toward making a significant contribution to the hospital's several programs—patient care, teaching, research, policy formulation, and program planning.

BIBLIOGRAPHY

Cohen, Gertrude. "Social Work Participation in the Beth Israel Hospital's Child Care Program," in *Social Work in Maternal and Child Health Programs.* Berkeley, Calif.: School of Public Health, University of California, June 1967.

Kravitz, Liebe. "The Patient Care Conference." *Hospitals* (Journal of the American Hospital Association), Chicago, July 16, 1974.

Kress, Helene, "Adaptation to Chronic Dialysis: A Two-Way Street." *Social Work in Health Care* 1, no. 1 (Fall 1975).

Nason, Frances, and Thomas Delbanco. "Soft Services: A Major Cost-Effective Component of Primary Medical Care." Paper presented at the meeting of the American Public Health Association, San Francisco, November 7, 1973.

16
PSYCHIATRIC SERVICES IN A COMMUNITY MENTAL HEALTH/ MENTAL RETARDATION CENTER

SHIRLEY MORRIS

The North West Center for Community Mental
Health/Mental Retardation Programs,
Philadelphia, Pennsylvania

HISTORICAL BACKGROUND

The history of the Community Mental Health and Mental Retardation (CMH/MR) programs can be traced in part to a vast national planning effort which culminated in the unanimous adoption by Congress in 1955 of the Mental Health Study Act. The purpose of this act was to study national mental illness problems and to arrive at recommendations for better utilization of and improvements to national mental health resources. The Joint Commission on Mental Health and Illness, a study group originated earlier in 1955 by the American Psychiatric Association, undertook the responsibility of implementing the congressional act. The commission found that mental illness and mental retardation were among the nations most critical problems. They occurred more frequently, affected more people, required more prolonged treatment, and caused more suffering by the families of those afflicted, thus wasting more human resources and constituting more of a financial drain than any other single condition.

In 1961 the commission published its final report, "Action for Mental Health," which made recommendations in three areas: pursuit of new knowledge, better use of existing knowledge and experience, and costs. The conclusions and recommendations of this committee led to President Kennedy's message to Congress on February 5, 1963, in which he outlined the much needed "bold new approach" to mental illness and called for the states to "retain in and return to the community the mentally ill and mentally retarded, and thus to restore and revitalize their lives and reinforce the will and capacity of . . . communities to meet those problems."

Congress acted on President Kennedy's message and on October 31, 1963, the "Mental Retardation Facilities and Community Mental Health Centers Construction Act of 1963" was signed into law. It required each state to draw up a state plan for centers based on a state-wide inventory of existing facilities and a survey of need. This act further called for catchment areas of not less than 75,000 nor more than 200,000 people to be established as service districts. In each catchment area there would be a community Mental Health Center which would carry the ultimate responsibility for providing at least "five basic services" to anyone in the catchment area who needed them regardless of ability to pay or other factors. Those five services were Emergency, In-Patient, Out-Patient, Partial Hospitalization, and Consultation and Education.

In 1966 Pennsylvania passed an act which provided funds for Base Service Units, a concept unique to Pennsylvania. This funding enabled catchment areas to provide a core of services for their residents. These included (1) the assessment of problems and the development of a treatment plan; (2) information, referral, and follow-up services when needed; (3) liaison with the public and private in-patient institutions regarding patients returning to the community; (4) assurance of continuing care; (5) education of the patient's immediate family about the full array of services provided in case other family members are at risk; and (6) the performance of monitoring the advocacy functions. It was also expected that, when appropriate, the Base Service Units would work closely with the patient if she or he was having difficulty receiving service at other health, social, rehabilitative, legal, or government agencies.

DEFINITION OF SERVICE

The five mandated services reflect a perception of levels of service that a mental health center should offer to be appropriate to a wide range of individual and community needs. As such they differ in the intensity of client contact. The common goal of each level of service is to help the client to remain in the community.

The Emergency service is designed to respond to a crisis which requires immediate attention, such as a suicide attempt, an acute psychotic episode, or a serious family problem. It seeks to provide immediate relief to the situation and a disposition for follow-up services. The Out-Patient Service offers treatment services to people who have emotional problems such as school adjustment problems or marital problems but who can remain in the community and continue to function in other areas of their lives. The Partial Hospitalization service is conceived as an alternative to full-time hospital care. It works with individuals who live in the community and come to the mental health center regularly during the day or in the evening for both resocialization and rehabilitation services. The In-Patient Service is available for those who have a psychiatric crisis of such severity that they cannot be maintained in the community. The transition from institution to community is eased by continued contact between the mental health center and the hospital during the patient's stay. Consultation and Education is the one mandated service that is not primarily for direct client service. This arm of the agency is seen as a preventative program that works with community agencies and groups.

To provide these mandated services the mental health centers employ a variety of professional persons. Psychiatrists, psychologists, social workers, art therapists, occupational therapists, music therapists, nurses, and mental health workers combine their specific skills and common perceptions to offer a wide variety of services to meet the individual client's needs.

THE ROLE OF THE SOCIAL WORKER IN A MENTAL HEALTH SETTING

The role of the social worker in a mental health setting can be as varied as the mandated services. The social worker providing direct service to clients functions as part of a treatment planning team that includes psychiatrists and psychologists. As such, the worker offers counseling service to the client as well as facilitating other services required to meet the treatment goals. The social worker also assumes a monitoring function in the client's adjustment to the community. The social worker cannot control the client's decisions within the community but assumes responsibility for discussing with the client any question that might arise as a result of these decisions. To carry out this function the social worker must have knowledge of those agencies and resources within the community that have an effect upon the client.

The following case material is designed to illustrate the various roles the social worker uses in management of the client's treatment plan as well as her adjustment to the community. The material is taken from the Northwest Center for Community Mental Health, Mental Retardation Programs in Philadelphia.

Mrs. Bell, born September, 1912, was first seen at the mental health center in February, 1972, at the age of sixty. She was described as a Caucasian, divorced female with a diagnosis of paranoid schizophrenia. Mrs. Bell's psychiatric history included a two-year hospitalization in a private psychiatric hospital from 1940 to 1942. In 1944, at the age of thirty-two, she was admitted to a state hospital where she remained until 1958. The treatment extended to her in the state hospital included electro-shock treatments in 1952 and the introduction of psychotropic drugs in 1956. In 1958 Thorazine was administered to Mrs. Bell. After sixteen years of institutional living, Mrs. Bell's condition stabilized and she was put on extended visit from the hospital and a follow-up clinic was made available to her until her final discharge in May, 1969. Mrs. Bell was seen by a private physician for medication from 1969 to 1972, when she referred herself to the mental health center. At the time of the referral there was no available information on how intensive the follow-up care had been nor what kind of services had been offered.

At the time of the initial interview Mrs. Bell was sixty years old. She had lost a job as a nurse's aide and had little hope of getting another job because of her poor job references. Although Mrs. Bell came from a financially secure family, she was in debt. She had taken out a loan and her inability to budget made it impossible to repay the funds. She was living alone in a room in a private home. She indicated a desire "to give up and return to the hospital." Mrs. Bell was withdrawn, had no contact with family and no friends. It was the worker's assessment that Mrs. Bell needed an intensive treatment program and with Mrs. Bell's agreement, she was referred to the Partial Hospitalization program. Mrs. Bell's treatment plan was designed to provide help for her in the areas that her initial assessment indicated she needed help. Mrs. Bell's family did not maintain contact with her, she had no peer relationships, and she was living in a socially isolated situation. To meet these needs both individual and group therapy opportunities were offered to her. Her quiet, withdrawn personality and inability to express feelings were attended to by offering art therapy as a medium where she could begin to express herself. Her coping skills were inadequate and it was determined that the worker would see her individually to help her begin to manage her financial situation. Mrs. Bell was scheduled daily into the Partial Hospitalization program. Initially she showed little involvement in any activities. She used the program primarily for medication and financial counseling. She made one attempt to work which she could not sustain. The worker's role was primarily individual counseling and monitoring to see that Mrs. Bell came into the program and went to the scheduled activities. In the first few months she had one period of active psychosis. The worker increased her contact with Mrs. Bell to assure her daily attendance in the program, medication was reviewed, and Mrs. Bell was stabilized while in the community.

With Mrs. Bell's permission the worker actively entered into the process of helping her to resolve her financial situation, contacting those persons administering her trust fund to gain the clarification Mrs. Bell needed about her finances. Mrs. Bell was also specifically instructed in budget and money management.

Mrs. Bell was scheduled for three to five days of intensive day program per week. Without this she would begin to withdraw and hallucinate. As she began to socialize more with other clients and take a more active part in the day program, she asked the worker for help in relocating from her single room to a group living situation, where she could socialize with other women. The worker supported the positive intent of this request, as it reflected a major step forward for Mrs. Bell. However, the worker questioned the choice of setting that Mrs. Bell made. The worker was concerned that it might be too threatening for Mrs. Bell because of the structure provided in the setting. Because Mrs. Bell knew some of the women living in the home she persisted in the plan. After six months in her new home, Mrs. Bell began to feel the stress of the structure of the home. She wanted more independence and had made progress in her money management skills. With her increased socialization skills and her better ability to cope in the community this time, the client decided with the worker's support that she would move into her own apartment.

As Mrs. Bell began to assert herself more in her program participation, the worker began to develop wider resources for Mrs. Bell in addition to those therapeutic services offered through the day hospital program. In October, 1974, Mrs. Bell's expressed need to be with a group of people her own age was met as she was helped to become active at the local Center for Older Adults. The program was designed for independent older adults living in the community and Mrs. Bell's beginning efforts were encouraged by the worker at the mental health center in conjunction with the staff of the community program. Mrs. Bell's willingness to participate in the community program was seen as a good sign for her continued development of independence.

Because of the positive steps that Mrs. Bell has made within the Partial Hospitalization program and the success of her affiliation with the older adult program, Mrs. Bell was transferred to the medication and resocialization part of the day program. Since May, 1975, Mrs. Bell has been seen for twice-a-month therapy groups. The worker emphasis is now on the positive steps Mrs.

Bell has made and offers support to her continued efforts for independence and increased social relationships.

At this point Mrs. Bell knows that she has graduated from the day program and is able to take pride in this. She also knows that if she comes to the time when she needs more support than she receives in the twice-a-month therapy groups, she can return to the more intensive program. The worker anticipates that because of the long-term institutionalization Mrs. Bell has experienced, realistically the time may come when Mrs. Bell will need to make use of the day program. Both Mrs. Bell and the worker know that if that option needs to be used it will be an option that will permit Mrs. Bell to remain in the community.

In this instance the worker's efforts with Mrs. Bell were designed to provide a therapeutic environment which would help her to deal with her problems that were both emotional and reality-based. As Mrs. Bell improved in the therapeutic milieu, the worker's efforts were extended to the community to help her meet financial, housing, and social needs. Mrs. Bell was viewed as a total person whose treatment plan reached out of the clinic and into the community. This also shows the transition from long-term institutionalization to an intensive day treatment program to a maintenance program; a process that many institutionalized people do follow with the flexibility and continued reassessment of the social workers and program in a mental health center.

THE ROLE OF THE SOCIAL WORKER IN THE COMMUNITY

As it is the role of the Base Service Unit to determine through the evaluation and referral process what type of service would best serve the need of the individual coming to the mental health center for service, it is the role of the Consultation and Education Unit to determine what types of service will be most appropriate to the needs of the community. This determination is based, first, on an awareness of who lives in the community and what this particular mix of people implies in the way of service needs. For example, are there a great many older adults in the catchment area and what is their economic status? Are there large numbers of school age children or single-parent families? What is the school drop-out rate? The second consideration on which the unit bases its recommendations for services is what specific services and programs community groups have requested. These might include requests for workshops for volunteers in the Big Brother program, training activities for staff working with older adults, or resource consultation to school personnel. Once the service needs are assessed, a plan is then made to address the described areas. The Consultation and Education Unit works on the presumption of mental health. Those community groups and individuals that the Consultation and Education staff addresses are coping and functioning. Any Consultation and Education intervention seeks to promote the continued mental health of its consultees.

The following material is based upon a project that was three months in planning, implementation, and follow-up. It indicates several of the roles the social worker in a Consultation and Education Unit of a mental health center may play as he or she relates to other agencies and community residents.

When the director of a local Bar Association project made a request to the Consultation and Education Unit to provide group therapy to abused wives in the catchment area, the following process was initiated.

The consultant and director together assessed the request the women were making of the Law Project. It was determined that the women's initial request was for legal guidance to help them manage the abusive situation they were in. They wanted to know the legal rights of an abused wife. Second, they were concerned about their financial security if they left the current situation which afforded them economic assurances. Third, the women had come as individuals for help in these areas and were not in communication with each other.

The Law Project director was aware of the stress the women were under because of the physical abuse from their husbands. They had individually expressed to her feelings of fear, "If I report this my husband will be angry"; feelings of guilt, "I'm not sure what I do that makes him hit me"; and concern about the impact of parental behavior on the children. These were all indicative to the director that the women had need of the services of the mental health center. However, the mutual assessment of the Law Project director and the consultant was that (1) the expressions of emotional stress were reflections of a need the women had but did not indicate a readiness on their part to seek therapy, and (2) each of the women had come as an individual to ask for help of the Law Project—they did not know each other nor had most of them shared their problem with their own families or friends. Thus it was concluded that the women were not asking for therapeutic intervention.

It was determined that the Law Project would offer the women a series of resource workshops including legal rights, job opportunities, and mental health services. The consultant in the capacity of social worker would provide a resource consultation for the workshop on mental health services in the community. The goal of the workshops was to provide specific information for the women and a mechanism for them to meet each other and begin to draw upon each other for support.

The Law Project had the names of nine women who had come to them for help. These women were to form the base group of the workshops. In addition, the Law Project would publicize the meetings in the local newspapers to encourage other abused wives in the community to come. To facilitate attendance, baby sitting was provided and a social time was planned in advance of each workshop.

The expressed needs of the women were met by the format of the workshops. A female lawyer was the resource person for the workshop on legal rights. The content was specific, related to state laws affecting the women and how best to use the legal system in this situation, including steps the women could take to protect themselves and their children.

The second workshop again was very specific, presuming from the requests the women had made that they needed to move back into the job market. This material was covered by an employment counselor who advised the women on how to write a job application and prepare a resumé, what agencies were available to help in the job search, and what types of references were needed. The counselor also provided written material in these areas for the women to take home with them. Both of these workshops were basically lectures with time for clarifying questions.

The third area, mental health resources in the community, was handled on a discussion basis by the social work consultant. The discussion was opened by raising the question of what the group members felt was mental health. An older woman participant immediately responded by stating that the consultant should tell the group what mental health was. Wasn't the consultant the expert? The consultant's answer that there was no set answer to the question but that the response could be as varied as the people responding to it started the discussion going. Definitions ranged from "mental health is feeling good about oneself" to "mental health is being able to cope with day-to-day demands and activities" to "mental health is feeling happy. " There was much discussion around relationships as part of one's mental health—with parents, with children, with spouses, and with peers. The group discussed the changing nature of relationships, primarily in terms of husbands and spouses. Several of the younger women observed that they had changed in the relationship and would no longer accept abusive behavior from their husbands but did not feel that the man in the relationship had changed.

When the group members were able to discuss objectively and then subjectively their personal mental health needs, they then went on to share with each other. At this time the consultant's role changed from leading the discussion to clarifying the situations presented. The women were able to extend to each other in this context. A young woman whose husband beat her only when he was drinking described to the group the steps she had taken to seek help for herself. She described how she had worked out with a psychiatrist a way to get in touch with her own family network in times of crisis. One relative would help the husband to find the emergency care he needed, another would manage the children during the crisis, and the wife had been able to determine the limits of what she could honestly assume as her responsibility. She offered this in a tentative way and was given a great deal of support from other members of the group who could relate to her experience and appreciate the struggle she had been through as she achieved success in this area they were struggling with.

For the participants who had been able to move themselves out of an abusive situation, they reflected more on the areas of where to go to get help. There were a variety of opinions about this. Some of the group members expressed fear of being labeled if they went to a professional social worker for help. Others felt that if that was the case the individual might want to go to a self-help group first and then to an agency if she felt she needed an individualized helping situation. The consultant's role through much of this discussion was to summarize and reflect back on the earlier discussion of mental health needs. At the end of the discussion the consultant presented a brief overview of services available in the community that were supportive of women and children. In addition, printed articles and materials on services were handed out to each participant covering early childhood programs, day care, information on marital problems, and also specific information on the mental health center. The questions raised to the last were primarily in the area of what one could expect to have happen if she called the center for an appointment. The women were given specific names and telephone numbers of the Base Service Unit and were adivsed of the steps that would be taken at the time of the initial contact with the mental health center.

In this project, collaboration between the Law Project and the mental health center made possible the development of a program to be carried out under the auspices of a legal agency. The definitions of both agencies were recognized and the women were offered the resources they had indicated they were ready to receive.

CONCLUSION

The primary purpose of CMH/MR centers is to provide services which preserve and enhance the mental, emotional, and social functioning of persons living in their catchment areas. This chapter has dealt with two ways in which one such center responded to two expressed needs; the one, an assumption of responsibility for the aftercare of a mental patient following prolonged hospitalization, the other, a response to need expressed by the community for service to a group of persons who shared common problems.

Centers differ in what they offer and how they perceive their role in the community. All centers continually appraise their performance and evaluate how best to serve their residents and devise new ways of implementing their goals.

BIBLIOGRAPHY

Caplan, Gerald. *An Approach To Community Health,* New York: Greene & Stratton, 1961.

Caplan, Ruth. *Psychiatry and the Community in Nineteenth-Century America.* New York: Basic Books, 1969.

Ellsworth, Robert B. *Nonprofessionals in Psychiatric Rehabilitation.* New York: Appleton-Century-Crofts, 1968.

Freeman, Howard E., and Ozzie Simmons. *The Mental Patient Comes Home.* New York: John Wiley & Sons, 1963.

Joint Commission on Mental Illness and Health. *Action for Mental Health.* New York: Basic Books, 1961.

Lamb, Richard H., Don Heath, and Joseph J. Downing, eds. *Hand Book of Community Mental Health.* San Francisco: Jossey-Bass, 1969.

Lieberman, James E., ed. *Mental Health: The Public Health Challenge.* Washington, D.C.: American Public Health Association, 1975.

Noland, Robert L., ed. *Counseling Parents of the Mentally Retarded.* Springfield, Ill.: Charles C Thomas, 1970.

Raush, Harold L., and Charlotte L. Raush. *The Half-way House Movement: A Search for Identity.* New York: Appleton-Century-Crofts, 1968.

Silverstein, Max. *Psychiatric Aftercare: Planning for Community Mental Health Service.* Philadelphia: University of Pennsylvania Press, 1968.

17
SERVICES IN CRIMINAL AND JUVENILE JUSTICE

RENDELL A. DAVIS
The Pennsylvania Prison Society, Philadelphia

The field of criminal and juvenile justice is one of the most frustrating yet challenging areas in the delivery of social services. Society has always struggled with the effort to reform the offender, and in the past century, the entrance of professionals from the behavioral sciences into the correctional process led to an optimism that rehabilitation could be accomplished. In fact, however, the success of the rehabilitative ideal has yet to be demonstrated in any significant degree. This is the frustration.

The challenge, on the other hand, is that since we do not have a clear picture of what "works," the field is wide open for social workers to develop innovative and experimental methods and interventions at every point along the spectrum of justice systems. This spectrum reaches from arrest to discharge. Between these are pretrial incarceration and diversion, the courts, presentence investigations, probation, prisons, work release, and parole.

OBJECTIVES OF CRIMINAL JUSTICE SYSTEMS
AND THE NEEDS OF THE CLIENT

Most systems feel a mandate from the public that focuses on security. Citizens want protection from the offender; therefore, the bulk of our resources are devoted to police, prosecutors, the judiciary, prisons, and guards. Further, systems are so incredibly overburdened that the secondary objective is simply to survive and to operate with a minimum amount of trouble. Therefore, the individual needs of the accused and the convicted receive the lowest priority.

In this atmosphere, the social worker often feels lost and ineffectual. For example, in an average prison, for 1000 inmates there might be 250 guards, 30 persons in administrative and clerical positions, and 7 counselors or social workers. With a caseload of 150, one can barely know all the clients, much less have time for intensive counseling. The social worker may be saddled with many nonprofessional chores, such as arranging for outside telephone calls for inmates. A sensitive counselor may be ridiculed by the rest of the institution's staff and even have his or her work undermined by them.

But here again is the challenge! The objective is to make the most of limited resources. For example, one can draw on community resources, volunteers, and private agencies. Skillful social workers, without compromising the task, may consult with custodial officers and the administration to elevate their sensitivity to the human beings in their care. By enlisting guards in the task, the social worker may develop 250 aides throughout the prison. He or she may teach guards how to listen and what to listen for. These guards, in turn, may alert the social worker to critical cases or needs. We have often advised students entering this field to start as guards themselves for a short period. The experience will not only reveal the problems that guards face but will also give credibility to a social worker who must work with security personnel. At least one state system requires employees to work in both treatment and security areas before they can be promoted to positions in middle management.

THE DUAL ROLE OF THE SOCIAL WORKER

For people caught up as clients in the justice system there are few opportunities to develop inner directions. They are tossed about by the decisions of police, prosecutors, lawyers, judges, correctional personnel, parole boards, and probation and parole officers. These persons control the client's future and the client, in turn, learns to play games in an attempt to make things come out better. The social worker, too, cannot avoid having a definitive part in what happens to his or her clients. A probation or parole officer is in part a police officer with the power to revoke privileges or to send his or her charge to jail. A presentence investigator may have more to do with a sentence than the judge. A prison counselor monitors an inmate's prison record which may affect prison work assignments, preparole release programs, and parole board decisions. With so much power to reward or punish, how can social workers deal effectively and honestly with their clients?

The challenge is for the worker to build trust and mutual respect to overcome the obstacle. It requires an enormous amount of integrity, because the only basis left is for the client to believe that the counselor is fair and objective. Only then is it possible to develop the kind of nonmanipulative relationship where progress in treatment has any chance.

Some have recommended that social workers be stripped of all enforcement potential in order to avoid the ambiguity. This, however, would remove the counselor farther from the mainstream of the system and create further imbalance. There is much to be said for removing a great deal of the discretionary power from the entire system, but little would be gained by removing it only from social workers.

Some have suggested that counselors work only with those who request help, on the principle that this would create a better counseling relationship. Certainly voluntarism should be encouraged. However, in itself it will not reduce the effort to manipulate and might also distract attention from those who most need help.

Where the nonmanipulative relationship cannot be established by the social worker, community resources, volunteers, and private agencies should be enlisted.

MEASURABLE OUTCOMES

The new science of "management by objective" is of considerable value in any pursuit. Anyone in a profession or business wants to have visible reinforcements in terms of measurable success. Further, the lack of research in justice systems has led us to continue many programs that are based on unfounded assumptions.

Nevertheless, social work, particularly in corrections, is different from the physical sciences or from the business profit-and-loss orientation. Social workers often have to settle for less visible rewards. We often hear an ex-offender credit some particular worker's intervention as being most meaningful in the course of his life, but when this information is reported back, the worker expresses surprise over the effectiveness of his or her work. Because of the stigma upon the criminal offender or juvenile delinquent, our successful clients usually melt back into society's mainstream, preferring anonymity. Our failures are the ones we see again.

However, there are rewards. One that a social worker should seek is the joy of the process itself. If there is integrity; if there is the belief that helping matters; if there is caring, then the process can be enjoyable. Usually the deepest changes that intervention effects are the least visible, but there are many helping acts which are apparent and which should be considered as tasks equal in value to in-depth efforts. They are usually expediting functions, such as assisting the client in communicating with the family from whom he or she has been separated by geographic distance or prison walls. It may be in the process of cutting bureaucratic red tape to give a client a chance for equal justice. Most importantly, the social worker should never accept the justice system as it is but should always battle for positive change and for a recognition of the offender as a human being. Professionals can become as institutionalized as their clients. When one finds oneself giving uncritical acceptance to the system, it is time for either a vacation or a new job.

A SOCIAL WORKER'S STYLE

Many principles of social work have been developed, most of which are very sound. Even when scholars disagree, there are usually basic axioms to which they are mutually committed. Few textbooks or scholars, however, discuss the social worker's style, possibly because everyone must ultimately develop his or her own. It is this author's observations that effectiveness in correctional settings is as influenced by style as by approved methods, and it seems appropriate to discuss this briefly.

Most criminal offenders have a deep identity problem. They are scourged, cursed, and put down by all the forces of the system and are groping for some thread of self-worth. The social worker's best chance of success is to work on that thread of self-worth and help weave it into a sturdy rope. The worker's success will probably depend on his or her style, by which respect for the client is communicated, usually in nonverbal exercises.

For example, must we always demand that the client meet us on our turf, in our office? It may be more time-consuming, but a probation or parole officer meeting a client in a local restaurant over a cup of coffee may produce many times the effect of a sterile agency office. In a prison, walking the cell blocks may enhance the worker's image of accessibility and may encourage the clients to seek help voluntarily.

And smile! Again the identity problem can be dealt with more effectively by an expression of "welcome" or "glad to see you" than by hours of exhortation. A social worker will not get very far if the client does not feel the worker "likes" him or her.

Finally, we must remember that those who are involved in direct client contact, if they are good, are the most important people in the system—far more important than the supervisor who shuffles papers and gives out assignments. It is to be hoped we will reach the day when the good line worker will be rewarded substantially rather than forced into a supervisory role in order to earn a better living. As in the "Peter Principle," too many great workers become incompetent administrators. Good clinical social work is probably more of an art than a science. Those who excel in it should beware of the apparent green pastures of upward organizational mobility.

To care, to give of oneself, to help—these are the greatest experiences known to humanity, and the field of criminal and juvenile justice may well provide a clientele that has a greater need for these services than any other.

The bibliography accompanying Chapter 18 pertains to this chapter also.

18
SOCIAL WORK PRACTICE IN A CORRECTIONAL INSTITUTION

DONALD D. HUGHES
The Pennsylvania Prison Society, Philadelphia

Studies have shown that the average IQ of residents of correctional institutions throughout the United States is about the same as that of the general citizen population. College graduates do go to jail. This means that the social caseworker will have the opportunity to work with clients whose intelligence, general knowledge, and experience may be equal or superior to his or her own, as well as with those clients who have learning disabilities, very little formal education, and low intelligence.

Along with a broad spectrum of abilities, talents, interests, and cultural and religious differences, the large majority of clients have an extensive criminal history. In most adult correctional institutions offenses committed by residents are of a serious nature: murder, rape, assaults, sex offenses, drug sales, etc. At least in large metropolitan areas, persons committing minor property offenses and misdemeanors are not sentenced to state or even county institutions because of overcrowding in these institutions.

Mixed in with residents with long and serious criminal records are first-time offenders, young offenders with no established pattern of criminal behavior, and parole violators—those individuals who may or may not have committed a new offense, but who did violate the rules or regulations imposed on them by the state board of probation and parole when they were released from an institution on parole. The individual who has a long history of convictions for nonviolent crime such as burglary, larceny, or receiving stolen goods is also included in the population as is the person who steals to support his or her addiction to alcohol or drugs.

Having entered the institution after being processed through the criminal justice system, many residents share a common bond in their distrust of the system itself and those who are responsible for administering and maintaining it. There are various reasons for this distrust. An offender may have agreed to plead guilty to a lesser offense under pressure from a Public Defender, whom he may have met for the first or second time at his trial. Not wanting to risk a stiffer sentence by being tried before a jury with what he may feel is inadequate legal representation, he has been coerced into "plea bargaining" away his right to be regarded as innocent until proven guilty.

He may have sat in court awaiting his trial and watched other defendants with sufficient financial and legal resources be released from court or to probation authorities when their offenses were more serious than his own. He may know that the time that he is to serve at the institution will not be time spent in vocational programs that will provide him with marketable work skills or therapy programs that will improve his ability to deal more effectively with himself and his environment. It will be simply time spent.

After some time in the institution, he may or may not notice that the types of behaviors which are praised and rewarded in the outside world—assertiveness, leadership abilities, decision-making skills, ability to organize groups— are discouraged and perhaps even punished in the institution because they may be seen as threatening to administrative discipline. Instead, he will be tolerated for behavior such as eating when he is told to, showering when it is time to, and sleeping when it is time to turn out the lights.

All staff members have problems functioning in the system. These include administrators, guards, parole officers, work supervisors, and treatment staff. However, among these people are caring, helping and genuinely concerned persons.

Since the social caseworker is employed by this system, he or she is part of the problem. More importantly, however, he or she can be part of the solution.

The work of the caseworker is to build working relationships with those individuals who interest themselves in improving movement within the system, and to take an advocacy role on behalf of clients against those who would oppose positive improvement within the system. In addition to working within the system there is the task of improving social service delivery outside of the system. The caseworker must reach out to those individuals, community organizations, and social agencies that can provide the necessary supportive services for his clients since eventually he will be referring his clients to these significant others.

Within the structure of the institution the caseworker is expected to abide by guidelines and policies set down by the administration and to complete tasks in a manner that reflects these guidelines and policies and contributes to the maintainance and discipline of the institution.

The following case histories are used to illustrate different problem areas faced by the caseworker in corrections.

John, a tall, handsome, muscular black male had recently finished serving his minimum sentence of two and a half years of a two-and-a-half to five-year sentence for possession and sale of dangerous drugs (heroin). Although he had been arrested several times for this same offense, this was his first conviction and incarceration. For the last two months the caseworker had been having regularly scheduled casework sessions with John in preparation for John's appearance before the State Board of Probation and Parole. The caseworker was responsible for presenting a formal recommendation to the Parole board concerning John's readiness for parole. In order to help her make this recommendation, she had compiled a vocational and social history on John.

John was born twenty-six years ago in a ghetto community of a large city. The father deserted the family shortly after his birth and he was raised along with three sisters by his mother and grandmother. Although the family was never affluent, John, being the only boy in a rather large family, was spoiled by his immediate family as well as his relatives. It wasn't necessary for John to take the responsibility for providing himself with material things since others took this responsibility.

When John became a teen-ager, he joined the neighborhood gang under peer pressure. Going along with what the gang expected of him, John began experimenting with drugs. As he matured and his stature within the gang increased, John was given drugs to sell. Eventually he became a drug dealer. He enjoyed the status and recognition he received from other drug dealers and the community at large. He liked the easy money, expensive clothes, and cars, as well as the women who liked the easy money also.

However, John's problem with drugs, although slow in developing, became acute. He explained to the caseworker that his habit grew from one bag of heroin a day to twenty bags a day in a little less than a year. He began to be reckless in dealing drugs to support his habit and this led to his selling drugs to an undercover cop. He was broke at the time of his arrest. He blamed his conviction on his long arrest history.

Although John never finished vocational high school, he did have a certificate from the Board of Education stating that he had completed a course in welding. He had never held a steady job and had no work history. His work supervisor at the institution reported that John was among the most skilled workers in the maintenance department but was absent from work regularly and didn't work well without supervision. John impressed the caseworker as an intelligent, sensitive, dependent young man who was used to having things his own way. He could be charming and manipulative when it suited his purpose, but was more often passive and lethargic.

Several weeks before John appeared before the parole board the caseworker had challenged John about his lack of preparation prior to seeing the board. He had not entered a drug therapy program nor had he attempted to formulate a parole plan for the parole board. Although all the parole plan involved was a home and a job, John did not have either part of the plan worked out when he saw the board.

John responded to the worker's challenge by saying that his family would get the plan together for him, because they had always come to his rescue in the past. "Anyway," he said, "I won't need a job, I can always go back to dealing drugs."

The caseworker suspected that John's glib reply was part of his phony self-image—nothing seemed to bother him, he wasn't worried about anything or anybody. However, the worker was unable to break through this defense but had to make the report to the Parole Board on the facts, even though John had hoped to achieve parole at the expiration of his minimum sentence.

The decision from the board was that parole was not indicated because of John's lack of involvement in institutional programs. Instead, he would be reviewed again for parole six months from the date of this interview. Further, the board stipulated that he must involve himself in a group therapy program designed to help him with his drug addiction prior to his next review.

John was understandably upset by the board's decision. During the two and a half years spent at the institution he had not had a single misconduct. Although he had not participated in any programs offered by the institution, he had maintained a good rapport with residents, guards, and staff. He had been drug-free while in the institution and had not succumbed to the temptation of the drug traffic within the institution. However, he did realize that returning to his old neighborhood on parole would severely test his ability to stay off drugs.

Faced with the board's decision, he could now state in the next social work interview that he wanted help with his drug problem. The reason he had not involved himself in the group therapy program in the institution was his distrust of the program. The group leaders for the drug therapy program were not trained professionals. Inmate ex-addicts ran the groups. John wouldn't feel free to make disclosures about himself, since he didn't believe the group leaders could handle his problems. But more importantly, his self-disclosures would leave him vulnerable to any group member who might want to exploit his vulnerability on the cell block.

The caseworker realized that what John told him was a true report of the drug program's inadequacies. Without a trained professional group leader who could establish trust within the group and confidentiality among the group members, a member's problem would not be kept in confidence within the group. In a population that valued toughness and rigidity, emotional problems were seen as weaknesses.

The focus for the rest of the session was the question of how John could receive meaningful therapy and still fulfill the requirements of the parole board, which, being an independent agency responsible only to the governor of the state, was very jealous of its prerogatives and was unlikely to change its decision in John's favor. It might, however, be possible to petition the board for an early review of John's case, perhaps in a month or two.

Since the worker agreed with John that the institution could not provide a program to fit his needs, he could work toward making a referral to an agency in John's community that could provide professional therapy and could be included in his parole plan when he saw the board again. This would have to be discussed with the parole case specialist so that the board would know the caseworker's evaluation of John and John's problem.

The caseworker's task with John was to point out these alternatives to him and at the same time make clear to him that he would have to take steps on his own behalf if he were to pass the next review of the board. Together, then, they reviewed how John could take responsibility for himself, and set as a goal the meeting of requirements, including attendance, in the maintenance department.

A very different kind of situation and outcome involved Chris.

Chris was a twenty-one-year-old, slender blue-eyed blond who had recently arrived at the state institution from a juvenile facility. He was serving a ten- to twenty-year sentence for a series of aggravated robberies. Having spent four years at the juvenile facility and having reached adulthood, he had been transferred to the institution to serve the rest of his sentence.

Chris was raised in a rural farming community by his father and mother. Chris, being an only child and living several miles from the closest town, spent most of his early childhood without companions. His parents were devoutly religious. Chris said that his father was a strict disciplinarian and his mother was overly protective.

Chris rebelled against his parents' strictness by getting into minor scrapes with the law when he was in his early teens. He ran away from home when he was sixteen years old and traveled around the local rural communities doing odd jobs to support himself. When Chris was arrested for his current offense, his family disowned him. They never corresponded with him or visited him, feeling—according to Chris—"that God was justly punishing me for my evil ways."

What the correctional caseworker knew about Chris had been learned in three sessions with him. During these sessions, Chris was able to say that he could accept the responsibility for being incarcerated, yet saw his incarceration as a waste of time. He passed his time by reading and passively watching television. His major concern was fear of his current environment. He was suspicious and cautious in his dealings with other residents. When asked by the caseworker if he had any friends, he replied that he had only a few whom he had selected very carefully.

It seemed to the caseworker that self-preservation was Chris's first consideration. His withdrawal, caution, and selectivity were seen by the worker as good coping mechanisms, considering his environment. The focus for the next session was to have been working on his general inactivity: discussing future plans, acquainting Chris with the educational and vocational programs in the institution, and acquainting Chris with resident groups who shared common interests and therefore, would be less threatening to him.

But before their next meeting the caseworker learned from the custody staff that Chris had been confined to the Behavioral Adjustment Unit—more correctly designated by the residents as the "hole." During a routine "shake down" or search by the guards a shank—a weapon fashioned from a piece of metal and used like a knife—was found in his cell. In addition to this he received a major misconduct report for threatening another inmate. Chris's current crisis demanded immediate intervention on the part of the caseworker.

Reflecting on the previous sessions, the caseworker felt that he had provided an atmosphere that had allowed Chris to express himself freely. He had valued Chris's thoughts and feelings and had set the stage for the beginning of an empathic relationship. Yet he had felt that Chris had a hidden agenda —something he wasn't telling him. When he had expressed this feeling to Chris it appeared to be too threatening for him to deal with. The caseworker had dropped the issue, thinking he would bring it up again later.

The caseworker called the guard in the Behavioral Adjustment Unit and requested that Chris be escorted up to his office that afternoon. When Chris entered the office, he was highly agitated and seemed anxious to talk. After the guards left, Chris and the caseworker sat a few minutes until Chris could gain some composure.

The anxiety and fear Chris was feeling were quickly vented as anger. Chris had been under homosexual pressure from a group of residents who had threatened him with physical harm if he did not submit to their demands. In retaliation he had made the shank and had threatened to use it on the leader of the group. This had led to his misconduct and confinement in the Behavioral Adjustment Unit.

The caseworker involved himself in letting Chris vent his anger and frustration. Only rarely interrupting to help Chris clarify his feelings, the caseworker began to piece together the circumstances which prompted the homosexual pressure. A rumor had preceded Chris to the institution through the inmate grapevine that Chris had been a "punk" (a resident who provides sexual favors for another resident in turn for protection) at the juvenile facility. The fact that the rumor was untrue was immaterial to Chris's situation.

Chris explained that while at the juvenile institution he had not associated with any of the other inmates, preferring the company of a young man who shared the same cell with him. Because this young man had a reputation as an assaultive individual, the other residents left him and Chris alone. Although Chris admitted that this man was in fact protecting him, he explained that their relationship was not homosexual in nature. Chris had always preferred the company of a single person. He had never had many friends or acquaintances. He felt self-conscious around people and had always been pretty much a loner. In this new situation he reasoned that by using this shank on his tormentors, he would establish himself as someone who could take care of himself and the other residents would treat him with respect.

Despite the caseworker's feelings and values against taking another man's life, he treated the fact that Chris could take action against this group as a valid alternative or solution to his predicament. However, he made Chris look at the consequence of such action. If he assaulted another resident, he would be charged with another offense and tried in court. If convicted, he would serve another sentence following his current sentence. Such a course of action meant that Chris would spend most of the rest of his life in jail.

Chris did not want to spend any more time in jail but could not think of any alternative other than retaliation. Part of the problem was that he could not seek the protection of the guards. In doing so, he would have to provide the names of group members so that a disciplinary hearing could be held. At that hearing, they would be exposed and punished. A reputation as a "snitch" would follow Chris for the length of time he was incarcerated and could lead to his being shanked.

By nonjudgmentally accepting Chris's feelings and thoughts concerning his predicament, the counselor had provided an atmosphere of open trust wherein other alternatives and solutions could be examined. One other alternative was for Chris to move away from the members of the group to another cell block after he was released from the "hole" in a month or so. Chris felt that this alternative would only delay the inevitable. He could not avoid a confrontation with this group for very long. He would run into them in the exercise yard and other places within the institution.

The decision made by Chris after he and his caseworker had examined several possible alternatives was for Chris to be transferred to another state institution in another part of the state several hundred miles away which had a resident population with a more reasonable balance of older and younger men and which was better equipped to handle the kind of problem Chris presented.

In the meantime the caseworker appeared at the disciplinary hearing in Chris's defense. Because Chris was able to confide in him, the caseworker was able to intervene on his behalf and prevent Chris from being labeled by the institution as a troublemaker—a label which would have seriously affected his chances for being released when he became eligible for parole five years hence.

In these cases of John and Chris, a climate that was free enough for each to examine his feelings and deal with his concerns was provided by the caseworker. Obviously no permanent solutions were supplied in the institution for either John's drug dependency or Chris's right to serve his time without being subject to homosexual pressure from other residents. However, they are accurate descriptions of what alternatives really are available to a caseworker and his client in most correctional settings at the present time.

Despite the skills, talents, and philosophy that the effective social caseworker brings to the casework relationship—accepting and liking other human beings, genuineness, a sensitive empathy to clients' feelings, seeing clients as worthy, dependable, and able to deal with their own lives—positive changes, in the correctional system or in the human beings embroiled within the system, happen gradually, if at all.

This is the correctional caseworker's frustration, but it is also his challenge.

Here perhaps more than in any other setting a social worker realizes that there are few comprehensive solutions to the problems of those living in a closed social system. The challenges and rewards for the social worker lie in the quality of his relationships and the contributions he makes in bringing about some small changes in the lives of his clients and in the humanizing of the correctional setting.

BIBLIOGRAPHY

American Friends Service Committee, *Struggle for Justice.* New York: Hill and Wang, 1971.

Fogel, David. *We Are the Living Proof: The Justice Model in Corrections.* Cincinnati, Ohio: W. H. Anderson, 1975.

Giallombardo, Rose. *Society of Women: A Study of a Women's Prison.* New York: John Wiley & Sons, 1966.

Glaser, Daniel. *The Effectiveness of a Prison Aid Parole System.* Indianapolis: Bobbs-Merrill Company, 1969.

Griswold, Jack H., et al. *An Eye for an Eye.* New York: Holt, Rinehart and Winston, 1970.

James, Howard. *Children in Trouble.* New York: David McKay Co., 1970.

Keve, Paul. *Prison Life and Human Worth.* Minneapolis: University of Minnesota Press, 1974.

Morris, Norval. *The Future of Imprisonment.* Chicago: University of Chicago Press, 1974.

Studt, Eliot, Sheldon L. Messinger, and Thomas P. Wilson. *C-Unit: Search for Community in Prisons.* New York: Russell Sage Foundation, 1968.

Sykes, Gresham. *The Society of Captives.* Princeton, N. J.: Princeton University Press, 1966.

Wicker, James. *A Time to Die.* New York: Quadrangle Books, 1975.

19
OLDER ADULTS: POLICIES, PROGRAMS, SERVICES

ANN BILAS JOHNSON

**Coordinating Council for Senior Citizens,
Durham, North Carolina**

NATIONAL POLICIES

The Bicentennial Charter for Older Americans prepared by the Federal Council on the Aging points to "... certain basic human rights for older Americans based on the 'laws of nature and of nature's God' as set forth in the founding documents of this nation. ..."

These rights are delineated as:

I. The right to freedom, independence and the free exercise of individual initiative.

II. The right to an income in retirement which would provide an adequate standard of living.

III. The right to an opportunity for employment free from discriminatory practices because of age.

IV. The right to an opportunity to participate in the widest range of meaningful civic, educational, recreational and cultural activities.

V. The right to suitable housing.

VI. The right to the best level of physical and mental health services needed.

VII. The right to ready access to effective social services.

VIII. The right to appropriate institutional care when required.

IX. The right to a life and death with dignity.

This document sets goals for the United States as a nation to achieve. It also challenges the older persons to be responsible, as full partners with those of a younger age, in working toward accomplishment of the goals.

WHO ARE OLDER AMERICANS?

Older Americans age sixty and over are the fastest growing portion of the U.S. population. In 1900 there were 4.9 million (6.4 percent); by 1975 there were 31.6 million (14.8 percent); and it is expected by the year 2000 that there will be 42 million (16.6 percent).

Women have outnumbered men since 1930. In 1974 there were 143 women over age sixty-five for every 100 men of the same age bracket, and this is expected to increase to 154 for every 100 men by the year 2000.

About half of those over sixty-five live in seven states—California, Illinois, New York, Ohio, Pennsylvania, Texas, and Florida. Florida had the most, 16.1 percent, and Alaska the fewest, 2.4 percent.

An increase in life expectancy from an average age of forty-seven years in 1900 to seventy-one years in 1974 accounts for some of the increase in population. Reduced death rates for children and young adults during this same period is the major contributing factor.

Future projections will be affected by the rise or decline in number of births (fertility). The factors of mortality decline and immigration (unless of older age) will not contribute significantly to an increase.

Life expectancy differs both with race and sex. Women who reach age sixty-five can expect to live seventeen years as compared to thirteen years for men. Minority races face shorter life expectancy with some hope that increased medical care programs will affect this in a positive way.

The proportion of blacks over sixty-five in 1975 was 7.4 percent; Spanish origin, 3.6 percent; and whites 11.0 percent. The proportion of males to females for blacks and whites are roughly the same—whites 69 males to 100 females; blacks 73 males to 100 females. In those of Spanish origin however, the ratio is higher—87 males per 100 females. One contributing factor related to this is that males have dominated among immigrants of Spanish origin.[1]

The image of the elderly is clouded in myth. Sick, fragile, disabled, and sexless are words too often used to characterize and stereotype the elderly. Older persons are not all alike. Life styles are becoming more varied. There are many types differing from each other as much as infants differ from teen-agers.

Older persons do have more chronic ailments than the young; but only 10 percent are confined in a limiting way and only 5 percent are institutionalized.

Learning ability does not decline after sixty. Depression is found in all age groupings. Flexibility in relation to society and its environment must be a part of the older adult simply because his life span has caused him to experience so much change.

Some characteristics can be assumed. Reduced income in retirement, loss of family and friends leading to possible isolation, and some reduced mobility are generally accepted as part of the end-of-life picture. These are the challenges, not only for the older adult but for all of society.

LEGISLATION

The changing commitment of the United States to respond to the needs of its older citizens is reflected in the legislation passed since 1935.

Income during the retirement years was the first concern addressed in 1935 with passage of the Social Security Act. An insurance program, administered directly by the federal government, pays benefits to retired and disabled workers, their dependents, and survivors of deceased workers. An individual must work a certain number of quarters during which a portion of the wages was contributed by a payroll tax. This contributed amount is matched by employers or is at a different rate for those who are self-employed.

Benefits under the retirement section are based on amount contributed and may be applied for as early as age sixty-two. Earnings are limited after benefits are received by a set ceiling or a reduction in benefits for those earning amounts over the ceiling figure. No limitations on earnings are set for those over age seventy-two.

In 1965 the Social Security Act was amended in an effort to protect older adults from the financial disaster of medical bills. Title XVIII (Medicare) is a

---

[1]Demographic data in support of the foregoing paragraphs may be found in the following publications: U. S. Department of Health, Education, and Welfare, Office of Human Development, Administration on Aging, National Clearing House on Aging, DHEW Publication No. (OHD) 75-20006; and U. S. Bureau of the Census, "Demographic Aspects of Aging and the Older Population in the U. S.," *Current Population Reports,* ser. P-23, no. 59 (May 1976).

federal insurance program, uniform all over the United States, that pays medical bills for those covered by the insurance.

Title XIX (Medicaid) is a federal-state assistance plan, varying state by state, that pays medical bills of certain eligible low-income persons.

Medicare insurance coverage is divided. Part A covers hospital costs. Part B is the supplementary plan, available for a monthly premium, covering physician's services as well as drugs, x-ray and lab tests, therapy, medical equipment, ambulance service, physical therapy, and limited home health service visits.

Both parts of Medicare coverage require payment of a deductible amount and limit the total benefits. With rising costs of medical care over the years, the deductibles and limits to care raise serious questions about the benefits and point to a need for a better system of protection.

The year 1965 also brought enactment of the Older Americans Act. The *Older Americans Act of 1965* and amended 1967, 1969, 1972, and 1975 provides for the development of a network spanning federal, state, and local levels to ''. . . assist our older people to secure equal opportunity to . . . full and free enjoyment . . .'' through adequate income, best possible physical and mental health, suitable housing, services when needed, meaningful activity, opportunity for employment, and community service.

The network starts at the federal level with the Administration on Aging; regional offices covering sections of the United States; state units, area-wide agencies, and local services providers (agencies). State units are charged with planning, coordination, and evaluation of aging programs articulated in a developed state plan. Area-wide agencies become the focal point for planning of services, awarding some service contracts, securing input of older persons in the planning effort, and working toward a comprehensive, coordinated service delivery. (Title III.)

Amendments during recent years have increased service-related titles to include nutrition (Title VII) and Senior Centers (Title V). Training, education, research, and demonstration grants are also provided for in the act.

The *Age Discrimination Act of 1975* prohibits discrimination in employment for workers age forty-five to sixty-five. Efforts are being made to change the maximum age on the basis that the law itself sets an age discrimination.

Supplementary Security Income provided for by Social Security Act Amendments of 1972 became possible as of January 1, 1974, when this program replaced the Old Age Assistance, Aid to the Blind, and Aid to the Permanently and Totally Disabled programs in the fifty states and the District of Columbia.

The law establishes a national program to provide a guaranteed annual income floor for persons age sixty-five or older, or who are blind or disabled. The program is administered through the Social Security Administration of HEW with open-ended appropriations from the federal general revenues.

Monthly cash payments are made to eligible persons whose income is below the level established. Individuals may have assets including a car, house, and life insurance—all with limited value.

Benefits as of October, 1975, to an eligible individual with no other income amount to $157.70; benefits to an eligible couple amount to $236.60 per month. SSI beneficiaries are eligible for medical care services (Medicaid) in thirty-three states. Beneficiaries are also eligible for food stamps except in six states which cash out the food stamp benefit and include that amount in their supplementary payments.

The *Employee Retirement Income Security Act* was signed into law on Labor Day, 1974, by President Ford. It protects employees from the loss of pension benefits due to company or pension plan bankruptcy, merger, or mismanagement. Although companies or unions are not required to establish retirement plans, if they do, the plan must conform to the minimum federal standards. The law protects covered individuals by a vesting provision, but no mention is made in the legislation of transfer of benefit credits from one employer to another (portability).

Housing legislation affecting older persons is found in several laws.

The *Housing Act of 1937,* Section 8, as amended by the *Housing and Community Development Act of 1974,* provides for subsidy payments to make up the difference between the family contribution (15 to 25 percent) and the unit rental determined as no more than 10 percent over the fair market rent.

The *Housing Act of 1959,* Section 202, as amended by the *Housing and Community Development Act of 1974,* provides for direct federal construction loans to a nonprofit corporation or nonprofit consumer cooperative for housing projects for the elderly and handicapped. Tenants must be at least sixty-two years of age (or in the case of a family, the head of the household or spouse must be at least age sixty-two) or a handicapped person of any age whose impairment is expected to be of long, continued duration. This program is tied to the previously mentioned Section 8 legislation in that eligibility is dependent upon eligibility for Section 8.

The *National Housing Act,* amended in 1968, Section 236, provides for interest reduction payments to private enterprise developing low-income housing. At least 20 percent of the total federal units developed must be for the elderly or the handicapped. The benefit to the older person is the availability of lower rents as a result of lower cost to the developer. A moratorium on this program was instituted on January 5, 1973.

The *Housing and Urban Development Act of 1965,* Title I, Section 101, provides for monthly federal payments to housing owners renting to low-income tenants. Units must be located in low-income housing owned by nonprofit, cooperative, or limited-dividend organizations. Income eligibility for tenants is set at the maximum public housing limit for the area. Tenants must pay 25 percent of their adjusted income for rent. The January, 1973, moratorium included this program. Other laws affecting service include the following:

The *Economic Opportunity Act,* amended in 1967, established "Senior Opportunities and Services"—a program aimed at the poor over age sixty. Cash grants are made to community action agencies or other public and nonprofit agencies for specific services such as outreach and referral, transportation, and educational and legal services.

The *Urban Mass Transportation Act of 1975,* Section 16(b), provides for 80 percent of purchase price of vehicles and equipment to be used in transporting the elderly or disabled.

THE AGING NETWORK

The situation of a growing population of older persons isolated not only by circumstance but by choice, less valued because of diminished productivity forced upon them, trapped in a support system planned in relation to organization requirements rather than people needs, obviously demands change.

Evidence of forces to effect change are beginning to emerge. At the federal level we now have not only the Administration on Aging (AOA) in the Office of Human Development, Department of Health, Education, and Welfare (HEW), but also the National Institute on Aging (NIA), which is within the National Institutes of Health.

The NIA is developing a program aimed at the conduct and coordination of research into all aspects, biological, psychological, and social, of aging. A major focus of the AOA is an effort to develop agreements with every department of the federal system to assure cooperation in providing appropriate service to the older segment of the population.

Since the federal network reaches to states and local service providers, this effort can produce significant improvement in service provision. Part of the network, as stipulated in the Older Americans Act, provides for an area-wide planning agency with an advisory committee made up of a majority of consumers. This advisory committee is charged with involvement in the plan for services within the geographic area. Used wisely, this input gives a voice to older adults in not only what services are needed but how those services should be provided and by whom.

The area-wide agency as part of the aging network is developing as a strong control point between the local service provider agencies and the state agency responsible for state-wide planning. Some controversy exists as to whether this "middle layer" is necessary, effective, or even fair in judgment. As time goes on, some changes in the mandate to these agencies may be forthcoming as experience in operation provides models for shared responsibility among the state, area agency, and local providers, as well as among the agencies drawing funds from a wide variety of sources.

Another force exists within the older population. Memory of the impact of the Townsend movement in the 1930s is giving impetus to action-oriented organizations of older adults. The Golden Age Societies and clubs focusing on recreation and socialization are not the only organized groups of older adults. The American Association of Retired Persons, American Association of Retired Teachers, National Council of Senior Citizens, and National Caucus on the Black Aged are national organizations whose membership is composed largely of older persons. The National Council on the Aging is a membership organization for professionals and service providers but open to older persons. All these organizations actively engage in social action, developing policy statements, legislative platforms, and educational conferences and workshops.

Other professional organizations such as the Gerontological Society and American Geriatrics Society are more focused on membership of those interested in research and service provision.

The Gray Panthers is a more recent organized group of both the older and younger population. Highly visible because of the articulate, strong leadership of its founder, the organization is seeking nation-wide membership.

State and local organizations, often in the form of federations of club groups, are forming as realization of the power of numbers joining together in common goal achievement becomes apparent.

Consensus planning, relying only upon elected officials or the elite power structure, has been affected. Advocacy is recognized as a planning mode, not only in the acceptance of input initiated by organized groups, but in the requirement that public hearings be held for funding plans.

Services

Transportation is viewed by older persons as one of their greatest problems. The lack of mobility means the older adult is faced with isolation from relatives and friends, from health care and shopping, and from services even though they may exist. Increasingly, reduced fares for older persons are being used as one way to give relief. However, the individual who is handicapped may not be able to use public systems even though cost is not a factor. Agencies serving older persons are developing systems that include transportation plans with vehicles equipped with lifts, and a volunteer corps particularly for medical appointments.

Rural areas are challenged to find workable plans.

Protective services as a special unit is growing to serve the older adult who has become unable to care for himself.

In-home care is a broad category that covers such services as Homemaker, Friendly Visiting, Home Health Aid, Chore, Home Repair, and Telephone Reassurance. Many older persons prefer to remain in their own homes rather than go into institutions when their capacity to perform the various activities of daily living diminishes; these various services make it ever more possible for them to do so. The National Council for Homemaker—Home Health Aide Services has developed standards for such services, and as more and more agencies are receiving certification under the standards, funding has increased for such quality programs.

Day care is one alternative to residential institutional placement for the individual who does not need skilled nursing care. A variety of models have emerged. The medical model (sometimes called day hospital) puts emphasis on short-term rehabilitation; the mental health model focuses on psychological needs; and the social model concentrates on providing a protected environment using other community resources for medical and psychiatric care.

Day care programs may be developed as a part of medical complexes, mental health centers, nursing homes, and senior centers or as the total agency. Locations vary with sponsorship. Churches have opened their facilities, and the majority of programs have a five-day week.

Possible funding sources include, in addition to private contributions or fees, Title XX of the social security amendments, Title III of the Older Americans Act, SOS program of the Community Services Administration Act, as well as local public support.

Legal services protect the rights of older persons, both as individuals and as a group. National efforts such as the Legal Research and Services for the Elderly sponsored by the National Council of Senior Citizens are providing technical assistance to communities for development of legal aid programs.

The situations involving possible need for legal assistance vary greatly. Consumer-type complaints, denial of benefits under state or federal programs, commitment appeals, landlord-tenant disputes, as well as the writing of a will are all examples.

Employment after retirement may be an elective or a financial necessity. In either case, the older person faces difficulty. Myths about diminished capability support early retirement and reluctance to hire an older person. Special efforts are required to combat this situation. Employment security commissions often designate an older workers' specialist to process applications of those over age fifty-five. Other programs initiated primarily in voluntary or nonprofit private agencies range from counseling services to specialized job placement efforts.

In an economy that is struggling with an overall high rate of unemployment, it is highly unlikely that much effort will go into providing jobs for older people.

Information, referral, and counseling are regarded as threshold services. Older adults tend to "make do" with whatever exists. State-wide information systems, often computerized and available through a toll-free telephone number, require an ability to articulate specific questions. Older persons also show a reluctance to become involved with persons or programs with whom or with which they are not familiar. Agencies serving older adults are developing back-up local information services to support the larger systems and are training counselors not only in case work techniques but in the unique characteristics of older persons that require special consideration. Social workers are challenged in several ways by the problems of older people: to examine their own values concerning age and ability; to be satisfied with small gains in case movement; to persevere and understand pride; and to understand the difference between helping that encourages dependency and helping that fortifies and builds natural strengths.

Community service opportunities represent one way an older person may remain a productive, needed individual. A variety of programs exist. The Retired Senior Volunteer Program (RSVP) is a federally funded program to stimulate the provision of meaningful volunteer jobs for those who would not ordinarily seek this type of activity. Volunteer bureaus are finding that older persons are a tremendous resource of skills. Special outreach efforts and reorganization of volunteer job requirements are required to successfully recruit and assign older volunteers, who may work as case aides, "friendly visitors," paralegals, program assistants, as well as receptionists, typists, and clerks—just to mention a few of the possibilities.

SENIOR CENTERS

It is obvious that a myriad of service possibilities exist, but unless the persons for whom the services are intended know of their existence and unless these services are readily available, the services lose their worth. The Older Americans Act calls for the development of focal points to coordinate services. Although the act is very specific in designating the area-wide agency for the *planning* of that coordinated service, it does not designate the focal point for service *delivery*. However, Title V, OAA, refers to Senior Centers as multiservice delivery agents.

The Senior Center as a multiservice facility devoted totally to serving older people is emerging as the focal point for service delivery. The Senior Center of the past, existing as a social club, has mushroomed into a facility that both provides services to older people and assists other service agencies to provide their mandated services in a more accessible way. A Senior Center, is, moreover, more than just a conglomeration of services provided in one location. Its organizational philosophy stipulates that older persons themselves are engaged in planning, directing, and carrying out such activities. The following definition of a Senior Center was developed by the Task Force on Standards of the National Institute of Senior Centers, a department of the National Council on the Aging:

> A Senior Center is a focal point on aging for the community. It is where older persons as individuals or in groups come together to provide programs which enhance their dignity, support their independence and encourage their involvement in and with the community.
>
> A Senior Center provides services and activities which emanate from or take place within the Center. It is part of a comprehensive community strategy to meet the needs of older persons. These programs consist of a variety of services in such areas as education, culture, recreation, advocacy, employment, health, nutrition, social work, and other supportive services.
>
> The Center serves as a community resource for information and referral on aging. Furthermore, it trains professionals interested in older adult programs, provides a testing ground for new knowledge related to aging and helps develop new approaches to aging programs.

ONE COMMUNITY'S ANSWER TO FRAGMENTATION: DURHAM, NORTH CAROLINA

The Coordinating Council for Senior Citizens, Durham, Inc., is a nonprofit private agency with an elected board of directors of thirty members. Since 1951 the Coordinating Council (until 1968 the Golden Age Society) has worked to establish a coordinated delivery system of services for older persons. From the time of the acceptance of that goal, it was believed that the goal could be achieved only through the establishment of centers that physically symbolized the concept of a coordinated system.

County Character

The characteristics of Durham County offer both a challenge and a hope in the accomplishment of the goal. Geographically its area is contained in 299 square miles. Its present population is 138,000, with 14 percent, or about 19,000 persons, over age sixty. Thirty-two percent are members of minority groups and eighty-three percent are in the low-income category. Older people are concentrated chiefly in the only municipality—the City of Durham.

Community Resources

The resources of the area are many. Human services mandated in the county show a high level of commitment. The Department of Social Services is supported in one of the highest per capita budgets in North Carolina. The

Public Health Department offers a wide range of services including multiphasic screening. It is licensed as a Home Health Agency. The Mental Health Department is building its capacity to reach into the preventive areas of service. The Durham Housing Authority was one of the first in the country to provide housing for older persons. The Gary Street Project was a model for many years, and Oldham Towers, the first high-rise for the elderly, is a unique architectural design. It is unfortunate that budget constraints would not allow builders of a new high-rise for the elderly to incorporate some of the special features called for in the original design. However, $100,000 of city revenue-sharing money is designated to expand the square footage of community space planned for the new construction.

The Durham County Library, encouraged by a pilot program cooperatively funded by money from Title III of the Older Americans Act, earmarked in the Coordinating Council budget and county funds, has developed a special unit serving older persons in centers, in institutions, and in their own homes. Funding for two professionals as well as for books, van, and operating costs is now completely borne by the library budget.

The Agricultural Extension Service has built a program that touches both city and rural area residents. Operation Breakthrough came into existence as one of the first antipoverty agencies and has continued its influence in combating problems of low-income persons, not only by strong advocacy but by cooperative action with other agencies. Presently Operation Breakthrough places three full-time workers with the Coordinating Council. They are responsible for Outreach in two of the centers.

Durham Technical Institute is working toward a free-registration policy for those over age sixty-five. Its continuing education department is openly receptive to scheduling classes for older persons.

In the nonprofit private sector of human services, the United Fund has had difficult years in fund raising. Despite the difficulty, the allocations to the Coordinating Council for Senior Citizens has increased from $1300 in 1967 to $25,000 in 1977.

Since 1967 Duke University Center for the Study of Aging and Human Development has had a continuing community service project. Presently the Older Americans Resources and Services (OARS) project is a subcontract for clinical service with the Mental Health Department.

The Recreation Department is a city agency. Eight Golden Age Clubs, originally started by the Coordinating Council, are now sponsored by the Recreation Department.

Universities in the area are a resource. Students and faculty provide assistance in service provision to gain experience as a part of their training. Students work in such areas as social work, the ministry, vocational rehabilitation, recreation, nursing, law, the library, physical therapy, and as associates in mental health.

Community leadership at the political level is allocating money to services for older persons. The Community Development budget of the City of Durham for 1977–78 includes $21,000 for the Coordinating Council's Minor Home Repair program. The major part of the city's entire budget is earmarked for housing rehabilitation. It will be spent largely for older persons.

Community leadership in the churches is increasingly receptive to supporting programs for older persons. Three churches have allocated space for centers, and a fourth is aggressively pursuing establishment of a multiservice center for older persons in its own buildings.

With the advent of the "new federalism," greater resources are available at the local level. Compared to the national pattern in which less than half of 1 percent of such monies have been allocated to services related to older persons, Durham has done well. As already mentioned, $100,000 of revenue-sharing money is earmarked for additional community space in the new high-rise. The budget for the City Community Development proposal for 1977–78 increases the total allocation to $69,000. This sum will escalate the capacity of the Coordinating Council in the in-home services, particularly in the Minor Home Repair program and the Senior Centers services.

Durham-Orange Manpower Consortium funded under the Community Employment and Training Act (CETA) has supported services to older persons through the Coordinating Council in several ways. As of April 1, 1976, four emergency employment slots (three from the City of Durham and one from the county) were allocated for the Minor Home Repair program. This number is expected to be increased. Trainees in the Attendant Corps for the Elderly, a two months course, who qualified under CETA regulations have been paid the minimum wage while in training.

The Volunteer Services Bureau came into existence in 1974. It has served as a valuable recruitment and placement agency for volunteers needed in service programs. Originally the Retired Senior Volunteer Program was housed in the Volunteer Services Bureau. It has since been spun off and is a project of Durham Technical Institute.

Countywide information and referral services as part of the Community Planning Services of the United Fund are the most recent addition to total services for older persons. Provision of telephone and "walk-in" information and referral plus follow-up are the designated areas of service.

Problem Areas

Obviously, Durham is rich in resources. But two questions must be asked. How effectively are these resources addressing services to older persons? What are the gaps?

Durham's service delivery system is plagued by the same fragmentation found throughout the country. This fragmentation is difficult for people of all ages, but even more so for the older person. Reduced mobility because of physical decline, diminished income, and lack of feelings of self-worth result in lower motivation to grapple with the system. The prevailing attitude is that we will "make do" with what we have. This attitude results in increased isolation and pervasive low morale or even depression, which in turn lead to poorer health than might otherwise be the case.

Even though agencies' services include the elderly as a target group, most agencies give low priority to these services and few allocate budget or staff to the unique needs of older persons. Services are not publicized, or if they are, the media used are not reaching the older person who may not be able to read because of either illiteracy or diminished sight, to hear, or to have newspapers, radio, or television because of lack of income.

Older persons are reluctant to open the door, literally and figuratively, to strangers. Their lifetime experiences have produced a wariness if not an actual mistrust of agencies whose assistance has often meant control. The stigma attached to "welfare" and "mental health" as words meaning services only to individuals who are less worthy or "crazy" sets up barriers to the older person who might benefit from such services.

Agency staff, untrained or insensitive to the slower pace or diminished capabilities of older persons, fail to take time to translate complicated rules and regulations; or—perhaps even worse—workers treat the older person as a child, withholding complete information or making decisions for him. Too often the service deliverers are unconsciously guided by the knowledge that by society's standards older people comprise an unproductive class and don't have long to live anyway.

Role of Coordinating Council for Senior Citizens

Given the analysis of the system of services to older persons operating in Durham County, the role of the Coordinating Council becomes very sharp. The Coordinating Council attempts to fill the need for coordination of existing services, for providing access to services and disseminating knowledge about services, and for offering unique services not provided by other agencies.

The technique used by the agency is based on the concept of multiservice Senior Centers. For the last few years the agency's efforts have been toward developing a network of such centers located in areas demographically identified as having the greatest concentration of older persons. The multipurpose nature of the centers includes a commitment not only to provide services to persons able to come to the facility but also to provide services from the facility to those who are homebound or even institution-bound. Such centers provide also for the maximum utilization of self-government by older persons in recognition of their need to adjust to reduced acceptance by the salaried productive society.

Acting upon the maxim that "the whole is greater than the sum of its parts," the network of centers offers (1) agencies a way to increase their particular service delivery in a more efficient, usable way; (2) older persons not only a focal point for the development of trust in service providers but also peer support as, individually and collectively, they test their adjustment to new roles; (3) the broad community a way to tangibly show respect, concern, and care for older persons; and (4) mandated planning agencies a two-way communication to both older persons and agencies.

The Coordinating Council has five centers presently operating on a part-time basis. The long-range goal of a complete network would increase the number by at least two.

The Coordinating Council as a Service Resource

In addition to the "broker" or umbrella agency role, the Coordinating Council provides several direct services, one of which is part-time employment for forty-three persons over age fifty-five. Funded under Title IX of the Older Americans Act with local matching funds provided by the City of Durham, the Senior Aides program gives economic support to older persons who are assigned to community service jobs.

In addition, the council provides day care for thirty persons threatened by institutional placement. Older adults who are curtailed in physical or mental capacities but who do not need twenty-four-hour skilled nursing care are able to remain in their own residences because of placement at the Community Life Center. Funded under Title XX of the Social Security amendments and by the Durham County Commissioners, the Community Life Center provides a home away from home with individual service plans aimed at restoring the older person to or maintaining him at the highest level of independence of which he is capable.

Noontime meals consisting of one-third the daily nutritional requirement of older persons are offered. This five-day-a-week service is funded under Title VII of the Older Americans Act with 5 percent of the budget provided by the county.

The following services are funded under Title III of the Older Americans Act with local match requirements provided by the United Fund:

Coordination as a service function continues and increases the value of the center network.

Transportation is a linkage service. Senior Citizens in Durham have tried unsuccessfully for five years to secure reduced bus fares. The Coordinating

Council has been approved for receipt of three vehicles (one with hydraulic lift) by the North Carolina Transportation Department. Funding comes from authorizations of the Urban Mass Transit Act (UMTA) and Community Development money from the city of Durham.

In-home services have become more and more of a priority as the national policy of preventing inappropriate institutional care has gained momentum. Unless support services are provided as more older persons are expected to remain in their own homes, the plight of the elderly could become worse. The Coordinating Council provides training for home care personnel; a one-time major clean-up crew; and a minor home repair unit.

The Attendant Care for the Elderly (ACE) training program is a two-month course instituted six years ago. Trainees are taught homemaking and personal care skills. Included are courses in both first aid and home nursing.

In-home aides are placed in homes of older persons unable to get service from the Department of Social Services Chore Service or from the two home health aides hired by the Durham County Health Department. Salary of the aides is provided either by the City of Durham Community Development funds or by the Title IX Senior Aides Program.

The clean-up crew is sent to homes where individuals need assistance with heavy chores, such as washing windows, turning mattresses, scrubbing floors, changing drapes, and storing heavy boxes. The crew members are all senior aides.

The unit specializing in minor home repair averages one home per day to maintain in repair the residences of older home-owners who cannot do the repairs themselves. Senior aides serve as crew members; the coordinator and crew supervisors are paid by the city and county.

Counseling as a service aims to bridge the gap between the county-wide information and referral service and the casework or psychiatric counseling services provided by other agencies. Short-term counseling, home visits to disabled people needing counseling, and arrangements for group discussion of problems are included.

The Coordinating Council is the major force behind a program of exploratory meetings designed to examine the two areas of greatest concern to agencies: (1) in-home services and attendant difficulties as a result of the fragmentation among agencies, and (2) health care. With regard to the former, no projections can be made as to the outcome of present efforts as the committee concentrates on a planning process that will examine all possibilities for solutions to the problems posed in this area.

In the latter area, health care, it is possible that space in the new high-rise may be given to some designated aspect of health services. To this point the representatives of agencies providing health care see no need for fortifying the primary care system; rather, the problem to be addressed is how to implement access to and understanding of that system.

The Coordinating Council, through its board of directors and staff, works with other agencies and older persons to constantly reexamine the existing system and services and to effect necessary changes or add services so that the quality of life for all older persons in Durham will improve.

THE SOCIAL WORKER IN THE AGING
NETWORK

As described earlier, the aging network encompasses federal, regional, state, area-wide, and local levels. Each has a distinct function; each has a place for the professional social worker committed to fortifying the quality of life as the life span is lengthened. The skills related to working with individuals, groups, and communities in counseling, therapy, planning, and research to fortify practice are all needed in services to older persons.

Casework with individuals is placing renewed emphasis on case management and dealing with the multiple problems usually presented. It calls for greater emphasis on the social worker as technical advisor in the coordination of services that may exist outside the agency employing the social worker.

Social work in relation to medical settings has a long history. Hospitals, public health departments, and the newer community health clinics employ the social worker as a member of the treatment team. Nursing homes are slowly following this lead, particularly since third-party reimbursement is requiring inclusion of this professional. Mental health clinics are beginning to recognize the need for workers uniquely qualified to work with older clients as that client population increases.

Senior Centers are developing core teams to relate to several service packages. A social worker in such a setting may be involved in working with a nurse for in-home service or as a team consultant developing a service plan for a participant in a day care component or as a therapist with a group formed to discuss coping with widowhood.

Area-wide and state planning for older persons' agencies seek staff with not only an understanding of the planning process but also the ability to negotiate in order to coordinate service delivery.

Local departments of social services will continue to hire the most significant percentage of social workers. Their mandates to manage protective services as well as other specific programs needed in their locale have become more inclusive with the Title XX amendments to the Social Security Act which provide for a sliding scale of fees.

The present and future system of service to older persons will require some unique professionals. The ability to write a funding proposal; to negotiate cooperative agreements with other agencies; to staff a board or advisory committee; to supervise paid and volunteer staff; to prepare a public relations

335

plan; to conduct group therapy sessions; to gather demographic data; to compile statistical documentation of services provided; and to arrange for involvement of older persons as decision makers, service volunteers, and paid staff, as well as recipients of services, are emerging as qualifications for a new professional role growing out of the demand for "focal points" for services. Social work is challenged to produce the multifaceted worker who meets the requirements.

BIBLIOGRAPHY

Burgess, Ernest W. *Aging in Western Societies.* Chicago and London: University of Chicago Press, 1960.

Carp, Frances M., ed. *Retirement.* New York: Behavioral Publications, 1972.

Deichman, E. S., and C. P. O'Kane. *Working with the Elderly: A Training Manual.* Buffalo, N.Y.: D. O. K., 1975.

Leanse, Joyce. *Senior Centers: Report of Senior Group Programs in America.* Washington, D.C.: National Council on the Aging (National Institute of Senior Centers), 1975.

Lou Harris and Associates, Inc. *The Myth and Reality of Aging in America.* Washington, D.C.: National Council on the Aging, 1975.

Mannes, Marya. *They.* New York: Doubleday, 1968.

Pfeiffer, Eric, ed. *Successful Aging: A Conference Report.* Durham, N.C.: Duke University Center for the Study of Aging and Human Development, 1974.

Puner, Morton. *To the Good Long Life: What We Know about Growing Old.* New York: University Books, 1974.

Rich, Thomas G., and Alden S. Gilmore. *Basic Concepts of Aging: A Programmed Manual.* Tampa, Florida: University of South Florida, 1972.

Taber, Merlin A., et al. *Handbook for Community Professionals: An Approach for Planning and Action.* Springfield, Ill.: Charles C Thomas, 1972.

Tibbitts, Clark, ed. *Handbook of Social Gerontology: Societal Aspects of Aging.* Chicago and London: The University of Chicago Press, 1960.

Townsend, Claire. *Old Age: The Last Segregation.* New York: Grossman, 1971.

Vedder, Clyde B., and Annette S. Lefkowitz. *Problems of the Aged.* Springfield, Ill.: Charles C Thomas, 1965.

Index

Abbott, Edith, 9
Abbott, Grace, 9
ACORN (Association of Community Organizations for Reform Now), 232
Adams, W. G. S., 37-38
Addams, Jane, 9, 182
Administration on Aging (AOA), 325
adoption, 263-64
Age Discrimination Act of 1975, 323
aged, 76-79, 320-36; aging network, 325-26, 335-36; in Durham, N.C., 329-35; in-home care, 77, 327, 334; legislation and, 78, 84-87, 92, 322-25; national policies, 320-21; old-age pensions, early, 54; Senior Centers, 328-29; Supplementary Security Income, 84, 86, 87, 93, 94, 100, 323-24; transportation, 326, 333-34
Agency for International Development (AID), 20
Agriculture, Department of, 83, 88
Aid to the Blind, 86, 323
Aid to Dependent Children, 62
Aid to Families with Dependent Children (AFDC), 11, 62, 83, 84, 87, 88, 91-94, 100
Aid to the Permanently and Totally Disabled, 86, 323
Alinsky, Saul, 225
almshouse, 49-50
ambulatory care, 291-94
American Association of Group Workers, 184
American Association for Organizing Charity, 44
American Association for Organizing Family Social Work, 45
American Association of Retired Persons, 326
American Association of Retired Teachers, 326

American Geriatrics Society, 326
American Public Welfare Association (APWA), 11
applied research, 105
Association for Improving the Condition of the Poor (AICP), 39-40
Association of Schools of Social Work, 7
Augustus, John, 74

Barnett, Canon, 36
Bartlett, Harriet, 66
basic research, 105
Bateson, Gregory, 164
Beers, Clifford, 71
behavior modification, 185
Bettelheim, Bruno, 159
Beveridge, Sir William, 29, 31
Beveridge report, 29-31
Bicentennial Charter for Older Americans, The, 320-21
Black Death, 22-23
blind, 53, 54, 59, 86
Bowen, Murray, 174-75
Brace, Charles Loring, 60
Brett, S. Reed, 25
Brewster, Mary, 65
Briar, Scott, 168

Cabot, Richard C., 65
Campbell, Donald T., 126, 127
Cannon, Ida, 65
Carolina Action, 232
Carter, Jimmy, 19, 94-96
casework, *see* social casework
Chalmers, Thomas, 6, 36
Charity Organization Societies, 4, 6-7; in Great Britain, 36; in U.S., 40-44
child abuse, 88, 244-46, 264-65
child guidance clinics, 70-71